87-4057

AXIOMATIC BARGAINING GAME THEORY

THEORY AND DECISION LIBRARY

General Editors: W. Leinfellner (*Vienna*) and G. Eberlein (*Munich*)

Series A: Philosophy and Methodology of the Social Sciences

Series B: Mathematical and Statistical Methods

Series C: Game Theory, Mathematical Programming and Operations Research

Series D: System Theory, Knowledge Engineering and Problem Solving

SERIES C: GAME THEORY, MATHEMATICAL PROGRAMMING AND OPERATIONS RESEARCH

VOLUME 9

Editor: S. H. Tijs (University of Nijmegen); *Editorial Board:* H. Keiding (Copenhagen), J.-F. Mertens (Louvain-la-Neuve), H. Moulin (Durham), B. Peleg (Jerusalem), T. E. S. Raghavan (Chicago), J. Rosenmüller (Bielefeld), A. Roth (Pittsburgh), D. Schmeidler (Tel-Aviv), R. Selten (Bonn).

Scope: Particular attention is paid in this series to game theory and operations research, their formal aspects and their applications to economic, political and social sciences as well as to socio-biology. It will encourage high standards in the application of game-theoretical methods to individual and social decision making.

The titles published in this series are listed at the end of this volume.

AXIOMATIC BARGAINING
GAME THEORY

by

HANS J.M. PETERS

Department of Mathematics, University of Limburg, The Netherlands

KLUWER ACADEMIC PUBLISHERS

DORDRECHT / BOSTON / LONDON

Library of Congress Cataloging-in-Publication Data

```
Peters, H. J. M.
    Axiomatic bargaining game theory / H.J.M. Peters.
      p.   cm. -- (Theory and decision library. Series C, Game
  theory, mathematical programming, and operations research)
    Includes index.
    ISBN 0-7923-1873-0 (alk. paper)
    1. Game theory.  2. Negotiation--Mathematical models.
  3. Axiomatic set theory.   I. Title.  II. Series.
  HB144.P48  1992
  658.4'0353--dc20                                      92-21620
```

ISBN 0-7923-1873-0

Published by Kluwer Academic Publishers,
P.O. Box 17, 3300 AA Dordrecht, The Netherlands.

Kluwer Academic Publishers incorporates
the publishing programmes of
D. Reidel, Martinus Nijhoff, Dr W. Junk and MTP Press.

Sold and distributed in the U.S.A. and Canada
by Kluwer Academic Publishers,
101 Philip Drive, Norwell, MA 02061, U.S.A.

In all other countries, sold and distributed
by Kluwer Academic Publishers Group,
P.O. Box 322, 3300 AH Dordrecht, The Netherlands.

Printed on acid-free paper

Printed in the Netherlands

Preface

The main objective of this book is to present an up to date survey of axiomatic models of bargaining. It is intended to include those results which I think most researchers in the field would consider as important with, I grant, a natural bias towards my own work. I also think that the book is fairly complete: it includes, at the least, examples of the various kinds of models, and gives proofs of almost all results discussed. Most of the work in axiomatic bargaining which is not treated extensively in this book, is at least mentioned. Furthermore, chapters are added containing results on related noncooperative models, on solutions for coalitional bargaining games (that is, nonsidepayment games), and on some relevant elements from the theory of utility and risk.

Related books are Alvin Roth's *Axiomatic models of bargaining* (1979) and William Thomson's forthcoming book *Bargaining theory: the axiomatic approach* (1992). I owe much to both authors and their work. Also the book by Thomson and Lensberg (1989) on variable population bargaining must be mentioned here.

I want to thank all my coauthors in bargaining theory, and in particular Stef Tijs for introducing me to the field of game theory. Special thanks are due to Jean Derks and Peter Wakker for reading parts of the manuscript (any remaining errors...), and to my colleagues, in particular Koos Vrieze, for giving me the opportunity to finish this book. Very special thanks go to Marlies Haenen for the superb TEXjob and perfect drawing of figures.

Hans Peters   April 1992

Contents

Chapter 1

Preliminaries

1.1 Introduction

The main theme of this book is *axiomatic bargaining game theory*, as initiated by Nash's seminal paper of 1950. Axiomatic bargaining game theory is a mathematical discipline which studies the problem of bargaining between two or more parties by studying the mathematical properties of maps assigning an outcome to each *bargaining game* in some class of bargaining games. A bargaining game is a set of outcomes representing the utilities attainable by the parties or players involved, together with a disagreement outcome. The interpretation is that this last outcome results if the players are unable to reach a unanimous agreement on some other possible outcome. Maps as mentioned will be called *bargaining solutions*. Axiomatic bargaining game theory is concerned with a mathematical investigation of the properties of such bargaining solutions. Usually, following Nash (1950), one formulates desirable properties for these solutions, and then tries to characterize a solution or a class of solutions by its properties. Therefore, such properties are often referred to as axioms[1], which is a less neutral expression. We will use both terms, *axioms* as well as *properties*. In a nutshell, this is what this book is mainly about.

Bargaining games as described are also called *pure* bargaining games, in view of the assumption that unanimous decisions are required. A more general formulation is obtained by allowing (sub)coalitions of players to reach a decision on their own. If this is the case, we are dealing with so-called general cooperative games without sidepayments. Also these games have been studied (and are being studied) axiomatically, although not as extensively as pure bargaining games. The main results are treated in this book as well, see chapter 10; there, such games are called *coalitional bargaining games*.

All these games, pure bargaining games as well as coalitional bargaining games, are *cooperative* games. The main distinguishing feature of a cooperative game is that binding agreements are possible — as opposed to so-called noncooperative games. Methodologically, in cooperative game theory mostly the axiomatic method is applied, whereas noncooperative games are described by strategies and moves and analyzed by the investigation of some equilibrium concept, usually *Nash equilibrium* (Nash, 1951). Nash (1953) felt that both approaches should be combined. More specifically, he described a noncooperative, strategic

---

[1]See also footnote 2 in chapter 11.

game of which the (in a certain sense) unique Nash equilibrium led to the outcome assigned
by the (cooperative, "axiomatic") *Nash bargaining solution*. The idea to back up cooperative, axiomatic solution concepts by equilibria of strategic games, has sometimes been
entitled the *Nash program* (see Binmore and Dasgupta, 1987). Chapter 9 of this book deals
with noncooperative models for bargaining solutions.

So far we have described the main theme and two other important themes of this book.
In section 1.4 below, we will present a much more detailed outline of its contents. Section
1.2 introduces the main concepts and basic definitions of axiomatic bargaining. Section 1.3
presents a number of situations that give rise to bargaining games.

1.2   Basic definitions and concepts

By $N := \{1, 2, \ldots, n\}$, where $n \geq 2$, we denote the set of *players*. $\mathbb{R}^N$ denotes the set
of functions $N \to \mathbb{R}$, and is identified with the Cartesian product of n copies of the real
line $\mathbb{R}$ indexed by the elements of N. As usual, $\mathbb{R}^N_+ := \{x \in \mathbb{R}^N : x_i \geq 0 \text{ for all } i \in N\}$,
$\mathbb{R}^N_{++} := \{x \in \mathbb{R}^N : x_i > 0 \text{ for all } i \in N\}$. Similarly for subsets $M \subset N$; in particular,
elements of $\mathbb{R}^M$ are indexed by the coordinates (players) in M. A set $S \subset \mathbb{R}^N$ is called
comprehensive if for all $x \in S$ and $y \in \mathbb{R}^N$, $y \leq x$ implies $y \in S$. Here, $y \leq x$ means $y_i \leq x_i$
for every $i \in N$, and $y < x$ means $y_i < x_i$ for every $i \in N$; similarly for $\geq, >$. For $S \subset \mathbb{R}^N$,
the *comprehensive hull of S* is the set $\text{com}(S) := \{y \in \mathbb{R}^N : y \leq x \text{ for some } x \in S\}$.

Definition 1.1 A *bargaining game for N* is a pair (S, d) where

(i) S is a nonempty closed subset of $\mathbb{R}^N$,

(ii) $d \in S$,

(iii) $u_i(S) := \max\{x_i : x \in S\}$ exists for every $i \in N$.

By $\tilde{\mathcal{B}}^N$ the class of all bargaining games for N is denoted.

The interpretation of a bargaining game $(S, d) \in \tilde{\mathcal{B}}^N$ is as follows. The players in N try to
reach a unanimous agreement on some *outcome* $x \in S$, yielding utility x_i for player i. If
they fail, the *disagreement outcome* or *disagreement point* d results. The set S is called the
feasible set.

Some comments on (i), (ii), and (iii) in definition 1.1 are in order, and lead to further
conditions on bargaining games. Closedness of the feasible set S is required for mathematical convenience. Often, it will also be assumed that the feasible set S is comprehensive
($S = \text{com}(S)$). This may be interpreted as free disposibility of utility; it serves, however,
also mathematical convenience and, with a few exceptions (see, for instance, subsection
2.5.2) does not affect the results. $\overline{\mathcal{B}}^N$ denotes the class of bargaining games with comprehensive feasible sets. $\mathcal{B}^N$ denotes the subclass of $\overline{\mathcal{B}}^N$ and hence of $\tilde{\mathcal{B}}^N$ where the disagreement outcome is always an interior outcome, which in view of comprehensiveness, is
equivalent to requiring the existence of an outcome $x > d$. In a game in $\mathcal{B}^N$ each player has
an incentive to cooperate; most results will be derived for games in this class. Sometimes,
however, it is convenient to allow the disagreement point to be a boundary point; see, e.g.,
section 2.5.

The point $u(S) = (u_1(S), \ldots, u_n(S))$ in (iii) is called the *utopia point of S*. It is customary and natural to have some boundedness condition on the feasible sets, and in this book this is condition (iii); it can be relaxed without affecting most of the results.

As a general comment on definition 1.1, we note that in the literature there are many variations on the requirements with respect to a bargaining game (S, d). For this book, however, we have tried to find a unifying framework so that different results may be compared, at the loss of as little generality as possible.

As a final but very important restriction, we introduce the subclasses

$$\tilde{\mathcal{C}}^N \subset \tilde{\mathcal{B}}^N,\ \overline{\mathcal{C}}^N \subset \overline{\mathcal{B}}^N,\ \mathcal{C}^N \subset \mathcal{B}^N$$

of bargaining games with *convex* feasible sets. Convexity of a feasible set may be interpreted in several ways: see the next section. The class $\mathcal{C}^N$ of bargaining games with convex comprehensive feasible sets and interior disagreement points plays a central role in this book. The literature on bargaining games with nonconvex feasible sets is much smaller, but the main results will be reviewed: see section 8.4.

The notation $\mathcal{D}^N$ will mostly be used to denote some unspecified subclass of $\tilde{\mathcal{B}}^N$ or $\tilde{\mathcal{C}}^N$. If $N = \{1, 2\}$, fixed, the superscript N is often omitted. Some results are explicitly based on the possibility of a changing number of players: see chapter 7.

Let $\mathcal{D}^N$ be a subclass of $\tilde{\mathcal{B}}^N$. A *bargaining solution on $\mathcal{D}^N$* is a map $\varphi : \mathcal{D}^N \to I\!\!R^N$ such that $\varphi(S, d) \in S$ for every $(S, d) \in \mathcal{D}^N$. If no confusion is likely, φ is also called a *solution*. An outcome $\varphi(S, d)$ is called the *solution outcome* or *solution point*. As explained in the introductory section, the main theme of this book is the study of solutions φ and their properties.

Variations on the concept of a solution occur in this book as well. *Multisolutions*, formally introduced in section 8.2, assign to a bargaining game a subset of feasible outcomes rather than a single outcome. A *probabilistic solution* — see section 8.3 — assigns to a bargaining game a probability measure on the feasible set. *Variable population solutions* are defined not just for a fixed set of players, but for every finite subset of a given finite or infinite population of players. See section 7.2.

1.3 Examples

Bargaining games are rather abstract objects. In applications, however, bargaining games arise from specific situations. Examples of such situations are given in this section.

1.3.1 Expected utility bargaining situations

In this subsection we describe a class of bargaining situations giving rise to the class $\mathcal{C}^N$ of bargaining games with convex comprehensive feasible sets and interior disagreement points. We will use concepts and notations from section 11.2, but our presentation is self-contained, so that readers who are familiar with the concept of a von Neumann-Morgenstern utility function do not need to consult chapter 11.

For a nonempty set A let $\mathcal{L}(A)$ denote the set of lotteries (finite probability distributions) on A. A typical element $\ell \in \mathcal{L}(A)$ has the form $\ell = (p_i; a^i)_{i=1}^k$ where the p_i are probabilities summing to 1, and the a^i are elements of A. For a function $u : A \to I\!R$, $Eu(\ell) :=$ $\sum_{i=1}^{k} p_i u(a^i)$ denotes the expected utility of ℓ under u.

Definition 1.2 An *expected utility bargaining situation for* N is an $(n+2)$-tuple

$$\Gamma :=< A, \bar{a}, u^1, u^2, \ldots, u^n >$$

where

(i) A is a compact set of $I\!R^m$, for some $m \in I\!N$,

(ii) for every $i \in N$, u^i is a continuous function from A to $I\!R$,

(iii) $\bar{a} \in A$, such that for every $i \in N$ there is an $a \in A$ with $u^i(a) > u^i(\bar{a})$.

Elements of A are called *riskless alternatives*, whereas lotteries on A are *risky alternatives*. The alternative $\bar{a}$ is called the *disagreement alternative*. Define

$$S_\Gamma := \{x \in I\!R^N : x \leq (Eu^1(\ell), \ldots, Eu^n(\ell)) \text{ for some } \ell \in \mathcal{L}(A)\}$$
$$d_\Gamma := (u^1(\bar{a}), \ldots, u^n(\bar{a}))$$

then it is straightforward to check that $(S_\Gamma, d_\Gamma) \in \mathcal{C}^N$. Moreover, every $(S, d) \in \mathcal{C}^N$ can be obtained in this way. Namely, let $T \subset S$ be a compact set such that $d \in T$ and $S = \text{com}(T)$. Such a set T exists in particular in view of condition (iii) in definition 1.1. Define

$$\Gamma' := < T, d, \text{pr}^1, \ldots, \text{pr}^n >$$

where, for every $i \in N$, $\text{pr}^i(x) := x_i$ for every $x \in T$. Clearly, $S = S_{\Gamma'}$ and $d = d_{\Gamma'}$.

The explicit consideration of expected utility bargaining situations will be needed when we study risk properties of bargaining solutions in chapter 6. The assumption of underlying expected utility bargaining situations provides a justification for considering the class $\mathcal{C}^N$ of bargaining games with convex feasible sets. Other justifications are given below, in subsections 1.3.2–1.3.4.

Studying bargaining solutions defined on $\mathcal{C}^N$ or some other class of bargaining games entails the implicit position that only utilities matter, and not the possibly underlying "physical" situations. This position is often referred to as the *welfarist approach* (see section 8.5, in particular subsection 8.5.2). As an illustration, it is not hard to give an example of different expected utility bargaining situations Γ and Γ' such that $S_\Gamma = S_{\Gamma'}$ and $d_\Gamma = d_{\Gamma'}$. The welfarist approach may well exclude certain "solutions" defined in terms of the underlying bargaining situations. A simple example is given in subsection 1.3.2.

1.3.2   A division problem

Suppose there are two players ($N = \{1, 2\}$), who bargain over the division of one unit of a perfectly divisible good. Any division (ξ, η), meaning that player 1 receives ξ and 2 receives η, is allowed as long as $\xi + \eta \leq 1$. If the players fail to reach an agreement, they both receive nothing, i.e., the alternative $(0, 0)$ results. Let the players have utility functions u^1 and u^2 with $u^1(\xi, \eta)$ depending only on ξ, and $u^2(\xi, \eta)$ depending only on η. Assume that u^1 is nonconstant, concave, continuous and nondecreasing in ξ, that u^2 is nonconstant, concave, continuous and nondecreasing in η, and that $u^1(0,0) = u^2(0,0) = 0$. Define

$$S(u^1, u^2) \; := \; \{x \in I\!\!R^N : x \le (u^1(\xi,\eta), u^2(\xi,\eta)) \text{ for some}$$
$$\text{division } (\xi,\eta) \text{ with } \xi + \eta \le 1\}.$$

Clearly, $(S(u^1, u^2), 0) \in \mathcal{C}$ for every pair (u^1, u^2) satisfying the properties described; and for every $(S, 0) \in \mathcal{C}$ with $S = \text{com}(S \cap I\!\!R_+^N)$ there is a pair (u^1, u^2) with $S = S(u^1, u^2)$. The concavity of the utility functions in particular provides a justification for considering convex bargaining games.

If we are interested in solving this division problem for any pair of utility functions (u^1, u^2), then we might study bargaining solutions φ on the appropriate domain of bargaining games, select an in some way attractive solution φ, and pick a division (ξ,η) with $u^1(\xi,\eta) = \varphi_1(S(u^1, u^2), 0)$ and $u^2(\xi,\eta) = \varphi_2(S(u^1, u^2), 0)$. This would be the welfarist approach, as explained in the previous section. This approach reflects the view that everything that matters is captured by the utilities, i.e., the outcomes available in the feasible set $S(u^1, u^2)$. Although this view is quite defendable, it should nevertheless be noted that it puts a restriction on the possible division rules. For instance, the "natural" division rule "equal split of the good" leading to the division $(\frac{1}{2}, \frac{1}{2})$ independently of the utility functions (u^1, u^2) is not feasible under the welfarist approach. To see this, consider the utility functions $u^1(\xi,\eta) = \xi$, $u^2(\xi,\eta) = \sqrt{\eta}$, $\overline{u}^1(\xi,\eta) = \xi(2-\xi)$, $\overline{u}^2(\xi,\eta) = \eta$. Note that $S(u^1, u^2) = S(\overline{u}^1, \overline{u}^2)$. However, $u^1(\frac{1}{2}, \frac{1}{2}) = \frac{1}{2}$ whereas $\overline{u}^1(\frac{1}{2}, \frac{1}{2}) = \frac{3}{4}$. See further section 8.5, which deals with bargaining theory on economic environments.

1.3.3   Bimatrix games

Bargaining games may arise from noncooperative games. Two examples of well-known so-called *bimatrix games* are the *prisoners' dilemma* and the *battle of the sexes*.

Prisoners' dilemma

Consider the bimatrix game given by the following diagram:

$$\text{Player 1} \quad \begin{array}{c} \\ T \\ B \end{array} \begin{array}{c} \text{Player 2} \\ \begin{array}{cc} L & R \end{array} \\ \begin{bmatrix} (5,5) & (0,6) \\ (6,0) & (1,1) \end{bmatrix} \end{array} .$$

(In any of the four pairs, the first and second numbers are the payoffs to players 1 and 2, respectively.) Both player 1 and player 2 have two *pure strategies* (top (T) row and bottom (B) row, and left (L) and right (R) column, respectively), and an infinity of *mixed strategies*, e.g. for player 1: play T with probability p and B with probability $1 - p$ (where $p \in [0, 1]$). As an example, the payoffs to the players, if player 1 plays T with probability $1/3$ and B with probability $2/3$ and player 2 plays L with probability $1/2$ and R with probability $1/2$, are the (expected) payoffs

$$\tfrac{1}{3}(\tfrac{1}{2} \cdot 5 + \tfrac{1}{2} \cdot 0) + \tfrac{2}{3}(\tfrac{1}{2} \cdot 6 + \tfrac{1}{2} \cdot 1) = 3\tfrac{1}{6} \text{ for player 1 and}$$

$\frac{1}{2}(\frac{1}{3} \cdot 5 + \frac{2}{3} \cdot 0) + \frac{1}{2}(\frac{1}{3} \cdot 6 + \frac{2}{3} \cdot 1) = 2\frac{1}{6}$ for player 2.

The unique *Nash equilibrium* (Nash (1951)) of this game is the pair of pure strategies (B, R): no player gains by deviating, unilaterally, from this pair of strategies. Both players, however, strictly prefer the pair of payoffs $(5, 5)$ corresponding to the pair of strategies (T, L), to the payoff pair $(1, 1)$ corresponding to the Nash equilibrium of the game. The pair of payoffs $(5, 5)$ is unlikely to be the final outcome of the game unless the players have a way to make some binding agreement (e.g., sign a contract) to play (T, L).

By using mixed strategies, the players can achieve any pair of payoffs in the shaded area S in figure 1.1.

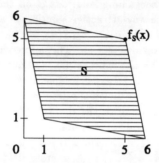

Figure 1.1: Prisoners' dilemma

Let $f_S : S \to S$ be a map, and suppose that the players agree to obey the following procedure: every player announces a mixed strategy, and the corresponding payoff pair $d \in S$ is calculated; and then a so-called *correlated strategy* is determined and carried out such that the corresponding pair of payoffs is $f_S(d)$. Such a correlated strategy has the form $(z_{TL}, z_{TR}, z_{BL}, z_{BR})$ where, e.g., z_{TL} is the joint probability that player 1 has to play T and player 2 has to play L. In this particular example, S is also the set of payoffs corresponding to correlated strategies. Suppose that f_S assigns to $d \in S$ the (by both players) most preferred point in S on the 45°-line through d. If, e.g., the players play the equilibrium pair of strategies (B, R), then $d = (1, 1)$, $f_S(d) = (5, 5)$, and $f_S(d)$ can be achieved by the correlated strategy $(1, 0, 0, 0)$. If we have, for every set S of this kind, a prespecified map f_S as above and a point d_S in S, then we can define a map φ which assigns to every S the point $f_S(d_S)$. Such a map φ is an example of a bargaining solution defined on some subclass of $\tilde{\mathcal{C}}^N$ — depending on the class of noncooperative games under consideration.

Battle of the sexes

Consider the following bimatrix game:

$$\begin{array}{cc} & \text{Player 2} \\ & \begin{array}{cc} L & \quad R \end{array} \\ \text{Player 1} \begin{array}{c} T \\ B \end{array} & \left[\begin{array}{cc} (2, 1) & (0, 0) \\ (0, 0) & (1, 2) \end{array} \right]. \end{array}$$

The shaded area in figure 1.2 is the set of payoffs attainable by mixed strategies. The set of payoffs attainable by correlated strategies is $\text{conv}\{(0,0), (2,1), (1,2)\} =: S$. (We denote by "conv" the convex hull.)

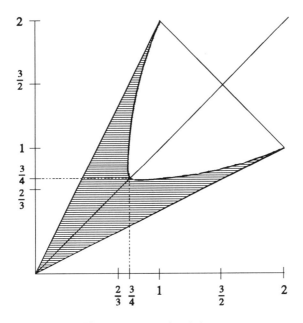

Figure 1.2: Battle of the sexes

For this game, there are three Nash equilibria: (T, L), (B, R), and (M, N), where M means: play T with probability $2/3$, and N means: play R with probability $2/3$. The corresponding payoff pairs are $(2,1)$, $(1,2)$, and $(2/3, 2/3)$, respectively, and if f_S is as above, then $f_S(2,1) = (2,1)$, $f_S(1,2) = (1,2)$, and $f_S(2/3, 2/3) = (3/2, 3/2)$; these payoffs can be achieved by the correlated strategies $(1,0,0,0)$, $(0,0,0,1)$, and $(1/2,0,0,1/2)$, respectively. The payoff pair $(3/2, 3/2)$ can only be obtained by a correlated strategy and not by a pair of mixed strategies; consequently, it can only be obtained by cooperation between the players since both of them have to consent to the use of the correlated strategy $(1/2,0,0,1/2)^2$.

Note that the game procedure, as a whole, is of a noncooperative nature: once the players have agreed to the use of correlated strategies and a "bargaining solution" φ, the final payoffs depend only on the strategies announced by the players. In the literature, these games are called *arbitration games*, and they were introduced by Nash (1953). See also Raiffa (1953), Luce and Raiffa (1957), and for a comprehensive study, see Tijs and Jansen (1982)[3]. For the stories behind the prisoners' dilemma and the battle of the sexes see also Luce and Raiffa (1957).

---

[2]However, this is subject to debate, since this particular correlated strategy is a so-called correlated equilibrium. See Aumann (1987a).

[3]Cf. section 9.8.

1.3.4   A wage-employment bargaining model

Bargaining games may arise from typical economic conflict situations like wage-employment bargaining between an employer and a union. McDonald and Solow (1981) describe a theoretical model for such a situation, part of which will be briefly reviewed here.

Denote the amount of labor (viz., employment, number of employed persons) by L and the wage rate by w. The union represents N members, all alike. It has a wage rate utility function U, and the total utility derived from a bargained combination (w, L) equals

$$V(w, L) := LU(w) + (N - L)U(\overline{w})$$

where $\overline{w} \geq 0$ is the reservation wage. The union bargains over (w, L) with a firm, which has revenue function R and profit function

$$G(w, L) := R(L) - wL.$$

R and U are assumed to be increasing and concave, and to have any other desirable properties: we do not go into the details. The *contract curve* of efficient (Pareto optimal) wage-employment combinations is given by the equation

$$\frac{U(w) - U(\overline{w})}{U'(w)} = w - R'(L) \tag{1.1}$$

as is easily verified. Let

$$S := \text{com}(\{(V(w, L), \ G(w, L)) : (w, L) \text{ satisfies } (1.1), w \geq \overline{w}, L \leq N\})$$

and

$$d := (V(\overline{w}, 0), \ G(\overline{w}, 0)) = (NU(\overline{w}), 0)$$

assuming that $R(0) = 0$. Under the appropriate conditions, $(S, d) \in \mathcal{C}$. McDonald and Solow apply the symmetric Nash bargaining solution, which will extensively be discussed in the next chapter and at many places elsewhere in this book. The symmetric Nash solution outcome is obtained by maximizing the product $(x_1 - d_1)(x_2 - d_2)$ on the set $\{x \in S : x \geq d\}$. Unconstrained maximization of the expression $(V(w, L) - NU(\overline{w}))G(w, L)$ combined with (1.1) gives the first order condition

$$w = \tfrac{1}{2}(R/L + R'(L)). \tag{1.2}$$

This is a surprising result: at the Nash bargaining solution, the wage is equal to the arithmetic mean of the average and marginal products of labor. In other words, it is a perfect compromise between what the union would ideally consider as fair ($w = R/L$) and what would maximize the firm's profit ($w = R'(L)$). This could be explained as a triumph for Nash bargaining theory and, more generally, for axiomatic bargaining theory, where the Nash bargaining solution is probably the most popular concept. But what is it worth? The fact that a nice formula such as (1.2) comes out, may be a matter of "pure" coincidence. The use of a concept like the Nash bargaining solution should be based on some axiomatic characterization or some noncooperative justification. To illustrate the former: it is not sufficient to simply refer to one of the existing characterizations, many of which are discussed in this book. A characterization here should be based on a class of bargaining games that explicitly correspond to a class of wage- employment bargaining situations as above, e.g., by varying the parameters $(V, R, N, \overline{w}, \ldots)$; the axioms should refer to or have an interpretation based on those underlying wage-employment conflicts. Consequently, one should be careful in applying the concepts and characterizations as presented for instance in this book, to specific economic problems. There is a lot of work in which — in particular — the Nash bargaining solution is applied but, unfortunately, this concerns almost always the "formula" and not the "foundation". Examples are, van Cayseele (1987), Grout (1984), and Svejnar (1986). The last paper is concerned with an empirical test of nonsymmetric Nash bargaining solutions (see chapter 2), and does provide a basis for the nonsymmetries in terms of wage bargaining power.

1.4   Outline of this book

In this section we first describe the contents of this book in a chapter by chapter, (sub)section by (sub)section fashion. Second, we provide the reader with some guidelines for the use of this book.

Chapter 2 deals with the Nash bargaining solution and its nonsymmetric or n-person extensions. In section 2.2 we mainly present the Nash bargaining solution and the well-known characterization based on the "independence of irrelevant alternatives" (IIA) axiom; this is practically Nash's original axiomatization, but formulated for n instead of two players. In section 2.3 we replace the symmetry axiom by an axiom of consistency, and obtain a characterization of a family of solutions based on given hierarchies within the set of players; this section is fairly technical, but gives an indication of the (mathematical) power of the symmetry axiom. Section 2.4 deals with four alternative characterizations of Nash bargaining solutions. Axioms called "independence of irrelevant expansions" and "multiplicativity" are central in subsections 2.4.2 and 2.4.3. Subsection 2.4.4 describes a player replication model, and in section 2.4.5 Nash bargaining solutions are derived as describing the utilities of playing certain positions in certain games. In section 2.5 characterizations of the Nash solutions are given which involve axioms concerning the disagreement point: "disagreement point convexity" in subsection 2.5.2, and related axioms in subsection 2.5.3. Chapter 2 is concluded by a discussion of related literature in section 2.6; in particular, it gives references to other axiomatizations in this book.

Chapter 3 studies the independence of irrelevant alternatives axiom from a "revealed preference" point of view. In contrast with most other chapters in this book, the sections of this chapter are part of a continuing story. The main results are theorem 3.20 and corollary 3.21 in section 3.5, in which large classes of solutions satisfying IIA (for two players) or the "strong axiom of revealed preference" (for n players) are characterized. The chapter concludes with related literature (section 3.6) and a technical appendix (section 3.7).

Chapter 4 deals with monotonicity properties. In section 4.2 we characterize a family of "individually monotonic" solutions for n players, without imposing symmetry; the familiar characterization of the Raiffa-Kalai-Smorodinsky solution follows as a corollary. A replication model for a class of individually monotonic solutions is discussed in section 4.3; the model also applies to Nash bargaining solutions. Individual monotonicity with respect to the "global utopia point" is studied in section 4.4. Section 4.5 focusses on so-called proportional solutions, with "strong monotonicity" as the main axiom; a variation based on the "disagreement point concavity" axiom is considered in subsection 4.5.2. We characterize the so-called equal-loss solution and lexicographic (Pareto optimal) versions of the egalitarian and equal-loss solutions in sections 4.6 through 4.8. Section 4.9 concludes this chapter with a discussion of related literature.

Chapter 5 focusses on additivity properties. The super-additive solution of Perles and Maschler is reviewed in section 5.2. Sections 5.4 and 5.5 present characterizations of proportional solutions and Nash solutions based on additivity axioms. In section 5.3 we discuss a game- and utility-theoretic basis for the use of additivity properties.

Chapter 6 deals with risk properties, which summarize, in several different ways, the possible effects on solution outcomes of changing risk attitudes of the players. It contains six sections. It is interesting to mention that section 6.5 gives a critical discussion of the practice of ascribing certain effects to changing risk attitudes; in this respect, section 6.6, which geometrically characterizes the main risk property ("risk sensitivity"), can be seen as inspired by the mentioned discussion.

Chapter 7 treats bargaining games where the number of players may vary, and axioms are formulated, based on this possibility. The "population monotonicity" axiom leads to Thomson's alternative characterization of the Raiffa-Kalai-Smorodinsky solution in section 7.3; the Nash solution is characterized in section 7.4 mainly with the aid of a stability axiom proposed by Lensberg. In section 7.5 we briefly discuss characterizations of the egalitarian and lexicographic solutions within this "variable population" model.

Chapter 8 deals with a number of different topics. Multisolutions (correspondences) and "probabilistic solutions" are studied in sections 8.2 and 8.3; the emphasis is on appropriate adaptations of the IIA axiom. We study bargaining games with nonconvex feasible sets in section 8.4; again, IIA and appropriate extensions of Nash solutions are central, and related to a dynamical process of bargaining in subsection 8.4.3. Sections 8.5 through 8.8 are relatively short sections dealing with bargaining on economic environments (in particular, problems of fair division), axiomatic bargaining models involving time, ordinal bargaining, and continuity properties, respectively.

Chapter 9 is devoted to noncooperative games related to bargaining games and bargaining solutions. The Harsanyi-Zeuthen procedure, Nash demand game, and Rubinstein bargaining model are treated in sections 9.2 through 9.4. Section 9.5 describes the one stage game of Anbar and Kalai. In section 9.6 we give an axiomatic characterization of the Raiffa-Kalai-Smorodinsky solution based on a so-called "reduced game property" and coupled with a noncooperative game that leads to the RKS solution outcome; sections 9.2–9.5 are all concerned with the Nash bargaining solution. In section 9.7 we present van Damme's model which enables a comparison between various bargaining solutions from a certain family via a noncooperative game; again, the Nash solution fares best. Section 9.8, finally, contains a few remarks about so-called arbitration games.

Chapter 10 deals with the (natural) extension of bargaining game theory to coalitional bargaining games, usually called nonsidepayment games. The Shapley solution and Harsanyi solution ("Shapley and Harsanyi NTU values") are characterized in sections 10.3 and 10.4, respectively; both solutions extend the Nash bargaining solution. The Kalai-Samet egalitarian solutions extend the proportional bargaining solutions and are characterized in section 10.5.

Chapter 11, finally, presents some elements of the theory of utility and risk, which play an implicit or explicit role in this book. Central topics are von Neumann-Morgenstern utility functions, risk aversion, strength of preference, and additive and multiplicative utility.

Guidelines for reading this book

By including an extensive notation and symbol index as well as a subject index and an author index, we have tried to facilitate separate reading of the various parts (chapters, sections) of this book. Still, the reader is advised to study at least sections 1.1 and 1.2 as a basis to understand the rest of the book. The first section of each chapter is introductory and outlines the contents of that chapter. Definitions, lemmas, propositions, theorems, corollaries, examples, and (most) remarks are numbered consecutively throughout each chapter; for instance, definition 2.1 is followed by lemma 2.2, etc.

The interest a reader may have in this book might range from just wanting to take notice of a few "classical" results of axiomatic bargaining, to diving into all kinds of technicalities associated with a thorough study of the axiomatic taxonomy. For most courses in game theory, for instance, it would suffice to treat some of the best known and perhaps less technical results. Therefore, I will describe a few possible trajectories through this book; each trajectory extends the previous one and, of course, many variations are possible.

Trajectory 1: Sections 1.1 and 1.2; 2.1, 2.2; 4.1, 4.2, 4.5; 5.1, 5.2, 5.5; 7.1, 7.2, 7.3; 9.1, 9.2, 9.3, 9.4.
Trajectory 2: Add 2.5; 5.3, 5.4; 7.4; 9.5, 9.6, 9.7.
Trajectory 3: Add 2.3, 2.4, chapter 3, ...
Etc.

The book contains no explicitly formulated exercises, but an easy algorithm to generate exercises works as follows. Take any result (lemma, theorem, ...) in the book. With high probability — especially in case of a theorem — such a result is an axiomatic characterization of a solution; then consider the consequences of dropping axioms or changing the domain of games. This procedure generates an abundance of exercises, many but not anywhere near all of which are answered in the book. Good luck!

Chapter 2

Nash bargaining solutions

2.1 Introduction

Any book on axiomatic bargaining game theory should start with Nash's 1950 article and with the Nash bargaining solution, and so will this one. Without any doubt the Nash bargaining solution is the most well-known and popular solution concept in bargaining — in the theoretical literature as well as in applied and empirical work. What could be the reasons for this popularity? Empirical evidence for the Nash bargaining solution certainly is not overwhelming and besides, lack of empirical results concerning other solution concepts makes any comparison difficult if not impossible. (For some empirical work see Svejnar (1986), or van Cayseele (1987).) Further, many experiments have been conducted — see Roth and Malouf (1979) for an overview — but also these are not unambiguously conclusive in favor of the Nash solution. Even, earlier experiments by Crott (1971) point in the direction of the next popular solution, the Raiffa-Kalai-Smorodinsky solution (Raiffa, 1953, Kalai and Smorodinsky, 1975; see chapter 4).

Thus, apart from historical or chronological considerations, the cause of the popularity of the Nash solution must be a theoretical one. Indeed, there have been developed many axiomatic characterizations of the Nash solution(s) — where the plural refers to the nonsymmetric extensions — and there are interesting noncooperative approaches to the bargaining problem which give support to the Nash solution(s). Nash solutions have their twins in Cobb-Douglas utility or production functions. The independence of irrelevant alternatives condition used by Nash to characterize his solution also occurs in decision theory (e.g., Luce, 1979) or consumer theory (e.g., Weddepohl, 1970, and Peters and Wakker, 1991a), and is in spirit related to the condition with the same name in social choice theory (Arrow, 1951). This and further chapters will review some of these topics.

Section 2.2 discusses Nash's original result in a somewhat wider setting. In section 2.3 we consider what happens if the symmetry axiom is dropped. In section 2.4 four other characterizations of Nash solutions are presented, based on Thomson (1981a), Binmore (1987a), Kalai (1977a), and Roth (1978). Section 2.5 presents an axiomatization in which axioms concerning the disagreement point are central. Section 2.6 concludes this chapter with a discussion of other relevant literature.

2.2   The bargaining problem

Axiomatic bargaining game theory started with the paper "The Bargaining Problem" (Nash, 1950). This article will be reviewed here in a somewhat different setting. Specifically, Nash considered the case of two players ($n = 2$), and convex compact feasible sets. We present Nash's characterization for an arbitrary number of players, and for bargaining solutions defined on the class of bargaining games with convex comprehensive feasible sets, and — as in Nash (1950) — with interior disagreement outcomes.

Let $\varphi : \mathcal{D}^N \to I\!\!R^N$ be a bargaining solution, where $\mathcal{D}^N$ is a subclass of $\tilde{\mathcal{B}}^N$. In order to define axioms for φ it is convenient to leave $\mathcal{D}^N$ unspecified for the time being. For $T \subset I\!\!R^N$, let

$$W(T) := \{x \in T : \text{there is no } y \in T \text{ with } y > x\}$$

denote the *weakly Pareto optimal subset* of T. Call $(S, d) \in \mathcal{D}^N$ *symmetric* if $d_1 = d_2 = \ldots = d_n$ and for every $x \in S$ any point $\tilde{x} \in I\!\!R^N$ arising from x by performing some permutation of its coordinates is also in S. For $x, y \in I\!\!R^N$, denote by xy the vector $(x_1 y_1, x_2 y_2, \ldots, x_n y_n)$ and for $T \subset I\!\!R^N$ let $xT := \{z \in I\!\!R^N : z = xy \text{ for some } y \in T\}$, and $x + T := T + x := \{z \in I\!\!R^N : z = y + x \text{ for some } y \in T\}$. Also, for $\alpha \in I\!\!R$, $\alpha x := (\alpha x_1, \alpha x_2, \ldots, \alpha x_n)$ and $\alpha T := \{\alpha x : x \in T\}$.

Nash proposed that φ should satisfy the following four axioms.

Symmetry (SYM): For every $(S, d) \in \mathcal{D}^N$, if (S, d) is symmetric, then $\varphi_1(S, d) = \varphi_2(S, d) = \ldots = \varphi_n(S, d)$.

A motivation for the symmetry axiom is that, if the description of the bargaining game does not contain any information that enables a meaningful distinction between the players, then the solution should not distinguish between the players either.

Weak Pareto Optimality (WPO): For every $(S, d) \in \mathcal{D}^N$, $\varphi(S, d) \in W(S)$.

The players should not be able to collectively improve upon the solution outcome.

Scale Transformation Covariance (STC): For every $(S, d) \in \mathcal{D}^N$ and all $a, b \in I\!\!R^N$ with $a > 0$ and $(aS + b, ad + b) \in \mathcal{D}^N$, we have $\varphi(aS + b, ad + b) = a\varphi(S, d) + b$.

The outcomes in S are usually interpreted as utility n-tuples which represent the players' preferences over some underlying set of alternatives. If these utility functions are "cardinal", e.g., von Neumann-Morgenstern, utility functions, then they represent the players' preferences uniquely only up to positive affine transformations (cf. theorem 11.2). The scale transformation covariance axiom requires the solution to be independent of the chosen representations of the preferences.

Independence of Irrelevant Alternatives (IIA): For all $(S, d), (T, e) \in \mathcal{D}^N$ with $d = e$, $S \subset T$ and $\varphi(T, e) \in S$, we have $\varphi(S, d) = \varphi(T, e)$.

Independence of irrelevant alternatives is Nash's main and also most criticized axiom. It states that if the feasible set shrinks but the solution outcome remains feasible, then the solution outcome for the smaller feasible set should be the same point. In other words, the solution outcome "beats" every outcome in T, so it certainly "beats" every outcome in $S \subset T$. An interpretation in this spirit will be elaborated in chapter 3. Most criticisms on IIA focus on the fact that it makes the solution insensitive to possibly important changes in the feasible set. See, in particular, Luce and Raiffa (1957, p. 132 ff.) and Kalai and Smorodinsky (1975). See also sections 4.1, 4.2.

Definition 2.1 For every $(S, d) \in C^N$, let $\nu(S, d)$ be the outcome of S where the function

$$x \mapsto \prod_{i \in N} (x_i - d_i) \tag{2.1}$$

is maximized over the set $\{x \in S : x \geq d\}$. The solution ν is called the (*symmetric*) *Nash* (*bargaining*) *solution*. The product in (2.1) is called the (*symmetric*) *Nash product*.

Thus, the Nash solution assigns to a convex bargaining game the point of the feasible set, dominating the disagreement outcome, where the product of the players' utility gains over their disagreement utilities is maximized.

We next argue that ν is well-defined, i.e., the maximum location in definition 2.1 is indeed unique, and derive a geometrical characterization for ν. First observe that the function in (2.1) is a strictly quasiconcave function on the convex set $\{x \in S : x > d\}$. Recall that $f : C \to I\!R$, with C a convex subset of $I\!R^m$ for some $m \in I\!N$, is *strictly quasiconcave* if $f(x) \geq f(x')$ implies $f(tx + (1-t)x') > f(x')$ for all $x \neq x' \in C$ and $0 < t < 1$. Strict quasiconcavity of the Nash product function in (2.1) can be derived directly, or for instance by applying theorem 5 in Arrow and Enthoven (1961). Uniqueness of the argmax of (2.1) now follows easily. Furthermore, by the Minkowsky separation theorem (Rockafellar, 1970, Section 11) the set S and the upper contour set

$$\{x \in I\!R^N : \prod_{i \in N} (x_i - d_i) \geq \prod_{i \in N} (\nu_i(S, d) - d_i)\} \tag{2.2}$$

can be separated by a hyperplane in $I\!R^N$. The equation of this hyperplane can be derived by differentiation of the Nash product function in (2.1). In that way, the following lemma is derived.

Lemma 2.2 Let $(S, d) \in C^N$ and $z \in W(S)$ with $z > d$. Then $z = \nu(S, d)$ if and only if the hyperplane in $I\!R^N$ with equation

$$\sum_{i \in N} \frac{x_i}{z_i - d_i} = \sum_{i \in N} \frac{z_i}{z_i - d_i}$$

supports S at z.

By way of an example, if $(S, d) \in C^N$ with $d = 0$ and $N = \{1, 2\}$, then $\nu(S, d)$ is the point of $W(S)$ at which there is a supporting line with slope equal to the negative of the slope of the straight line through $d = 0$ and $\nu(S, d)$.

Verification of the following proposition is left to the reader.

Proposition 2.3 Let $\mathcal{D}^N \subset C^N$. Then the Nash solution $\nu : \mathcal{D}^N \to I\!R^N$ satisfies SYM, WPO, STC, and IIA.

Nash's original result was that the four axioms in proposition 2.3 uniquely determine the Nash solution.

Proposition 2.4 *Let* $\varphi : C^N \to \mathbb{R}^N$ *be a bargaining solution satisfying SYM, WPO, STC and IIA. Then* φ *is the symmetric Nash bargaining solution.*

Proof Let $(S,d) \in C^N$. By STC, w.l.o.g.[1] $d = 0$ and $z := \nu(S,d) = (1,1,\ldots,1)$. We have to show that $\varphi(S,d) = z$. By lemma 2.2 the hyperplane with equation $\sum_{i \in N} x_i = n$ supports S at z. Take $K \in \mathbb{R}$, $K > 0$ so large that $S \subset T$ where

$$T := \{x \in \mathbb{R}^N : \sum_{i \in N} x_i \leq n, \ x \leq (K,K,\ldots,K)\}.$$

Since φ is symmetric and weakly Pareto optimal, $\varphi(T,d) = z$. Because $S \subset T$ and $\varphi(T,d) = z \in S$, by IIA: $\varphi(S,d) = z$. $\qquad\square$

By combining propositions 2.3 and 2.4 one obtains the result that Nash obtained for the case of two players.

Theorem 2.5 *The bargaining solution* $\varphi : C^N \to \mathbb{R}^N$ *satisfies SYM, WPO, STC, and IIA, if and only if* φ *is the symmetric Nash bargaining solution.*

In axiomatic characterizations, it is a good practice to check whether the axioms involved are independent, so that no axioms can be left out. In this case, starting with WPO, we have the following lemma.

Lemma 2.6 *Let* $\varphi : C^N \to \mathbb{R}^N$ *satisfy STC and IIA. Then either* φ *satisfies WPO or* $\varphi(S,d) = d$ *for all* $(S,d) \in C^N$.

Proof The proof consists of two steps. First, it will be shown that if $\varphi(S,d) \notin W(S)$ then $\varphi(S,d) = d$, for all $(S,d) \in C^N$. Second, we prove that, if $\varphi(S,d) = d$ for *some* $(S,d) \in C^N$, then $\varphi(S,d) = d$ for *all* $(S,d) \in C^N$.

For the first step, suppose $(S,d) \in C^N$ with $\varphi(S,d) \notin W(S)$. In view of STC, w.l.o.g. $d = 0$. We are done if $\varphi(S,d) = 0$. Suppose $\varphi(S,d) \neq 0$. Let $\alpha \in \mathbb{R}$, $\alpha > 1$ be such that $\alpha\varphi(S,d) \in W(S)$. By IIA, $\varphi(\alpha^{-1}S, \alpha^{-1}d) = \varphi(S,d)$, so by STC, $\alpha = 1$, a contradiction.

For the second step, let $(T,e) \in C^N$ with $\varphi(T,e) = e$. Take $(T',e') \in C^N$ arbitrarily. Take $a,b \in \mathbb{R}^N$ with $a > 0$ such that $ae + b = e'$, $T' \subset aT + b$. Then, by STC, $\varphi(aT + b, e') = a\varphi(T,e) + b = ae + b = e'$. So by IIA, $\varphi(T',e') = e'$. $\qquad\square$

The solution assigning to each bargaining game its disagreement point is called the *disagreement point solution*. An immediate consequence of lemma 2.6 and theorem 2.5 is the following theorem.

Theorem 2.7 *There are exactly two solutions on* C^N *satisfying SYM, STC, and IIA, namely the symmetric Nash bargaining solution and the disagreement point solution.*

---

[1]without loss of generality

Theorem 2.7 describes the consequences of dropping weak Pareto optimality in the characterization of the symmetric Nash bargaining solution. The disagreement point solution can be excluded by requiring the following axiom, stated for a solution $\varphi : \mathcal{D}^N \to \mathbb{R}^N$, where $\mathcal{D}^N \subset \tilde{\mathcal{B}}^N$.

Strong Individual Rationality (SIR): For every $(S, d) \in \mathcal{D}^N$ and $i \in N$, $\varphi_i(S, d) \geq d_i$, with strict inequality whenever $x_i > d_i$ for some $x \in S$.

For later reference, we also define:

Individual Rationality (IR): For every $(S, d) \in \mathcal{D}^N$, $\varphi(S, d) \geq d$.

An immediate consequence of theorem 2.7 is the following corollary.

Corollary 2.8 *The symmetric Nash bargaining solution is the unique solution on $\mathcal{C}^N$ satisfying SYM, STC, SIR, and IIA.*

Corollary 2.8 was first proved by Roth (1977a).

Dropping the main axiom, IIA, gives a plethora of solutions. The most well-known of these is probably the Raiffa-Kalai-Smorodinsky solution, see section 4.2. A solution satisfying symmetry, weak Pareto optimality, and independence of irrelevant alternatives, is the egalitarian solution, see section 4.5. The consequences of dropping the symmetry axiom are discussed in the next section.

2.3   Nonsymmetric Nash solutions

In this section, we consider the consequences of dropping the symmetry axiom in theorem 2.5 — the characterization of the symmetric Nash bargaining solution.

Apart from showing that the axioms in theorem 2.5 are independent, what is the importance of considering nonsymmetric solutions? There is the intrinsic value of the thorough investigation of a mathematical model. More important for applications, nonsymmetries may arise from exogenous factors, which are not determined by the abstract model of the bargaining game, but come from properties of the underlying situation. An example is given in subsection 2.4.4. See also section 9.4.

Because this section is rather technical, readers not interested in the proof of the main result may skip the part before theorem 2.32, starting with proposition 2.16. Intermediate results are corollaries 2.24 and 2.25.

We start by showing that weak Pareto optimality, scale transformation covariance, and independence of irrelevant alternatives no longer imply individual rationality of the bargaining solution.

Example 2.9 Let $N = \{1, 2\}$, and let $\varphi : \mathcal{C}^N \to \mathbb{R}^N$ assign to each $(S, d) \in \mathcal{C}^N$ the point $\varphi(S, d)$ with $\varphi_2(S, d) := u_2(S)$ and $\varphi_1(S, d) := \max\{x_1 : (x_1, u_2(S)) \in S\}$. Clearly, φ satisfies WPO, STC, and IIA, but not IR.

Because individual rationality seems to be a compelling property for a solution, it will be required explicitly below. The next example defines a 2-person solution satisfying WPO, STC, IIA, and IR.

Example 2.10 Let $N = \{1,2\}$ and let $\varphi : \mathcal{C}^N \to \mathbb{R}^N$ assign to each $(S,d) \in \mathcal{C}^N$ the point $\varphi(S,d)$ with $\varphi_1(S,d) := d_1$ and $\varphi_2(S,d) := \max\{x_2 : (d_1,x_2) \in S\}$.

Contrary to the symmetric Nash bargaining solution, the solution of example 2.10 does not have the following property. For $T \subset \mathbb{R}^N$, let

$$P(T) := \{x \in T : \text{there is no } y \in T \text{ with } y \geq x, \ y \neq x\}$$

denote the *Pareto optimal subset* of T. Let $\varphi : \mathcal{D}^N \to \mathbb{R}^N$ be a solution.

Pareto Optimality (PO): For every $(S,d) \in \mathcal{D}^N$, $\varphi(S,d) \in P(S)$.

In this section, in order to further restrict the class of solutions, we will exclude those that are only weakly Pareto optimal. In other words, we will require PO instead of WPO. The next example describes a 4-person bargaining solution which satisfies IR, PO, STC, and IIA.

Example 2.11 Let $N = \{1,2,3,4\}$, and let $\varphi : \mathcal{C}^N \to \mathbb{R}^N$ be defined as follows. For $(S,d) \in \mathcal{C}^N$, let $\varphi_4(S,d) := \max\{x_4 : x \in S, \ x \geq d\}$. Let $Z := \{(x_1,x_2,x_3) \in \mathbb{R}^3 : (x_1,x_2,x_3,\varphi_4(S,d)) \in S\}$. If $z > (d_1,d_2,d_3)$ for some $z \in Z$, then let $\varphi(S,d)$ be such that $(\varphi_1(S,d),\varphi_2(S,d),\varphi_3(S,d))$ maximizes the product $(x_1 - d_1)(x_2 - d_2)(x_3 - d_3)$ on $\{x \in Z : x \geq (d_1,d_2,d_3)\}$. Otherwise, let $(\varphi_1(S,d),\varphi_2(S,d),\varphi_3(S,d))$ be the lexicographical maximum of this set[2]. It is straightforward to verify that, indeed, φ satisfies IR, PO, STC, and IIA.

The next example shows that the solution of example 2.11 violates a property which will be introduced afterwards. First, we need a few notations: for a set $X \subset \mathbb{R}^N$, $\text{conv}(X)$ denotes the convex hull of X, and $\text{comv}(X) := \text{com}(\text{conv}(X))$ denotes the comprehensive convex hull of X.

Example 2.12 Let (S,d) and (T,d) in $\mathcal{C}^N$ $(N = \{1,2,3,4\})$ be defined by $d := 0$, $S := \text{comv}\{(1,0,0,1),(0,1,0,1),(0,0,1,1)\}$, and $T := \text{comv}\{(1,0,0,0), (0,\frac{2}{3},0,1),(0,0,\frac{2}{3},1)\}$. Let φ be the solution of example 2.11. Then $\varphi(S,d) = (\frac{1}{3},\frac{1}{3},\frac{1}{3},1)$ and $\varphi(T,d) = (0,\frac{2}{3},0,1)$. Fix in the game (S,d) player 1's utility at $\frac{1}{3}$. The "slice" remaining for the other players is the set

$$\{(x_2,x_3,x_4) : (\varphi_1(S,d),x_2,x_3,x_4) \in S\} = \text{com}\{(\tfrac{2}{3}-\alpha,\alpha,1) : 0 \leq \alpha \leq \tfrac{2}{3}\}.$$

Analogously, in the game (T,d):

$$\{(x_2,x_3,x_4) : (\varphi_1(T,d),x_2,x_3,x_4) \in T\} = \text{com}\{(\tfrac{2}{3}-\alpha,\alpha,1) : 0 \leq \alpha \leq \tfrac{2}{3}\}.$$

Nevertheless, $(\varphi_2(S,d),\varphi_3(S,d),\varphi_4(S,d)) = (\frac{1}{3},\frac{1}{3},1) \neq (\frac{2}{3},0,1) = (\varphi_2(T,d), \varphi_3(T,d), \varphi_4(T,d))$.

Example 2.12 shows that the properties IR, PO, STC, and IIA do not imply the following property. In order to define this property, some additional notation is required. For $x \in \mathbb{R}^N$ and $\emptyset \neq M \subset N$, x_M denotes the vector in $\mathbb{R}^M$ obtained by deleting the coordinates of x belonging to $N\backslash M$. For $T \subset \mathbb{R}^N$, $T_M := \{y_M : y \in T\}$. Further, $(T,x)_M := \{y_M : y \in T, y_{N\backslash M} = x_{N\backslash M}\}$. For $(T,d) \in \mathcal{D}^N$ and a solution $\varphi : \mathcal{D}^N \to \mathbb{R}^N$,

---

[2]This is obtained by first maximizing the first coordinate, conditionally on this maximizing the second coordinate, conditionally on this maximizing the third coordinate.

$$(T, d, \varphi)_M := (T, \varphi(T, d))_M$$

is called the *feasible set for M with respect to (T, d) and φ.* It consists of those utility $|M|$-tuples available for the collective M, if the players i outside M receive $\varphi_i(T, d)$. Because, in this chapter, the set of players is assumed to be fixed, feasible sets for coalitions of players are not identified with bargaining games for those coalitions. This last approach will be adopted in chapter 7. Finally, as usual we write $x_i, T_i, \ldots$ instead of $x_{\{i\}}, T_{\{i\}}, \ldots$ Let $\varphi : \mathcal{D}^N \to I\!\!R^N$ be a bargaining solution.

Consistency (CONS): For all $(S, d), (T, d) \in \mathcal{D}^N$ and every $\emptyset \neq M \subset N$, if $(S, d, \varphi)_M = (T, d, \varphi)_M$, then $\varphi_M(S, d) = \varphi_M(T, d)$.

This consistency property is an example of a well-known general principle in game theory, see for instance Thomson (1990) and Driessen (1991). In the framework where the number of players may vary, it is intimately related to Lensberg's (1988) *stability* property: see section 7.4, and the end of this section. Harsanyi (1959) was the first to use a consistency property like this one.

    The remainder of this section will be devoted to the characterization of all solutions on $\mathcal{C}^N$ satisfying IR, PO, STC, IIA, and CONS. We start with the following definition.

Definition 2.13 A *weighted hierarchy H of N* is an ordered $(k + 1)$-tuple of the form

$$H = < N^1, N^2, \ldots, N^k, \omega >$$

where $(N^1, N^2, \ldots, N^k)$ is a partition of N (i.e., the sets N^ℓ are pairwise disjoint nonempty sets whose union equals N) and $\omega \in I\!\!R_{++}^N$ with $\sum_{i \in N^\ell} \omega_i = 1$ for every $\ell = 1, 2, \ldots, k$. The set N^ℓ is called the ℓth *class of H*. By $\mathcal{H}^N$ the family of all weighted hierarchies of N is denoted.

With each weighted hierarchy $H \in \mathcal{H}^N$ a bargaining solution φ for N will be associated, by lexicographically maximizing "nonsymmetric Nash products" in a bargaining game (S, d) according to the partition and weights in H. Before we can give a formal definition, we need some more definitions and notations, and a lemma.

Definition 2.14 (i) Let $\emptyset \neq L \subset M \subset N, V \subset I\!\!R^M, z \in I\!\!R^M$. Denote by

$$L_+(V, z) := \{i \in L : \text{there exists } x \in V \text{ with } x_i > z_i\}$$

the subset of players in L for which there is an element of V strictly dominating z. (If, in particular, V is convex, it follows that there is an $x \in V$ with $x_{L_+(V,z)} > z_{L_+(V,z)}$, provided $L_+(V, z) \neq \emptyset$.)
(ii) For $V \subset W \subset I\!\!R^N$ and a function $f : W \to I\!\!R^N$ we use the (somewhat loose) notation

$$\operatorname{argmax}\{f(x) : x \in V\} := \{x \in V : f(x) \geq f(y) \text{ for all } y \in V\}.$$

(iii) Let $H = < N^1, N^2, \ldots, N^k, \omega >$ be a weighted hierarchy of N, and let $(S, d) \in \mathcal{C}^N$. For $\ell = 0, 1, 2, \ldots, k$ the sets S^ℓ are defined as follows:

$$S^0 := \{x \in I\!\!R^N : x \in P(S), x \geq d\}$$

$$S^1 \;:=\; \text{argmax}\{\textstyle\prod(x_i - d_i)^{\omega_i} : i \in N^1, x \in S^0\}$$

$$S^2 \;:=\; \begin{cases} \text{argmax}\{\prod(x_i - d_i)^{\omega_i} : i \in N^2_+(S^1, d),\; x \in S^1\} \text{ if } N^2_+(S^1, d) \neq \emptyset, \\ S^1 \text{ otherwise} \end{cases}$$

$$\vdots$$

$$S^\ell \;:=\; \begin{cases} \text{argmax}\{\prod(x_i - d_i)^{\omega_i} : i \in N^\ell_+(S^{\ell-1}, d),\; x \in S^{\ell-1}\} \text{ if } N^\ell_+(S^{\ell-1}, d) \neq \emptyset, \\ S^{\ell-1} \text{ otherwise} \end{cases}$$

$$\vdots$$

$$S^k \;:=\; \begin{cases} \text{argmax}\{\prod(x_i - d_i)^{\omega_i} : i \in N^k_+(S^{k-1}, d),\; x \in S^{k-1}\} \text{ if } N^k_+(S^{k-1}, d) \neq \emptyset, \\ S^{k-1} \text{ otherwise.} \end{cases}$$

Lemma 2.15 *Let $H = <N^1, N^2, \ldots, N^k, \omega> \in \mathcal{H}^N$. Let $(S, d) \in \mathcal{C}^N$ and let S^k be the set described in definition 2.14 (iii). Then $|S^k| = 1$.*

Proof Since S is convex and every "Nash product" $\prod(x_i - d_i)^{\omega_i}$ strictly quasi-concave if the number of indices i is greater than 1, we have, for every $\ell \in \{1, 2, \ldots, k\}$ and all $x, y \in S^\ell$ (see definition 2.14), that $x_i = y_i$ for all $i \in \bigcup_{j=1}^{\ell} N^j$. In particular, $x = y$ for all $x, y \in S^k$.   □

In view of lemma 2.15, the solution $\varphi^H : \mathcal{C}^N \to I\!\!R^N$ assigning the unique element of S^k to every $(S, d) \in \mathcal{C}^N$, is well-defined. The solution φ^H is called the *bargaining solution corresponding to the weighted hierarchy H*. Observe that, if $H = <N, (\frac{1}{n}, \ldots, \frac{1}{n})>$, then φ^H equals ν, the symmetric Nash bargaining solution.

Proposition 2.16 *Let $H = <N^1, N^2, \ldots, N^k, \omega> \in \mathcal{H}^N$. Then $\varphi^H : \mathcal{C}^N \to I\!\!R^N$ satisfies IR, PO, STC, IIA, and CONS.*

Before proving this proposition, we need some additional notation.

Definition 2.17 Let $\emptyset \neq L \subset M \subset N$. By $e^L \in I\!\!R^N$ we denote the vector with $e_i^L = 1$ if $i \in L$, $e_i^L = 0$ otherwise. In particular, we write e^i instead of $e^{\{i\}}$, if $L = \{i\}$. For $x \in I\!\!R^L$, we denote by $O^M(x) \in I\!\!R^M$ the vector with $O^M(x)_i = x_i$ if $i \in L$, $O^M(x)_i = 0$ otherwise; and by $E^M(x) \in I\!\!R^M$ the vector with $E^M(x)_i = x_i$ if $i \in L$, $E^M(x)_i = 1$ otherwise. For $S \subset I\!\!R^L$, we denote $O^M(S) := \{O^M(x) : x \in S\}$ and $E^M(S) := \{E^M(x) : x \in S\}$.

Proof of proposition 2.16 The proof of IR, PO, STC, and IIA of φ^H is left to the reader. We are left to show that φ^H is consistent. Let $(S, d), (T, d) \in \mathcal{C}^N$ and $\emptyset \neq M \subset N$. Suppose that $(S, d, \varphi^H)_M = (T, d, \varphi^H)_M$. It must be proved that

$$\varphi^H_M(S, d) = \varphi^H_M(T, d). \tag{2.3}$$

Let $L := N \setminus M$. W.l.o.g. $L \neq \emptyset$, otherwise (2.3) follows immediately. Let $L^1 := \{i \in L : \varphi_i^H(S, d) = d_i\}$ and $L^2 := \{i \in L : \varphi_i^H(S, d) > d_i\}$. Similarly, $L^3 := \{i \in L : \varphi_i^H(T, d) = d_i\}$ and $L^4 := \{i \in L : \varphi_i^H(T, d) > d_i\}$. In view of STC of φ^H, w.l.o.g. suppose $d = 0$, $L^2 = \{i \in L : \varphi_i^H(S, d) = 1\}$, $L^4 = \{i \in L : \varphi_i^H(T, d) = 1\}$. Let $Z := O^N((S, d, \varphi^H)_M) = O^N((T, d, \varphi^H)_M)$, i.e., Z is the "slice" for the players of M in S or T at the solution outcome, embedded in $I\!\!R^N$ by adding zeros.

If there is an $i \in M$ with $z_i \leq 0$ for all $z \in Z$, then $\varphi_i^H(S,d) = \varphi_i^H(T,d) = 0$, which proves (2.3) for such an i. For the determination of $\varphi_j^H(S,d)$ and $\varphi_j^H(T,d)$ for all other j ($\neq i$) we might, by definition of φ^H, restrict attention to $\{x \in S : x_i = 0\}$ and $\{x \in T : x_i = 0\}$ from the start; in other words, it is without loss of generality to assume that $M_+(Z,d) = M$ (cf. definition 2.14 (i)).

Now let $V := \mathrm{comv}(Z \cup \{\alpha e^{L^1}\} + e^{L^2})$ and $W := \mathrm{comv}(Z \cup \{\beta e^{L^3}\} + e^{L^4})$, where α and β are chosen such that $\alpha e^{L^1} \in S$, $\beta e^{L^3} \in T$. Also, $e^{L^2} = O^N(\varphi_{L^2}^H(S,d)) \in S$ and $e^{L^4} = O^N(\varphi_{L^4}^H(T,d)) \in T$, so $V \subset S$, $W \subset T$. Since $(V,d),(W,d) \in \mathcal{C}^N$, $\varphi^H(S,d) \in V$, $\varphi^H(T,d) \in W$, IIA implies:

$$\varphi^H(S,d) = \varphi^H(V,d), \quad \varphi^H(T,d) = \varphi^H(W,d). \tag{2.4}$$

Because we may restrict attention to Z for the determination of both $\varphi^H(V,d)$ and $\varphi^H(W,d)$, we conclude $\varphi_M^H(V,d) = \varphi_M^H(W,d)$. In combination with (2.4), this implies (2.3). $\qquad\square$

Our main objective is to show that the converse of proposition 2.16 also holds:

Proposition 2.18 *Let $\varphi : \mathcal{C}^N \to \mathbb{R}^N$ be a bargaining solution satisfying IR, PO, STC, IIA, and CONS. Then there exists a weighted hierarchy $H \in \mathcal{H}^N$ such that $\varphi = \varphi^H$.*

Before we can prove this proposition, we need some more definitions and lemmas.

Denote $\Delta^M := \mathrm{comv}\{e^i \in \mathbb{R}^M : i \in M\}$, for $\emptyset \neq M \subset N$, and call $\overline{\Delta}^M := \mathrm{com}(E^N(\Delta^M))$ the *standard bargaining game for $M \subset N$*. A solution with the five properties listed in proposition 2.18 will be characterized by the outcomes it assigns to standard bargaining games.

Definition 2.19 *Let $\varphi : \mathcal{C}^N \to \mathbb{R}^N$ be a bargaining solution and $H = <N^1,N^2,\ldots,N^k,$ $\omega> \in \mathcal{H}^N$ a weighted hierarchy. We say that φ determines H (on standard bargaining games) if*

$$\varphi(\Delta^N, 0) = O^N(\omega_{N^1})$$
$$\varphi(\overline{\Delta}^{\cup_{\ell=2}^k N^\ell}, 0) = e^{N^1} + O^N(\omega_{N^2})$$
$$\varphi(\overline{\Delta}^{\cup_{\ell=3}^k N^\ell}, 0) = e^{N^1 \cup N^2} + O^N(\omega_{N^3})$$
$$\vdots$$
$$\varphi(\overline{\Delta}^{N^k}, 0) = e^{\cup_{\ell=1}^{k-1} N^\ell} + O^N(\omega_{N^k}). \tag{2.5}$$

The following lemma and its proof are similar to lemma 2.2 and its proof. Therefore, the proof is omitted.

Lemma 2.20 *Let $(S,d) \in \mathcal{C}^N$, $\omega \in \mathbb{R}_{++}^N$ with $\sum_{i \in N} \omega_i = 1$, and $z \in P(S)$ with $z \geq d$. Then z maximizes the product $\prod_{i \in N}(x_i - d_i)^{\omega_i}$ on $\{x \in P(S) : x \geq d\}$ if and only if the hyperplane with equation*

$$\sum_{i \in N} \frac{\omega_i x_i}{z_i - d_i} = \sum_{i \in N} \frac{\omega_i z_i}{z_i - d_i}$$

supports S at z.

We first show (lemma 2.21) that every Pareto optimal and individually rational bargaining solution defined on C^N determines a (unique) weighted hierarchy. Further, every φ^H determines H.

Lemma 2.21 *(i) For every $H \in \mathcal{H}^N$, φ^H determines H. (ii) If the bargaining solution $\varphi : C^N \to \mathbb{R}^N$ determines H and H' in $\mathcal{H}^N$, then $H = H'$. (iii) Every Pareto optimal and individually rational bargaining solution $\varphi : C^N \to \mathbb{R}^N$ determines some $H \in \mathcal{H}^N$.*

Proof (i) follows with the aid of lemma 2.20. (ii) follows by definition, that is, by (2.5). Also (iii) follows from (2.5), as follows. Let φ satisfy IR and PO. Let $N^1 := \{i \in N : \varphi_i(\Delta^N, 0) > 0\}$ and, for $i \in N^1$, $\omega_i := \varphi_i(\Delta^N, 0)$. If $N \neq N^1$, let $N^2 := \{i \in N \backslash N^1 : \varphi_i(\overline{\Delta}^{N \backslash N^1}, 0) > 0\}$, and, for $i \in N^2$, $\omega_i := \varphi_i(\overline{\Delta}^{N \backslash N^1}, 0)$. Etc.   □

Next, we consider two special cases.

Lemma 2.22 *Let the bargaining solution $\varphi : C^N \to \mathbb{R}^N$ satisfy IR, STC, and IIA, and let φ determine $H = \,< N, \omega > \,\in \mathcal{H}^N$. Then $\varphi = \varphi^H$.*

Proof The proof is similar to the proof of proposition 2.4. Let $(S, d) \in C^N$. In view of STC, w.l.o.g. assume $d = 0$. By IR and IIA, w.l.o.g. assume $S = \text{com}\{x \in S : x \geq 0\}$. In view of STC, w.l.o.g. assume $\varphi^H(S, d) = \omega$. From lemma 2.20 it follows that the hyperplane with equation $\sum_{i=1}^n x_i = 1$ supports S at ω. Therefore, $S \subset \Delta^N$. Furthermore, since φ determines H, $\varphi(\Delta^N, 0) = \omega$. So IIA implies $\varphi(S, d) = \omega$. Hence, $\varphi(S, d) = \varphi^H(S, d)$.   □

Lemma 2.23 *Let $N = \{1, 2\}$ and let $\varphi : C^N \to \mathbb{R}^N$ satisfy IR, PO, STC, and IIA. Then $\varphi = \varphi^H$ for some $H \in \mathcal{H}^N$.*

Proof Let H be the unique weighted hierarchy determined by φ (cf. lemma 2.21, (ii) and (iii)). If H is of the form $< N, \omega >$, then we are done by lemma 2.22. Otherwise, either $H = \,< \{1\}, \{2\}, (1,1) >$ or $H = \,< \{2\}, \{1\}, (1,1) >$. Assume the first, the second case is similar. Thus, $\varphi(\Delta^N, 0) = (1, 0)$. Let $(S, d) \in C^N$ and suppose $\varphi(S, d) \neq \varphi^H(S, d)$. We will derive a contradiction which completes the proof.

Note that $\varphi^H(S, d)$ is the point of $P(S)$ weakly dominating d with maximal first coordinate. Therefore, $\varphi_1(S, d) < \varphi_1^H(S, d)$. In view of STC, it is without loss of generality to assume that $d = 0$, $\varphi_1^H(S, d) = 1$, $\varphi_1(S, d) + \varphi_2(S, d) = 1$.

Let $W := \text{comv}\{(\varphi_1^H(S, d), d_2), \varphi(S, d)\} = \text{comv}\{(1, 0), \varphi(S, d)\}$. Then $(W, d) \in C^N$, $W \subset S$, $\varphi(S, d) \in W$. So IIA implies $\varphi(W, d) = \varphi(S, d)$. On the other hand $W \subset \Delta^N$, $\varphi(\Delta^N, 0) = (1, 0) \in W$, so by IIA: $\varphi(W, d) = (1, 0) \neq \varphi(S, d)$. This is the desired contradiction.   □

Lemma 2.23 and proposition 2.16 immediately imply:

Corollary 2.24 *The bargaining solution $\varphi : C^{\{1,2\}} \to \mathbb{R}^{\{1,2\}}$ satisfies IR, PO, STC, and IIA, if and only if $\varphi = \varphi^H$ for some $H \in \mathcal{H}^{\{1,2\}}$.*

Corollary 2.24 was first proved in de Koster *et al.* (1983). Observe that the consistency axiom is not used: if $n = 2$, CONS follows from PO.

Lemmas 2.22, 2.6, and proposition 2.16, imply:

Corollary 2.25 *The bargaining solution* $\varphi : C^N \to \mathbb{R}^N$ *satisfies SIR, STC, and IIA, if and only if* $\varphi = \varphi^H$ *for some* $H \in \mathcal{H}^N$ *of the form* $H = <N, \omega>$.

Note that corollary 2.8 immediately follows from corollary 2.25. Lemma 2.22 corresponds to theorem 3 in Roth (1979a).

The proof of proposition 2.18 will be based on lemma 2.23 and the following induction hypothesis:

For all $2 \le k < n$, for all $K \subset N$ with $|K| = k$, and for all $H \in \mathcal{H}^K$, if the solution

$\varphi : C^K \to \mathbb{R}^K$ satisfies IR, PO, STC, IIA, and CONS, and determines H,

then $\varphi = \varphi^H$.   (2.6)

For an n-person bargaining solution $\varphi : C^N \to \mathbb{R}^N$, we define solutions for subclasses of the player set N, as follows.

Definition 2.26 Let $\varphi : C^N \to \mathbb{R}^N$ be a bargaining solution, and $\emptyset \ne M \subset N$. We denote by $M\varphi : C^M \to \mathbb{R}^M$ the solution for M defined by $M\varphi(S, d) := \varphi_M(\text{com}(E^N(S)), O^N(d))$ for every $(S, d) \in C^M$.

Lemma 2.27 *Let the solution* $\varphi : C^N \to \mathbb{R}^N$ *satisfy IR, PO, STC, IIA, and CONS, and let* $\emptyset \ne M \subset N$. *Then also* $M\varphi : C^M \to \mathbb{R}^M$ *has these properties.*

Proof We only show that $M\varphi$ is consistent, and leave verification of the other properties to the reader. Let $(S, d), (T, d) \in C^M$, $\emptyset \ne L \subset M$, $L \ne M$, such that $(S, d, M\varphi)_L = (T, d, M\varphi)_L$. Then $(\text{com}(E^N(S)), O^N(d), \varphi)_L = (\text{com}(E^N(T)), O^N(d), \varphi)_L$, so by CONS of φ we have $M\varphi_j(S, d) = M\varphi_j(T, d)$ for all $j \in L$. We conclude that $M\varphi$ is consistent. $\square$

The next lemma shows that the induced solution $M\varphi$ determines a corresponding induced weighted hierarchy.

Lemma 2.28 *Let the solution* $\varphi : C^N \to \mathbb{R}^N$ *determine* $<N^1, N^2, \ldots, N^k, \omega> \in \mathcal{H}^N$, *where* $k \ge 2$. *Let* $M := N \backslash N^1$. *Then* $M\varphi$ *determines* $<N^2, N^3, \ldots, N^k, \omega_M> \in \mathcal{H}^M$.

Proof $M\varphi(\overline{\Delta}^M, 0) = \varphi_M(\overline{\Delta}^M, 0) = O^M(\omega_{N^2})$, $M\varphi(\text{com}(E^M(\Delta^{M \backslash N^2})), 0) = \varphi_M(\overline{\Delta}^{M \backslash N^2}, 0) = \varphi_M(\overline{\Delta}^{N \backslash (N^1 \cup N^2)}, 0) = e^{N^2} + O^M(\omega_{N^3})$, etc. $\square$

The following lemma treats the case in which the first class of the weighted hierarchy determined by a solution with the five properties of proposition 2.18, consists of exactly one player.

Lemma 2.29 *Let the solution* $\varphi : C^N \to \mathbb{R}^N$ *satisfy IR, PO, STC, IIA, and CONS, and let* φ *determine* $H = <N^1, N^2, \ldots, N^k, \omega>$ *with* $|N^1| = 1$. *Suppose furthermore that the induction hypothesis (2.6) holds. Then* $\varphi = \varphi^H$.

Proof W.l.o.g. let $N^1 = \{1\}$. Take $(S, d) \in C^N$, w.l.o.g. $d = 0$, and let $z \in P(S)$, $z \ge 0$, with $z_1 < u_1 := \max\{x_1 : x \in S, x \ge d\}$. Take $\beta > 0$ so large that $z \in V := \text{comv}\{u_1 e^1, \beta e^i \in \mathbb{R}^N : i = 2, \ldots, n\}$, which is possible since $z_1 < u_1$. By STC and $\varphi(\Delta^N, 0) = e^1$, we have $\varphi(V, 0) = u_1 e^1$. Therefore, $\varphi(S, d) \ne z$ since otherwise, by IIA, $\varphi(V \cap S, 0) = u_1 e^1$ as well as $\varphi(V \cap S, 0) = z$, which is a contradiction. Thus, we have proved:

For every $(T, e) \in \mathcal{C}^N, \varphi_1(T, e) = \varphi_1^H(T, e)$.   (2.7)

Let $M := N \backslash \{1\}$, and let $L := \{i \in M: \text{there is an } x \in (S, d, \varphi)_M \text{ with } x_i > d_i\}$. Suppose $M \backslash L \neq \emptyset$. Note that $\varphi_i(S, d) = 0$ for all $i \in M \backslash L$ and that, in view of (2.7), $(S, d, \varphi)_L = (e^{M \backslash L} + S, d, \varphi)_L$, so, in view of CONS: $\varphi_L(S, d) = \varphi_L(e^{M \backslash L} + S, d)$. Consequently, it is without loss of generality to assume that $M = L$, i.e., $M \backslash L = \emptyset$. In view of STC we may assume $u_1 = 1$, so by IIA: $\varphi(S, d) = \varphi(\text{com}(E^N(S, d, \varphi)_M)), d)$, hence $\varphi_M(S, d) = M\varphi((S, d, \varphi)_M, 0) = \varphi_M^H(S, d)$, where the last equality follows from lemmas 2.27 and 2.28, and induction hypothesis (2.6). So we have proved that $\varphi_i(S, d) = \varphi_i^H(S, d)$ for all $i \in N$.
$\square$

Another special case is where the first class of the induced hierarchy contains at least two, but not all players.

Lemma 2.30 *Let the solution $\varphi : \mathcal{C}^N \to I\!\!R^N$ satisfy IR, PO, STC, IIA, and CONS. Let φ determine $H = <N^1, N^2, \ldots, N^k, \omega> \in \mathcal{H}^N$, with $1 < |N^1| < n$. Let $(S, d) \in \mathcal{C}^N$ and $z = \varphi(S, d)$. Then:*

$$\prod_{i \in N^1} (z_i - d_i)^{\omega_i} = \max\{ \prod_{i \in N^1} (x_i - d_i)^{\omega_i} : x \in S, x \geq d \}.$$ (2.8)

Proof W.l.o.g. let $N^1 = \{1, 2, \ldots, s\}$ with $1 < s < n$ and $d = 0$. Let $M := N \backslash N^1$ and $q \in S$ with $q_M = 0$ and $\prod_{i=1}^s q_i^{\omega_i} = \max\{\prod_{i=1}^s x_i^{\omega_i} : x \in S \cap I\!\!R_+^N, x_M = 0\}$. As a consequence of lemma 2.20, there is a hyperplane Y in $I\!\!R^{N^1}$, supporting $\{x_{N^1} \in I\!\!R^{N^1} : x \in S, x_M = 0\}$ at q_{N^1}, with equation $\sum_{i=1}^s \omega_i q_i^{-1} x_i = 1$. In view of STC, we may suppose that $q_i = \omega_i$ ($i = 1, 2, \ldots, s$). Let $\bar{z} := O^N(z_{N^1})$. We distinguish three cases.

Case (i). $z_{N^1} = q_{N^1}(= \omega_{N^1})$. Then $\prod_{i=1}^s z_i^{\omega_i} = \prod_{i=1}^s q_i^{\omega_i} = \max\{\prod_{i=1}^s x_i^{\omega_i} : x \in S \cap I\!\!R_+^N, x_M = 0\} = \max\{\prod_{i=1}^s x_i^{\omega_i} : x \in S \cap I\!\!R_+^N\}$. So for this case (2.8) holds.

Case (ii). $z_{N^1} \notin Y$. Then $z_{N^1} \in \text{int}(\Delta^{N^1})$, so $\bar{z} \in \text{relint}(O^N(\Delta^{N^1}))$. Therefore we can find $\delta > 0$ so large that $z \in V := \text{comv}(O^N(\Delta^{N^1}) \cup \{\delta e^i \in I\!\!R^N : i \in M\}) \in \mathcal{C}^N$. By STC and the equalities $\varphi(\Delta^N) = O^N(\omega_{N^1}) = q$, we have $\varphi(V) = q$. Then, by IIA, $\varphi(V \cap S) = q$, and also $\varphi(V \cap S) = z$. In particular we have $q_{N^1} = z_{N^1}$ and $z_{N^1} \in Y$. From this contradiction we conclude that case (ii) cannot occur.

Case (iii). $z_{N^1} \in Y$, $z_{N^1} \neq q_{N^1}$. In this case, let $y \in S$ with $y_M = 0$ and $y_{N^1} = \frac{1}{2}(z_{N^1} + q_{N^1})$. Then $\prod_{i=1}^s y_i^{\omega_i} = \max\{\prod_{i=1}^s x_i^{\omega_i} : x \in a\Delta^{N^1}\}$ where $a \in I\!\!R_{++}^{N^1}$ is defined by $a_i = y_i q_i^{-1}$ for every $i = 1, 2, \ldots, s$. A tedious but elementary calculation then shows that $z_{N^1} \in \text{int}(a\Delta^{N^1})$, so $\bar{z} \in \text{relint}(O^N(a\Delta^{N^1}))$, which brings us in a case analogous to case (ii) above. The conclusion that also case (iii) cannot occur, completes the proof. $\square$

Lemma 2.31 *Let φ satisfy the conditions in lemma 2.30, and let the induction hypothesis (2.6) hold. Then $\varphi = \varphi^H$.*

Proof Let $(S, d) \in \mathcal{C}^N$. In view of lemma 2.30 we have:

$$\varphi_{N^1}(S, d) = \varphi_{N^1}^H(S, d).$$ (2.9)

By (2.9) and an argument similar to the one used in the proof of lemma 2.29, which was based on the consistency of φ, we may w.l.o.g. suppose that $M_+((S,d,\varphi)_M, d_M) = M$, where $M := N\backslash N^1$. In view of STC, we may further suppose that $d = 0$ and $\varphi_{N^1}(S,d) = e^{N^1} \in \mathbb{R}^{N^1}$. Hence, by IIA: $\varphi(S,d) = \varphi(\text{com}(E^N(S,d,\varphi)_M), 0)$, so $\varphi_M(S,d) = M\varphi((S,d,\varphi)_M, 0) = \varphi_M^H(S,d)$, where the last equality follows from lemmas 2.27 and 2.28, and induction hypothesis (2.6). $\qquad\qquad\qquad\qquad\qquad\qquad\qquad\qquad\qquad\qquad\qquad\qquad\qquad\qquad$ $\square$

We are finally in a position to prove proposition 2.18.

Proof of proposition 2.18 Let $H \in \mathcal{H}^N$ be the unique (lemma 2.21) weighted hierarchy determined by φ, say $H = < N^1, N^2, \ldots, N^k, \omega >$ with $k \geq 1$. If $k = 1$, then $\varphi = \varphi^H$ by lemma 2.22. If $k > 1$ and $|N^1| = 1$, then $\varphi = \varphi^H$ by lemmas 2.29 and 2.23. Finally, if $k > 1$ and $1 < |N^1| < n$, then $\varphi = \varphi^H$ by lemmas 2.31 and 2.23. $\qquad\qquad\qquad\qquad$ $\square$

Combining propositions 2.16 and 2.18, we conclude:

Theorem 2.32 *The bargaining solution* $\varphi : \mathcal{C}^N \to \mathbb{R}^N$ *satisfies IR, PO, STC, IIA, and CONS, if and only if* $\varphi = \varphi^H$ *for some* $H \in \mathcal{H}^N$.

Are the axioms in theorem 2.32 independent? Examples 2.9 and 2.10 showed that both IR and PO cannot be omitted. Examples 2.11 and 2.12 showed that CONS is indispensable; of course, if $n = 2$, then CONS is implied by PO, see corollary 2.24 and the comment following that result. Also STC cannot be omitted: for instance, the egalitarian solution (see section 4.5) satisfies the remaining axioms but not STC.

The next example shows that IIA cannot be omitted. It is a 3-person example; if $n = 2$, then CONS is implied by PO and so dropping IIA would leave us with only IR, PO, and STC.

Example 2.33 Let $N = \{1, 2, 3\}$. Let the solution $\varphi : \mathcal{C}^N \to \mathbb{R}^N$ be defined as follows. For $(S,0) \in \mathcal{C}^N$ such that $aS = \text{comv}\{(\frac{3}{2}, \frac{3}{2}, 0), (1,1,1)\}$ for some $a \in \mathbb{R}^3_{++}$, let $\varphi(S,0) := (a_1^{-1}, a_2^{-1}, a_3^{-1})(\frac{5}{4}, \frac{5}{4}, \frac{1}{2})$. For every other $(S,0) \in \mathcal{C}^N$, let $\varphi(S,0) := \varphi^H(S,0)$, where $H = < N, (\frac{1}{3}, \frac{1}{3}, \frac{1}{3}) >$. Extend the definition to arbitrary (S,d) by translation: $\varphi(S,d) := \varphi(S - d, 0) + d$. The reader may verify that this solution φ satisfies IR, PO, STC, CONS, but not IIA.

Example 2.33 is based on Lensberg (1988, p. 339). Lensberg gives a characterization of the symmetric Nash bargaining solution $\varphi^H : \mathcal{C}^N \to \mathbb{R}^N$, where $H = < N, (\frac{1}{n}, \ldots, \frac{1}{n}) >$, for arbitrary $n \in \mathbb{N}$, without using the IIA property: instead, he uses a stability property which is closely related to CONS, but which is required in a framework where the number of players may vary and, in this case, may be arbitrarily large. See chapter 7.

As is apparent from corollary 2.25, CONS, IR, and PO may together be replaced by SIR in order to characterize the family of solutions φ^H where H contains exactly one class. In light of this result, it is interesting to note that, loosely speaking, in many cases the conclusion of CONS follows by applying IIA. The CONS axiom is needed in order to take care of "degenerate" cases, where players in "slices" of the feasible set cannot reach a positive gain.

The results in this section are based mainly on section 28 in Peters (1986a).

2.4   Alternative characterizations of nonsymmetric Nash solutions

2.4.1   Introduction

In this section four alternative characterizations of nonsymmetric Nash solutions are presented. The first three of these concern 2-person solutions, the last one n-person solutions.

The first characterization is based on an axiom called *independence of irrelevant expansions*, introduced by Thomson (1981a). Recall that the independence of irrelevant alternatives axiom considers the behavior of a solution when the feasible set shrinks. The independence of irrelevant expansions axiom does the opposite: it puts a requirement on the solution outcome if the feasible set is expanded in a certain way.

Next, in subsection 2.4.3, 2-person nonsymmetric Nash solutions are characterized by means of the axiom of Pareto optimality and the so-called *multiplicativity* axiom. This characterization is based on a result by Binmore (1987a). It is of a technical nature, since the axiom requires a kind of "multiplication invariance"; a utility-theoretic foundation, however, is also provided, based on section 11.6.

In subsection 2.4.4 a model proposed by Kalai (1977a) is discussed, which gives not so much an axiomatic characterization but rather an interpretation in terms of replications of bargaining games. A 2-person bargaining game is replicated in a specific way, where it is assumed that the replicated players are of two different types in a certain proportion. The symmetric Nash bargaining solution is then applied to the resulting n-person game, and the result translated back to the original 2-person game where it gives rise to a nonsymmetric Nash bargaining solution. Thus, the nonsymmetry is explained by referring to different types of players.

Finally, in subsection 2.4.5, nonsymmetric Nash bargaining solutions are characterized as describing the players' possible preferences over playing different positions in different games. This approach, based on Roth (1978), provides an explanation of nonsymmetries in terms of, what Roth calls, the strategic risk posture of the players.

Because, as in the preceding sections, the scale transformation covariance axiom will always be assumed to hold, it is without loss of generality to take the disagreement point equal to 0, whenever convenient. Thus, we let $\mathcal{C}_0^N$ denote the subclass of $\mathcal{C}^N$ consisting of bargaining games with zero disagreement point. More generally, adding the subscript 0 to the notation for some class of bargaining games will mean that the disagreement points of games in that class are equal to zero. Furthermore, it is notationally convenient to write S instead of $(S, 0)$, for bargaining games in $\mathcal{C}_0^N$. Recall from section 1.2 that the superscript N will often be omitted if $N = \{1, 2\}$.

2.4.2   Independence of irrelevant expansions

For $x, y \in \mathbb{R}^n$, denote by $x \cdot y$ the inner product $\sum_{i=1}^n x_i y_i$. Let φ be a solution $\mathcal{C}_0 \to \mathbb{R}^2$, where $\mathcal{C}_0$ is as defined in the previous subsection. The following axiom for φ plays a central role in the present subsection.

Independence of Irrelevant Expansions (IIE): For every $S \in \mathcal{C}_0$ there exists a vector $p \in \mathbb{R}_+^2$ with $p_1 + p_2 = 1$ such that:

(i) $p \cdot x = p \cdot \varphi(S)$ is the equation of a supporting line of S at $\varphi(S)$,

(ii) for all $T \in \mathcal{C}_0$ with $S \subset T$ and $p \cdot x \leq p \cdot \varphi(S)$ for all $x \in T$, we have $\varphi(T) \geq \varphi(S)$.

The IIE axiom is illustrated in figure 2.1. It was introduced in Thomson (1981a).

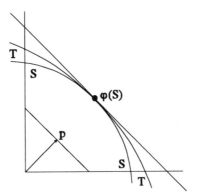

Figure 2.1: Independence of irrelevant expansions

IIE states that, if a bargaining game S is expanded to a game T by adding utility pairs below a specific supporting line of S at $\varphi(S)$, then the solution outcome of T should weakly Pareto dominate the solution outcome of S. Observe that, unless this supporting line is horizontal or vertical, this implies that actually the solution outcome of T equals that of S. One way of looking at this property is as follows. The slope of the (or a) supporting line at the solution outcome reflects the proportion of the utilities, or rate of utility transfers, on which, apparently, the players agree. Now suppose the solution outcome is Pareto optimal and the supporting line unique. In that case, any expansion of the feasible set in which the original solution outcome is still Pareto optimal, has the same unique supporting line at that outcome. It would then be natural to assume that the players will agree on the same outcome, since there the rate of utility transfers is still the preferred one. The IIE axiom is actually stronger, mainly in the sense that it takes care also of the cases where a supporting line is not unique. Further, Thomson (1981a) requires the vector p in the formulation of IIE to be strictly positive. Consequently, his result concerns the solutions φ^H where H has the form $H = <N, \omega>$. In the version presented below, also the "dictator solutions" corresponding to $H = <\{i\}, \{j\}, (1,1)>$ for $i, j \in \{1, 2\}$, are included.

Call a set V in some Euclidean space *smooth* at a boundary point x if V has a unique supporting hyperplane at x. The remarks in the preceding paragraph make it clear that smoothness is an important property in relation with the IIE axiom. This is not a coincidence. The smoothness condition, often interpreted as small utility transfers between the players being well-determined, plays an important role in several axioms satisfied by Nash bargaining solutions and related concepts. In this book see subsection 2.5.3, and sections 5.5, 10.2–10.4.

We start with a lemma which is a formal representation of the intuitively strong relationship between IIE and IIA. Observe, by the way, that IIE implies WPO.

Lemma 2.34 *Let $\varphi : C_0 \to \mathbb{R}^2$ be a solution satisfying IIE, let S be smooth at $\varphi(S)$, and let $T \in C_0$ with $S \subset T$ and $\varphi(S) \in P(T)$. Then $\varphi(T) = \varphi(S)$.*

Proof Let ℓ be the unique supporting line of S at $\varphi(S)$. Since $\varphi(S) \in P(T)$, it is in view of IIE of φ sufficient to show that ℓ supports T at $\varphi(S)$. Let ℓ' be a supporting line of T at $\varphi(S)$. Then ℓ' also supports S at $\varphi(S)$, therefore $\ell = \ell'$. So ℓ supports T at $\varphi(S)$. □

The main result in this section is that in corollary 2.24 IIA may be replaced by IIE. That is, we have the following theorem.

Theorem 2.35 *Let $\varphi : C_0 \to \mathbb{R}^2$ be a 2-person bargaining solution. Then φ satisfies IR, PO, STC, and IIE, if and only if $\varphi = \varphi^H$ for some $H \in \mathcal{H}^{\{1,2\}}$.*

For the proof of theorem 2.35, we need the following lemma. For a subset X of some Euclidean space, $\text{int}(X)$ denotes its (topological) interior. The notation $p(\varphi, S)$ will be used for the set of vectors p in the definition of IIE. If S is smooth at $\varphi(S)$, then $p(\varphi, S)$ contains exactly one element, which, with an abuse of notation, will also be denoted by $p(\varphi, S)$.

Lemma 2.36 *Let $v, w \in \mathbb{R}^2$ with $v_1, w_2 > 0$ and $v_2, w_1 < 0$ and such that $0 \in \text{int}(V)$ where $V := \text{comv}(\{v, w\})$. Let $\varphi : C_0 \to \mathbb{R}^2$ be a solution satisfying IR, PO, STC and IIE, and such that $\varphi_1(V) > 0$. Let $z \in P(V)$, $z \geq 0$, $z_1 < \varphi_1(V)$, and $y \in \text{int}(V)$ with $w_1 < y_1 < 0$ and $z_2 < y_2$. Finally, let $T := \text{comv}(\{v, z, y\})$, and $W := \text{comv}(\{v, u\})$ where $u \in P(V)$ with $u_2 = y_2$. Then $\varphi(T) = \varphi(V) = \varphi(W)$.*

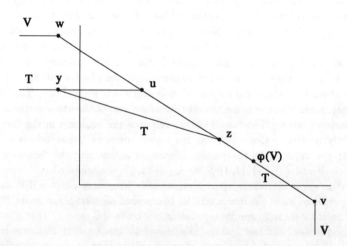

Figure 2.2: Proof of lemma 2.36

Proof (See figure 2.2.) First we show that $\varphi(T) = \varphi(V)$. Suppose that $\varphi_1(T) \leq z_1$. If $\varphi_1(T) < z_1$, then, necessarily, $x_1 < p_1(\varphi, V)$ for every $x \in p(\varphi, T)$, and if $\varphi(T) = z$, then

also $x_1 < p_1(\varphi, V)$ for every $x \in p(\varphi, T)$, since otherwise we would contradict IIE applied
to $T \subset V$. Now perform the scale transformation $a \in I\!\!R^2_{++}$ to V such that $p(\varphi, aV) = p$
for some $p \in p(\varphi, T)$ and $z \in P(aV)$. It follows that $a_2 < 1$, and $T \subset aV$. Further,
$p \cdot x = p(\varphi, aV) \cdot x \leq p(\varphi, aV) \cdot \varphi(T)$ for all $x \in aV$. So by IIE, $\varphi(aV) \geq \varphi(T)$, hence
by STC, $a\varphi(V) \geq \varphi(T)$, which contradicts $a_2 < 1$ and $\varphi_2(V) < \varphi_2(T)$. So we must have
$\varphi_1(T) > z_1$, and hence by lemma 2.34 applied to $T \subset V : \varphi(T) = \varphi(V)$.

Finally, by lemma 2.34 applied to $T \subset W$, we obtain $\varphi(T) = \varphi(W)$. $\qquad\square$

Proof of theorem 2.35 First, suppose $\varphi = \varphi^H$ for some $H \in \mathcal{H}^{\{1,2\}}$. By corollary
2.24, φ satisfies IR, PO, and STC. Take $S \in \mathcal{C}_0$. If $\varphi = \varphi^H$ for $H =< \{1\}, \{2\}, (1,1) >$,
then φ satisfies IIE with $(1,0) \in p(\varphi, S)$ if $\varphi^H_2(S) > 0$, and with as an element of $p(\varphi, S)$,
e.g., the vector with maximal first coordinate among all normal vectors of length 1 of
supporting lines of S at $\varphi^H(S)$, otherwise. A similar argument holds if $\varphi = \varphi^H$ with
$H =< \{2\}, \{1\}, (1,1) >$. If $\varphi = \varphi^H$ with $H =< \{1,2\}, (t, 1-t) >$ for some $0 < t < 1$, then,
by lemma 2.20, φ satisfies IIE with a multiple of the vector $(t\varphi_1(S)^{-1}, (1-t)\varphi_2(S)^{-1})$ as
an element of $p(\varphi, S)$.

Second, suppose φ satisfies IR, PO, STC, and IIE. In view of corollary 2.24 the proof is
complete if we show that φ satisfies IIA. So let S and T in $\mathcal{C}_0$ with $S \subset T$ and $\varphi(T) \in S$.
We have to prove:

$$\varphi(S) = \varphi(T). \tag{2.10}$$

Suppose, to the contrary, that $\varphi(S) \neq \varphi(T)$. W.l.o.g. assume $\varphi_1(S) < \varphi_1(T)$. We distinguish two cases: (a) $p(\varphi, T) \ni (1,0)$; (b) $x > 0$ for all $x \in p(\varphi, T)$ $(p(\varphi, T) \ni (0,1)$ is
excluded by PO).

(a) $p(\varphi, T) \ni (1,0)$. Note that $p(\varphi, S) \not\ni (1,0)$. If $p(\varphi, S) \ni (0,1)$, then take $x, y \in I\!\!R^2_{++}$
with $x_2 = \varphi_2(S)$ and $\varphi_1(S) < x_1 < \varphi_1(T)$, $y_1 = \varphi_1(T)$ and $\varphi_2(T) < y_2 < \varphi_2(S)$. (Cf.
figure 2.3 (a).) Then $S \subset \text{comv}(\{x, y\})$. By IIE and PO applied to $S \subset \text{comv}(\{x, y\})$, we
obtain $\varphi(\text{comv}(\{x, y\})) = x$, hence $\varphi_1(\text{comv}(\{x, y\})) < \varphi_1(T)$. On the other hand, we
can perform a scale transformation $(1, a_2) \in I\!\!R^2_{++}$ with $a_2 > 1$ on $\text{comv}(\{x, y\})$ such that
$T \subset (1, a_2)\text{comv}(\{x, y\})$ and, then, by IIE, $\varphi((1, a_2)\text{comv}(\{x, y\}) \geq \varphi(T)$, contradicting, by
STC, $\varphi_1(\text{comv}\{x, y\}) < \varphi_1(T)$.

Next, suppose $p > 0$ for some $p \in p(\varphi, S)$. (Cf. figure 2.3 (b).) Denote by ℓ the
straight line with equation $p \cdot x = p \cdot \varphi(S)$, and take points v and w on this line as in
lemma 2.36, and such that $S \subset V := \text{comv}(\{v, w\})$. By IIE, $\varphi(V) = \varphi(S)$. By lemma 2.36
(interchanging there the roles of the players), we then obtain $\varphi(W) = \varphi(V) = \varphi(S)$ where
$W := \text{comv}(\{w, x\})$ and $x \in \ell$ with $\varphi_1(S) < x_1$ and $x_2 > 0$. Apply a scale transformation
$(x_1^{-1}\varphi_1(T), a_2) \in I\!\!R^2_{++}$ to W with $a_2 > 1$ such that $T \subset (x_1^{-1}\varphi_1(T), a_2)W$. By IIE and
STC, $x_1^{-1}\varphi_1(T)\varphi_1(W) \geq \varphi_1(T)$, hence $\varphi_1(W) \geq x_1$, and so $\varphi_1(S) \geq x_1$, a contradiction.
So for the case $p(\varphi, T) \ni (1,0)$, we have proved (2.10).

(b) $x > 0$ for all $x \in p(\varphi, T)$. Let now $q \in p(\varphi, T)$ and ℓ be the straight line with equation
$q \cdot x = q \cdot \varphi(T)$, and choose points v and w on this line as in lemma 2.36 such that $T \subset$
$\text{comv}(\{v, w\}) =: V$. By IIE, we obtain $\varphi(V) = \varphi(T)$. If $p(\varphi, S) \ni (0,1)$, then let u be
the point of intersection of ℓ with the straight line $x_2 = \varphi_2(S)$. (Cf. figure 2.4(a).) Then,
by IIE applied to $S \subset \text{comv}(\{v, u\})$, we obtain $\varphi(\text{comv}(\{v, u\})) = u$, but this contradicts
lemma 2.36.

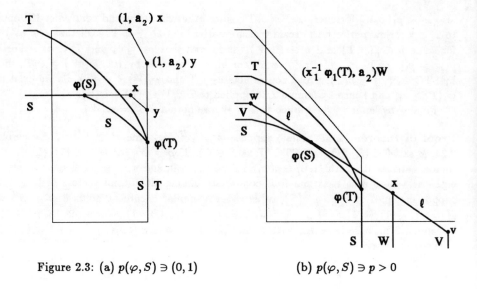

Figure 2.3: (a) $p(\varphi, S) \ni (0,1)$ (b) $p(\varphi, S) \ni p > 0$

Finally, suppose $p > 0$ for some $p \in p(\varphi, S)$, and let z be the point of intersection of ℓ with the straight line m with equation $p \cdot x = p \cdot \varphi(S)$. (Cf. figure 2.4(b).) Note that $z_1 < \varphi_1(V)$. Choose $y \in m$ as in lemma 2.36, with y_2 so large that $S \subset \text{comv}(\{v, z, y\})$ (if necessary, we have to rechoose w in order to find an appropriate y). By IIE, $\varphi(S) = \varphi(\text{comv}(\{v, z, y\}))$, so by lemma 2.36 $\varphi(S) = \varphi(V) = \varphi(T)$. $\qquad\square$

The axioms in theorem 2.35 are independent. Without IR, consider the solution of example 2.9. With WPO instead of PO, see example 2.10. Without STC, consider the egalitarian solution (section 4.5). Without IIE, there are many possibilities, for instance the Raiffa-Kalai-Smorodinsky solution (section 4.2).

2.4.3 Multiplicativity

Given the fact that nonsymmetric Nash bargaining solutions, i.e., bargaining solutions corresponding to weighted hierarchies, are determined by maximizing certain products — Nash products, see definitions 2.1, 2.14 — it is not surprising that such solutions can be characterized by multiplicativity as well as additivity properties. Additivity properties will be discussed in chapter 5; in the present section a specific multiplicativity property is employed. Such characterizations are of only technical interest if no interpretation of the axiom(s) under consideration is provided. Therefore, at the end of this subsection, a utility-theoretic foundation will be given for the multiplicativity axiom. That is, the appropriateness of the axiom depends on the specific assumptions made concerning the underlying preferences or utility functions. The utility-theoretic foundation as meant here is based on section 11.6. The characterization itself, viewed as a technical exercise, can be understood without knowledge of this part of utility-theory.

For $V, W \subset \mathbb{R}^2$, denote by VW the set $\{z \in \mathbb{R}^2 : z = vw \text{ for some } v \in V, w \in W\}$.

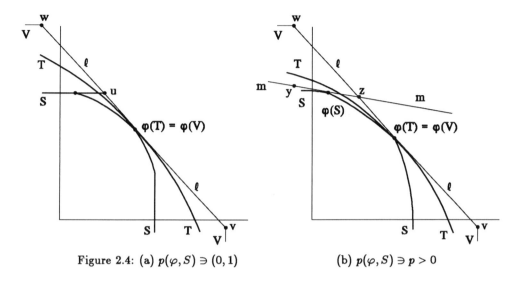

Figure 2.4: (a) $p(\varphi, S) \ni (0,1)$ (b) $p(\varphi, S) \ni p > 0$

For $S, T \in C_0$, let $S * T$ denote the set $\mathrm{com}((S \cap \mathbb{R}_+^2)(T \cap \mathbb{R}_+^2))$. Let $\varphi : C_0 \to \mathbb{R}^2$ be a bargaining solution.

Multiplicativity (MUL): For all $S, T \in C_0$, if $S * T \in C_0$, then $\varphi(S * T) = \varphi(S)\varphi(T)$.

Observe that the condition $S * T \in C_0$ in the formulation of MUL is needed, since $S * T$ does not have to be a convex set. For instance, the set $\Delta^{\{1,2\}} * \Delta^{\{1,2\}}$ is not convex. The main result in this part is the following theorem.

Theorem 2.37 *Let* $\varphi : C_0 \to \mathbb{R}^2$ *be a solution. Then* φ *is Pareto optimal and multiplicative, if and only if* $\varphi = \varphi^H$ *for some* $H \in \mathcal{H}^{\{1,2\}}$.

For the proof of this theorem we need two lemmas.

Lemma 2.38 *Let the solution* $\varphi : C_0 \to \mathbb{R}^2$ *satisfy PO and MUL. Then* φ *satisfies IR and STC, and* $\varphi(S) = \varphi(\mathrm{com}(S \cap \mathbb{R}_+^2))$ *for every* $S \in C_0$.

Proof Let $S \in C_0$ and $a \in \mathbb{R}_{++}^2$. Let $T := \mathrm{comv}(\{(1,1)\}) \in C_0$. Then, by MUL and PO, $\varphi(aS) = \varphi(aS)\varphi(T) = \varphi(aS * T) = \varphi(S * aT) = a\varphi(S)$. So STC holds and, taking $a = (1,1)$, we obtain $\varphi(S) = \varphi(S * T) = \varphi(\mathrm{com}(S \cap \mathbb{R}_+^2))$. This also implies IR.   □

Lemma 2.39 *Let* $S \in C_0$ *with* $u(\mathrm{com}(S \cap \mathbb{R}_+^2)) = (1,1)$. *Then there exists a* $T \in C_0$ *with* $u(\mathrm{com}(T \cap \mathbb{R}_+^2)) = (1,1)$ *and* $S * T = \Delta^{\{1,2\}}$.

Proof Let $V := \{y \in \mathbb{R}_+^2 : x \cdot y \le 1 \text{ for all } x \in S, x \ge 0\}$. Then V is convex, V is bounded (for every $y \in V$, $(1,0) \cdot y \le 1$ and $(0,1) \cdot y \le 1$ imply $y \le (1,1)$), and closed ($V = \bigcap_{x \in S,\ x \ge 0}\{y \in \mathbb{R}_+^2 : x \cdot y \le 1\}$). Further, $(1,0), (0,1) \in V$ and $(\alpha, 0), (0, \alpha) \notin V$ if $\alpha > 1$, so $T := \mathrm{com}(V) \in C_0$ with $u(T) = (1,1)$. By definition of V, $S * T \subset \Delta^{\{1,2\}}$. We still have to show: $\Delta \subset S * T$. Since $(1,0), (0,1) \in S \cap T$, we have $(1,0), (0,1) \in S * T$. Let

$(t, 1-t) \in P(\Delta^{\{1,2\}})$ with $0 < t < 1$. Let $z := \varphi^H(S)$ where $H = < \{1,2\}, (t, 1-t) >$. Then $(tz_1^{-1}, (1-t)z_2^{-1}) \in T$ by lemma 2.20. Therefore, $(t, 1-t) = (z_1, z_2)(tz_1^{-1}, (1-t)z_2^{-1}) \in S * T$. It follows that $\Delta \subset S * T$.   □

Proof of theorem 2.37 If $\varphi = \varphi^H$ for some $H \in \mathcal{H}^{\{1,2\}}$, one easily verifies that, besides PO, φ satisfies MUL. Now suppose φ satisfies PO and MUL, and let $S \in \mathcal{C}_0$. By lemma 2.38, we may assume w.l.o.g. that $u(\text{com}(S \cap I\!R_+^2)) = (1,1)$. Let T be as in lemma 2.39. If $\varphi(\Delta^{\{1,2\}}) = (1,0)$, then, by MUL, $\varphi_1(S)\varphi_1(T) = 1$, so $\varphi_1(S) = 1$ and therefore $\varphi(S) = \varphi^H(S)$ with $H = < \{1\}, \{2\}, (1,1) > \in \mathcal{H}^{\{1,2\}}$. Similarly, $\varphi(\Delta^{\{1,2\}}) = (0,1)$ implies $\varphi(S) = \varphi^H(S)$ with $H = < \{2\}, \{1\}, (1,1) >$. Let now $\varphi(\Delta^{\{1,2\}}) = (t, 1-t)$ for some $0 < t < 1$. Let $H := < \{1,2\}, (t, 1-t) >$ and $x \in S$ with $x \neq \varphi^H(S)$. Then $x_1^t x_2^{1-t} \varphi_1(T)^t \varphi_2(T)^{1-t} < [\varphi_1^H(S)\varphi_1^H(T)]^t [\varphi_2^H(S)\varphi_2^H(T)]^{1-t}$, therefore $x\varphi(T) \neq \varphi^H(\Delta^{\{1,2\}}) = \varphi(\Delta^{\{1,2\}}) = \varphi(S)\varphi(T)$. We conclude that $\varphi(S) = \varphi^H(S)$.   □

The last part of this subsection is devoted to the announced utility-theoretic foundation of the multiplicativity property. Let $\Gamma_1 = < A, \bar{a}, u^1, u^2 >$ and $\Gamma_2 = < B, \bar{b}, v^1, v^2 >$ be two expected utility bargaining situations as introduced in definition 1.2. Let $\Gamma = < C, \bar{c}, w^1, w^2 >$ be an expected utility bargaining situation with $C = A \times B$, $\bar{c} = (\bar{a}, \bar{b})$, and such that conditions (11.14) and (11.15) in section 11.6 hold. Then, in view of theorem 11.16, we may assume: $w^1(a,b) = u^1(a)v^1(b)$ and $w^2(a,b) = u^2(a)v^2(b)$ for all $a \in A$ and $b \in B$.

Let φ be a bargaining solution. If, for every $\ell \in \mathcal{L}(A \times B)$, there are $\ell_1 \in \mathcal{L}(A)$ and $\ell_2 \in \mathcal{L}(B)$ such that $(Ew^1(\ell), Ew^2(\ell)) = (Eu^1(\ell_1)Ev^1(\ell_2), Eu^2(\ell_1) Ev^2(\ell_2))$, then the MUL property requires that the same equality holds for lotteries ℓ, ℓ_1, ℓ_2, the expected utilities of which are the solution outcomes of the bargaining games S_Γ, S_{Γ_1}, S_{Γ_2}, respectively. Suppose now, that ℓ_1 results in $a^k \in A$ with probability p_k, ℓ_2 in $b^j \in B$ with probability q_j, then, for $i = 1, 2$, $Eu^i(\ell_1)Ev^i(\ell_2)$ is the expected utility Ew^i of the lottery in $\mathcal{L}(A \times B)$ which results with probability $p_k q_j$ in (a^k, b^j). So, according to the MUL property, each player is indifferent between this lottery and the lottery ℓ; hence, the MUL property may be interpreted as requiring each player to be indifferent between either playing Γ_1 and Γ_2 (ending in (a^k, b^j) with probability $p_k q_j$) or playing Γ (ending in the lottery ℓ).

The multiplicativity property was introduced in Binmore (1987a) under the name "convention consistency". The theorem presented here is a slight generalization of Binmore's result.

2.4.4 Replications of 2-person bargaining

As argued at the beginning of section 2.3, nonsymmetries in bargaining may be studied for their intrinsical value, for instance in a mathematical sense, but also because in specific applications factors which are no longer present in the abstract model considered here, may lead to nonsymmetries. This subsection, which is based on Kalai (1977a), provides an interpretation of 2-person nonsymmetric Nash solutions $\varphi^H (H \in \mathcal{H}^{\{1,2\}})$ by considering replications of 2-person bargaining games.

The intuition is roughly as follows. Suppose the two bargainers each represent their families, which may have different sizes. The bargainer with the larger family may be tougher, because his share has to be divided among more persons. Alternatively, he may be considered more powerful since he has a larger family to back him up. The right way to model a situation like this is subject to discussion. Two different approaches are given by Kalai (1977a) and Thomson (1986). The model by Kalai is discussed here and leads to 2-person nonsymmetric Nash bargaining solutions. The extension to bargaining solutions φ^H with H of the form $H =< N, \omega >$ for $n = |N| > 2$ is straightforward: see Thomson and Lensberg (1989, chapter 12); the extension, however, to solutions φ^H for general $\varphi^H \in \mathcal{H}^N$ is still an open question. Thomson's model leads to nonsymmetric extensions of the Raiffa-Kalai-Smorodinsky as well as the Nash solution. See section 4.3.

Kalai (1977a) proposes replications of 2-person bargaining games, as follows. For m, $\ell \in \mathbb{N}$, let $\mathbb{R}^{m,\ell} := \{x \in \mathbb{R}^{m+\ell} : x_i = x_j$ for all $1 \le i, j \le m$ and all $m+1 \le i, j \le m+\ell\}$. Define the *Kalai (m, ℓ)-replicating function* $K^{m,\ell} : \mathbb{R}^2 \to \mathbb{R}^{m,\ell}$ by $K^{m,\ell}(x)_i := x_1$ if $1 \le i \le m$, $K^{m,\ell}(x)_i := x_2$ if $m+1 \le i \le m+\ell$. Let $N = M \cup L$ with $M \cap L = \emptyset$, $M, L \ne \emptyset$, $M = \{1, 2, \ldots, m\}$, $L = \{m+1, \ldots, m+\ell\}$. A bargaining game $(S, d) \in \mathcal{C}^N$ is a *Kalai (m, ℓ)-replication* of a bargaining game $(S', d') \in \mathcal{C}^{\{1,2\}}$ if $d = K^{m,\ell}(d')$ and $S = \text{com}(K^{m,\ell}(S'))$. As before, let ν denote the symmetric Nash bargaining solution, corresponding to the weighted hierarchy $< N, (\frac{1}{n}, \ldots, \frac{1}{n}) > \in \mathcal{H}^N$. If H is the weighted hierarchy $< \{1,2\}, (\frac{m}{m+\ell}, \frac{\ell}{m+1}) >$ then $K^{m,\ell}(\varphi^H(S', d')) = \nu(S, d)$, as is straightforward to verify. In other words, the Kalai replication method provides an interpretation of 2-person nonsymmetric Nash solutions corresponding to weighted hierarchies $< \{1,2\}, \omega >$ with ω rational, by looking at the symmetric Nash solution applied to the appropriately replicated bargaining game. If ω is irrational, then there are sequences $m_1, m_2, \ldots$ and $\ell_1, \ell_2, \ldots$ of natural numbers with $\lim_{i \to \infty} m_i(m_i + \ell_i)^{-1} = \omega_1$ and $\lim_{i \to \infty} \ell_i(m_i + \ell_i)^{-1} = \omega_2$. Moreover, for $(T, e) \in \mathcal{C}^{\{1,2\}}$, $\{x \in T : x \ge e\}$ is a compact set and for z in this set, $\lim_{i \to \infty} (z_1 - e_1)^{m_i(m_i+\ell_i)^{-1}} (z_2 - e_2)^{\ell_i(m_i+\ell_i)^{-1}} = (z_1 - e_1)^{\omega_1} (z_2 - e_2)^{\omega_2}$. It follows that solutions corresponding to weighted hierarchies $< \{1,2\}, \omega >$ with ω irrational can be obtained as limits of solutions obtainable by the above replication method. A similar argument and conclusion holds for the extreme cases φ^H corresponding to $H =< \{1\}, \{2\}, (1,1) >$ and $< \{2\}, \{1\}, (1,1) >$.

This subsection is concluded by an example, taken from Kalai (1977a) and illustrating the intuition formulated above.

Example 2.40 Consider two players, 1 and 2, who have one dollar to divide between them. If they do not come to an agreement on how to divide the dollar they lose it, and each receives nothing. Each player has utility α for α units of money that he receives. Thus, the players play the bargaining game $\Delta^{\{1,2\}} \in \mathcal{C}_0^{\{1,2\}}$, and any Pareto optimal symmetric solution, e.g. the symmetric Nash bargaining solution, would prescribe the dollar to be divided evenly between the players. Now assume that player 1 has an enthusiastic supporter 1', (say a mother), who also has utility α for α units of money that 1 receives. In addition, 1' has to agree to the decisions that 1 makes. The 2-person game becomes a 3-person game which is a $(2,1)$-replication of the original game. The symmetric Nash solution assigns the outcome $(\frac{2}{3}, \frac{2}{3}, \frac{1}{3})$ to this game, leading to a $(\frac{2}{3}, \frac{1}{3})$ division of the dollar in the original 2-person game. As Kalai states, it is not clear whether this is reasonable. In this example, the Raiffa-Kalai-Smorodinsky solution would assign an even division of the dollar also after replication: see sections 4.2 and 4.3.

2.4.5　The utility of playing a bargaining game

Let $\mathcal{D}^N$ be some collection of bargaining games for the (fixed) player set N. An individual — one of the players in N, or some outsider, or the writer of this book — may prefer to be (say) player i in the bargaining game (S, d) to (say) player j in the bargaining game (T, e). Such a preference may be based on the fact that the individual expects to obtain a larger payoff as player i in (S, d) than as player j in (T, e). Suppose our individual is able to assess his preferences over all positions in all games, including lotteries of the kind "play i in (S, d) with probability p or j in (T, e) with probability $1 - p$". Under certain conditions, such a preference relation is representable by a von Neumann-Morgenstern utility function. By assuming additional properties of the preference relation, the representing utility function may be described by the payoff assigned to a player in a game by some bargaining solution. In this section, additional properties are imposed that lead to a nonsymmetric Nash bargaining solution of the form $\varphi^{<N,\omega>}$. Specifically, the number ω_i will be seen to reflect our individual's *strategic risk posture* with respect to playing the position of player i in a given bargaining game. Suppose n players divide one dollar. If our individual expects to obtain exactly (less than; more than) one n^{th} of the dollar as player i in this bargaining game, then we say that he is *neutral* (*averse; attracted*) *to strategic risk*.

In the formal presentation of this approach, which is based on Roth (1978), we use the following domain of bargaining games for N:

$$\overline{C}_*^N := \{S \in \overline{C}_0^N : S = \text{com}(S \cap \mathbb{R}_+^N)\}.$$

Recall that $\overline{C}_0^N$ is the class of bargaining games with convex comprehensive feasible sets and disagreement outcome normalized to 0, which may be a point on the boundary of the feasible set. Within this class, attention is restricted to bargaining games with feasible sets of which the Pareto optimal boundaries are included in the nonnegative orthant. The reason for considering this class is mainly convenience of presentation. However, allowing the disagreement outcome 0 to be a boundary point enables us to include a "zerogame" as a game of reference in certain properties concerning the preference relation.

For completeness, we extend the definition of nonsymmetric Nash solutions φ^H for $H \in \mathcal{H}^N$ of the form $H = < N, \omega >$ to the class $\tilde{C}^N$, as follows. For every $(S, d) \in \tilde{C}^N$ and $H = < N, w > \in \mathcal{H}^N$, if $d \in P(S)$ then $\varphi^H(S, d) := d$, and if $d \notin P(S)$, then $\varphi^H(S, d)$ is the unique element of $\text{argmax}\{\prod_{i \in N_+(S,d)}(x_i - d_i)^{\omega_i} : x \in P(S), x \geq d\}$. It is obvious that this extension of definition 2.14 is needed since d may now be a boundary point of S.

The preference relation

Let $\mathcal{L} = \mathcal{L}(N \times \overline{C}_*^N)$ be the set of lotteries over the alternatives of the form (i, S), where $i \in N$ will be called a *position* and $S \in \overline{C}_*^N$ is a bargaining game. Let $\succeq$ be a preference relation on $\mathcal{L}$ satisfying the continuity and independence axioms formulated in subsection 11.2.1. Theorems 11.1 and 11.2 imply that $\succeq$ can be represented by a von Neumann-Morgenstern utility function (see subsection 11.2.2) u, which is uniquely determined up to a positive affine transformation. Additionally, we impose the following conditions on the preference relation $\succeq$. Let $\succ$ and $\sim$ denote the asymmetric and symmetric parts of $\succeq$, respectively. For a permutation π of N, and $x \in \mathbb{R}^N$, let $\pi x \in \mathbb{R}^N$ be defined by $\pi x := (x_{\pi(1)}, x_{\pi(2)}, \ldots, x_{\pi(n)})$. For $V \subset \mathbb{R}^N$, $\pi V := \{\pi x : x \in V\}$.

(P1) For every $i \in N$, $S \in \overline{C}_*^N$ and permutation π of N: $(i, S) \sim (\pi(i), \pi S)$.

(P2) (a) For every $S \in \overline{C}_*^N$ and $i \notin N_+(S, 0)$: $(i, S) \sim (i, \mathrm{com}\{0\})$.

   (b) For all $x, y \in \mathbb{R}_+^N$ and every $i \in N$, if $x_i = y_i$ then $(i, \mathrm{com}\{x\}) \sim (i, \mathrm{com}\{y\})$, and if $x_i > y_i$ then $(i, \mathrm{com}\{x\}) \succ (i, \mathrm{com}\{y\})$.

   (c) For every $\emptyset \neq M \subset N$ and $i \in N$ with $M \neq \{i\}$, $(i, \mathrm{com}\{e^i\}) \succ (i, \mathrm{com}\, O^N(\Delta^M))$.

   (d) For every $S \in \overline{C}_*^N$ with $N_+(S, 0) \neq \emptyset$, there is an $i \in N_+(S, 0)$ with $(i, S) \succ (i, \mathrm{com}\{0\})$.

(P3) For every $S \in \overline{C}_*^N$, $i \in N$, and $a \in \mathbb{R}_{++}^N$ with $a_i \geq 1$, $(i, S) \sim (a_i^{-1}; (i, aS), 1 - a_i^{-1}; (i, \mathrm{com}\{0\}))$.

(P4) For all $x \in \mathbb{R}_+^N$, $i \in N$, $S, T \in \overline{C}_*^N$, if $\mathrm{com}\{x\} \subset S \subset T$, $x \in P(T)$, and $(i, \mathrm{com}\{x\}) \sim (i, T)$, then $(i, \mathrm{com}\{x\}) \sim (i, S)$.

Condition (P1) expresses that the particular axis on which a player's (position's) utility is measured should not influence the preference relation. (P2) says, first, that our individual is indifferent between playing the zerogame com$\{0\}$ or some position in some other game in which there is nothing to be gained; second, that among games with unique Pareto optimal outcomes the preference for a position is determined by the corresponding coordinate of the Pareto optimal outcome; third, that the individual prefers a position in a game where that position can yield 1 and the other positions only 0, to the same position in a game where, at the best, the payoff of 1 has to be shared with other positions; and fourth, that among the "non-dummy" positions in a game there is at least one that the individual expects to be profitable. Condition (P3) says that, if the payoffs available in a game are multiplied by positive constants, then the individual is indifferent between playing the old game, or participating in the appropriate lottery involving the new game. Condition (P4), finally, corresponds to the independence of irrelevant alternatives axiom. It says that if the individual is indifferent between playing the same position in a game com$\{x\}$ or in a game T with a larger feasible set, then he is also indifferent between playing that position in com$\{x\}$ or a game S which contains com$\{x\}$ and is contained in T.

Until further notice, let $i \in N$ be fixed. Since the utility function u representing $\succ$ is unique only up to positive affine transformations, it may, in view of $(\mathrm{P2}(c, a))$, be normalized by setting $u(i, \mathrm{com}\{0\}) = 0$ and $u(i, \mathrm{com}\{e^i\}) = 1$. The following lemmas follow easily from (P1)–(P3).

Lemma 2.41 *(i) Let $S \in \overline{C}_*^N$ with $i \notin N_+(S, 0)$. Then $u(i, S) = 0$.*
(ii) Let $x, y \subset \mathbb{R}_+^N$ with $x_i = y_i$. Then $u(i, \mathrm{com}\{x\}) = u(i, \mathrm{com}\{y\})$.

Proof (i) This follows immediately from (P2(a)). (ii) Immediately from (P2(b)). $\square$

Lemma 2.42 *Let $S \in \overline{C}_*^N$ and $a \in \mathbb{R}_{++}^N$. Then $u(i, aS) = a_i u(i, S)$.*

Proof Suppose $a_i \geq 1$. Then by (P3), $u(i,S) = a_i^{-1}u(i,aS) + (1 - a_i^{-1})u(i,\text{com}\{0\}) = a_i^{-1}u(i,aS)$. Suppose $a_i < 1$. Then let $b_j := a_j^{-1}$ for every $j \in N$. It follows that $b_i > 1$, hence $u(i,S) = u(i,b(aS)) = b_i u(i,aS)$. $\qquad\square$

Lemma 2.43 *Let $x \in I\!\!R_+^N$. Then $u(i,\text{com}\{x\}) = x_i$.*

Proof By lemma 2.42, $u(i,\text{com}\{x_i e^i\}) = x_i$. By lemma 2.41, $u(i,\text{com}\{x\}) = x_i$. $\qquad\square$

Lemma 2.44 *Let $M \subset N$ with $i \in M$. Let $m := |M|$. Then there is a unique number $f(m)$ with $(i,\text{com}(O^N(\Delta^M))) \sim (i,f(m)\text{com}\{e^i\})$. Furthermore, $0 < f(m) \leq 1$, and $f(m) = 1 \Leftrightarrow M = \{i\}$. Finally, if $M' \subset N$ with $i \in M'$ and $|M'| = m$, then $(i,\text{com}(O^N(\Delta^{M'}))) \sim (i,f(m)\text{com}\{e^i\})$.*

Proof First suppose $u(i,\text{com}(O^N(\Delta^M))) \leq 0$. By applying the appropriate permutations π of N with $\pi(M) = M$ and using (P1), it follows that $u(j,\text{com}(O^N(\Delta^M))) \leq 0$ for all $j \in M$. This, however, contradicts (P2(d)). Therefore, $u(i,\text{com}(O^N(\Delta^M))) > 0$. By (P2(c)), if $M \neq \{i\}$, then $u(i,\text{com}(O^N(\Delta^M))) < u(i,\text{com}\{e^i\}) = 1$. Define $f(m) := u(i,\text{com}(O^N(\Delta^M)))$, then, by lemma 2.43, $f(m)$ satisfies the properties desired in the lemma. Finally, if $i \in M' \subset N$ with $|M'| = m$, then $(i,\text{com}(O^N(\Delta^{M'}))) \sim (i,\text{com}(O^N(\Delta^M)))$ by applying a permutation σ of N with $\sigma(i) = i$, $\sigma(M') = M$, and using (P1). This proves the last statement of the lemma. $\qquad\square$

The number $f(m)$ in lemma 2.44 expresses the worth to our individual of being one of m strategic players ("non-dummies") who have to divide a payoff of 1. In other words, receiving the utility $f(m)$ for certain is for our individual equivalent to the "risky" situation of being one of m players who have to divide 1 unit of utility. If $f(m) = 1/m (< 1/m; > 1/m)$ we say that the individual (or the preference relation) is *strategic risk neutral* (*averse*; *attracted*). Note that, by (P1), $u(j,\text{com}(O^N(\Delta^M))) = f(m)$ for *every* $j \in M$. This does not mean that every player in the actual bargaining game will receive $f(m)$; it just means that our individual judges the worth of every position in this game to be equal to $f(m)$. The values of $f(m)$ $(2 \leq m \leq n)$ will completely determine the utility function u. (Note that $f(1) = 1$ by normalization.) In what follows, i is no longer fixed. The main result of this subsection is the following theorem.

Theorem 2.45 *Let $S \in \overline{C}_*^N$ and $k \in M := N_+(S,0)$. Let $m := |M|$ and $H = \langle N, \omega \rangle \in \mathcal{H}^N$ be any weighted hierarchy such that $\omega_k (\sum_{i \in M} \omega_i)^{-1} = f(m)$. Then $u(k,S) = \varphi_k^H(S)$.*

Theorem 2.45 completely determines the utility function u: the utility of playing a position in a certain game is equal to the payoff ascribed to that position in the game by a nonsymmetric Nash solution, whereby the weight corresponding to that position is proportional to the strategic risk posture of our individual. Thus, this approach provides another interpretation for the nonsymmetries of solutions corresponding to weighted hierarchies. Note that the theorem implies that the other weights are relatively unimportant: if $H' = \langle N, \omega' \rangle$ with $\omega_k' (\sum_{i \in M} \omega_i')^{-1} = f(m)$, then $\varphi_k^{H'}(S) = u(k,S) = \varphi_k^H(S)$.

Proof of theorem 2.45 Let $z := \varphi^H(S)$, and let the vector $a \in I\!\!R_{++}^N$ be defined by $a_i := \omega_k z_i (\omega_i f(m))^{-1}$ if $i \in M$, $a_i := 1$ if $i \notin M$. Let $T := a \text{ com}(O^N(\Delta^M)) \in \overline{C}_*^N$, then

$S \subset T$ and $z \in P(T)$ by lemma 2.20. By lemma 2.42, $u(k,T) = a_k u(k,\text{com}(O^N(\Delta^M)))$. Hence, $u(k,T) = a_k f(m) = z_k$. Since $\text{com}\{z\} \subset S \subset T$, $z \in P(T)$, and $z_k = u(k, \text{com}\{z\}) = u(k,T)$, we can apply (P4) and obtain $u(k,S) = z_k = \varphi_k^H(S)$. $\square$

A consequence of theorem 2.45 is that, if our individual is strategic risk neutral, then his utility for a certain position in a certain game is exactly the payoff of the symmetric Nash bargaining solution to that position in the game.

It seems safe to conjecture that different bargaining solutions can be obtained by imposing different conditions on the preference relation $\succeq$. This subject is open for further research. More generally, Roth's method as described here can be applied to other classes of games as well. So far, it has been used in Roth (1977b) to derive the Shapley value for transferable utility games.

2.5 Disagreement point axioms

2.5.1 Introduction

Most of the axioms proposed in the bargaining theory literature concern changes in the solution outcome resulting from changes in the feasible sets. The disagreement outcome usually only plays an implicit role. Consider, for example, Nash's IIA axiom where the disagreement outcomes of the two compared games are required to be equal.

It seems to be equally natural to consider axioms where the disagreement point is varied while the feasible set remains fixed. In the recent literature on bargaining, several axioms of this variety have been proposed, and characterizations of bargaining solutions based mainly on such axioms have been obtained. An obvious advantage is that the role of the disagreement outcome is made more explicit. Further, such characterizations are based on the existence of only *one* feasible set together with some sets derived from it in a natural way. To see why this may be an advantage, notice that implicit in the axiomatic approach as proposed by Nash is the assumption that the solution outcome should be independent of all characteristics of a bargaining situation that are not captured by the pair (S,d). For instance, the conclusion of the IIA axiom is supposed to hold for all bargaining games satisfying the premises, even though the shrunken set S may well have arisen from an underlying physical situation that cannot be obtained by deleting physical alternatives in the situation leading to the larger set T. See also the discussion in subsections 1.3.1 and 1.3.2. Here, we merely wish to point out that a characterization based on disagreement outcome axioms may be easier to adapt to specific bargaining situations. Finally, let us note that the disagreement point approach can serve as a starting point of a dynamic theory of bargaining. See, in particular, Furth (1990); cf. subsection 8.6.1.

In this section, we concentrate on a characterization of the class of nonsymmetric Nash solutions corresponding to weighted hierarchies of the form $< N, \omega >$. This characterization and the (new) axioms involved are discussed in subsection 2.5.2. Related literature is discussed in 2.5.3.

The results in subsection 2.5.2 are based on Peters and van Damme (1991).

2.5.2 Disagreement point convexity

In what follows, a characterization of nonsymmetric Nash solutions is presented on the domain $\overline{C}^N$ of bargaining games with convex comprehensive feasible sets and with disagreement outcomes that may be boundary points[3]. Considering this domain instead of C^N mainly serves mathematical convenience: specifically, it will enable us to apply the Brouwer fixed point theorem in lemma 2.48 below. This does not imply that the extension from C^N to $\overline{C}^N$ is harmless: see the discussion on the domain at the end of this subsection.

Let $\mathcal{D}^N$ be some subclass of $\tilde{C}^N$ and let $\varphi : \mathcal{D}^N \to I\!\!R^N$ be a solution. The first axiom we want to introduce is in a sense the "dual" of the super-additivity axiom of Perles and Maschler (1981), see section 5.2. Suppose that a feasible set S is given, and that d^i will be the disagreement point with probability p^i (i from a finite index set). Suppose that all solution outcomes $\varphi(S, d^i)$ are equal. So, if the players only meet after the disagreement point uncertainty has been resolved, they will always agree on the same outcome. Will they also agree on this outcome ex ante? Answering this question affirmatively corresponds to imposing the following axiom:

Convexity (CONV): For all $(S, d), (S, e) \in \mathcal{D}^N$, all $0 < \mu < 1$ and all $x \in S$, if $\varphi(S, d) = \varphi(S, e) = x$ and $(S, \mu d + (1 - \mu)e) \in \mathcal{D}^N$, then $\varphi(S, \mu d + (1 - \mu)e) = x$.

This axiom is actually well-known: in 2-person bargaining with variable threat point, together with a few standard axioms it suffices to guarantee that Nash's threat game (Nash, 1953) has an equilibrium (see, for example, Tijs and Jansen (1982); see also section 9.8). In the 2-person case, Nash's symmetric solution satisfies this axiom; however, CONV is a surprisingly strong axiom. If there are more than two bargainers, then on $\overline{C}^N$ CONV is inconsistent with Pareto optimality and the strong individual rationality axiom (SIR, see section 2.2). To prove this, let φ be a solution satisfying these three axioms, and let S be the comprehensive convex hull of the points $(1, 0, 0)$, $(0, 1, 0)$, $(0, 0, 1)$, and $(1, 1, 0)$. By PO and SIR the points $d = (1, 0, 0)$ and $d = (0, 1, 0)$ of S result in the outcome $\varphi(S, d) = (1, 1, 0)$, but then CONV implies $\varphi(S, d) = (1, 1, 0)$ for $d = (\frac{1}{2}, \frac{1}{2}, 0)$ and this contradicts SIR. Note that this example uses the fact that the disagreement point may be a boundary point; it is an open problem whether PO, CONV, and SIR are inconsistent if this is not allowed.

In the characterization of nonsymmetric Nash solutions below, an axiom will be used that is considerably weaker than CONV. Specifically, we require that a convex combination of a disagreement point and the corresponding solution point give rise to the same solution point, hence:

Disagreement Point Convexity (DPC): For all $(S, d) \in \mathcal{D}^N$ and all $0 \leq \mu \leq 1$ if $(S, \mu d + (1 - \mu)\varphi(S, d)) \in \mathcal{D}^N$, then $\varphi(S, \mu d + (1 - \mu)\varphi(S, d)) = \varphi(S, d)$.

This requirement can be motivated as above by referring to exogenous uncertainty about the disagreement point.

(Another motivation is obtained by the following informal argument concerning en-

---

[3]Bargaining games in $\overline{C}^N$ may still be derived from expected utility bargaining situations if we relax condition (iii) in definition 1.2 in the appropriate way.

dogenous (strategic) uncertainty. Consider a 2-person bargaining problem (S, d) and suppose player 1 firmly adheres to the (PO, SIR) solution φ. If $\varphi_2(S, e) > \varphi_2(S, d)$ for $e = (d + \varphi(S, d))/2$, then player 2 has an incentive to behave strategically: he could threaten to toss a coin and to accept $\varphi(S, d)$ if heads comes up and to walk away from the bargaining table in case of tails. By this behavior the disagreement point is effectively converted to e, so player 1 will offer $\varphi(S, e)$ in order to avoid disagreement, which is to the advantage of player 2. DPC excludes manipulating behavior of this kind.)

The following axiom is a minimal continuity requirement. It states that, for a fixed feasible set of outcomes, the solution outcome should depend continuously on the disagreement outcome.

Disagreement Point Continuity (DCONT): For every sequence $(S, d), (S, d^1), (S, d^2), \ldots$ in $\mathcal{D}^N$, if $d^i \to d$, then $\varphi(S, d^i) \to \varphi(S, d)$.

The next axiom does *not* refer to just one feasible set. For $(S, d) \in \tilde{\mathcal{B}}^N$, let $S_d := \text{com}(\{x \in S : x \geq d\})$.

Independence of Non-Individually Rational Outcomes (INIR): For every $(S, d) \in \mathcal{D}^N$, if $(S_d, d) \in \mathcal{D}^N$, then $\varphi(S, d) = \varphi(S_d, d)$.

The INIR axiom was first formally used in Peters (1986b), and amounts to a very weak form of Nash's IIA. Still it is far from being harmless, although many authors assume it to hold implicitly by their choices of the domain of bargaining games. For example, Kalai and Smorodinsky (1975, p. 514) defend the axiom, or rather their restriction to bargaining games (S, d) with $S = S_d$, on the ground that "if this [i.e., $S = S_d$] is not the case, we can disregard all the points of S that fail to satisfy this condition [i.e., of dominating d], because it is impossible that both players will agree to such a solution" [i.e., a non-individually rational solution outcome]. Note that actually Kalai and Smorodinsky need a stronger argument to defend the criterion "$S = S_d$": non-individually rational outcomes should not only never occur as solution outcomes, but they should also never influence the solution outcome. This argument amounts to imposing INIR. Most solutions occurring in this book satisfy INIR. For a notable exception, see section 4.4. Further, it is not always natural to impose INIR. See the discussion in section 5.3.

In what follows, a characterization is given of the class of solutions φ^H with $H \in \mathcal{H}^N$ of the form $H = <N, \omega>$. To be precise, we prove the following theorem.

Theorem 2.46 *A solution* $\varphi : \overline{C}^N \to \mathbb{R}^N$ *satisfies STC, SIR, INIR, DCONT, and DPC, if and only if* $\varphi = \varphi^H$ *for some H of the form* $H = <N, \omega>$.

We have already seen that the CONV axiom is inconsistent with PO and SIR if $n > 2$. It is worthwhile to note that, also if we restrict attention to bargaining games in the class C^N, where the disagreement outcome is not allowed to be a boundary point, the nonsymmetric Nash solutions in theorem 2.46 still do not satisfy CONV; this can be seen by taking, in the previous example, points of the form $(1 - \alpha, \alpha, 0)$ and $(\beta, 1 - \beta, 0)$ instead of $(1, 0, 0)$ and $(0, 1, 0)$ as disagreement points, for suitably chosen α and β, sufficiently small. However, these solutions do satisfy DPC: this follows straightforwardly from lemma 2.20. Verification of the other axioms for φ^H in theorem 2.46 is left to the reader. In order to prove the converse, we need some lemmas.

Lemma 2.47 *Let $\varphi : \overline{C}^N \to I\!R^N$ satisfy DPC and SIR. Then φ satisfies PO.*

Proof Let $(S, d) \in \overline{C}^N$. DPC of φ implies $\varphi(S, \varphi(S, d)) = \varphi(S, d)$. Pareto optimality now immediately follows from applying SIR.   □

The following axiom is a considerable strengthening of DPC.

Disagreement Point Linearity (DLIN): For every $(S, d) \in \mathcal{D}^N$, and $\mu \in I\!R$, if $(S, \mu d + (1 - \mu)\varphi(S, d)) \in \mathcal{D}^N$, then $\varphi(S, \mu d + (1 - \mu)\varphi(S, d)) = \varphi(S, d)$.

The next lemma is a crucial step in the proof of theorem 2.46. It derives DLIN from (three of) the axioms in the theorem with the aid of a fixed point argument.

Lemma 2.48 *Let $\varphi : \overline{C}^N \to I\!R^N$ satisfy DPC, DCONT, and SIR. Then φ satisfies DLIN.*

Proof Let φ satisfy DPC, DCONT, and SIR, and let (S, d) be a bargaining game in $\overline{C}^N$. Let $e := \mu d + (1 - \mu)\varphi(S, d)$ be as in the statement of DLIN with $\mu > 1$ (the case $\mu \leq 1$ follows from DPC). Let M be the subset of players such that $i \in M$ if and only if $x_i > d_i$ for some $x \in S$, i.e., $M = N_+(S, d)$. Then note that $\varphi_i(S, e) = \varphi_i(S, d) = d_i$ for all $i \notin M$, in view of SIR. We want to show that $\varphi_i(S, e) = \varphi_i(S, d)$ also for all $i \in M$.

For all $x, y \in S$, $x \neq y$, write $\varphi(x)$ instead of $\varphi(S, x)$, and let $\ell(x, y)$ be the straight line through x and y; by $[x, y]$ denote the line segment with endpoints x and y. Then, for $x \in T := \{x \in S : x \geq e\}$, define $\psi(x)$ as the other (i.e., $\neq \varphi(x)$) point of intersection of $\ell(d, \varphi(x))$ with relbd(T), i.e., with the boundary of T relative to the $|M|$-dimensional subspace containing T. This map is well-defined since d is in the interior, relint(T), of T relative to that same $|M|$-dimensional subspace, and continuous since φ is continuous by DCONT. Since T is compact and convex, by Brouwer's fixed theorem there exists $z \in T$ such that $\psi(z) = z$. Then $z \in$ relbd(T) and $d \in \ell(z, \varphi(z))$. By PO, $d \geq \varphi(z)$ would imply $d = \varphi(z)$ which contradicts $d \in$ relint(T). Further, $d \leq z$ with $d \neq z$ would imply $z \in$ relint(T), also a contradiction. So we must have $d \in [z, \varphi(z)]$, so $\varphi(d) = \varphi(z)$ by DPC. In particular we also have $e \in \ell(z, \varphi(z))$. But then we must have $z = e$ since $e \in$ relbd(T). So $\varphi(e) = \varphi(z) = \varphi(d)$.   □

In his 1953 paper on 2-person cooperative games, Nash justifies the IIA axiom as follows. "This axiom is equivalent to an axiom of "localization" of the independence of the solution point on the shape of the set S. The localization of the solution point on the upper right boundary of S is determined only by the shape of any small segment of the boundary that extends to both sides of it. It does not depend on the rest of the boundary curve" (Nash (1953), p. 138; our notation). Formally, one may state this "localization" axiom as follows (see also Lensberg (1987, p. 953)):

Localization (LOC): For all (S, d), $(T, d) \in \mathcal{D}^N$, if $U \cap S = U \cap T$ for an open neighborhood U of $\varphi(S, d)$, then $\varphi(T, d) = \varphi(S, d)$.

Clearly this axiom is closely related to IIA. However, it is neither weaker nor stronger than

IIA. The relationship between the two axioms will be discussed in more detail at the end of this subsection.

It is easy to prove that (four of) the axioms in theorem 2.46 imply LOC:

Lemma 2.49 Let $\varphi : \overline{C}^N \to \mathbb{R}^N$ satisfy DPC, DCONT, SIR, and INIR. Then φ satisfies LOC.

Proof Assume (S,d), $(T,d) \in \overline{C}^N$ satisfy the conditions stated in LOC, and let e be a convex combination of d and $\varphi(S,d)$ sufficiently close to $\varphi(S,d)$ such that $S_e = T_e$. Such a point e exists in particular since f satisfies PO, see lemma 2.47. Then from INIR and $\varphi(S_e, e) = \varphi(T_e, e)$ we conclude $\varphi(S,e) = \varphi(T,e)$, so $\varphi(S,d) = \varphi(T,d)$ follows from DLIN (lemma 2.48). $\qquad\square$

We are now sufficiently equipped to prove theorem 2.46.

Proof of theorem 2.46 Let $\omega := \varphi(\Delta^N, 0)$. By SIR and lemma 2.47, $\omega > 0$ and $\sum_{i \in N} \omega_i = 1$. Let $H := \langle N, \omega \rangle \in \mathcal{H}^N$ and $(S,d) \in \overline{C}^N$. We will prove that $\varphi(S,d) = \varphi^H(S,d)$. We may suppose that d is not a boundary point of S, i.e., $(S,d) \in C^N$, for boundary points are taken care of by DCONT of φ and φ^H: boundary points can be approximated by interior points, so it is sufficient to give the proof for interior disagreement points. In view of STC, and SIR, we may further assume that $d = 0$ and $\varphi_i(S,d) = 1$ for every $i \in N$. We write $z = \varphi^H(S,d) > 0$, and suppress $d = 0$ from notation: so we write $\varphi(S)$ instead of $\varphi(S,0)$, etc. In view of SIR and INIR, we may also assume $S = S_0$. We denote, for $\omega \in \mathbb{R}^N$, $\omega > 0$:

$$L(\omega) := \{x \in \mathbb{R}^N : \sum_{i \in N} \omega_i x_i z_i^{-1} = 1\}$$

and

$$K(\omega) := \text{com}(\{x \in L(\omega) : x \geq 0\}).$$

By lemma 2.20, $S \subset K(z)$, so $\varphi(S) \in K(z)$. We first show that actually $\varphi(S) \in L(z)$. Suppose not (see figure 2.5). Then $\sum_i \omega_i \varphi_i(S) z_i^{-1} = \sum \omega_i z_i^{-1} < 1$, so we can choose an $\alpha > 0$ such that $\sum_i \omega_i z_i^{-1} < 1 - \alpha$, and let $T := S \cap K((1-\alpha)z)$. Then T coincides with S in a neighborhood of $\varphi(S)$ so that, by LOC (lemmas 2.48 and 2.49), $\varphi(S) = \varphi(T)$. Now lemma 2.20 implies that $\varphi^H(T) = (1 - \alpha)z$, so that $\varphi^H(T)$ is an interior point of S. This in turn implies that, in a neighborhood of $\varphi^H(T)$, T coincides with the set $K((1-\alpha)z)$. Then STC and the fact that $\varphi(\Delta^N) = \varphi^H(\Delta^N)$ imply $\varphi(K((1-\alpha)z)) = \varphi^H(K((1-\alpha)z)) = \varphi^H(T)$, hence, by LOC of φ, $\varphi(T) = \varphi^H(T)$. However, $\varphi^H(T) \notin P(S)$, in contradiction with PO of φ, since $\varphi^H(T) = \varphi(T) = \varphi(S)$. Consequently, $\varphi(S) \in L(z)$ and $\sum_i \omega_i z_i^{-1} = 1$.

Now assume $z \neq \varphi(S)$ $(= (1, 1, \ldots, 1))$ and let $y = \frac{1}{2}z + \frac{1}{2}\varphi(S) \in S$. Since the function h on $\mathbb{R}_+$ with $h(\beta) = \beta^{-1}$ is strictly convex we have $h(\frac{1}{2}(1) + \frac{1}{2}(z_i)) < \frac{1}{2}h(1) + \frac{1}{2}h(z_i)$ i.e.

$$y_i^{-1} = (\tfrac{1}{2} + \tfrac{1}{2}z_i)^{-1} < \tfrac{1}{2} + \tfrac{1}{2}z_i^{-1} \text{ if } z_i \neq 1 = \varphi_i(S)$$

so that

$$\sum_i \omega_i y_i^{-1} < \tfrac{1}{2} + \tfrac{1}{2}\sum_i \omega_i z_i^{-1} = 1 \text{ if } z \neq \varphi(S). \tag{2.11}$$

Consider the set $S' = S \cap K(y)$. Then lemma 2.20 implies $\varphi^H(S') = y$. Furthermore, S' and S coincide in a neighborhood of $\varphi(S) = (1,1,\ldots,1)$ in view of (2.11), so that $\varphi(S) = \varphi(S')$ by LOC. However, the previous part of the proof applied to S' implies $\varphi(S') \in L(y)$, so $\varphi(S) \in L(y)$ but this contradicts (2.11). Consequently, we must have $\varphi^H(S) = z = \varphi(S)$.

□

This section is concluded by a discussion of the sensitivity of the results — in particular of

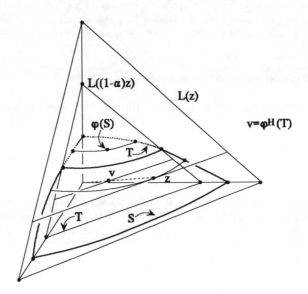

Figure 2.5: Proof of theorem 2.46

theorem 2.46 — to the choice of the domain of bargaining games, and the independence of the axioms.

The domain

Theorem 2.46 is derived for the domain $\overline{C}^N$ of bargaining games where the disagreement outcome may be a boundary point. We conjecture that a modified version of this theorem can be derived for the domain C^N. However, this is not straightforward: it is easy to see that lemmas 2.47 and 2.48 and their proofs cannot be maintained in their present form on the domain C^N.

Chun and Thomson (1990a) derive a strongly related theorem on a domain of bargaining games where the disagreement outcome must be an interior point. However, their set of axioms differs in a few respects from the list used in theorem 2.46. For instance, they use a stronger continuity axiom, and manage to give a more elementary and direct proof, in the sense that they do not need a fixed point argument. It is not clear to us whether stronger conditions are needed if the disagreement point is not allowed to be a boundary point. A detailed account of the mentioned results of Chun and Thomson is given in subsection 2.5.3.

A second consideration concerning the domain is the comprehensiveness assumption. The following example shows that lemma 2.48 no longer holds for solutions on the class $\tilde{C}^N$.

Example 2.50 Let $S := \text{conv}\{(0,0),(2,2),(1,3)\}$. Then, for every $x \in S$, $(S,x) \in \tilde{C}^{\{1,2\}}\backslash\overline{C}^{\{1,2\}}$. Let $D = \{x \in \mathbb{R}^2 : x = (\alpha,\alpha) \text{ for some } \alpha \le 1\}$. For $x = (\alpha,\alpha)$, $x \in D \cap S$, define $\varphi(S,x) = (1+\alpha, 3-\alpha)$. Note that $\{\text{conv}(x,\varphi(S,x)) : x \in D\}$ is a partition of S so that φ can be extended from D to S by the requirement of DPC. Then φ satisfies DPC, DCONT, and SIR but not DLIN. (This solution φ can be extended to $\tilde{C}^{\{1,2\}}$ in any arbitrary way, as long as it satisfies DPC, DCONT and SIR.)

Suppose that φ is a solution on $\tilde{C}^N$ satisfying the five axioms of theorem 2.46. It is easy to see that $\varphi(S,d) = \varphi(\text{com}(S),d)$ for every $(S,d) \in \tilde{C}^N$. It follows that theorem 2.46 still holds on the domain $\tilde{C}^N$. Indeed, it is not possible to extend the solution in example 2.50 to $\tilde{C}^{\{1,2\}}$ in such a way that it satisfies INIR. The formulation of INIR in Peters and van Damme (1991) is weaker, so that in their case theorem 2.46 does not extend to $\tilde{C}^N$ if $n > 2$. For details see the mentioned paper.

The axioms

The following example shows that none of the axioms in theorem 2.46 can be omitted: for SIR, DCONT, DPC, INIR, and STC, see example 2.51 (a), (b), (c), (d) and (e), respectively. In each example, φ is a solution on $\overline{C}^N$.

Example 2.51 (a) $\varphi(S,d) = d$ for all $(S,d) \in \overline{C}^N$. (b) Let $n = 3$ and $(S,d) \in \overline{C}^N$. If d is an interior point of S then $\varphi(S,d) := \varphi^{H'}(S,d)$, and otherwise, $\varphi(S,d) := \varphi^H(S,d)$, with $H =< N, (\frac{1}{2},\frac{1}{4},\frac{1}{4}) >$ and $H' =< N, (\frac{1}{3},\frac{1}{3},\frac{1}{3}) >$. (c) Let $n = 2$ and let φ be the Raiffa-Kalai-Smorodinsky solution (see section 4.2). (d) Let $n = 2$ and let φ be the Kalai-Rosenthal solution (see section 4.4). (e) Let φ be the lexicographic egalitarian solution (see section 4.7).

Adding the axiom SYM to the list of axioms in theorem 2.46 would of course single out the symmetric Nash solution. The question then arises whether one or more of the other axioms can be dropped. The answer to this question is negative as regards SIR, DPC, or STC: cf. example 2.51 (a), (c) or (e). However, the question is open as regards DCONT and INIR because the corresponding examples above are nonsymmetric.

We finally examine more closely the relation between IIA and LOC. Under certain lists of additional assumptions the two axioms are equivalent, e.g., the list in theorem 2.46. Lensberg (1987, p. 953, lemma 15) shows that IIA and LOC are equivalent for a solution that is feasible set continuous (this axiom will be introduced in section 3.4). In general, however, IIA and LOC are not logically related. To show that IIA does not imply LOC, let $\varphi : \overline{C}^{\{1,2\}} \to \mathbb{R}^2$ be defined as follows. Let $(S,d) \in \overline{C}^{\{1,2\}}$, let $v := \varphi^{<\{1\},\{2\},(1,1)>}(S,d)$ and $w := \varphi^{<\{2\},\{1\},(1,1)>}(S,d)$. Then $\varphi(S,d) := v$ if $v_1 - d_1 \ge w_2 - d_2$, $\varphi(S,d) := w$ otherwise.

This solution φ satisfies IIA but not LOC. An example of a solution $\varphi' : \overline{C}^{\{1,2\}} \to I\!\!R^2$ satisfying LOC but not IIA is as follows. If $(S,d) \in \overline{C}^{\{1,2\}}$ is such that $\{x \in S : x \geq d\}$ is a subset of a horizontal or vertical straight line, let φ' assign the unique Pareto optimal point weakly dominating d. Otherwise, let φ' assign the disagreement outcome. This last example, though, is rather trivial, and it is still an open question, e.g., whether PO suffices to obtain the implication LOC $\Rightarrow$ IIA.

2.5.3 Related literature

As remarked in subsection 2.5.2 (see the discussion concerning the domain there) a result strongly related to theorem 2.46 was obtained by Chun and Thomson (1990a). Their central axiom is called "restricted disagreement point linearity". Here, it will be called "Modified Convexity". It is formulated for a solution $\varphi : C^N \to I\!\!R^N$.

Modified Convexity (MCONV): For all $(S, d^1), (S, d^2) \in C^N$ and all $0 \leq \alpha \leq 1$, if $\alpha\varphi(S, d^1) + (1-\alpha)\varphi(S, d^2) =: x \in P(S)$ and S is smooth at both $\varphi(S, d^1)$ and $\varphi(S, d^2)$, then $\varphi(S, \alpha d^1 + (1 - \alpha)d^2) = x$.

Recall (see subsection 2.4.2) that smoothness of S at some point y means that S has a unique supporting hyperplane at that point. The modified convexity axiom is neither stronger nor weaker than CONV. Without the smoothness assumption, it would imply CONV and therefore be not satisfied by the symmetric Nash bargaining solution for $n > 2$ (see the paragraph following theorem 2.46). With the smoothness assumption, it can be verified that it is fulfilled by the Nash solution[4]. See also the discussion following the definition of the IIE axiom in subsection 2.4.2. This discussion focusses on the smoothness condition as requiring that utility transfers are possible at the same rate in all directions. For another interpretation, we quote Chun and Thomson (1990a, p. 217): "If a solution outcome x is a Pareto optimal point where $P(S)$ is not smooth, then it could be a *forced* compromise: an agent who has conceded along $P(S)$ until x might be willing to concede further at the same rate. He does not concede further because the rate at which a loss to him is converted into a gain for the others changes discontinuously; suddenly, concessions have become relatively more costly. As a result, the selection of $\varphi(S, d)$ as a compromise for (S, d) does not fully reflect the extent to which agents were willing to concede. Our axiom [MCONV] does not apply to situations where solution outcomes are so forced".

The following axiom was introduced in Peters (1986c). Let $\varphi : D^N \to I\!\!R^N$ be a solution, where $D^N \subset \tilde{B}^N$.

Pareto Continuity (PCONT): For every sequence $(S, d), (S^1, d), (S^2, d), \ldots \in D^N$, if $P(S^i) \to P(S)$ in the Hausdorff metric, then $\varphi(S^i, d) \to \varphi(S, d)$.

The main result of Chun and Thomson (1990a) is the following theorem, which we present here without a proof. The proof given by Chun and Thomson is more direct and elementary than the proof of theorem 2.46, and in particular does not use a fixed point argument.

---

[4]This shows that MCONV does not imply CONV. The construction of an example reflecting the converse implication is left to the reader.

Theorem 2.52 *The solution $\varphi : \mathcal{C}^N \to \mathbb{R}^N$ satisfies PO, SYM, STC, INIR, PCONT, and MCONV, if and only if φ is the symmetric Nash bargaining solution.*

The MCONV axiom in theorem 2.52 can be replaced by the following axiom, which *is* weaker than CONV.

Restricted Convexity (RCONV): For every $(S, d) \in \mathcal{C}^N$ and $x \in S$ such that S is smooth at x, $\{e \in S : \varphi(S, e) = x\}$ is a convex set.

This axiom was first used in an axiomatization by Livne (1988).

2.6 Nash bargaining solutions: further results

Several other axiomatizations of Nash bargaining solutions are presented in the remaining chapters of this book. In section 5.5 we characterize the family of two-person nonsymmetric Nash solutions $\varphi^H (H \in \mathcal{H}^{\{1,2\}})$ with as main axiom the restricted additivity axiom. Lensberg's (1988) axiomatization of the symmetric Nash bargaining solution in a context where the number of players may vary is reviewed in section 7.4. Sections 8.2–8.4 consider, among other topics, extensions of Nash solutions as multisolutions, as probabilistic solutions, and to bargaining games with nonconvex feasible sets. In chapter 9 some noncooperative approaches to the bargaining problem are considered, most of which are related to the Nash solution; in particular see section 9.2 on the Harsanyi-Zeuthen procedure, 9.3 on the Nash demand game, 9.4 on the Rubinstein bargaining model, and 9.5 on a single-stage game leading to the Nash outcome. Also in section 9.7, where a noncooperative comparison between several solutions is made, the Nash bargaining solution plays a central role. Extensions to coalitional bargaining games (NTU games) are reviewed in chapter 10, see sections 10.2–10.4 in particular.

We conclude by mentioning some literature that is not further discussed in this book. Aumann and Kurz (1977) introduce a concept "fear of ruin", which is related to the idea of risk aversion (chapter 6) or "risk limit" (section 9.2) and which can be used to derive the Nash bargaining solution. Chun (1988b) presents a characterization of the Nash bargaining solution based on an axiom referring to uncertainty concerning the feasible set, as opposed to uncertainty concerning the disagreement point: cf. section 2.5.

An early application of the Nash bargaining solution can be found in Mayberry *et al.* (1953). An axiomatization of the Nash bargaining solution based on underlying preferences is obtained by Rubinstein *et al.* (1990); axioms are defined in terms of preferences rather than in terms of utilities, i.e., of the feasible set. Thomson (1981c) studies the relationship between utilitarian choice rules (functions maximizing a weighted sum of the players' utilities over the feasible set) and the Nash bargaining axioms. Thomson (1981b) extends the Nash bargaining model by considering so-called reference functions instead of fixed disagreement points. Buch and Tauman (1989), finally, consider a modification of the bargaining problem where the disagreement point is determined endogenously, by negotiations between subsets of players; they appeal to a version of IIA but obtain a characterization of a utilitarian-type solution rather than of the Nash bargaining solution.

Chapter 3

Independence of irrelevant alternatives and revealed preferences

3.1 Introduction

Chapter 2 dealt with the Nash bargaining solution and its nonsymmetric extensions. The first characterization of the Nash bargaining solution, by Nash (1950), was based on the independence of irrelevant alternatives (IIA) axiom. This chapter is a further exploration into the consequences of this axiom. This exploration is based on the concept of revealed preference, in the wider context of choice functions and choice situations.

In consumer demand theory the concept of revealed preference is based on the assumption that, by choosing from budget sets, a consumer reveals his preferences over the available commodity bundles. Analogously, in bargaining theory the agreements reached in bargaining games may be thought to reveal the preferences of the bargainers as a group. Alternatively, these agreements may be regarded as reflecting the preferences of some arbitrator. In this chapter we consider, more generally, single-valued choice functions defined on a class of convex compact subsets of the nonnegative orthant of $I\!R^N$. These subsets are called choice situations. In bargaining game theory choice functions correspond to bargaining solutions and choice situations correspond to bargaining games. In consumer demand theory choice functions are called demand functions and choice situations are called budget sets. Compact convex budget sets may be regarded as "generalized" budget sets where certain commodity bundles from the full simplices (linear budget sets) are not available. An example is the case of piecewise linear budget sets, see Hausman (1985); the results in this chapter would remain valid under the restriction to this case as well. Works concerned with revealed preference in consumer demand theory are, e.g., Richter (1971), Varian (1982), and Pollak (1990). The latter discusses generalized budget sets.

One purpose of this chapter is to establish conditions under which a choice function maximizes a real-valued function. In consumer demand theory such a function is called the consumer's utility function. Another purpose is to provide a thorough study of the IIA condition. A result of this study is a characterization of a large class of bargaining solutions satisfying this condition.

We will first observe that a choice function maximizes a binary relation if and only if it satisfies IIA. Next we show that the combination of Pareto optimality and IIA for a choice function in general only excludes cycles of length 1 or 2 in the revealed binary relation. If the dimension is 2, then also cycles of length 3 are excluded, but cycles of length at least 4 may still occur. For the latter case (i.e., $n = 2$), adding a weak form of continuity called Pareto continuity (see subsection 2.5.4) suffices to exclude circularity of the revealed binary relation; in general, however, even "full" (feasible set) continuity does not exclude cycles. For the case of 2-dimensional linear budget sets, related work was done by Samuelson (1948) and Rose (1958).

The main result in this chapter is obtained by strengthening Pareto continuity to feasible set continuity: this condition together with Pareto optimality, and IIA for $n = 2$ or the (stronger) strong axiom of revealed preference for $n > 2$, is sufficient for the existence of a function representing the revealed binary relation, i.e., of a function which is maximized by the choice function. We finally show that this representing function must be strongly monotonic and strongly quasiconcave and, conversely, that the existence of a representing function with these properties implies the conditions of feasible set continuity, Pareto optimality, IIA, and the strong axiom of revealed preference for the choice function.

This chapter is organized as follows. Section 3.2 gives definitions and considers the role of IIA. Sections 3.3 and 3.4 study the (a)cyclicity of revealed preference without and with continuity, respectively. Section 3.5 is devoted to the aforementioned main result and briefly discusses the consequences for bargaining game theory. Section 3.6 contains concluding remarks and a short discussion of related literature. Section 3.7 is a technical appendix, in which a choice function is constructed for dimension $n = 3$, satisfying feasible set continuity, PO and IIA, but not the strong axiom of revealed preference.

The material in this section is based on Peters and Wakker (1991a).

3.2   The role of IIA

A *choice situation* is a compact convex subset S of $I\!\!R_+^N$ which is comprehensive relative to $I\!\!R_+^N$ (i.e., $y \in S$ whenever $0 \leq y \leq x$ and $x \in S$) and which additionally satisfies $P(S) \subset I\!\!R_{++}^N$ i.e., all Pareto optimal points are strictly positive. The last condition is added to avoid problems on the boundary of $I\!\!R_+^N$ when representation of revealed preference is discussed (see section 3.5 and the domain discussion in section 3.6). Note that a choice situation S is an element of $\tilde{C}_0^N$, the class of bargaining games with convex feasible sets and zero disagreement outcomes. Thus, $\Sigma^N \subset \tilde{C}_0^N$, where Σ^N denotes the class of all choice situations.

A *choice function* is a map $\varphi : \Sigma^N \to I\!\!R^N$ with $\varphi(S) \in S$ for every $S \in \Sigma^N$. So a choice function is *single-valued* by definition. If Σ^N is viewed as a class of bargaining games, then a choice function is simply a bargaining solution. Therefore, axioms and concepts related to bargaining solutions are defined also for choice functions. From a choice function φ we derive a binary relation R on $I\!\!R_+^N$ as follows: xRy ("x is *directly revealed preferred to* y") if there is an $S \in \Sigma^N$ with $x = \varphi(S)$, $y \in S$. If no confusion is likely to arise, dependence of R on φ is suppressed from notation.

Sometimes choice functions can be derived from binary relations. A binary relation $\succeq$ on $\mathbb{R}_+^N$ *represents* a choice function φ if for every choice situation S we have:

$$\{\varphi(S)\} = \{x \in S : x \succeq y \text{ for every } y \in S\}, \tag{3.1}$$

i.e., φ uniquely maximizes $\succeq$ on S. Obviously, not every binary relation represents a choice function, and not every choice function can be represented by a binary relation. The IIA axiom plays a central role here, as is demonstrated by the following simple but basic theorem.

Theorem 3.1 *The choice function $\varphi : \Sigma^N \to \mathbb{R}^N$ can be represented by a binary relation $\succeq$ if and only if φ satisfies IIA.*

Proof First suppose φ is represented by $\succeq$. Let $S, T \in \Sigma^N$ with $S \subset T$ and $\varphi(T) \in S$. By definition $\{\varphi(T)\} = \{x \in T : x \succeq y \text{ for every } y \in T\}$. So $\{\varphi(T)\} = \{x \in S : x \succeq y \text{ for every } y \in S\}$. From this we conclude that φ satisfies IIA.

In order to prove the converse, suppose φ satisfies IIA. Define $\succeq := R$. Then, for every $S \in \Sigma^N$, $\varphi(S) \succeq y$ for every $y \in S$. We still have to show that $\varphi(S)$ uniquely maximizes $\succeq$ on S, for every $S \in \Sigma^N$. Suppose there is an $S \in \Sigma^N$ with $y \in S$ and $y \succeq \varphi(S)$, i.e., $yR\varphi(S)$. Then there is a $T \in \Sigma^N$ with $\varphi(S) \in T$ and $y = \varphi(T)$, so by IIA applied twice, $y = \varphi(T \cap S) = \varphi(S)$ (observe that $T \cap S \in \Sigma^N$). This completes the proof. $\square$

In defending the IIA condition Nash (1950, p. 195) argues that (two) rational individuals, agreeing on a common choice x from T, should find the agreement to choose x from $S \subset T$ "of lesser restrictiveness" than the agreement to choose x from T, and thus should also agree to choose x from S. Theorem 3.1 and formula (3.1) clarify how the presence of fewer points in S may make it "of lesser restrictiveness" to agree on the choice x from S: in S the players must agree on $[x \succeq y]$ for fewer points y. Thus, theorem 3.1 clarifies two ideas which may have been underlying Nash's intuition: first, that the two players should choose in accordance with a binary "group preference" relation, and, second and more basic, the idea that the two players may be considered as one decision unit on which consistency requirements can be imposed.

Let us further note that theorem 3.1 essentially depends on the assumption that the choice function is single-valued and has a domain which is intersection closed. Under more general circumstances many other conditions for choice functions have been formulated in the literature which in the context of this chapter are equivalent to IIA. We mention the weak axiom of revealed preference (see Samuelson (1938)), property α and property β of Sen (1971), renamed nonincreasing eligibility and nondecreasing eligibility in Wakker (1989a), the independence of/from irrelevant alternatives of Luce (1979) and Kaneko (1980), and the V-axiom of Richter (1971). Most of these properties were studied in the context of consumer demand theory. Arrow (1959) showed that IIA (called C4 there) is necessary and sufficient for the existence of a transitive complete representing binary relation under the restrictive assumption that the domain of the choice function contains all finite subsets of (in our context) $\mathbb{R}_+^N$.

The next two sections deal with the (a)cyclicity of the binary relation in theorem 3.1. In section 3.3 we consider choice functions without the (Pareto) continuity property, in section 3.4 we will add Pareto continuity and feasible set continuity.

3.3   (A)cyclicity of revealed preference without continuity

Let φ be a choice function and R the corresponding directly revealed preference relation. We write xPy if there exists an $S \in \Sigma^N$ with $x = \varphi(S)$, and $y \in S$, $y \neq \varphi(S)$. P is called the *directly revealed strict preference relation*.

Some elementary facts concerning the binary relations R and P are collected in the following lemma. For a set $V \subset I\!R_+^N$, denote by $\mathrm{cc}(V)$ the comprehensive convex hull of V relative to $I\!R_+^N$, i.e., $\mathrm{cc}(V) := \{y \in I\!R_+^N : y \leq x \text{ for some } x \in \mathrm{conv}(V)\}$.

Lemma 3.2 *Let $x, y \in I\!R_+^N$ with $x \neq y$. Let φ be a choice function. Then:*
(i)   Not xPx, and $xRy \Leftrightarrow xPy$.
(ii) If φ satisfies PO and $x > 0$, then xRx.
(iii) If φ satisfies IIA, and xRy, then $\varphi(S) = x$ for every $S \in \Sigma^N$ with $x \in S \subset \mathrm{cc}\{x, y\}$.

Proof (i) [Not xPx] is obvious since $x = x$. The equivalence is obvious since $x \neq y$.
(ii) Follows from: $x = \varphi(\mathrm{cc}\{x\})$ if φ is Pareto optimal.
(iii) If $\mathrm{cc}\{x, y\} \notin \Sigma^N$, we are done. Otherwise, by IIA and xRy, $x = \varphi(\mathrm{cc}\{x, y\})$. The desired statement then follows by IIA. $\square$

The following property for a choice function φ is well-known from revealed preference theory.

Definition 3.3 The choice function φ satisfies the *strong axiom of revealed preference* (SARP) if there does not exist a *cycle* $x = x^0 P x^1 P x^2 \ldots x^{k-1} P x^k = x$, where $k > 0$ is the *length* of the cycle.

The condition SARP and the following result (formulated here in a way suited for our context) have been obtained by Ville (1946) and, independently, Houthakker (1950) for general contexts. Kim (1987) has shown that slight weakenings of the transitivity of the binary relation do not affect the characterizing condition.

Theorem 3.4 *There exists a transitive binary relation representing φ if and only if φ satisfies SARP.*

The following question arises: Are there in our context simpler and more appealing conditions which are still strong enough to imply SARP? In view of theorem 3.1, IIA is a necessary condition. Further, we have the following lemma:

Lemma 3.5 *Let the choice function φ satisfy IIA. Then there do not exist cycles of length 1 or 2 in the revealed preference relation.*

Proof Cycles of length 1 are excluded by lemma 3.2(i). The proof of the nonexistence of cycles of length 2 is analogous to the second half of the proof of theorem 3.1. $\square$

The last property in lemma 3.5, nonexistence of cycles of length 2, is known as the *weak axiom of revealed preference* (WARP), see e.g., Richter (1971). Further discussion is postponed until the end of the next section.

In the sequel we shall always assume Pareto optimality. In consumer demand theory it is an implicit condition, in bargaining game theory it is fairly standard. The next step is to show that for $n = 2$ ($N = \{1, 2\}$) also cycles of length 3 are excluded for a choice function satisfying PO and IIA. Bossert (1992) proves that this is true also without Pareto optimality.

In what follows $\ell(a, b)$ denotes the straight line through the points $a \neq b$ in $\mathbb{R}^N$.

Lemma 3.6 *Let* $\varphi : \Sigma^{\{1,2\}} \to \mathbb{R}^{\{1,2\}}$ *satisfy PO and IIA. Then there do not exist cycles of length 3 in the corresponding directly revealed strict preference relation.*

Proof Assume the following situation:

$$a, b, x \in \mathbb{R}_+^{\{1,2\}} \text{ satisfy } aPb, \ x\not\!Rb. \qquad (3.2)$$

Observe that (3.2) implies $a \neq b$, $a \neq x$, $b \neq x$. The lemma follows by proving that $x\not\!Ra$; in some cases the additional requirement bPx will be assumed for this. Note that $a > 0$ by PO of φ, since $P(S) \subset \mathbb{R}_{++}^2$ for all $S \in \Sigma^{\{1,2\}}$. W.l.o.g. also $x > 0$ otherwise we are done.

In order to prove $x\not\!Ra$, we list the following cases, which essentially exhaust all possible configurations of $\{a, b, x\}$.

(3.2.a) $a \geq b$
(3.2.b) $b_1 < a_1,\ b_2 > a_2$
(3.2.b.1) $x_1 < b_1$, x on or above $\ell(a, b)$
(3.2.b.2) $x_1 < b_1$, $x_2 > b_2$, x strictly below $\ell(a, b)$
(3.2.b.3) $x \in \text{cc}\{a, b\}$
(3.2.b.4) $x_1 > a_1$, x on or below $\ell(a, b)$
(3.2.b.5) $x_2 < a_2$, x strictly above $\ell(a, b)$
(3.2.b.6) $x_1 \geq a_1$, $a_2 \leq x_2 < b_2$
(3.2.b.7) $x_1 < a_1$, $x_2 < b_2$, x strictly above $\ell(a, b)$.

Note that the case $b \geq a$ is excluded by aPb and PO. Also the case $x \geq b$ is excluded by $x\not\!Rb$ and PO. Further, the cases with $b_1 > a_1$, $b_2 < a_2$ are analogous to (3.2.b.1)–(3.2.b.7) and are therefore omitted. The proof of $x\not\!Ra$ is given in two steps.

Step 1: In the cases (3.2.a), (3.2.b.1), (3.2.b.3), and (3.2.b.4), we have $x\not\!Ra$.

Proof:
(3.2.a): xRa would by lemma 3.2 imply $x = \varphi(\text{cc}\{x, a, b\})$, contradicting $x\not\!Rb$.
(3.2.b.1): Same proof as for case (3.2.a).
(3.2.b.3): By aPb and lemma 3.2 we have $a = \varphi(\text{cc}\{a, b, x\})$, so aPx, hence $x\not\!Ra$.
(3.2.b.4): Let $S := \text{cc}\{x, a, b\}$. If $\varphi(S) \in \text{cc}\{a, b\}$ then $\varphi(S) = a$ and hence aPx. If $\varphi(S) \in \text{cc}\{a, x\}$ then $\varphi(S) \neq x$ since otherwise xRb; so by IIA also $\varphi(\text{cc}\{a, x\}) \neq x$, which by lemma 3.2 implies $x\not\!Ra$.

Step 2: Suppose bPx. Then $x\not\!Ra$ in the cases (3.2.b.2), (3.2.b.5)–(3.2.b.7)

Proof:
(3.2.b.2): Let $S := \text{cc}\{x, a, b\}$. If $\varphi(S) \in \text{cc}\{a, b\}$ then $\varphi(S) = a$ by IIA, so aPx. If $\varphi(S) \in \text{cc}\{x, b\}$ then $\varphi(S) = b$ since bPx, which leads to the contradiction bPa.
(3.2.b.5), (3.2.b.6): By lemma 3.2, bPx, and $a \in \text{cc}\{b, x\}$, we would have bPa, a contradiction.

(3.2.b.7): Let $T := cc\{a, b, x\}$. If $\varphi(T) \in cc\{b, x\}$, then $\varphi(T) = b$, which would imply bPa, a contradiction. So $\varphi(T) \in cc\{x, a\}$ and $\varphi(T) \neq x$ since otherwise xPb. So by IIA, $\varphi(cc\{x, a\}) \neq x$, hence $x\not{R}a$ by lemma 3.2. $\square$

The following example shows that (for $n = 2$) IIA and PO are not sufficient to exclude cycles of length greater than 3.

Example 3.7 We define the following subsets of $\mathbb{R}_+^2$ (see figure 3.1).

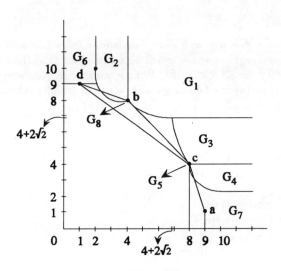

Figure 3.1: Example 3.7

$G_1 := \{x \in \mathbb{R}_+^2 : x_1 \geq 4, \ x_2 \geq 4 + 2\sqrt{2}\} - \{(4,8)\} - \{x \in \mathbb{R}_+^2 : x_1 \leq 4 + 2\sqrt{2}, \ x_2 \leq 8,$
$\quad (x_1 - 4 - 2\sqrt{2})^2 + (x_2 - 8 - 2\sqrt{2})^2 > 16\}$
$G_2 := \{x \in \mathbb{R}_+^2 : 2 \leq x_1 < 4\} - \{x \in \mathbb{R}_+^2 : x_2 \leq 10, \ (x_1 - 4)^2 + (x_2 - 10)^2 > 4\}$
$G_3 := \{x \in \mathbb{R}_+^2 : 4 \leq x_2 < 4 + 2\sqrt{2}\} - \{(8,4)\} - \{x \in \mathbb{R}_+^2 : x_1 \leq 8,$
$\quad (x_1 - 8 - 2\sqrt{2})^2 + (x_2 - 4 - 2\sqrt{2})^2 > 16\}$
$G_4 := \{x \in \mathbb{R}_+^2 : 2 \leq x_2 < 4\} - \{x \in \mathbb{R}_+^2 : x_1 \leq 10, (x_1 - 10)^2 + (x_2 - 4)^2 > 4\}$
$G_5 := \{(8,4)\}$
$G_6 := \{x \in \mathbb{R}_+^2 : x_2 \geq 9\} - G_1 - G_2$
$G_7 := \{x \in \mathbb{R}_+^2 : x_1 > 8\} - G_1 - G_3 - G_4$
$G_8 := \{(4,8)\}$
$G_9 := \mathbb{R}_+^2 \backslash (G_1 \cup \ldots \cup G_8)$.

Further $a := (9,1)$, $b := (4,8)$, $c := (8,4)$, and $d := (1,9)$. Let the transitive binary relation $\stackrel{\sim}{\succeq}$ on $\mathbb{R}_+^2$ be defined as follows:

(i) $x\stackrel{\sim}{\succ}y$ for all $i < j$, $x \in G_i$, $y \in G_j$, $i, j \in \{1, 2, \ldots, 9\}$.

(ii) On $G_1, G_4, G_5, G_7, \stackrel{\sim}{\succeq}$ is the lexicographic order.

(iii) On $G_2, G_3, G_6, G_8, \stackrel{\sim}{\succeq}$ is the reversed lexicographic order (first maximizing the second coordinate).

(iv) On G_9, $\overset{\sim}{\succeq}$ maximizes the product $x_1 x_2$.

We define $\overset{\sim}{\varphi}$ as the choice function maximizing $\overset{\sim}{\succeq}$. It can be seen that $\overset{\sim}{\varphi}$ is well-defined, and satisfies IIA, PO, and SARP. We define $\succeq$ to be equal to $\overset{\sim}{\succeq}$ with one exception: $b \succeq c$ instead of $c \overset{\sim}{\succeq} b$. So $\succeq$ is not transitive. We define φ as the choice function maximizing $\succeq$. Then also φ is well-defined and satisfies PO and IIA (by theorem 3.1), but φ does not satisfy SARP: $aPbPcPdPa$, a cycle of length 4.

This section is concluded by an example showing that if $n > 2$, IIA and PO admit cycles of length 3.

Example 3.8 Let $N = \{1, 2, 3\}$ and let the choice function $\varphi : \Sigma^N \to I\!\!R^N$ be defined as follows. Let $Y := \{x \in I\!\!R^N : x \geq (1, 1, 1)\}$ and let $S \in \Sigma^N$. If S contains an interior point of Y, then let $\varphi(S)$ be the unique point of $Y \cap S$ where the product $(x_1 - 1)(x_2 - 1)(x_3 - 1)$ is maximized on this set; then $\varphi(S) > (1, 1, 1)$. If $S \cap Y = \emptyset$, then let $\varphi(S)$ be the unique point of S where the product $x_1 x_2 x_3$ is maximized on S. If $S \cap Y \neq \emptyset$ and x_1 (resp. x_2, x_3) $= 1$ for all $x \in S \cap Y$ then let $\varphi(S)$ be the Pareto optimal point of $S \cap Y$ with maximal third (resp. first, second) coordinate. Then φ can be seen to be a well-defined choice function satisfying IIA and PO. The corresponding revealed preference relation contains cycles of length 3, e.g. $(2, 1, 1)P(1, 1, 2)P(1, 2, 1)P(2, 1, 1)$.

3.4   (A)cyclicity of revealed preference with continuity

The Pareto continuity condition (PCONT) has been introduced in subsection 2.5.3. For a choice function, it means that if the Pareto optimal subsets of a sequence of choice situations converge, then also the outcomes assigned by the choice function converge to the outcome assigned to the limit choice situation. A strictly stronger condition is the feasible set continuity axiom, which, in view of future reference, is defined here for a (bargaining) solution φ defined on some subclass $\mathcal{D}^N$ of $\overset{\sim}{\mathcal{B}}{}^N$.

Feasible Set Continuity (SCONT): For every sequence $(S, d), (S^1, d), (S^2, d) \dots \in \mathcal{D}^N$, if $S^i \to S$ in the Hausdorff metric, then $\varphi(S^i, d) \to \varphi(S, d)$.

Feasible set continuity is strictly stronger than Pareto continuity. For instance, on $\Sigma^{\{1,2\}}$, the solutions φ^H corresponding to the weighted hierarchies $H = < \{1\}, \{2\}, (1, 1) >$ or $H = < \{2\}, \{1\}, (1, 1) >$ are choice functions satisfying PO, IIA, and PCONT, but not SCONT (as is easily verified). Note that for choice functions φ satisfying PO and IIA we have $\varphi(S) = \varphi(T)$ whenever $P(S) = P(T)$; so for such φ, requiring Pareto continuity instead of feasible set continuity seems reasonable.

The remainder of this section is devoted, first, to proving that the combination of PO, PCONT, and IIA for a choice function φ implies SARP if $n = 2$; second, to showing that for $n > 2$ these conditions, even with SCONT instead of PCONT, do not suffice to exclude cycles. For $x \neq y$, $\ell_x(y)$ denotes the intersection with $I\!\!R_+^N$ of the straight closed halfline through x and y with endpoint x.

Lemma 3.9 *Let the choice function* $\varphi : \Sigma^N \to I\!\!R^N$ *satisfy PO, IIA, and PCONT. Let* $v, w \in I\!\!R_+^N$ *with* $v \neq w$.

(i) If wPv then wPx for all $x \in \ell_w(v)\backslash\{w\}$, and wPx' for all $x' \leq x$ where $x \in \ell_w(v)$, $x' \neq w$.

(ii) For all $x \in \text{conv}\{v,w\}\backslash\{v,w\}$ with $x > 0$, we have xPv or xPw; and for all $x' \geq x \in$ $\text{conv}\{v,w\}$, $x' \notin \{v,w\}$, $x' > 0$, we have $x'Pv$ or $x'Pw$.

Proof (i) Suppose wPv. By convexity of choice situations this immediately implies wPx for all $x \in \text{conv}\{v,w\}\backslash\{w\}$. The case remains where $x \in \ell_w(v)$, x not between v and w. Let $S := \text{cc}\{x,w\}$. If $\varphi(S) \in \text{conv}\{v,w\}$ then, by IIA, $\varphi(S) = \varphi(\text{cc}\{v,w\}) = w$, so wPx. The case remains where $\varphi(S) \notin \text{conv}\{v,w\}$. We will show that this case cannot occur. By PCONT the function $y \mapsto \varphi(\text{cc}\{y,w\})$ is continuous on $\ell(v,w)$. Its image must be connected, so there is a $y \in \text{conv}\{x,v\}$ such that $\varphi(\text{cc}\{y,w\}) = v$. This and $\varphi(\text{cc}\{v,w\}) = w$ contradict IIA. So everything concerning x in (i) has been proved. The result concerning x' follows from consideration of $\text{cc}\{x,w\}$.

(ii) Let x' as in the statement of (ii), possibly $x' \in \text{conv}\{v,w\}$. We are done if $x' \geq v$ or $x' \geq w$ (by PO of φ). Otherwise note that $\text{conv}\{w,x'\} \cup \text{conv}\{x',v\}$ is the Pareto optimal subset of $\text{cc}\{w,x',v\}$. W.l.o.g. suppose $\varphi(\text{cc}\{w,x',v\}) \in \text{conv}\{w,x'\}$. By PCONT the function $y \mapsto \varphi(\text{cc}\{y,x',v\})$ from $\text{conv}\{w,x'\}$ to $\text{conv}\{w,x'\} \cup \text{conv}\{x',v\}$ is continuous. Its image must be connected, hence $\varphi(\text{cc}\{y,x',v\}) = x'$ for some $y \in \text{conv}\{x',w\}$. This implies $x'Pv$. $\qquad\square$

Up to theorem 3.14 we make the following assumption.

$N = \{1,2\}$ and $\varphi : \Sigma^N \to \mathbb{R}^N$ is a choice function satisfying PO, IIA and PCONT.   (3.3)

We show that under this condition P has no cycles, by induction based on lemma 3.6, which says that there are no cycles of length 3. Fix a sequence $a, b, \dots, y, x$ of length at least 4 with $aPbP\dots PyPx$. We want to show: $x\cancel{R}a$. The induction hypothesis is that no cycles of length smaller than the length of $(a,b,\dots,y,x)$ exist. This implies:

> For all v and w in this sequence with $vP\dots Pw$ and not both $v = a$ and $w = x$,
>
> we have $w\cancel{R}v$. Further, $x\cancel{R}a$ if there are v and w in the sequence with w
>
> not the immediate successor of v and vPw.   (3.4)

Note that aPb and $x\cancel{R}b$. Again (3.2.a)–(3.2.b.7), distinguished in the proof of lemma 3.6, are essentially all possible cases. Step 1 in the proof of lemma 3.6 (in which only $x\cancel{R}b$ is used) implies the following lemma.

Lemma 3.10 *Assume (3.3) and (3.4). Then $x\cancel{R}a$ in the cases (3.2.a), (3.2.b.1), (3.2.b.3) and (3.2.b.4).*

The remaining cases are treated in the following lemmas.

Lemma 3.11 *Assume (3.3) and (3.4). In case (3.2.b.2), $x\cancel{R}a$. Case (3.2.b.6) cannot occur.*

Proof In case (3.2.b.2), it follows from lemma 3.9(i) with a in the role of w and b in the role of v, that (even) aPx. In case (3.2.b.6), yPx and $x \geq a$ imply $y = \varphi(\text{cc}\{a,y,x\})$. So yPa, in contradiction with (3.4). Hence, this case cannot occur. $\qquad\square$

Lemma 3.12 *Assume (3.3) and (3.4). Then case (3.2.b.7) cannot occur.*

Proof We consider all possible locations of y. If $y_1 \leq a_1$ and y on or below $\ell(a,b)$ then aPy in view of lemma 3.9(i), so from (3.4) we obtain $x\mathcal{R}a$. Since by (3.4) also $x\mathcal{R}b$, a contradiction with lemma 3.9(ii) follows. If $y_1 > a_1$, and y on or below $\ell(x,a)$, then xPa would by lemma 3.9(i) imply xPy which is a contradiction. So $x\mathcal{R}a$, but as before that is also impossible. If $y_2 \geq b_2$ and y on or above $\ell(a,b)$, then $b \in cc\{x,y\}$, so yPb by lemma 3.2(iii) (since yPx), in contradiction with (3.4). If $y_2 \leq a_2$ and y on or above $\ell(x,a)$, then $a \in cc\{x,y\}$, so yPa (since yPx), in contradiction with (3.4). Also $y \geq a$ would imply the contradiction yPa. The only possibility left is: y strictly above $\ell(a,b)$, $y_2 < b_2$, $y_1 < a_1$. In that case, yPa or yPb by lemma 3.9(ii), in contradiction with (3.4). $\square$

Lemma 3.13 *Assume (3.3) and (3.4). In case (3.2.b.5), we have $x\mathcal{R}a$.*

Proof Suppose xPa. Then $xPaPb\ldots Py$, and yPx. By the previous lemmas, yPx is excluded in all possible configurations except for the configuration described in this lemma, so $a_1 < x_1$, $a_2 > x_2 > y_2$, y strictly above $\ell(x,a)$. If z is the immediate predecessor of y, then $yPxPaPb\ldots Pz$ and zPy. Again, the only possible configuration for this is: $x_1 < y_1$, $x_2 > y_2 > z_2$, z strictly above $\ell(y,x)$. Repeating this argument we find for the final step $bPcP\ldots PzPyPxPa$ and $aPb : c_1 < b_1$, $c_2 > b_2 > a_2$, a strictly above $\ell(b,c)$. In particular, $b_1 > c_1 > \ldots > y_1 > x_1 > a_1 > b_1$, an obvious impossibility. $\square$

Lemmas 3.5 and 3.6 and lemmas 3.10–3.13 imply the following theorem.

Theorem 3.14 *Let $N = \{1,2\}$ and let the choice function $\varphi : \Sigma^N \to \mathbb{R}^N$ satisfy PO, IIA and PCONT. Then φ satisfies SARP.*

Samuelson (1948) and Rose (1958) essentially showed that PO and WARP suffice to exclude cycles, for a single-valued choice function defined on only 2-dimensional linear choice situations (i.e., budget sets of the form $cc\{(a,0), (0,b)\}$ where $a,b \in \mathbb{R}_+$). Theorem 3.14 extends this result to choice functions defined on nonlinear 2-dimensional budget sets, while weakening WARP to IIA.

The next question is whether theorem 3.14 still holds if $n > 2$. Gale (1960) has provided an example of a continuous demand function defined on 3-dimensional linear budget sets which satisfies PO and WARP but not SARP. In other words, the result of Rose (1958) mentioned before does not have to hold if there are more than two commodities. In section 3.7 it is shown that Gale's example can be extended to 3-dimensional nonlinear budget sets (our choice situations) as well. The extension to higher dimensions, also for linear budget sets, is given in Peters and Wakker (1991b). For linear budget sets a theoretical (nonconstructive) argument can be found in Kihlstrom, Mas-Colell, and Sonnenschein (1976, p. 975).

Another interesting question is whether IIA can be strengthened in an appealing way in order to imply SARP. For instance, for each dimension n, can one find a natural number $k(n)$ such that requiring the exclusion of cycles of length smaller than or equal to $k(n)$, instead of IIA, implies SARP? For linear budget sets the answer is negative, as follows from Shafer (1977). For our case the answer is also negative: this can be shown by extending Shafer's 3-dimensional example to nonlinear budget sets in the same way as is done in section 3.7 with Gale's example.

3.5   Representation of revealed preference

Let φ be a choice function. $x \in I\!\!R_+^N$ is *revealed preferred to* $y \in I\!\!R_+^N$, notation $x\overline{R}y$, if there exists a sequence $x = x^0, x^1, \ldots, x^k = y$ in $I\!\!R_+^N$ with $x^0 Rx^1 R \ldots Rx^k$. If in this sequence $x^i Px^{i+1}$ for some $i \in \{0, 1, \ldots, k-1\}$, x is *revealed strictly preferred to* y, notation $x\overline{P}y$. By Wakker (1989b, Corollary I.2.12, (vi) and (vii), and Theorem I.2.5, (ii) and (vi)), F satisfies SARP if and only if $\overline{P}$ is the asymmetric part of $\overline{R}$. Note that in our case, by lemma 3.2(i), if $x \neq y$ and $x\overline{R}y$, then $x\overline{P}y$.

$\overline{R}$ does not have to be complete. ($\overline{R}$ is *complete* if $x\overline{R}y$ or $y\overline{R}x$ for all x, y.) For instance, if $n = 2$ and φ is the "Nash choice function", maximizing the product $x_1 x_2$ on every $S \in \Sigma^N$, then neither $(1,2)\overline{R}(2,1)$ nor $(2,1)\overline{R}(1,2)$. By our choice of domain, in particular the requirement $P(S) \subset I\!\!R_{++}^N$ for every $S \in \Sigma^N$, $\overline{R}$ is never complete if the choice function φ is Pareto optimal. However, the relation $\overline{R}$ induced by the choice function $\varphi = \varphi^H$ where $H = < \{1\}, \{2\}, (1,1) > \in \mathcal{H}^{\{1,2\}}$ is complete on the positive orthant $I\!\!R_{++}^2$.

Since, in what follows, only Pareto optimal choice functions will be considered, it is natural to restrict attention to $I\!\!R_{++}^N$. In deriving representation results, this will avoid boundary problems. Thus, we say that the function $f : I\!\!R_{++}^N \to I\!\!R$ *represents* the binary relation $\succeq$ if $[x \succ y \Rightarrow f(x) > f(y)]$ and $[x \succeq y \Rightarrow f(x) \geq f(y)]$ for all $x, y \in I\!\!R_{++}^N$, where $\succ$ is the asymmetric part of $\succeq$. It is well-known that not every binary relation is representable in this way. For instance, if $\overline{R}$ is revealed by $\varphi^{<\{1\},\{2\},(1,1)>}$, then $\overline{R}$ is the lexicographic order which is well-known not to be representable by a real-valued function.

The main purpose of this section is to find sufficient conditions for φ such that the corresponding revealed preference relation $\overline{R}$ is representable by a real-valued function f. Such a function will be called a *utility function* (of the consumer, or the group of bargainers). It will be shown that f is strongly monotonic and strongly quasi-concave.

The following lemma can be derived from corollary 1 in Jaffray (1975).

Lemma 3.15 *Let $\overline{P}$ be a transitive asymmetric partial order on $I\!\!R_{++}^N$. If there exists a countable subset A of $I\!\!R_{++}^N$ such that for all $x, y \in I\!\!R_{++}^N$ with $x\overline{P}y$ there is an $a \in A$ with $x\overline{P}a\overline{P}y$, then there exists a function $f : I\!\!R_{++}^N \to I\!\!R$ such that for all $x, y \in I\!\!R_{++}^N$, $x\overline{P}y$ implies $f(x) > f(y)$.*

Remark: Lemma 3.15 is a variation on a result by Debreu (1954, Lemma II); the latter holds for weak orders (transitive complete binary relations). Actually, given an enumeration $A = \{a_1, a_2, \ldots\}$ of the set A, a function f as in lemma 3.15 is easily defined: $f : x \mapsto \sum_{k: x\overline{P}a_k} 2^{-k-1}$. See Jaffray (1975) for further details.

Lemma 3.16 *Let the choice function $\varphi : \Sigma^N \to I\!\!R^N$ satisfy PO, SCONT, and SARP. Let*

$$A := \{a \in I\!\!R_{++}^N : a = \varphi(\text{cc}\{v, w\}) \text{ for some } v, w \in Q_{++}^N\}.$$

Let $x, y \in I\!\!R_{++}^N$ with $x\overline{P}y$. Then there exists an $a \in A$ with $x\overline{P}a\overline{P}y$.

Proof First assume xPy. Choose sequences $\{x^j\}, \{y^j\} \subset Q_{++}^N$ with $x^j \to x$, $y^j \to y$, and with for all j : $x^j < x$, $y^j > y$, and $\frac{1}{2}x^j + \frac{1}{2}y^j \in \text{cc}\{x, y\}$. By SCONT of φ we have $\varphi(\text{cc}\{x^j, y^j\}) \to \varphi(\text{cc}\{x, y\}) = x$ which implies: there is some $k \in I\!\!N$ such that $a := \varphi(\text{cc}\{x^k, y^k\}) \in \text{cc}\{x, y\}$. So $a \in A$, and xPa in view of lemma 3.2(iii). Since $y \in \text{cc}\{a, y^k\}$, also aPy. So this point a has the desired properties.

Next assume $x\overline{P}y$. Then $x = x^0Rx^1\ldots Rx^{j-1}Rx^j\ldots Rx^k = y$ with, say, $x^{j-1}Px^j$. So by the first part of the proof we have $x^{j-1}Pa Px^j$ for some $a \in A$, hence also $x\overline{P}a\overline{P}y$.   □

Observe that in the proof of lemma 3.16 feasible set continuity cannot be replaced by Pareto continuity; if, for instance, $x, y \in \mathbb{R}^2$ with $x_2 > y_2$ and $x_1 = y_1$, the proof does not work. Indeed, the choice function $\varphi^{<\{1\},\{2\},(1,1)>}$ is Pareto continuous but the corresponding lexicographic order is not representable by a real-valued utility function.

For a choice function φ and a real-valued function f on $\mathbb{R}^N_{++}$, φ *maximizes* f if $\varphi(S) > 0$ and $f(\varphi(S)) > f(x)$ whenever $S \in \Sigma^N$, $x \in S$, $x \neq \varphi(S)$, $x > 0$.

Theorem 3.17 *Let φ be a Pareto optimal feasible set continuous choice function. Then the following two statements are equivalent:*

(a) φ satisfies SARP.

(b) φ maximizes a real-valued function f on $\mathbb{R}^N_{++}$.

Proof Suppose φ satisfies SARP. Then by lemmas 3.15 and 3.16 there is an $f : \mathbb{R}^N_{++} \to \mathbb{R}$ with $x\overline{P}y \Rightarrow f(x) > f(y)$ for all $x, y \in \mathbb{R}^N_{++}$. Since $\varphi(S)Px$ for all $\varphi(S) \neq x \in S$ and $S \in \Sigma^N$, φ maximizes f. The implication (b) $\Rightarrow$ (a) is straightforward.   □

Next, it will be shown that the function f in theorem 3.17 is *strongly monotonic* (i.e., strictly increasing in each coordinate) and *strongly quasiconcave*. The latter means that for all $0 < \alpha < 1$ and $x, y \in \mathbb{R}^N_{++}$ with $f(y) \geq f(x)$, we have that $\alpha x + (1 - \alpha)y$ is an interior point of the set $\{z \in \mathbb{R}^N_{++} : f(z) \geq f(x)\}$.

Lemma 3.18 *Let the choice function φ on Σ^N be Pareto optimal and feasible set continuous, and suppose it maximizes a real-valued function f on $\mathbb{R}^N_{++}$. Then f is strongly monotonic and strongly quasiconcave.*

Proof Let $x, y \in \mathbb{R}^N_{++}$ with $x \geq y$, $x \neq y$. Then $\varphi(cc\{x, y\}) = x$ by PO of φ, so $f(x) > f(y)$. This proves strong monotonicity of f.

Next, let $z \in \mathbb{R}^N_{++}$ and $T := \{x \in \mathbb{R}^N_{++} : f(x) \geq f(z)\}$. Let $x, x' \in T$ with $x \neq x'$ and $y = \alpha x + (1 - \alpha)x'$ where $0 < \alpha < 1$. By lemma 3.9(ii), we have yPx or yPx', so $f(y) > f(z)$ and $y \in T$. In particular, T is convex.

If $v \neq w \in T$ and $conv\{v, w\}$ contains an interior point t of T, then by convexity of T all points in $conv\{v, w\}\backslash\{v, w\}$ are interior. For contradiction, assume that $conv\{v, w\}$ does not contain an interior point of T. Let $\varphi(cc\{v, w\}) = v$ (otherwise continue the proof with $\varphi(cc\{v, w\})$ in the role of v if $\varphi(cc\{v, w\}) \neq w$, or with the roles of v and w reversed if $\varphi(cc\{v, w\}) = w$). Note that $f(v) > f(w) \geq f(z)$. Also, $f(x) < f(z)$ for every x in the interior of $cc\{v, w\}$ since otherwise, by PO, $conv\{v, w\}$ would contain an interior point of T. Let $v^1, v^2, \ldots \in \mathbb{R}^N_{++}$ be a sequence in the interior of $cc\{v, w\}$ converging to v. Then $\varphi(cc\{v^k, w\}) = w$ for every $k \in \mathbb{N}$ whereas $\varphi(cc\{v, w\}) = v$. This contradicts SCONT of φ.   □

Lemma 3.19 *Let the choice function φ on Σ^N maximize a strongly monotonic and strongly quasiconcave real-valued function f on $\mathbb{R}^N_{++}$. Then φ satisfies PO and SCONT.*

Proof Pareto optimality of φ is an immediate consequence of strong monotonicity of f. Next, suppose for contradiction that φ does not satisfy SCONT. Using compactness, subsequences, and IIA, we can arrange sequences $p, p^1, p^2, \ldots$ and $q, q^1, q^2, \ldots$ in $I\!\!R^N_{++}$ with $p^k \to p$, $q^k \to q$, $\varphi(\text{cc}\{p^k, q^k\}) = p^k$, $\varphi(\text{cc}\{p, q\}) = q$. From $f(q) > f(p)$ and strong quasiconcavity of f it follows that $\frac{1}{2}p + \frac{1}{2}q$ is an interior point of $\{x : f(x) \geq f(p)\}$; so $f(\frac{1}{2}p + \frac{1}{2}q) > f(p)$ by monotonicity of f. Similarly $\frac{3}{4}q + \frac{1}{4}p$ is an interior point of $\{x : f(x) \geq f(\frac{1}{2}p + \frac{1}{2}q)\}$, so by monotonicity of f there is a $\hat{q} < \frac{3}{4}q + \frac{1}{4}p$ such that $f(\hat{q}) > f(\frac{1}{2}p + \frac{1}{2}q)$. Further, there is a $\hat{p} > p$ such that $\frac{1}{2}p + \frac{1}{2}q > \hat{w}$ for some $\hat{w} \in \text{conv}\{\hat{p}, \hat{q}\}$. Then $f(\hat{q}) > f(\frac{1}{2}p + \frac{1}{2}q) > f(\hat{w})$. By strong quasiconcavity of $f : f(\hat{w}) \geq \min\{f(\hat{p}, f(\hat{q})\}$. We conclude that $f(\hat{p}) < f(\hat{q})$.

So $\hat{q} < \frac{3}{4}q + \frac{1}{4}p$, $\hat{p} > p$, $f(\hat{p}) < f(\hat{q})$. Take $k \in I\!\!N$ so large that $p^k < \hat{p}$ and $\hat{q} \in \text{cc}\{p^k, q^k\}$. Then $f(p^k) < f(\hat{p}) < f(\hat{q})$ whereas $\varphi(\text{cc}\{p^k, q^k\}) = p^k$. This contradicts $\hat{q} \in \text{cc}\{p^k, q^k\}$. $\square$

Theorem 3.17 and lemmas 3.18 and 3.19 imply the following theorem.

Theorem 3.20 *For a choice function φ on Σ^N the following two statements are equivalent:*

(a) *φ satisfies SCONT, PO, and SARP.*

(b) *φ maximizes a strongly monotonic strongly quasiconcave real-valued function f on $I\!\!R^N_{++}$.*

For $N = \{1, 2\}$, theorems 3.14 and 3.17 imply the following corollary, which further illustrates the meaning of Nash's IIA.

Corollary 3.21 *Let $N = \{1, 2\}$ and let the choice function φ on Σ^N be Pareto optimal and feasible set continuous. Then the following two statements are equivalent:*

(a) *φ satisfies IIA.*

(b) *φ maximizes a real-valued function f on $I\!\!R^N_{++}$.*

The function f in theorem 3.20 may fail to be continuous. This can be inferred from the straightforward adaptation of Example 1 and Remark 4 in Hurwicz and Richter (1971) to our context.

The strong quasiconcavity condition is neither stronger nor weaker than the strict quasiconcavity condition defined in section 2.2. For instance, a constant function on the positive orthant of $I\!\!R^2$ is strongly but not strictly quasiconcave. A strongly monotonic strongly quasiconcave function, however, is also strictly concave. It is possible to construct an example of a strongly monotonic strictly quasiconcave function that is not strongly quasiconcave, and such that the choice function maximizing this function is not feasible set continuous. These considerations show that strong quasiconcavity can be replaced by strict quasiconcavity in lemma 3.18 but not in lemma 3.19 (and, consequently, not in theorem 3.20).

We conclude this section with a few remarks on the consequences for bargaining theory. Theorem 3.1 and corollary 3.21 characterize large classes of bargaining solutions with the IIA property. These solutions can be interpreted as generalizations of the Nash bargaining solutions that allow for interaction between players, and payments in perhaps more realistic quantities than von Neumann-Morgenstern utilities. Similarly, theorem 3.20 characterizes a large class of n-person solutions with the SARP property.

3.6   Concluding remarks and related literature

As remarked at the beginning of section 3.2, the condition $P(S) \subset \mathbb{R}^N_{++}$ $(S \in \Sigma^N)$ was added to avoid boundary problems related to the representation of revealed preference — for instance, a point $\hat{q}$ as in the proof of lemma 3.19 would not have to exist without this condition. Up to that lemma, however, everything essentially remains true without this condition. Instead of this condition, a requirement like "$\varphi(S) > 0$" for all $S \in \Sigma^N$ would do as well. With the appropriate modifications in the proofs, the results in this chapter would essentially remain true for some other domain choices: see Peters and Wakker (1991a) for more details.

One of the conclusions from this chapter is that the IIA condition, combined with Pareto optimality and continuity, only has strong implications in the 2-dimensional case. This case is relatively important: bargaining situations often include two parties; in consumer demand theory, many situations can be modeled as involving only two goods by considering composite goods. Nevertheless it is unfortunate that, in general, we obtain the n-dimensional analogue only by strengthening IIA to SARP.

Closely related to the material in this chapter is the work by Bossert (1992) and Lensberg (1987). Bossert obtains almost similar results for the 2-person case, but the proofs are quite different and to a larger extent use results from revealed preference theory, notably Hurwicz and Richter (1971), and from Lensberg (1987). In a context where the dimension may vary and where a choice function is a (countably infinite) list of prescriptions (one for each dimension) Lensberg shows that a condition called Multilateral Stability is necessary and sufficient for a Pareto optimal continuous choice function to maximize an additively separable strictly quasiconcave function. Further, if the dimension may vary but has an upper bound of at least 3, then Lensberg shows that this result still holds under the weaker condition of Bilateral Stability. Interesting as these results are, it should be noted that additive separability excludes interactions between dimensions. It has been discussed in many contexts, see Wakker (1989b, section II.5). In consumer theory where dimensions refer to commodities which may have physical interaction, and even more in group decision making where dimensions refer to individuals who may have social interaction, violations of additive separability are of considerable interest.

3.7   Violation of SARP for $n > 2$

In this technical section, a choice function φ on $\Sigma^{\{1,2,3\}}$ is constructed that satisfies SCONT, PO, and IIA, but not SARP. This shows that theorem 3.14 cannot be extended to higher dimensions. The choice function φ extends a demand function proposed by Gale (1960) and shows that WARP does not imply SARP if there are at least three goods. This demand function is based on the matrix

$$A := \begin{bmatrix} -3 & 4 & 0 \\ 0 & -3 & 4 \\ 4 & 0 & -3 \end{bmatrix}.$$

For all ("price") vectors $p, q > 0$ with ("demand") vectors $Ap \geq 0$, $Aq \geq 0$, the following implication holds (see Gale, 1960, section 3):

$$[pAq \leq pAp \text{ and } qAp \leq qAq] \Rightarrow Ap = Aq. \tag{3.5}$$

Implication (3.5) is the standard definition of WARP. Let $B := A^{-1}$, i.e.,

$$B = \frac{1}{37} \begin{bmatrix} 9 & 12 & 16 \\ 16 & 9 & 12 \\ 12 & 16 & 9 \end{bmatrix}.$$

Let $S \in \Sigma^{\{1,2,3\}}$ be fixed, and let $M := \{x \in S: \text{ there is no } y \in S \text{ with } x_i = y_i \text{ for all } i \neq 1 \text{ and } x_1 < y_1\}$. For every $x \in M$ let $\pi(x) \in \mathbb{R}^3_+$ be defined by $\pi(x)_i = x_i$ for all $i \neq 1$, $\pi(x)_1 = 0$, i.e., π is the projection on the hyperplane $x_1 = 0$. Then $\pi : M \to \pi(M)$ is a homeomorphism, and $\pi(M)$ is nonempty, compact, and convex.

Further, for every $x > 0$ let $H(x)$ be the supporting hyperplane of S with normal x and such that S is below $H(x)$. Then the correspondence $I : x \mapsto H(x) \cap S = H(x) \cap P(S)$ for every $x > 0$ is upper semi-continuous (as can be shown directly, or as a consequence of the Maximum Theorem: see Hildenbrand and Kirman, 1976).

Finally, let the correspondence $\mu : \pi(M) \to \pi(M)$ be defined by

$$\mu(x) = \pi\big(I(B(\pi^{-1}(x)))\big) \text{ for every } x.$$

Then clearly μ is convex-valued and uppersemicontinuous, so by Kakutani's fixed point theorem there exists a fixed point $x^* \in \mu(x^*)$.

Next, we show that such a fixed point x^* is unique. Suppose $z^* \in \mu(z^*)$ is another fixed point. Then $\pi^{-1}(x^*) \in I(B(\pi^{-1}(x^*)))$ and $\pi^{-1}(z^*) \in I(B(\pi^{-1}(z^*)))$. So by definition of I:

$$\big(B\pi^{-1}(z^*)\big)\pi^{-1}(x^*) \leq \big(B\pi^{-1}(z^*)\big)\pi^{-1}(z^*) \text{ and}$$
$$\big(B\pi^{-1}(x^*)\big)\pi^{-1}(z^*) \leq \big(B\pi^{-1}(x^*)\big)\pi^{-1}(x^*).$$

Hence

$$\big(B\pi^{-1}(z^*)\big)A\big(B\pi^{-1}(x^*)\big) \leq \big(B\pi^{-1}(z^*)\big)A\big(B\pi^{-1}(z^*)\big) \text{ and}$$
$$\big(B\pi^{-1}(x^*)\big)A\big(B\pi^{-1}(z^*)\big) \leq \big(B\pi^{-1}(x^*)\big)A\big(B\pi^{-1}(x^*)\big).$$

From these inequalities and (3.5), we conclude $\pi^{-1}(x^*) = \pi^{-1}(z^*)$, and so $x^* = z^*$.

Let φ assign the point $\pi^{-1}(x^*)$ to every choice situation, with x^* the unique fixed point as above. Then φ is a well-defined choice function. PO and IIA of φ follow straightforwardly from its definition. Next, we prove that φ is feasible set continuous.

Let $S, S^1, S^2, \ldots \in \Sigma^{\{1,2,3\}}$, $S^i \to S$ in the Hausdorff-metric, and $\varphi(S^i) = y^i \to y \in S$. For every i let $p^i = B(y^i)$; by construction, p^i is a normal of a supporting hyperplane of S^i at y^i. Since $y^i \to y$, we have $B(y^i) \to B(y) =: p$, so $p^i \to p$. It is straightforward to show that $\{x : p \cdot x = p \cdot y\}$ supports S at y. (Incidentally, it also follows that $p = B(y) > 0$, since all entries of B are positive. Hence $y \in P(S)$.) So $\pi^{-1}(y)$ is the fixed point of μ, and $\varphi(S) = y$ follows.

Finally, a violation of SARP is obtained, adapting the example of Gale (1960, section 5). The following observation will be used. Let $S \in \Sigma^{\{1,2,3\}}$ be such that $P(S) \subset \{x \in X : p \cdot x = c\}$ for some vector $p > 0$ and some constant $c > 0$. If the point $c(pAp)^{-1}Ap$ is an element of $P(S)$, then by construction of φ it is equal to $\varphi(S)$. We now turn to the example.

Let $x^1 = (1, 0.001, 0.001)$, $x^2 = (0.6, 0.001, 0.3)$, $x^3 = (0.3, 0.001, 0.6)$, $x^4 = (0.001, 0.001, 1)$, and let $p^1 = (9.028, 16.021, 12.025)$, $p^2 = (10.212, 13.209, 9.916)$, $p^3 = (12.312, 12.009, 9.016)$, $p^4 = (16.021, 12.025, 9.028)$. Then each x^i is a multiple of Ap^i. Further, we have:

$$p^1 \cdot x^1 > p^1 \cdot x^2, \quad \text{so} \quad \varphi(\text{cc}\{x^1, x^2\}) = x^1,$$
$$p^2 \cdot x^2 > p^2 \cdot x^3, \quad \text{so} \quad \varphi(\text{cc}\{x^2, x^3\}) = x^2,$$
$$p^3 \cdot x^3 > p^3 \cdot x^4, \quad \text{so} \quad \varphi(\text{cc}\{x^3, x^4\}) = x^3.$$

So x^1 is revealed preferred to x^4, i.e., $(1, 0.001, 0.001)$ is revealed preferred to $(0.001, 0.001, 1)$. By interchanging the appropriate numbers one similarly shows that $(0.001, 0.001, 1)$ is revealed preferred to $(0.001, 1, 0.001)$, and that $(0.001, 1, 0.001)$ is revealed preferred to $(1, 0.001, 0.001)$. So φ violates SARP.

Chapter 4

Monotonicity properties

4.1 Introduction

Both foregoing chapters dealt with solutions depending on only local properties of the Pareto optimal subset of a bargaining game. Chapter 2 extensively discussed nonsymmetric Nash bargaining solutions, and chapter 3 led us to conclude that, at least for the case of two players and in the presence of Pareto optimality and (feasible set) continuity, the independence of irrelevant alternatives axiom implies the maximization of a strongly monotonic, strongly quasiconcave function (corollary 3.21, lemma 3.18): again a quite local phenomenon. The localization axiom (LOC) explicitly expresses this solution property (see section 2.5). As remarked at the end of subsection 2.5.2, feasible set continuity of a solution suffices to imply the equivalence of IIA and LOC. Thus, it is not surprising that the critical discussion in the literature has focussed on this localization property of the symmetric Nash bargaining solution, and on the IIA axiom.

One of the first critical notes concerning the IIA axiom is from Luce and Raiffa (1957, p. 132). Their criticism on IIA is exemplified by the following situation. Let S be the convex comprehensive hull of the points $(10,0)$ and $(0,100)$ in $\mathbb{R}^2$, and let $T :=$ comv$\{(10,0),(5,50)\}$. Suppose a solution assigns the outcome $(5,50)$ to $(S,(0,0))$. The IIA axiom would imply the same outcome for $(T,(0,0))$. Player 1, however, could argue that this is not fair since, in $(T,(0,0))$, player 2 obtains his maximum and does not have to make any concession. *Mutatis mutandis*, if in $(T,(0,0))$ the players would reach an agreement reflecting the "levels of aspiration" of the players, say some outcome strictly between $(10,0)$ and $(5,50)$, and after that they are told that actually the game is $(S,(0,0))$, it is reasonable for player 2 to argue that he now deserves more[1]. This last consideration could induce one to impose the following axiom. Let $\varphi : \mathcal{D}^N \to \mathbb{R}^N$ be a solution, where $\mathcal{D}^N$ is some subclass of $\tilde{\mathcal{B}}^N$.

Strong Monotonicity (SMON): For all $(S,d), (T,d) \in \mathcal{D}^N$ with $S \subset T$, $\varphi(T,d) \geq \varphi(S,d)$.

---

[1]Luce and Raiffa (1957, p. 133) then conclude that this again would be a violation of IIA. This conclusion is overhasty since the agreed upon outcome in S might be a point not in T, and then IIA does not apply. From chapter 3, however, we know that under reasonable additional assumptions a violation of IIA does follow.

In general, strong monotonicity is inconsistent with Pareto optimality. For instance, suppose $(\text{comv}\{(2,1)\},(0,0))$, $(\text{comv}\{(1,2)\},(0,0))$, and $\text{comv}\{(3,0),(0,3)\}$, $(0,0))$ are in $\mathcal{D}^{\{1,2\}}$. A strongly monotonic Pareto optimal solution would assign the outcomes $(2,1)$ and $(1,2)$ to the first two games, respectively. Clearly, there is no feasible point in the third game dominating both $(2,1)$ and $(1,2)$. The present chapter can be viewed as discussing several ways out of this inconsistency[2].

Section 4.2 is devoted to the *individual monotonicity* property proposed by Kalai and Smorodinsky (1975). We will present a characterization of a family of nonsymmetric solutions on a class of n-person bargaining games. These solutions are Pareto optimal. The (2-person) result by Kalai and Smorodinsky follows as a corollary.

Section 4.3 discusses a replication method proposed by Thomson (1986), which gives rise to an interpretation of a family of nonsymmetric 2-person individually monotonic solutions. This section parallels subsection 2.4.4. In section 4.4, a family of globally individually monotonic solutions is characterized; such solutions depend on the utopia point of the feasible set (the point $u(S)$ defined in section 1.2) and not on the utopia point of the individually rational part of the feasible set (see section 4.2).

Instead of weakening strong monotonicity, we may require weak Pareto optimality instead of Pareto optimality. This leads to so-called proportional or egalitarian solutions, or equal-loss solutions: see sections 4.5 and 4.6 respectively. By refining these solutions by some lexicographic procedure, the Pareto optimality property can be restored. Such lexicographic solutions are discussed in sections 4.7 and 4.8. The chapter is concluded by section 4.9, which mentions related work in this book and elsewhere.

It should be noted that, although this chapter starts by advancing monotonicity properties as alternatives for IIA, nevertheless many of the solutions occurring in it — specifically, the proportional solutions and their lexicographic versions — do satisfy IIA. Therefore, these solutions can be regarded as representing compromises between monotonicity and independence axioms.

4.2   Individual Monotonicity

Kalai and Smorodinsky (1975) propose an axiom of monotonicity as an alternative for IIA. They criticize the (2-person symmetric) Nash bargaining solution by means of the following example.

Example 4.1 Let $S := \text{comv}\{(1,0),(0,1),(\frac{3}{4},\frac{3}{4})\}$ and $T := \text{comv}\{(1,0),(0,1),(1,\frac{7}{10})\}$. Then $\nu(S,0) = (\frac{3}{4},\frac{3}{4})$ and $\nu(T,0) = (1,\frac{7}{10})$. Thus, although in T for every utility level of player 1, player 2's maximal utility level has increased compared to S, he obtains less if the Nash bargaining solution is employed.

This example shows that the Nash bargaining solution violates the following axiom, which reduces to Kalai and Smorodinsky's monotonicity axiom for the 2-person case. For a bargaining game $(S,d) \in \tilde{\mathcal{B}}^N$, let $h(S,d)$, defined by

---

[2] An axiom like SMON heavily relies on the so-called "welfarism" assumption discussed in subsection 1.3.1. An underlying assumption one should at least make is that in all games under consideration each individual is using the same multiplicity scale for his utility function (cf. Kalai, 1977b).

$h_i(S, d) := \max\{x_i : x \in S, x \geq d\}$ for every $i \in N$,

denote the *utopia point of* (S, d). Observe that $h(S, d) = u(\text{com}\{x \in S : x \geq d\})$. Let $\mathcal{D}^N$ be some subclass of $\tilde{\mathcal{B}}^N$, and let $\varphi : \mathcal{D}^N \to I\!\!R^N$ be a bargaining solution.

Individual Monotonicity (IM): For all (S, d), $(T, d) \in \mathcal{D}^N$ and $i \in N$, if $S \subset T$ and $h_j(S, d) = h_j(T, d)$ for all $j \in N\backslash\{i\}$, then $\varphi_i(T, d) \geq \varphi_i(S, d)$.

Unfortunately, imposing this axiom leads to the following "impossibility" result, which is closely related to Theorem 3 in Roth (1979a).

Theorem 4.2 *Let $n > 2$. There exists no bargaining solution on $\mathcal{C}^N$ which is Pareto optimal and individually monotonic.*

Proof For every $i \in N$, let y^i be the vector in $I\!\!R^N$ with i th coordinate 0 and all other coordinates equal to 1, and let $V^i := \text{comv}\{y^j : j \in N, j \neq i\} \in \mathcal{C}^N$. Let further $V := \text{comv}\{y^i : i \in N\}$. Suppose $\varphi : \mathcal{C}^N \to I\!\!R^N$ satisfies PO and IM. By PO, we have $\varphi_i(V^i, 0) = 1$ for every $i \in N$. By IM, $\varphi_i(V, 0) \geq \varphi_i(V^i, 0)$ for every $i \in N$. Hence $\varphi(V, 0) \geq (1, 1, \ldots, 1) \notin V$, a contradiction. $\qquad\square$

We will avoid this impossibility result by imposing an additional condition on the class of bargaining games. Thomson (1980) requires all weakly Pareto optimal points in the individually rational subset of the feasible set to be the Pareto optimal, i.e., for $(S, d) \in \mathcal{C}^N$, he imposes the condition $W(S) \cap I\!\!R^N_+ \subset P(S)$. Such a restriction is justified, for instance, if S is the image in utility space of the set of feasible distributions of a fixed bundle of commodities, assumed to be freely disposable among a group of consumers with continuous, concave and strongly monotonic utility functions (Thomson, 1980, p. 227).

Since, in what follows, the scale transformation covariance (STC) axiom will be imposed, we restrict attention to the class $\mathcal{C}^N_0$ and formulate the following additional condition an $S \in \mathcal{C}^N_0$.

> For each $x \in S$, $x \geq 0$, and each $i \in N$ we have: if $x \notin P(S)$
> and $x_i < h_i(S)$, then there exists an $\varepsilon > 0$ such that $x + \varepsilon e^i \in S$. (4.1)

(As before, $e^i \in I\!\!R^N$ denotes the vector with i th coordinate 1 and the other coordinates 0.) Observe that the set V in the proof of theorem 4.2 satisfies (4.1) but not Thomson's condition; the sets V^i do not satisfy (4.1). Also, every $S \in \mathcal{C}^{\{1,2\}}_0$ satisfies (4.1). Denote by I^N the subclass of bargaining games in $\mathcal{C}^N_0$ satisfying condition (4.1).

We first characterize a family of individually monotonic solutions on the class I^N. Kalai and Smorodinsky's (1975) result follows as corollary 4.14. We start by collecting some properties of bargaining games in I^N. For $S \in I^N$ we use the notation

$$\alpha(x, v) := \sup\{\beta \in [0, \infty) : x + \beta v \in S\}$$

where $x \in S$ and $v \in I\!\!R^N_+$, $v \neq 0$.

Lemma 4.3 *Let $S \in I^N$, $x \in I\!\!R^N_+ \cap S$, and $v \in I\!\!R^N_+$, $v \neq 0$. Then*

(i) $x + \beta v \in S$ *for each* $\beta \in [0, \alpha(x, v)]$,

(ii) $x + \alpha(x,v)v \in P(S)$ *or there is an* $i \in N$ *with* $v_i > 0$ *and* $x_i + \alpha(x,v)v_i = h_i(S)$,

(iii) $\alpha(0, h(S))h(S) \in P(S)$.

Proof (i) The set $\{\beta \in [0,\infty) : x + \beta v \in S\}$ is a closed and bounded interval containing 0. Hence, $\alpha(x,v) \in I\!R$ and $x + \beta v \in S$ for all $\beta \in [0, \alpha(x,v)]$.

(ii) Suppose $x + \alpha(x,v)v \notin P(S)$ and $x_i + \alpha(x,v)v_i < h_i(S)$ for all $i \in N$ with $v_i > 0$. Because $x + \alpha(x,v)v \in S \cap I\!R_+^N$ (by (i)), there is, in view of (4.1), an $\varepsilon > 0$ such that

$$(x + \alpha(x,v)v) + \varepsilon v_i e^i \in S \text{ for all } i \in N.$$

Then $x + (\alpha(x,v) + n^{-1}\varepsilon)v = n^{-1}\sum_{i=1}^n (x + \alpha(x,v)v) + \varepsilon v_i e^i$. Hence $x + (\alpha(x,v) + n^{-1}\varepsilon)v \in S$ because S is convex. But that is in contradiction with the definition of $\alpha(x,v)$. So we have proved (ii).

(iii) This follows from (ii) with 0 in the role of x and $h(S)$ in the role of v, if we note that $h(S) > 0$. □

The following lemma gives a further characterization of the class I^N. Let $U^N := \text{com}\{e^N\}$ where, as before, e^N is the vector of $I\!R^N$ with all coordinates to 1. Further, "cl" denotes (topological) closure.

Lemma 4.4 *For every* $S \in \mathcal{C}_0^N$, *we have* $S \in I^N$ *if and only if* $S = h(S)U^N$ *or* $S \cap \text{cl}(h(S)U^N \backslash S) \cap I\!R_+^N = P(S) \cap I\!R_+^N$.

Proof Let $S \in \mathcal{C}_0^N$. W.l.o.g. we assume $h(S) = e^N$. We first show the "only if" part of the lemma. Let $S \in I^N$, and suppose $S \neq U^N$. Let $x \in P(S)$, $x \geq 0$. Then $y \in U^N \backslash S$ for every $y \in \text{conv}\{x, e^N\}$ with $y \neq x$, so $x \in \text{cl}(U^N \backslash S)$. We conclude that $P(S) \cap I\!R_+^N \subset \text{cl}(U^N \backslash S) \cap I\!R_+^N$.

Next, let $x \in S \backslash P(S)$, $x \geq 0$. By (4.1), there exists for every $i \in N$ with $x_i < 1$, an $\varepsilon^i > 0$ such that $x + \varepsilon^i e^i \in S$. Let $\varepsilon := \min\{\varepsilon^i : i \in N \text{ with } x_i < 1\}$ and let Q be the ball with center x and radius $n^{-1}\varepsilon$. Then, for $y \in Q \cap U^N$, we have $y_i \leq x_i$ if $x_i = 1$ and $y_i \leq x_i + n^{-1}\varepsilon$ if $x_i < 1$. Let, for $i \in N$, $x^i \in S$ be defined by $x^i := x$ if $x_i = 1$ and $x^i := x + \varepsilon^i e^i$ if $x_i < 1$. Because S is convex, $n^{-1}\sum_{i=1}^n x^i \in S$. Now $y \in Q \cap U^N$ implies $y \leq n^{-1}\sum_{i=1}^n x^i$, so $y \in S$. We have shown that $Q \cap U^N \subset S$, hence $Q \cap U^N = Q \cap S$, which implies $x \notin \text{cl}(U^N \backslash S)$. We have proved: $S \cap \text{cl}(U^N \backslash S) \cap I\!R_+^N \subset P(S) \cap I\!R_+^N$, which completes the proof of the "only if" part.

For the "if" part: if $S = U^N$, then $S \in I^N$ straightforwardly; now suppose $S \neq U^N$, and $S \cap \text{cl}(U^N \backslash S) \cap I\!R_+^N = P(S) \cap I\!R_+^N$. Let $x \in S$, $x \geq 0$, $x \notin P(S)$, and $i \in N$ with $x_i < 1 = h_i(S)$. Then $x \notin \text{cl}(U^N \backslash S)$. For every $\varepsilon \in [0, 1 - x_i]$, we have $x + \varepsilon e^i \in U^N$; so $x + \varepsilon e^i \notin S$ for every $\varepsilon \in (0, 1 - x_i]$ would imply $x \in \text{cl}(U^N \backslash S)$, and hence a contradiction. We have proved (4.1), so $S \in I^N$. □

Our main objective is to characterize all bargaining solutions on I^N satisfying PO, STC, and IM. We first observe that PO and IM together imply individual rationality (IR).

Lemma 4.5 *Let* $\varphi : I^N \to I\!R^N$ *be a bargaining solution satisfying PO and IM. Then:*

(i) $\varphi(S) = \varphi(\text{com}(S \cap I\!R_+^N))$ *for every* $S \in I^N$.

(ii) φ *satisfies IR.*

Proof Let $S \in I^N$. By PO, $\varphi(\text{com}(S \cap \mathbb{R}^N_+)) \geq 0$, hence (ii) follows from (i). For (i), note that $h(S) = h(\text{com}(S \cap \mathbb{R}^N_+))$ and $\text{com}(S \cap \mathbb{R}^N_+) \subset S$, and apply IM n times, to obtain $\varphi(S) \geq \varphi(\text{com}(S \cap \mathbb{R}^N_+))$; hence $\varphi(S) = \varphi(\text{com}(S \cap \mathbb{R}^N_+))$ by PO.   □

The individual monotonicity axiom is closely related to the following property. Let $\varphi : \mathcal{D}^N \to \mathbb{R}^N$ be a solution, where $\mathcal{D}^N \subset \tilde{\mathcal{B}}^N$.

Restricted Monotonicity (RM): For all (S, d), $(T, d) \in \mathcal{D}^N$ with $S \subset T$ and $h(S, d) = h(T, d)$, we have $\varphi(T, d) \geq \varphi(S, d)$.

Lemma 4.6 *Let* $\varphi : I^N \to \mathbb{R}^N$ *be a bargaining solution satisfying PO and STC. Then* φ *satisfies IM if and only if* φ *satisfies RM.*

Proof The implication IM $\Rightarrow$ RM is straightforward. Suppose that φ satisfies RM. Take $i \in N$ and $S, T \in I^N$ with $S \subset T$ and $h_j(S) = h_j(T)$ for all $j \in N \backslash \{i\}$. We have to prove that $\varphi_i(S) \leq \varphi_i(T)$. In view of lemma 4.5, which can be easily seen to hold with RM instead of IM, we may assume $S = \text{com}(S \cap \mathbb{R}^N_+)$, $T = \text{com}(T \cap \mathbb{R}^N_+)$. Clearly $0 < h_i(S) \leq h_i(T)$. Let $K := \{x \in T : x_i \leq h_i(S)\}$. Then $K \in I^N$, $S \subset K$, and $h(S) = h(K)$. Consequently, by RM:

$$\varphi(S) \leq \varphi(K). \tag{4.2}$$

Let $\alpha := h_i(S)^{-1} h_i(T) \geq 1$. Then $\alpha e^i K \in I^N$ and $h(T) = h(\alpha e^i K)$. Furthermore, $T \subset \alpha e^i K$ because for each $t \in T$ we have $t = \alpha e^i (\alpha^{-1} e^i t)$, and $\alpha^{-1} e^i t \in K$ by definition of K. By RM:

$$\varphi(T) \leq \varphi(\alpha e^i K). \tag{4.3}$$

STC together with (4.3) implies $\varphi_j(T) \leq \varphi_j(K)$ for all $j \neq i$. Because $\varphi(K) \in P(T)$ and $\varphi(T) \in P(T)$ we conclude that $\varphi_i(T) \geq \varphi_i(K)$. Combining this with (4.2) yields $\varphi_i(S) \leq \varphi_i(T)$.   □

In order to define the family of bargaining solutions on I^N satisfying PO, STC, and IM, we need to introduce another concept.

Definition 4.7 A *monotonic curve (for N)* is a map $\lambda : [1, n] \to \{x \in \mathbb{R}^N_+ : x \leq e^N, 1 \leq \sum_{i=1}^n x_i \leq n\}$ satisfying the following condition:

$$\text{For all } 1 \leq s \leq t \leq n \text{ we have } \lambda(s) \leq \lambda(t) \text{ and } \sum_{i=1}^n \lambda_i(s) = s. \tag{4.4}$$

By Λ^N we denote the family of all monotonic curves for N.

Every map $\lambda \in \Lambda^N$ is continuous since $\sum_{i=1}^n |\lambda_i(t) - \lambda_i(s)| = |t - s|$ for all $s, t \in [1, n]$. With every monotonic curve a bargaining solution will be associated. We need the following lemma.

Lemma 4.8 *For each* $\lambda \in \Lambda^N$ *and* $S \in I^N$ *with* $h(S) = e^N$, *the set* $P(S) \cap \{\lambda(t) : t \in [1, n]\}$ *contains exactly one point.*

Proof Let $\lambda \in \Lambda^N$ and $S \in I^N$ with $h(S) = e^N$, and denote $L := \{\lambda(t) : t \in [1,n]\}$. In view of condition (4.4) and the definition of $P(S)$, the set $L \cap P(S)$ contains at most one point. Let $m := \sup\{t \in [1,n] : \lambda(t) \in S\}$. From $\lambda(1) \in S$, the continuity of λ and the closedness of S, we conclude $\lambda(m) \in S$. If $m = n$, then $L \cap P(S) = \{e^N\}$ and the proof is completed. Otherwise, $\{\lambda(t) : t \in (m,n]\} \subset U^N \backslash S$, hence $\lambda(m) \in \mathrm{cl}(U^N \backslash S)$. So by lemma 4.4 we conclude that $\lambda(m) \in P(S)$. $\qquad \square$

By lemma 4.8, the following definition is correct.

Definition 4.9 For each $\lambda \in \Lambda^N$, we denote by ρ^λ the bargaining solution on I^N which assigns to every $S \in I^N$ with $h(S) = e^N$ the unique point in $P(S) \cap \{\lambda(t) : t \in [1,n]\}$, and to every other $S \in I^N$ the point $h(S)z$ with $z := \rho^\lambda((h_1(S)^{-1}, h_2(S)^{-1}, \dots, h_n(S)^{-1})S)$. We call ρ^λ the *bargaining solution corresponding to* $\lambda \in \Lambda^N$.

We leave the following proposition for the reader to verify.

Proposition 4.10 *Every* $\rho^\lambda : I^N \to \mathbb{R}^N$ *satisfies PO, STC, and RM.*

The converse of proposition 4.10 is also true:

Proposition 4.11 *Let the bargaining solution* $\varphi : I^N \to \mathbb{R}^N$ *satisfy PO, STC and RM. Then* $\varphi = \rho^\lambda$ *for some* $\lambda \in \Lambda^N$.

Proof For each $t \in [1,n]$ let

$$V(t) := \{x \in \mathbb{R}^N : x \le e^N, \sum_{i=1}^n x_i \le t\}.$$

Then $V(t) \in I^N$ and $h(V(t)) = e^N$ for each $t \in [1,n]$. Define $\lambda : [1,n] \to \mathbb{R}^N$ by $\lambda(t) := \varphi(V(t))$ for each $t \in [1,n]$. For $1 \le s \le t \le n$ we have by RM: $\lambda(s) = \varphi(V(s)) \le \varphi(V(t)) = \lambda(t)$. Furthermore, for each $t \in [1,n]$, $\lambda(t) \in P(V(t)) = \{x \in V(t) : \sum_{i=1}^n x_i = t\}$. Hence, $\sum_{i=1}^n \lambda_i(t) = t$. So $\lambda \in \Lambda^N$. Note that

$$\varphi(V(t)) = \rho^\lambda(V(t)) \text{ for each } t \in [1,n]. \tag{4.5}$$

We want to prove that $\varphi = \rho^\lambda$. In view of STC it is sufficient to show that $\varphi(S) = \rho^\lambda(S)$ where $S \in I^N$ with $h(S) = e^N$. Let $s := \sum_{i=1}^n \rho_i^\lambda(S)$, and let $W := V(s) \cap S$. Then $W \in I^N$ with $h(W) = e^N$.
Since $\rho^\lambda(S) \in P(S) \cap P(V(s))$, we have in view of (4.5):

$$\rho^\lambda(W) = \rho^\lambda(S) = \rho^\lambda(V(s)) = \varphi(V(s)) \in P(W) \cap P(S) \cap (P(V(s)). \tag{4.6}$$

In view of RM, $\varphi(W) \le \varphi(V(s))$. Since, by (4.6), $\varphi(V(s)) \in P(W)$, we obtain

$$\varphi(W) = \varphi(V(s)). \tag{4.7}$$

In view of RM, $\varphi(W) \le \varphi(S)$. By (4.6) and (4.7): $\varphi(W) \in P(S)$. So

$$\varphi(W) = \varphi(S). \tag{4.8}$$

Combining (4.6) and (4.8) we may conclude that $\varphi(S) = \rho^\lambda(S)$.   □

The main result of this section is the following theorem.

Theorem 4.12 *Let $\varphi : I^N \to I\!\!R^N$ be a bargaining solution. Then φ satisfies PO, STC, and IM, if and only if $\varphi = \rho^\lambda$ for some $\lambda \in \Lambda^N$.*

Proof Combine propositions 4.10 and 4.11, and lemma 4.6.   □

Let $\lambda^* \in \Lambda^N$ be defined by $\lambda^*(t) := tn^{-1}e^N$ for every $t \in [1, n]$. Theorem 4.12 immediately implies the following corollary.

Corollary 4.13 *Let $\varphi : I^N \to I\!\!R^N$ be a bargaining solution. Then φ satisfies PO, STC, IM, and SYM, if and only if $\varphi = \rho^{\lambda^*}$.*

The solution ρ^{λ^*} can be seen as an extension, on I^N, of a solution for 2-person bargaining games first proposed by Raiffa (1953) and axiomatically characterized by Kalai and Smorodinsky (1975). We call this solution, i.e., the solution $\rho^{\lambda^*} : C_0^{\{1,2\}} \to I\!\!R^{\{1,2\}}$, the *Raiffa-Kalai-Smorodinsky solution* (RKS solution) and denote it by ρ. (Recall that $C_0^N = I^N$ for $N = \{1, 2\}$.) Summarizing, we have the following corollary of theorem 4.12.

Corollary 4.14 *Let $\varphi : C_0^{\{1,2\}} \to I\!\!R^{\{1,2\}}$ be a bargaining solution. Then φ satisfies PO, STC, and IM, if and only if $\varphi = \rho^\lambda$ for some $\lambda \in \Lambda^{\{1,2\}}$. Moreover, the Raiffa-Kalai-Smorodinsky solution ρ is the unique solution on $C_0^{\{1,2\}}$ satisfying, besides PO, STC, and IM, the symmetry axiom.*

Of course, on $C^{\{1,2\}}$, the Raiffa-Kalai-Smorodinsky solution ρ assigns to a bargaining game (S, d) the unique Pareto optimal point on the line segment connecting d and $h(S, d)$. Obviously, ρ does not satisfy IIA. It turns out that, on I^N, there are exactly $n!$ solutions satisfying PO, STC, IM, and IIA. For a permutation $\pi : N \to N$, $x \in I\!\!R^N$ and $T \subset I\!\!R^N$, the notations πx and πT were introduced in subsection 2.4.5.

Theorem 4.15 *The bargaining solution $\varphi : I^N \to I\!\!R^N$ satisfies PO, STC, IM, and IIA, if and only if there is permutation $\pi : N \to N$ such that, for every $S \in I^N$, $\pi\varphi(S)$ is the lexicographical maximum of $S \cap I\!\!R_+^N$.*

Proof For the "if" part: let π be a permutation of N with, for every $S \in I^N$, $\varphi(S) \in S$ such that $\pi\varphi(S)$ is the lexicographical maximum of $S \cap I\!\!R_+^N$. Then note that $\varphi = \varphi^H$: $I^N \to I\!\!R^N$ with $H = <\{\pi(1)\}, \{\pi(2)\}, \ldots, \{\pi(n)\}, e^N>$ (see section 2.3). So φ satisfies PO, STC, and IIA (proposition 2.16). Note further that $\varphi = \rho^{\lambda_0}$ where $\lambda_0 \in \Lambda^N$ has graph $\mathrm{conv}\{e^{\pi(1)}, e^{\pi(1)} + e^{\pi(2)}\} \cup \mathrm{conv}\{e^{\pi(1)} + e^{\pi(2)}, e^{\pi(1)} + e^{\pi(2)} + e^{\pi(3)}\} \cup \ldots \cup \mathrm{conv}\{\sum_{i=1}^{n-1} e^{\pi(i)}, e^N\}$. So φ satisfies IM (theorem 4.12). For the "only if" part, let $\lambda \in \Lambda^N$ be such that λ is not of the form λ_0 above. In view of theorem 4.12, it is sufficient to show that the corresponding $\rho^\lambda : I^N \to I\!\!R^N$ does not satisfy IIA. Note that λ is not of the form λ_0 if and only if there is a point on the graph of λ with at least two coordinates unequal to 0 and 1. W.l.o.g. we may suppose, for some $t_0 \in [1, n)$:

$$0 < \lambda_1(t_0) < 1, \; 0 < \lambda_2(t_0) < 1. \tag{4.9}$$

We may further suppose that $\lambda_1(t) > \lambda_1(t_0)$ or $\lambda_2(t) > \lambda_2(t_0)$ for all $t > t_0$, say:

$$\lambda_2(t) > \lambda_2(t_0) \text{ for all } t > t_0. \tag{4.10}$$

Let $V := \{x \in U^N : \sum_{i=1}^n x_i \leq t_0\}$. Then $V \in I^N$ and $\rho^\lambda(V) = \lambda(t_0)$. Choose $\alpha \in (\lambda_1(t_0), 1)$, and let $W := \{x \in V : x_1 \leq \alpha\}$, then $W \in I^N$. Suppose, contrary to what we want to prove, that ρ^λ satisfies IIA. Then, because $W \subset V$ and $\rho^\lambda(V) = \lambda(t_0) \in W$, we have

$$\rho^\lambda(W) = \lambda(t_0). \tag{4.11}$$

On the other hand, $\rho^\lambda(W) = \alpha e^N \pi^\lambda(\alpha^{-1}e^N W) = \alpha e^N \lambda(t)$ for some $t > t_0$ since $\lambda(t_0) \in (\alpha^{-1}e^N W) \backslash P(\alpha^{-1}e^N W)$. So, in view of (4.10) and (4.11), we have $\rho_2^\lambda(W) = \lambda_2(t) > \lambda_2(t_0) = \rho_2^\lambda(W)$, an impossibility. We conclude that ρ^λ does not satisfy IIA. $\qquad\square$

Remark 4.16 The axioms in theorem 4.12 are independent. The next section presents a family of solutions that satisfy IM, STC, and WPO but not PO. The 2-person lexicographic egalitarian solution (see section 4.7) satisfies PO and IM but not STC.

Remark 4.17 The material in this section is based mainly on Peters and Tijs (1984, 1985a).

4.3 Replication invariance of bargaining solutions

In subsection 2.4.4 we discussed a replication method introduced by Kalai (1977a), which provided an interpretation of 2-person nonsymmetric Nash bargaining solutions. Here, we present a different and, in a certain way, more general model introduced by Thomson (1986). This model leads to an interpretation of a family of 2-person nonsymmetric individually monotonic solutions, but also of the nonsymmetric Nash solutions appearing in Kalai's model.

Let a bargaining game $S \in \mathcal{C}_0^{\{1,2\}}$ be given, as well as natural numbers m, ℓ. Let $I_m := \{1, 2, \dots, m\}$ and $J_\ell := \{m+1, \dots, m+\ell\}$. The interpretation is that I_m contains m players of type 1, and J_ℓ contains ℓ players of type 2. For a pair $(i, j) \in I_m \times J_\ell$, let

$$S_{ij} := \{x \in \mathbb{R}^{m+\ell} : \exists (x_1', x_2') \in S[x_i = x_1', x_j = x_2', x_k = 0 \text{ whenever } k \neq i, j]\}.$$

The *Thomson (m, ℓ)-replication* of S is defined as $S^{m,\ell} := \text{comv}\{S_{ij} : (i, j) \in I_m \times J_\ell\}$.

Thomson's basic idea can be illustrated as follows. (See figure 4.1.) Suppose player 2 is, in some sense or another, twice as powerful as player 1, and suppose that they play a bargaining game $S \in \mathcal{C}_0^{\{1,2\}}$. Split player 2 in two players of his type; with notation as above, $m = 1$, $\ell = 2$, $I_m = \{1\}$, $J_\ell = \{2, 3\}$. Consider the game $S^{1,2}$. This is a three-player game, in which we view the three players as "equal", so that we wish to apply an anonymous solution. (A bargaining solution $\varphi : \mathcal{D}^N \to \mathbb{R}^N (\mathcal{D}^N \subset \tilde{\mathcal{B}}^N)$ is *anonymous* (AN) if $\varphi(\pi S) = \pi \varphi(S)$ for all $S \in \mathcal{D}^N$ and permutations π of N with $\pi S \in \mathcal{D}^N$.) The payoffs to players 1 and 2 in the original game S are then obtained by taking the sums of the payoffs for the players of the corresponding types in the three-player game. By the anonymity property of φ and the fact that $S^{m,\ell}$ is by construction symmetric for the players in I_m as well as for the players in J_ℓ, this amounts to multiplying the payoff in $S^{m,\ell}$ for a player of type 1 (a player in I_m) by m and the payoff for a player of type 2 (a player in J_ℓ) by ℓ. As a matter of fact, given an anonymous bargaining solution for every number of players (i.e., a list of solutions, one for each cardinality of the player set N), this method can be used to define a family of (nonsymmetric) 2-person bargaining solutions parametrized by a pair $(m, \ell) \in I\!N \times I\!N$.

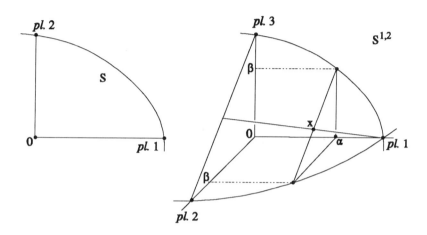

Figure 4.1: Replication of a bargaining game

The construction is illustrated in figure 4.1, where we assume x is the point assigned by the anonymous 3-person solution, and (α, β) the solution outcome induced in S. Note that player 1 obtains α in $S^{1,2}$, whereas players 2 and 3 obtain $\frac{\beta}{2}$ in $S^{1,2}$.

Thomson shows that, if the method is applied to the n-person symmetric Nash bargaining solution ν then, as in Kalai's model, we obtain nonsymmetric Nash bargaining solutions for the original 2-person game. When applied to the Raiffa-Kalai-Smorodinsky solution ρ, a family of nonsymmetric individually monotonic 2-person solutions results.

We now first define these solutions. Let $p \in I\!R^2_+$, $p_1 + p_2 = 1$, then the solution $\rho^p : C_0^{\{1,2\}} \to I\!R^2$ assigns to an $S \in C_0^{\{1,2\}}$ the unique point of $W(S)$ on the straight line through 0 and $ph(S)$. Note that $\rho^{(\frac{1}{2}, \frac{1}{2})}$ coincides with the Raiffa-Kalai-Smorodinsky solution ρ. Also note that every ρ^p is scale transformation covariant and individually monotonic, but only ρ is Pareto optimal. Therefore, only $p^{(\frac{1}{2}, \frac{1}{2})} = \rho$ belongs to the family of solutions characterized in corollary 4.14. If we would further restrict attention to those two-person bargaining games where all nonnegative weakly Pareto optimal points are Pareto optimal, then $\{\rho^p\}$ would be a subfamily of $\{\rho^\lambda : \lambda \in \Lambda^{\{1,2\}}\}$.

Let ρ also denote the n-person *Raiffa-Kalai-Smorodinsky solution*, which assigns the unique point of $W(S)$ on the line segment connecting 0 and $h(S)$ to every $S \in C_0^N$. Of course, on I^N, $\rho = \rho^{\lambda^*}$, cf. corollary 4.13.

The following theorem corresponds to Theorem 1 in Thomson (1986).

Theorem 4.18 *For each $(m,\ell)\in \mathbb{N}\times \mathbb{N}$ and each $S\in C_0^{\{1,2\}}$, $m\rho_i(S^{m,\ell})=\rho_1^{(m+\ell)^{-1}(m,\ell)}(S)$ for each $i\in I_m$ and $\ell\rho_j(S^{m,\ell})=\rho_2^{(m+\ell)^{-1}(m,\ell)}(S)$ for each $j\in J_\ell$.*

Proof Write $\rho^{m,\ell}$ instead of $\rho^{(m+\ell)^{-1}(m,\ell)}$. Let $(\alpha,\beta):=\rho^{m,\ell}(S)$ and let $x\in \mathbb{R}^{m+\ell}$ be defined by $x_i:=\alpha/m$ for each $i\in I_m$ and $x_j:=\beta/\ell$ for each $j\in J_\ell$. We will prove that $x=\rho(S^{m,\ell})$.

Let $\alpha',\beta'\in \mathbb{R}$ be such that the line of equation $\alpha'x_1'+\beta'x_2'=\alpha'\alpha+\beta'\beta$ supports S at (α,β). Given each $(i,j)\in I_m\times J_\ell$, let $x^{ij}\in \mathbb{R}^{m+\ell}$ be defined by $x_i^{ij}:=\alpha$, $x_j^{ij}:=\beta$ and $x_k^{ij}:=0$ for any other coordinate k. Clearly $x^{ij}\in S_{ij}$ and the hyperplane $H\subset \mathbb{R}^{m+\ell}$ of equation $\alpha'\sum_{I_m}x_i'+\beta'\sum_{J_\ell}x_j'=\alpha'\alpha+\beta'\beta$ supports S_{ij} at x^{ij}. Since $S^{m,\ell}=\mathrm{comv}\{S_{ij}: (i,j)\in I_m\times J_\ell\}$, H supports $S^{m,\ell}$ as well. Note that $x=\frac{1}{m\ell}\sum_{(i,j)\in I_m\times J_\ell}x^{ij}$. Therefore x is a point of $S^{m,\ell}$ undominated by any other point of $S^{m,\ell}$. We will be done if we can show that $x=\lambda h(S^{m,\ell})$ for some $\lambda\in \mathbb{R}$.

Since $(\alpha,\beta)=\rho^{m,\ell}(S)$, $(\alpha,\beta)=\mu(mh_1(S),\ell h_2(S))$ for some μ. Also, $h_i(S^{m,\ell})=h_1(S)$ for all $i\in I_m$ and $h_j(S^{m,\ell})=h_2(S)$ for all $j\in J_\ell$. The argument concludes by recalling the definition of x. (λ turns out to be equal to μ.) □

A similar result holds for the Nash bargaining solution. The following result corresponds to Theorem 2 in Thomson (1986).

Theorem 4.19 *For each $(m,\ell)\in \mathbb{N}\times \mathbb{N}$ and each $S\in C_0^{\{1,2\}}$, $m\nu_i(S^{m,\ell})=\varphi_1^H(S)$ for each $i\in I_m$ and $\ell\nu_j(S^{m,\ell})=\varphi_2^H(S)$ for every $j\in J_\ell$, where $H:=<\{1,2\},(m+\ell)^{-1}(m,\ell)> \in \mathcal{H}^{\{1,2\}}$.*

Proof Let $x\in \mathbb{R}^{m+\ell}$ be as in the proof of theorem 4.18 with (α,β) designating $\varphi^H(S)$ instead of $\rho^{m,\ell}(S)$. We claim that $x=\nu(S^{m,\ell})$. Consider the hyperplane H' with equation $m\alpha^{-1}(\sum_{I_m}x_i')+\ell\beta^{-1}(\sum_{J_\ell}x_j')=m+\ell$. Note that x is an element of this hyperplane. In order to show that $x=\nu(S^{m,\ell})$, it is in view of lemma 2.20 sufficient to show that H' supports $S^{m,\ell}$ at x. Let the points x^{ij} $(i\in I_m,\ j\in J_\ell)$ be defined as in the proof of theorem 4.18. Because, by lemma 2.20, the line with equation $m\alpha^{-1}x_1'+\ell\beta^{-1}x_2'=m+\ell$ supports S at (α,β), it follows that H' supports the sets S_{ij} at the points x^{ij}. Consequently, H' supports S at x. □

Theorems 4.18 and 4.19 show that nonsymmetric 2-person solutions with "rational weights" can be obtained by replicating bargaining games and applying symmetric (or rather: anonymous) solutions to the replicated games. As in subsection 2.4.4, other weights can be obtained by appealing to a limiting argument. Further, the method may also be applied to n-person games instead of 2-person games. See Thomson and Lensberg (1989, chapter 12) for details.

Applying the replication method presented here to example 2.40, we obtain the Thomson $(2,1)$-replication $\Delta^{\{1,2,3\}}\in C_0^{\{1,2,3\}}$ with $I_m=\{1,2\}$ and $J_\ell=\{3\}$. Any symmetric (weakly) Pareto optimal solution would assign the outcome $(\frac{1}{3},\frac{1}{3},\frac{1}{3})$ to $\Delta^{\{1,2,3\}}$, leading to $(\frac{2}{3},\frac{1}{3})$ in the original bargaining game $\Delta^{\{1,2\}}$. Recall that the Kalai $(2,1)$-replication of the same game is the game $T=\mathrm{comv}\{(1,1,0),(0,0,1)\}$, so $\nu(T)=(\frac{2}{3},\frac{2}{3},\frac{1}{3})$ whereas $\rho(T)=(\frac{1}{2},\frac{1}{2},\frac{1}{2})$. As remarked before, according to Kalai's method only the Nash solution gives rise to the division $(\frac{2}{3}, \frac{1}{3})$ in the original game. The difference between the two methods is somewhat reminiscent of the distinction between public and private goods. Kalai's method proposes juxtaposition of utilities and would be appropriate in a public goods environment. Thomson's method proposes the splitting of utility between players of the same type, and is therefore appropriate in a private goods context.

4.4 Global individual monotonicity

The individual monotonicity axiom is formulated with respect to the utopia point $h(S, d)$ of the individually rational part of the feasible set S. It can also be formulated with respect to the utopia point $u(S)$ of S, which is independent of the disagreement outcome d. This leads to the following definition, for a bargaining solution $\varphi : \mathcal{D}^N \to I\!\!R^N$, where $\mathcal{D}^N$ is some subclass of $\tilde{\mathcal{B}}^N$.

Global Individual Monotonicity (GIM): For all (S, d), $(T, d) \in \mathcal{D}^N$ and $i \in N$, if $S \subset T$ and $u_j(S) = u_j(T)$ for all $j \in N\backslash\{i\}$, then $\varphi_i(T, d) \geq \varphi_i(S, d)$.

The utopia point $u(S)$ of a bargaining game (S, d) may be determined by points of S that are not individually rational. Yet, such points may be relevant for the determination of the (individually rational) solution outcome. This discussion is similar in spirit to the discussions in subsection 2.5.2 with respect to the INIR axiom, and section 5.3.

In this section, we limit our attention to the 2-person case. The extension to the general case can be given along the lines of section 4.2, and is omitted. Because STC will be required, attention may be further restricted to the class $\mathcal{C}_0^{\{1,2\}}$. Recall (lemma 4.5) that individual monotonicity and Pareto optimality together imply individual rationality. With GIM, this is no longer the case. The following example shows that, in the presence of STC and GIM, IR is not implied by PO, nor PO by IR.

Example 4.20 Let $\varphi : \mathcal{C}_0^{\{1,2\}} \to I\!\!R^2$ assign the point $(0, h_2(S))$ to every $S \in \mathcal{C}_0^{\{1,2\}}$. Let $\psi : \mathcal{C}_0^{\{1,2\}} \to I\!\!R^2$ assign to every $S \in \mathcal{C}_0^{\{1,2\}}$ the point of $P(S)$ with second coordinate $u_2(S)$. Then φ and ψ satisfy GIM and STC, φ satisfies IR, WPO, but not PO, and ψ satisfies PO but not IR.

If the comprehensiveness assumption on a bargaining game is dropped, then it can be shown that, in the presence of IM or GIM, WPO implies PO. For a proof see Peters and Tijs (1985a) on which this section is based. This is a(nother) case where the choice of domain is quite relevant.

We will work towards a characterization of all solutions satisfying STC, GIM, IR and PO. The first lemma shows that such solutions depend only on the individually rational part and the utopia point of the feasible set.

Lemma 4.21 *Let* $\varphi : \mathcal{C}_0^{\{1,2\}} \to I\!\!R^{\{1,2\}}$ *be a solution satisfying PO, IR, and GIM. Let* $S, T \in \mathcal{C}_0^{\{1,2\}}$ *with* $u(S) = u(T)$ *and* $S \cap I\!\!R_+^2 = T \cap I\!\!R_+^2$. *Then* $\varphi(S) = \varphi(T)$.

Proof Choose $\alpha \in I\!\!R$ so small that $(\alpha, u_2(S)) = (\alpha, u_2(T)) \in S \cap T$, and choose $\beta \in I\!\!R$ so small that $(u_1(S), \beta) = (u_1(T), \beta) \in S \cap T$. Let $V := \text{comv}(\{(\alpha, u_2(S)), (u_1(S), \beta)\} \cup (S \cap$

$I\!R_+^2$)) then $V \in C_0^{\{1,2\}}$, $V \subset S$, $V \subset T$, $u(V) = u(S) = u(T)$, and $V \cap I\!R_+^2 = S \cap I\!R_+^2 = T \cap I\!R_+^2$. By applying IR, PO, and GIM twice, we find that $\varphi(V) = \varphi(S)$. Similarly, $\varphi(V) = \varphi(T)$. So $\varphi(S) = \varphi(T)$. $\square$

The following lemma is the analogon of lemma 4.6. Its proof is also analogous, and therefore omitted. (We note, however, that in the proof of lemma 4.6 we needed lemma 4.5, but here we do not need lemma 4.21.)

Lemma 4.22 *Let* $\varphi : C_0^{\{1,2\}} \to I\!R^{\{1,2\}}$ *be a solution satisfying PO, IR, and STC. Then* φ *satisfies GIM if and only if* $\varphi(S) \leq \varphi(T)$ *for all S and T in $C_0^{\{1,2\}}$ with $S \subset T$ and* $u(S) = u(T)$.

The GIM solutions that will be characterized correspond again to a family of "monotonic curves".

Definition 4.23 By Θ, we denote the family of maps $\theta : [0,2] \to \mathrm{cc}(\{(1,1)\})$ which satisfy

$$\text{for all } s,t \in [0,2] : \theta(s) \leq \theta(t) \text{ if } s \leq t, \text{ and } \theta_1(s) + \theta_2(s) = s. \tag{4.12}$$

Similarly as in section 4.2 for $\lambda \in \Lambda$, it follows from (4.12) that $\theta \in \Theta$ is a continuous map. Further, note that, for every $S \in C_0^{\{1,2\}}$, the set $P(S) \cap \{\theta(t) : t \in [0,2]\}$ contains exactly one element.

Definition 4.24 For $\theta \in \Theta$, the solution $\psi^\theta : C_0^{\{1,2\}} \to I\!R^{\{1,2\}}$ is defined by: for every $S \in C_0^{\{1,2\}}$ with $u(S) = (1,1)$, $\{\psi^\theta(S)\} := P(S) \cap \{\theta(t) : t \in [0,2]\}$, and $\psi^\theta(S) := u(S)\psi^\theta((u_1(S)^{-1}, u_2(S)^{-1})S)$ otherwise. We call ψ^θ *the solution corresponding to* θ.

Proposition 4.25 *For every $\theta \in \Theta$, ψ^θ satisfies IR, PO, STC, and GIM.*

Proof ψ^θ satisfies IR, PO, and STC by definition. GIM follows easily with the aid of lemma 4.22. $\square$

Proposition 4.26 *Let* $\varphi : C_0^{\{1,2\}} \to I\!R^{\{1,2\}}$ *be a solution satisfying IR, PO, STC, and GIM. Then $\varphi = \psi^\theta$ for some $\theta \in \Theta$.*

Proof The proof is very much like the proof of proposition 4.11. First, we construct a map θ with the aid of φ. To this end, let, for each $t \in (0,1)$, $L(t) := \mathrm{comv}(\{(-1,1),(0,t),(t,0),(1,-1)\})$, and let, for each $t \in [1,2]$, $L(t) := \mathrm{comv}\{(t-1,1),(1,t-1)\}$. Define $\theta : [0,2] \to I\!R^2$ by $\theta(0) := (0,0)$ and $\theta(t) := \varphi(L(t))$ if $t \in (0,2]$. Similarly as in the proof of proposition 4.11, now using lemma 4.22, we have $\theta \in \Theta$ and

$$\varphi(L(t)) = \psi^\theta(L(t)) \text{ for each } t \in (0,2]. \tag{4.13}$$

Let $S \in C_0^{\{1,2\}}$. We shall prove

$$\varphi(S) = \psi^\theta(S). \tag{4.14}$$

In view of STC we may suppose $u(S) = (1,1)$. Let $s := \psi_1^\theta(S) + \psi_2^\theta(S)$. By definition of s and of ψ^θ, and by PO, we have

$$\psi^\theta(S) = \psi^\theta(L(s)) \in P(S) \cap P(L(s)) \subset P(S \cap L(s)). \tag{4.15}$$

In view of lemma 4.22, $\varphi(L(s)) \geq \varphi(S \cap L(s))$. In view of PO, (4.13) and (4.15), we obtain $\varphi(L(s)) = \varphi(S \cap L(s))$. By lemma 4.22 again, $\varphi(S) \geq \varphi(S \cap L(s)) = \varphi(L(s))$, hence

$$\varphi(S) = \varphi(L(s)), \tag{4.16}$$

since $\varphi(L(s)) \in P(S)$ by (4.13) and (4.15). Now (4.14) follows if we combine (4.13), (4.15) and (4.16). $\qquad\square$

Propositions 4.25 and 4.26 lead to the main results of this section.

Theorem 4.27 *A bargaining solution* $\varphi : C_0^{\{1,2\}} \to \mathbb{R}^{\{1,2\}}$ *satisfies IR, PO, STC, and GIM, if and only if* $\varphi = \psi^\theta$ *for some* $\theta \in \Theta$.

The unique symmetric member of the family $\{\psi^\theta : \theta \in \Theta\}$ corresponds to $\theta \in \Theta$ with $\theta(t) := (t/2, t/2)$ for each $t \in [0,2]$. This solution is sometimes called the *Kalai-Rosenthal solution* (cf. Kalai and Rosenthal (1978)). The solutions $\varphi^{H'}$ and $\varphi^{H''}$ corresponding to the weighted hierarchies $H' =< \{1\}, \{2\}, (1,1) >$ and $H'' =< \{2\}, \{1\}, (1,1) >$, coincide with the solutions $\psi^{\theta'}$ and $\psi^{\theta''}$, respectively, where $\theta'(t) = (t,0)$ and $\theta''(t) = (0,t)$ for each $t \in [0,1]$, and $\theta'(t) = (1, t-1)$ and $\theta''(t) = (t-1, 1)$ for each $t \in [1,2]$.

We conclude with the following corollary of theorems 4.15 and 4.27, and corollary 2.24.

Corollary 4.28 *Let the solution* $\varphi : C_0^{\{1,2\}} \to \mathbb{R}^{\{1,2\}}$ *satisfy IR, PO, and STC. Let* θ', $\theta'' \in \Theta$ *as above. Then* $\varphi \in \{\psi^{\theta'}, \psi^{\theta''}\}$ *if and only if* φ *satisfies at least two of the three properties IIA, IM, and GIM.*

Proof If $\varphi = \psi^{\theta'}$ or $\varphi = \psi^{\theta''}$, then φ satisfies IIA, IM and GIM (e.g. theorems 4.15 and 4.27). Let now φ satisfy IR, PO and STC. If φ satisfies IIA as well as IM, then $\varphi \in \{\psi^{\theta'}, \psi^{\theta''}\}$ by theorem 4.15. Suppose φ satisfies IIA and GIM. Let $0 \leq t \leq 1$ with $(t, 1-t) = \varphi(\Delta^{\{1,2\}})$. By STC, $\varphi(\alpha\Delta) = (\alpha t, \alpha(1-t))$ for every $\alpha \in \mathbb{R}, \alpha > 0$. So by PO, IR, and IIA applied to $\alpha\Delta \subset \text{comv}\{(\alpha-1,1),(1,\alpha-1)\}$, we have $\varphi(\text{comv}\{(\alpha-1,1),(1,\alpha-1)\}) = (\alpha t, \alpha(1-t))$ for every $\alpha \in \mathbb{R}, \alpha > 0$. This means, in view of theorem 4.27, that φ corresponds to a curve $\theta \in \Theta$ with

$$\theta(s) = (ts, (1-t)s) \text{ for } 0 \leq s \leq 1. \tag{4.17}$$

Consider $V := \text{comv}\{(-1,1),(1,0)\}$. By IR, PO, STC, and IIA applied to $(1, \frac{1}{2})\Delta^{\{1,2\}} \subset V$, we obtain $\varphi_1(V) = t$. By (4.17), we have $\varphi_1(V) = t/(2-t)$. So either $t = 1$ or $t = 0$, which, in view of corollary 2.24, implies $\varphi \in \{\psi^{\theta'}, \psi^{\theta''}\}$.

Finally, suppose φ satisfies IM and GIM. Let again $\varphi(\Delta^{\{1,2\}}) = (t, 1-t)$ for some $0 \leq t \leq 1$. In the same way as in the previous part of the proof (replace IIA by IM everywhere) we have that either $t = 1$ or $t = 0$. But then it follows with the aid of theorem 4.27, that $\varphi \in \{\psi^{\theta'}, \psi^{\theta''}\}$. $\qquad\square$

4.5   Proportional solutions

4.5.1   Strong monotonicity

In the introductory section (4.1) of this chapter, we saw that the strong monotonicity axiom is incompatible with Pareto optimality. In section 4.2 strong monotonicity was weakened to individual monotonicity in order to restore Pareto optimality, at least on a reasonable subclass of bargaining games. Here, we pick up again the strong monotonicity axiom for solutions on the class $\mathcal{C}^N$, the class of bargaining games with convex comprehensive feasible sets and interior disagreement points, and start by requiring WPO and the following axiom for a solution φ on $\mathcal{D}^N \subset \tilde{\mathcal{B}}^N$.

Homogeneity (HOM): For every $(S, d) \in \mathcal{D}^N$ and all $\alpha \in I\!R_{++}$ and $b \in I\!R^N$, if $(\alpha S + b, \alpha d + b) \in \mathcal{D}^N$, then $\varphi(\alpha S + b, \alpha d + b) = \alpha \varphi(S, d) + b$.

The homogeneity axiom can be justified by regarding it as a weakening of scale transformation covariance, assuming of course that in the situation under consideration this latter property makes sense. A different interpretation is in terms of uncertainty concerning the feasible set (cf. Kalai, 1977b). Let, for the sake of argument, $S \in \overline{\mathcal{C}}_0^N$ and let α be a nonnegative real number, smaller than 1. Suppose, with probability α S is the game to be played, and with probability $1 - \alpha$ the game is $0 - I\!R_+^N$. Let φ be an individually rational solution. Then homogeneity requires that the expected outcome $\alpha \varphi(S)$ equals the outcome of the expected game $\varphi(\alpha S)$.

   Kalai (1977b) offers another justification for imposing homogeneity by an example based on an experiment performed by Nydegger and Owen (1975). In this experiment, individuals 1 and 2 have linear utility for money and they are given one hundred chips to divide among themselves. In the first game each player can cash in each chip for one dollar. In the second game player 1 can cash in each chip for 3 dollars while player 2 can still cash in each chip for one dollar. The Nydegger-Owen experiment showed that while the players would divide the chips 50-50 in the first situation, they would divide them 25-75 in the second situation. In other words, they tend to equally divide the money and not the chips. This seems to be a violation of scale transformation covariance, and supports the so-called *egalitarian solution*, to be defined below. This solution satisfies HOM but not STC.

   A final argument for homogeneity, also proposed by Kalai (1977b), is that the solution outcome should depend on the shape of the feasible set. If this set is "blown up" by some factor, then the solution outcome should be "blown up" accordingly.

   Our first observation is that homogeneity and strong monotonicity together imply individual rationality.

Lemma 4.29 *Let the solution* $\varphi : \mathcal{C}_0^N \to I\!R^N$ *satisfy HOM and SMON. Then* φ *satisfies IR.*

Proof Suppose not, and let $S \in \mathcal{C}_0^N$ and $i \in N$ with $\varphi_i(S) < 0$. Let $\alpha > 1$. By HOM, $\varphi_i(\alpha S) = \alpha \varphi_i(S) < \varphi_i(S)$. This, combined with $S \subset \alpha S$, contradicts SMON.   □

A next observation is that weak Pareto optimality does *not* follow from HOM and SMON. For instance, let $N = \{1, 2\}$, let for every $S \in \mathcal{C}_0^N$, $E(S)$ be the point of $W(S)$ with equal coordinates; then the solution which assigns $\frac{1}{2}E(S)$ to every S satisfies HOM, SMON, but not WPO. Therefore, WPO will be required additionally. We show that every solution on $\mathcal{C}_0^N$ satisfying HOM, SMON, and WPO, must be proportional. A solution $\varphi : \mathcal{D}^N \to I\!\!R^N$ is called *proportional* if there exists a vector $p \in I\!\!R_+^N$ with $\sum_{i \in N} p_i = 1$ such that for every $(S, d) \in \mathcal{D}^N$ (where, as usual, $\mathcal{D}^N \subset \tilde{\mathcal{B}}^N$), $\varphi(S, d)$ is the maximal (w.r.t. the usual ordering) point of S on the straight line through d and $d+p$. If the *weight vector* p has all coordinates equal (to $1/n$) then the corresponding solution is called *egalitarian*. A proportional solution with weight vector p is denoted by E^p. The egalitarian solution is also denoted by E.

Theorem 4.30 *Let* $\varphi : \mathcal{C}_0^N \to I\!\!R^N$ *be a bargaining solution. Then* φ *satisfies HOM, SMON, and WPO, if and only if it is proportional.*

Proof Clearly every proportional solution satisfies the three axioms. For the converse, assume that φ satisfies the three axioms. Let $p := \varphi(\Delta^N)$. Let $S \in \mathcal{C}_0^N$. The proof will be completed by proving the following three statements.

(i) $\varphi(S) \geq E^p(S)$.

(ii) If $E^p(S) \in P(S)$ then $\varphi(S) = E^p(S)$.

(iii) $\varphi(S) \leq E^p(S)$.

For $\varepsilon > 0$ with $\varepsilon < \min\{1 - p_i : i \in N, \ p_i < 1\}$, let $V^\varepsilon := \mathrm{comv}\{p, (p_i + \varepsilon)e^i : i \in N, \ p_i < 1\}$. Then $V^\varepsilon \subset \Delta^N$, so by SMON, WPO and lemma 4.29, $\varphi(V^\varepsilon) = p = E^p(V^\varepsilon)$. For every $\delta < 1$ there exists such an ε with $\delta \alpha V^\varepsilon \subset S$, where α is defined by $\alpha p := E^p(S)$. By SMON and HOM, $\varphi(S) \geq \varphi(\delta \alpha V^\varepsilon) = \delta E^p(S)$. Statement (i) follows. Statement (ii) follows immediately from (i). To show (iii), let $\beta \in I\!\!R$ with $\beta > 1$, and let $S^\beta := \mathrm{comv}(S \cup \{\beta E^p(S)\})$. Then $S \subset S^\beta$, $E^p(S^\beta) = \beta E^p(S)$, and $E^p(S^\beta) \in P(S^\beta)$. So by (ii), $E^p(S^\beta) = \varphi(S^\beta)$, and by SMON, $\varphi(S) \leq E^p(S^\beta)$. Letting $\beta \downarrow 1$, (iii) follows. $\square$

Observe that adding symmetry to the list of axioms in theorem 4.30 singles out the egalitarian solution E. Moreover, the following theorem shows that homogeneity is then implied by the other three axioms.

Theorem 4.31 *Let* $\varphi : \mathcal{C}_0^N \to I\!\!R^N$ *be a bargaining solution. Then* φ *satisfies SYM, SMON, and WPO, if and only if it is the egalitarian solution* E.

Proof E satisfies the three axioms. Conversely, suppose φ satisfies the three axioms and let $S \in \mathcal{C}_0^N$. By applying the three axioms to $\mathrm{comv}\{E(S)\} \subset S$, we obtain $\varphi(S) \geq E(S)$. We are done if $E(S) \in P(S)$. Otherwise, consider $S \subset \mathrm{comv}(S \cup \{\beta E(S)\}) =: S^\beta$ for $\beta > 1$. By the previous step, $\varphi(S^\beta) = E(S^\beta)$. By SMON, $\varphi(S) \leq E(S^\beta)$. So $E(S) \leq \varphi(S) \leq E(S^\beta)$, and by letting $\beta \downarrow 1$, $\varphi(S) = E(S)$. $\square$

Theorem 4.30 is a minor extension of Theorem 1 in Kalai (1977b). Alternatively, proportional solutions may be characterized by the following axiom. This axiom is a kind of additivity axiom, cf. section 5.4. We formulate it for a solution φ on $\mathcal{C}_0^N$.

Step-by-Step Negotiations (SSN): For all $S, T \in \mathcal{C}_0^N$ with $S \subset T$ and $T - \varphi(S) \in \mathcal{C}_0^N$, we have $\varphi(T) = \varphi(S) + \varphi(\text{comv}((T - \varphi(S)) \cap \mathbb{R}^N_+))$.

Also this axiom is introduced in Kalai (1977b). Its justification (Kalai, 1977b, p. 1627) can be summarized as follows. Instead of playing the larger bargaining game T, the players could first play S, and the agreement reached in S could then serve as disagreement point in the remainder of T. The SSN axiom requires a decomposition like this not to affect the final outcome reached in T.

Theorem 4.32 *Let $\varphi : C_0^N \to \mathbb{R}^N$ be a bargaining solution. Then φ satisfies HOM, SSN, WPO, and IR, if and only if it is proportional.*

Proof In view of theorem 4.30, it is sufficient to show that the four axioms imply strong monotonicity of φ. (It is straightforward to see that a proportional solution satisfies SSN.) Let $S, T \in C_0^N$ with $S \subset T$. For every $0 < \alpha < 1$, $\text{comv}((T - \varphi(\alpha S)) \cap \mathbb{R}^N_+) \in C_0^N$, and hence SSN, IR, and HOM imply $\varphi(T) \geq \varphi(\alpha S) = \alpha\varphi(S)$. Since this holds for every $\alpha < 1$, it follows that $\varphi(T) \geq \varphi(S)$. $\square$

In this theorem, WPO cannot be left out (same example as the one following lemma 4.29), but this time also IR cannot be left out. (For example, consider the solution assigning to each $S \in C_0^N$ the (unique) weakly Pareto optimal point on the straight line through 0 and $(-1, 1, 1, \ldots, 1) \in \mathbb{R}^N$.) Probably, the homogeneity axiom is implied by the other axioms (cf. Kalai, 1977b, p. 1628), but a precise proof of this remains to be constructed. The step-by-step negotiations axiom as formulated by Kalai is a version of another axiom, modified to apply to bargaining games with zero normalized disagreement outcomes. This axiom is called "decomposability" by Roth (1979b). It is formulated here for a solution $\varphi : \mathcal{D}^N \to \mathbb{R}^N$ where, as usual, $\mathcal{D}^N$ is some subclass of $\tilde{\mathcal{B}}^N$.

Decomposability (DEC): For all $(S, d), (T, d) \in \mathcal{D}^N$ with $S \subset T$ and $(T, \varphi(S, d)) \in \mathcal{D}^N$, we have $\varphi(T, d) = \varphi(T, \varphi(S, d))$.

The interpretation of decomposability is similar to that of step-by-step negotiations. For characterizations of proportional solutions involving the decomposability axiom, see Roth (1979a,b).

It is interesting to notice that proportional solutions have some other appealing properties, like independence of irrelevant alternatives and individual monotonicity, which have also been used in characterizations (e.g. Kalai, 1977b, Theorem 3; Roth, 1979b).

4.5.2   Disagreement point concavity

The strong monotonicity axiom, by which the proportional solutions were characterized in the foregoing section, involves a comparison of two feasible sets with the same disagreement outcome. Instead, different disagreement outcomes within the same feasible set may be compared. Recall that such an approach led to a characterization of nonsymmetric Nash solutions in section 2.5. In the present section an axiom in this spirit will be formulated on the basis of which we will derive an alternative characterization of proportional solutions. The axioms and the characterization result are due to Chun and Thomson (1990b). Let $\mathcal{D}^N \subset \tilde{\mathcal{B}}^N$ and let φ be a solution on $\mathcal{D}^N$.

Disagreement Point Concavity (DCAV): For all $(S,d),(S,d') \in \mathcal{D}^N$ and all $\alpha \in [0,1]$ with $(S, \alpha d + (1-\alpha)d') \in \mathcal{D}^N$, we have $\varphi(S, \alpha d + (1-\alpha)d') \geq \alpha\varphi(S,d) + (1-\alpha)\varphi(S,d')$.

The disagreement point concavity axiom can be interpreted in a similar spirit as the disagreement point convexity axiom in subsection 2.5.1. Suppose the players face a bargaining game where the disagreement outcome is still uncertain (e.g., as in the axiom, it will be d with probability α and d' with probability $1-\alpha$). They may either wait until the uncertainty is resolved, resulting in the (in general Pareto-dominated) expected bargaining outcome $\alpha\varphi(S,d) + (1-\alpha)\varphi(S,d')$, or they may bargain on the basis of the expected disagreement outcome — which will lead to a (weakly) Pareto optimal outcome if the solution φ is (weakly) Pareto optimal. The DCAV condition ensures that all players are willing to bargain on the basis of the expected disagreement outcome and, thus, reach a (weakly) Pareto optimal outcome. (As a practical example, Chun and Thomson consider management-labor bargaining, where the exact consequences of disagreement, i.e., of a strike, are not known with certainty.)

The announced characterization is as follows.

Theorem 4.33 *Let* $\varphi : \mathcal{C}^N \to I\!\!R^N$ *be a solution. Then* φ *satisfies WPO, INIR, SCONT, and DCAV, if and only if it is proportional.*

The independence of non-individually rational outcomes (INIR) axiom was defined and discussed in subsection 2.5.2. Feasible set continuity (SCONT) was introduced in section 3.4. Since the Nash bargaining solution ν satisfies WPO, INIR, and SCONT, apparently it does not satisfy DCAV. Indeed, let $S := \text{comv}\{(48,0),(30,30),(0,48)\}$ and let $d := (30,0)$, $d' := (0,18)$. Then $(S,d),(S,d'),(S,\frac{1}{2}d+\frac{1}{2}d') \in \mathcal{C}^{\{1,2\}}$, $\nu(S,d) = (39,15)$, $\nu(S,d') = (25,33)$, $\nu(S,\frac{1}{2}d+\frac{1}{2}d') = (30,30)$, so that DCAV is violated: the expected payoff to player 1 from waiting until the uncertainty concerning the disagreement outcome is resolved, equals 32 and therefore dominates the payoff of 30 resulting from bargaining on the basis of the expected disagreement outcome. Thus, although the expected outcome from waiting $(32,24)$ is not attractive from the viewpoint of efficiency (e.g., it is dominated by $(33,25)$), player 1 will oppose against bargaining before the resolution of the uncertainty.

The proof of theorem 4.33 is by way of several lemmas.

Lemma 4.34 *Let the solution* $\varphi : \mathcal{C}^N \to I\!\!R^N$ *satisfy WPO, INIR, and SCONT. Then* φ *satisfies IR.*

Proof Suppose not, let $(S,d) \in \mathcal{C}^N$ and $i \in N$ with $\varphi_i(S,d) < d_i$. By INIR and WPO, $\varphi(S,d) \in W(S)\backslash P(S)$. Let $(x^k)_{k \in I\!\!N}$ be a sequence of points in $I\!\!R^N$ with $x^k \to \varphi(S,d)$, $x^k > \varphi(S,d)$ and $x_i^k < d_i$ for every $k \in I\!\!N$. Let $S^k := \text{comv}(S \cup \{x^k\})$ for every $k \in I\!\!N$. Then $x^k \in P(S^k)$ for every k, so, by WPO and INIR, $\varphi(S^k,d) \neq x^k$ for every $k \in I\!\!N$. Since $S^k \to S$, this violates SCONT. $\qquad\qquad \square$

For a subset V of $I\!\!R^N$, let $\text{int}(V)$ denote the interior of V with respect to $I\!\!R^N$, and let $\text{relint}(P(V))$ denote the relative interior of $P(V)$ with respect to $W(V)$.

Lemma 4.35 *Let* $\varphi : \mathcal{C}^N \to I\!\!R^N$ *be a solution satisfying WPO, IR, and DCAV. Let* $(S,d) \in \mathcal{C}^N$ *with* $\varphi(S,d) \in \text{relint}(P(S))$. *Let* ℓ *be the straight line through* d *and* $\varphi(S,d)$, *and* $x \in \ell \cap \text{int}(S)$. *Then* $\varphi(S,x) = \varphi(S,d)$.

Proof   We distinguish two cases. (The case $x = d$ is trivial.)

(a) $x = \lambda d + (1 - \lambda)\varphi(S, d)$ for some $0 < \lambda < 1$. Let $(\lambda^k)_{k \in \mathbb{N}}$ be a sequence of numbers strictly between 0 and λ with $\lambda^k \to \lambda$, and let x^k be determined by $(1 - \lambda^k)x^k + \lambda^k d = x$ for every $k \in \mathbb{N}$. Then $(S, x^k) \in \mathcal{C}^N$ for every k. By DCAV, $\varphi(S, x) \geq \lambda^k \varphi(S, d) + (1 - \lambda^k)\varphi(S, x^k)$. As $k \to \infty$, $x^k \to \varphi(S, d)$, and by IR and the fact that $\varphi(S, d) \in P(S)$, $\varphi(S, x^k) \to \varphi(S, d)$. Therefore, $\varphi(S, x) \geq \varphi(S, d)$. Since $\varphi(S, d) \in P(S)$, $\varphi(S, x) = \varphi(S, d)$.

(b) $d = \overline{\lambda} x + (1 - \overline{\lambda})\varphi(S, d)$ for some $0 < \overline{\lambda} < 1$. By a similar argument as in (a), we can show that $\varphi(S, d) \geq \varphi(S, x)$. Because $\varphi(S, d) \in \mathrm{relint}(P(S))$ and by WPO $\varphi(S, x) \in W(S)$, we have $\varphi(S, x) = \varphi(S, d)$.   □

Lemma 4.36 *Let $\varphi : \mathcal{C}^N \to \mathbb{R}^N$ satisfy WPO, IR, and DCAV. Let $(S, d^1), (S, d^2) \in \mathcal{C}^N$. Let $\varphi(S, d^1) \in \mathrm{relint}(P(S))$ and $\alpha\varphi(S, d^1) + (1 - \alpha)\varphi(S, d^2) \in P(S)$ for all $0 \leq \alpha \leq 1$. For $k = 1, 2$, let ℓ^k be the straight line through d^k and $\varphi(S, d^k)$. Then ℓ^1 and ℓ^2 are parallel.*

Proof   By lemma 4.35, $\varphi(S, y) = \varphi(S, d^1)$ for all $y \in \ell^1 \cap \mathrm{int}(S)$. Let $d^3 \in \ell^1 \cap \mathrm{int}(S)$ with $d^3 \neq d^1$. W.l.o.g. suppose d^3 is strictly inbetween d^1 and $\varphi(S, d^1)$. Let $z^i := \frac{1}{2}d^i + \frac{1}{2}d^2$ for $i = 1, 3$. By DCAV,

$$\varphi(S, z^i) \geq \tfrac{1}{2}(\varphi(S, d^i) + \varphi(S, d^2)) = \tfrac{1}{2}(\varphi(S, d^1) + \varphi(S, d^2)) =: x$$

for $i = 1, 3$.

Since $x \in P(S)$, we have $\varphi(S, z^i) = x$ for $i = 1, 3$. Let ℓ^3 be the straight line through z^1 and z^3. For all $z \in \ell^3 \cap \mathrm{int}(S)$ such that $z^3 = \lambda z^1 + (1 - \lambda)z$ for some $0 < \lambda < 1$, by DCAV and $\lambda < 1$, we have $x \geq \varphi(S, x)$. Since $\varphi(S, d^1) \in \mathrm{relint}(P(S))$ and $\varphi(S, d^2) \in P(S)$ imply $x \in \mathrm{relint}(P(S))$, we have by WPO, $\varphi(S, z) = x$. By IR, $x \in \ell^3$. This is only possible if ℓ^1 and ℓ^2 are parallel.   □

Let Γ denote the collection of all subsets S of $\mathbb{R}^N$ such that $(S, d) \in \mathcal{C}^N$ for some $d \in S$. Let $P := \{p \in \mathbb{R}_+^N : \sum_{i \in N} p_i = 1\}$.

Lemma 4.37 *Let $\varphi : \mathcal{C}^N \to \mathbb{R}^N$ be a solution. Then φ satisfies WPO, IR, SCONT, and DCAV, if and only if there is continuous map $\delta : \Gamma \to P$ such that for all $(S, d) \in \mathcal{C}^N$, $\varphi(S, d) = E^{\delta(S)}(S, d)$.*

Proof The "if" part is obvious. For the "only if" part, assume φ satisfies the four axioms. Let $(S, d) \in \mathcal{C}^N$ such that $\mathrm{relint}(P(S)) \neq \emptyset$ and S polygonal, i.e., there are $S^1, S^2, \ldots, S^k$ such that $S = \bigcap_{i=1}^{k} S^i$ where S^i has the form $S^i := \{x \in \mathbb{R}^N : x \leq u(S), \ p^i \cdot x \leq c^i$ for some $p^i \in P$ and $c^i \in \mathbb{R}\}$. Take $i \in \{1, 2, \ldots, k\}$ with $p^i > 0$ (such an i exists because $\mathrm{relint}(P(S)) \neq \emptyset$). By WPO and IR, there exists an $x \in \mathrm{int}(S)$ such that $\varphi(S, x) \in \mathrm{relint}(P(S) \cap P(S^i))$. By lemma 4.36, for all $d' \in \mathrm{int}(S)$, if $\varphi(S, d') \in P(S) \cap P(S^i)$ then the straight line through x and $\varphi(S, x)$ is parallel to the line through d' and $\varphi(S, d')$. Let this common direction be denoted by $\delta(S^i)$. By IR, we may assume $\delta(S^i) \in P$. Also, for all $d' \in \mathrm{int}(S)$, if the straight line through d' with direction $\delta(S^i)$ intersects $P(S^i)$ in a point y with $y \in \mathrm{relint}(P(S))$, then $\varphi(S, d') = y$. Indeed, let $A^i := \mathrm{relint}(P(S^i) \cap P(S))$. If $y \in A^i$ then the statement follows from lemma 4.36. If $y \notin A^i$, let $y^1 \in A^i$, $d^1 := y^1 - \delta(S^i)$, $d^2 := \frac{1}{2}d' + \frac{1}{2}d^1$, $y^2 := \frac{1}{2}y + \frac{1}{2}y^1$. By DCAV,

$$\varphi(S, d^2) \geq \frac{1}{2}\varphi(S, d^1) + \frac{1}{2}\varphi(S, d') = \frac{1}{2}(y^1 + \varphi(S, d')).$$

Since $y^1 \in A^i$, $\varphi(S, d^2) = y^2$. Therefore, $y \geq \varphi(S, d')$, and because $y \in \text{relint}(P(S))$, WPO of φ implies $y = \varphi(S, d')$, as desired.

Next, let i and j be such that $P(S^i) \cap P(S^j) \cap \text{relint}(P(S)) \neq \emptyset$. W.l.o.g. let $i = 1$, $j = 2$. We claim that $\delta(S^1) = \delta(S^2)$. To prove this, let $a \in P(S^1) \cap P(S^2) \cap \text{relint}(P(S))$, $z^1 \in A^1$, $f^1 := z^1 - \delta(S^1)$, $f^2 := a - \delta(S^2)$. By the previous step, $\varphi(S, f^1) = z^1$ and $\varphi(S, f^2) = a$. By lemma 4.36 applied to f^1 and f^2, the line through f^1 and z^1 is parallel to the line through f^2 and a. Therefore, $\delta(S^1) = \delta(S^2)$. Repeating the argument, we have $\delta(S^i) = \delta(S^1)$ for every S^i with $p^i > 0$. We denote this common direction by $\delta(S) \in P$.

We now claim that $\varphi(S, d) = E^{\delta(S)}(S, d)$. If $E^{\delta(S)}(S, d) \in \text{relint}(P(S))$ then this holds by the previous argument. Otherwise, let $\{(S^m, d) : m \in \mathbb{N}\}$ be a sequence in $\mathcal{C}^N$ with S^m polygonal for every m, such that $S^m \to S$ and $\{z \in P(S^m) : z \geq d\} \subset \text{relint}(P(S^m))$ for every m. By the previous argument, $\varphi(S^m, d) = E^{\delta(S^m)}(S^m, d)$ for every m. SCONT of φ implies $\delta(S^m) \to \delta(S)$ and therefore also $\varphi(S, d) = E^{\delta(S)}(S, d)$.

The lemma follows by SCONT since each bargaining game in $\mathcal{C}^N$ can be approximated by bargaining games with polygonal feasible sets. Continuity of δ (in the Hausdorff topology) follows from SCONT of φ. $\square$

Proof of theorem 4.33 Clearly, every proportional solution satisfies the four axioms. Conversely, let φ be a solution on $\mathcal{C}^N$ satisfying the four axioms. By lemma 4.34, φ satisfies IR. By lemma 4.37, there is a continuous map $\delta : \Gamma \to P$ such that, for all $(S, d) \in \mathcal{C}^N$, $\varphi(S, d) = E^{\delta(S)}(S, d)$. Let $S \in \Gamma$ such that $\text{relint}(P(S)) \neq \emptyset$, and let $x \in \text{relint}(P(S))$. We claim that $\delta(S) = \delta(\text{comv}\{x\})$. Let $\ell := \{x - \lambda\delta(S) : \lambda > 0\}$ and let $\{d^k\}$ be a sequence of points in ℓ with $d^k \to x$ and finally let $S^k := \text{comv}\{y \in S : y \geq d^k\}$ for every k. By INIR we have, for all k, $\varphi(S, d^k) = \varphi(S^k, d^k) = x$, which implies that $\delta(S^k) = \delta(S)$. Since $S^k \to \text{comv}\{x\}$, the continuity of δ implies that $\delta(\text{comv}\{x\}) = \delta(S)$. For an arbitrary element $S \in \Gamma$ and $x \in W(S)$, we apply SCONT to conclude that $\delta(\text{comv}\{x\}) = \delta(S)$.

Finally, let $S^1, S^2 \in \Gamma$. Let $T \in \Gamma$ be such that $W(T) \cap W(S^1) \neq \emptyset$ and $W(T) \cap W(S^2) \neq \emptyset$. The above argument applied twice gives $\delta(T) = \delta(S^1)$ and $\delta(T) = \delta(S^2)$. Therefore, $\delta(S^1) = \delta(S^2)$ for all $S^1, S^2 \in \Gamma$, which completes the proof. $\square$

Observe that, in view of lemma 4.34, replacing INIR by IR would be a weakening of the list of axioms in theorem 4.33. Actually, all solutions on $\mathcal{C}^N$ satisfying WPO, IR, SCONT and DCAV are described by lemma 4.37, which, therefore, is an important result by itself.

Clearly, WPO or DCAV cannot be omitted from the list in theorem 4.33. Without WPO, the *disagreement solution* would be allowed. Without SCONT, consider for instance the solution assigning $E^{(1,0,\dots,0)}(S, d)$ to every (S, d) with $S = \text{comv}\{u(S)\}$, and $E^{(0,0,\dots,1)}(S, d)$ otherwise. This solution satisfies DCAV, WPO and INIR, but not SCONT.

Finally, in Chun and Thomson (1990c) some variations on theorem 4.33 are presented.

4.5.3 Strong transfer responsiveness

An alternative characterization of the egalitarian solution E is presented by Bossert (1991). This characterization is based on the following axiom for a solution φ on $\mathcal{D}^N \subset \tilde{\mathcal{B}}^N$.

Strong Transfer Responsiveness (STR): For all $(S, d), (S, d') \in \mathcal{D}^N$ and $i, j \in N$, if $d'_i > d_i$, $d'_j < d_j$, and $d'_k = d_k$ for all $k \in N \setminus \{i, j\}$, then

(i) $\varphi_i(S, d') - \varphi_i(S, d) \geq \max_{k \in N} \{0, \varphi_k(S, d') - \varphi_k(S, d)\}$,

(ii) $\varphi_j(S, d') - \varphi_j(S, d) \leq \min_{k \in N} \{0, \varphi_k(S, d') - \varphi_k(S, d)\}$.

If a solution φ is strongly transfer responsive and in a certain bargaining game the disagreement point changes in favor of player i and to the disadvantage of player j while remaining the same for all other players, then player i gains, at least as much as any other player, and player j looses, also at least as much as any other player. The STR axiom is a strengthening of *disagreement point monotonicity* and *strong disagreement point monotonicity* discussed by Thomson (1987).

Bossert (1991) obtains the following characterization of the egalitarian solution, which we state here without a proof.

Theorem 4.38 *Let $n \geq 3$ and let $\varphi : C^N \to I\!\!R^N$ be a solution. Then φ satisfies SCONT, DCONT, IR, WPO, and STR, if and only if φ is the egalitarian solution E.*

Observe that no axiom of symmetry is needed in this theorem. Apparently, symmetry follows from STR (in combination with the other axioms). For $n = 2$, the STR axiom reduces to Thomson's (1987) strong disagreement point monotonicity axiom, which (for $n = 2$) is satisfied by most well-known solutions like the Nash solution and the Raiffa-Kalai-Smorodinsky solution. Thomson provides an interesting explanation for this axiom, which applies to STR as well. For completeness, we formulate it, for φ on $\mathcal{D}^N \subset \tilde{\mathcal{B}}^N$.

Strong Disagreement Point Monotonicity (SDMON): For all $(S, d), (S, d') \in \mathcal{D}^N$ and $i, j \in N$, if $d'_i > d_i$, $d'_j < d_j$, and $d'_k = d_k$ for all $k \in N \backslash \{i, j\}$, then

(i) $\varphi_i(S, d') \geq \varphi_i(S, d)$,

(ii) $\varphi_j(S, d') \leq \varphi_j(S, d)$.

Suppose a bargaining game reflects the problem of dividing a bundle of goods in an exchange economy, the disagreement outcome corresponding to the utilities of the players' initial endowments. Suppose player j gives part of his initial endowment to player i, for instance to repay a debt, then the SDMON axiom makes sure that no "transfer paradox" occurs (which would be the case if by his gift player j would be better off himself).

4.6   The equal-loss solution

The egalitarian solution to the bargaining problem equalizes the gains of the players relative to their disagreement point utilities. Alternatively, one can equalize the players' losses relative to their maximal "claims", where the utopia point of a bargaining game (S, d) can be seen as representing these maximal claims. The bargaining solution based on this idea was first proposed and characterized by Chun (1988a).

The equal-loss principle has received much attention in the literature on bankruptcy and taxation problems. "Two hold a garment; one claims it all, the other claims half. The one is awarded $\frac{3}{4}$, the other $\frac{1}{4}$". This story from a Mishna is quoted by O'Neill (1982) and Aumann and Maschler (1985), and presents a clear example of the equal-loss principle; each claimant loses the same amount, $\frac{1}{4}$.

In bargaining, Yu (1973) and Freimer and Yu (1976) have introduced a class of solutions obtained by minimizing the distance to the utopia point measured by some norm. The equal-loss solution to be discussed below, coincides with one of the Yu-solutions for the two-person case. Yu offers no characterization of these solutions.

Definition 4.39 Let $\mathcal{D}^N \subset \tilde{\mathcal{B}}^N$. The *equal-loss solution*, denoted by E^*, assigns to every $(S,d) \in \mathcal{D}^N$ the maximal point of the set $\{x \in S : h_i(S,d) - x_i = h_j(S,d) - x_j \text{ for all } i,j\}$.

The equal-loss solution outcome depends only on the disagreement outcome insofar as this affects the utopia point. A drawback is that E^* is individually rational on $\mathcal{C}^N$ if and only if $n = 2$, as can easily be checked. Also, E^* is Pareto optimal if and only $n = 2$. For $n > 2$, E^* is only weakly Pareto optimal, but a lexicographic version can be found that satisfies Pareto optimality; see section 4.8.

Like the proportional solutions, the equal-loss solution satisfies the following axiom, formulated here for a solution φ on $\mathcal{D}^N \subset \tilde{\mathcal{B}}^N$.

Translation Covariance (TC): For all $(S,d) \in \mathcal{D}^N$ and $x \in \mathbb{R}^N$, if $(S + x, d + x) \in \mathcal{D}^N$, then $\varphi(S + x, d + x) = x + \varphi(S,d)$.

In the main characterization of the proportional solutions, theorem 4.30 — and at many other places in this book as well — the translation covariance axiom is implicitly assumed by the choice of the domain, e.g., $\mathcal{C}_0^N$ instead of $\mathcal{C}^N$ in theorem 4.30. In the characterization below it is more convenient to consider the class $\mathcal{C}^N$ and impose TC explicitly.

The main axiom in the characterization of the equal-loss solution is the following one.

Strong Monotonicity relative to the Utopia Point (SMON*): For all $(S^1, d^1), (S^2, d^2) \in \mathcal{D}^N$, if $S^1 \subset S^2$ and $h(S^1, d^1) = h(S^2, d^2)$, then $\varphi(S^1, d^1) \le \varphi(S^2, d^2)$.

SMON* requires that, if the feasible set expands and the disagreement point changes without affecting the utopia point, then no player should lose. It is the utopia-point analogon of strong monotonicity (SMON). The main result in Chun (1988a) is the following theorem.

Theorem 4.40 *The solution $\varphi : \mathcal{C}^N \to \mathbb{R}^N$ satisfies WPO, SYM, TC, and SMON*, if and only if φ is the equal-loss solution E^*.*

Proof E^* satisfies the four axioms. Let φ be a solution satisfying the four axioms, and let $(S,d) \in \mathcal{C}^N$ with $[y \in W(S), y \ge d \Rightarrow y \in P(S)]$. By TC, we may assume that $h(S,d) = (1, \ldots, 1)$. Let $x := E^*(S,d)$ and $S^1 := \text{comv}\{y \in S : y \ge d\}$. Let $p \in \Delta^N$ be the normal vector to a supporting hyperplane of S at x, $H^-(x) := \{y \in \mathbb{R}^N : p \cdot y \le p \cdot x\}$, and $S^2 := \{y \in H^-(x) : y \le h(S,d)\}$. Now let y^i, for all i, be the maximal weakly Pareto optimal point of S^2 such that $y_i^i = h_i(S,d) = 1$ and $y_j^i = y_k^i =: \alpha^i$ for all $j,k \ne i$. Let $\alpha^* := \min_{i \in N} \alpha^i$ and for all i, let z^i be such that $z_i^i = h_i(S,d) = 1$ and $z_j^i = \alpha^*$ for all $j \ne i$. Finally, let $S^3 := \text{comv}\{x, z^1, \ldots, z^n\}$.

By setting $d^* := (\alpha^*, \ldots, \alpha^*)$, we have $h(S^3, d^*) = (1, \ldots, 1)$ and by WPO and SYM, $\varphi(S^3, d^*) = x$. By SMON* applied to (S^*, d^*) and (S^2, d^*) we have $\varphi(S^2, d^*) = x$, and by SMON* applied to (S^2, d^*) and (S^2, d), we have $\varphi(S^2, d) = x$. Now we apply SMON* twice, to the pairs (S^2, d) and (S^1, d), and (S^1, d) and (S, d), to conclude that $\varphi(S, d) = x$.

By applying SMON* again, we obtain the desired conclusion for an arbitrary element of $\mathcal{C}^N$.   □

This theorem is the counterpart of theorem 4.31, in which the egalitarian solution E is characterized on $\mathcal{C}_0^N$ by the axioms WPO, SYM, and SMON. Chun (1988a) also gives an alternative characterization of the equal-loss solution E^*.

4.7   The lexicographic egalitarian solution

The egalitarian solution E combines many appealing properties. It is strongly monotonic, independent of irrelevant alternatives, homogeneous, and weakly Pareto optimal. In this section, we discuss an adaptation of E, the so-called *lexicographic egalitarian solution*, that is also Pareto optimal. We characterize this solution on the class $\mathcal{C}_0^N$. This characterization is based on Chun and Peters (1988). An alternative characterization based on a disagreement point axiom — but using a similar interiority condition as is presented below — was given by Chun (1989). Another characterization is provided by Thomson and Lensberg (1989, chapter 9). An explicit investigation of the 2-person case without symmetry can be found in Chun and Peters (1989). Other solutions that were lexicographically extended in a similar way are the Raiffa-Kalai-Smorodinsky solution (see Imai, 1983, and the end of the present section) and the equal-loss solution (see the next section).

The lexicographic egalitarian solution is Pareto optimal and violates the egalitarian principle only inasmuch as some players may receive lower utilities than others but still receive at least the utilities they would obtain at the egalitarian outcome. The idea behind this solution is akin to Rawls's maximin principle (Rawls, 1971) and also to Schmeidler's nucleolus (Schmeidler, 1969). See also Sen (1970), who suggests a lexicographic extension of the Rawlsian maximin criterion, which corresponds to the lexicographic extension of the egalitarian bargaining solution discussed below.

In order to define the lexicographic egalitarian solution, denoted L, let $S \in \mathcal{C}_0^N$. Let z^1 be the maximal point of S with all coordinates equal. If $z^1 \in P(S)$, then $L(S) := z^1 (= E(S))$. Otherwise, let $N^1 := \{i \in N: \text{there exists } x \in S \text{ with } x \geq z^1 \text{ and } x_i > z_i^1\}$. So $N^1 \subset N$ is the largest possible subset of players whose utilities can be equally increased in a nonnegative direction starting from z^1. Then let z^2 be the maximal point of S of the form $z^1 + \varsigma e^{N^1} (\varsigma > 0)$. If $z^2 \in P(S)$, then $L(S) := z^2$. Otherwise, let $N^2 := \{i \in N^1: \text{there exists } x \in S \text{ with } x \geq z^2 \text{ and } x_i > z_i^2\}$, and let z^3 be the maximal point of S of the form $z^2 + \varsigma e^{N^2} (\varsigma > 0)$. Etc. This procedure leads to a unique Pareto optimal point $z =: L(S)$. Observe that both comprehensiveness and convexity are needed for this procedure to be well-defined. With respect to the first condition, consider the feasible set $\text{conv}\{(0,0), (1,0), (1, \frac{1}{2})\} \subset \mathbb{R}^2$. As to the latter condition, convexity, consider $\text{com}\{(2,1), (1,2)\} \subset \mathbb{R}^2$.

An alternative way to define L is as follows. Let $>^\ell$ denote the *lexicographic ordering* on $\mathbb{R}^N$, i.e., $x >^\ell y$ $(x, y \in \mathbb{R}^N)$ if there is an $i \in N$ with $x_i > y_i$ and $x_j = y_j$ for all $j < i$. Let $\alpha : \mathbb{R}^N \to \mathbb{R}^N$ be such that for each $x \in \mathbb{R}^N$ there is a permutation π of N with $\alpha(x) = \pi x$ and $\alpha_1(x) \leq \alpha_2(x) \leq \ldots \leq \alpha_n(x)$. The *lexicographic maximin ordering* $>^{\ell m}$ on $\mathbb{R}^N$ is defined by $x >^{\ell m} y$ $(x, y \in \mathbb{R}^N)$ if $\alpha(x) >^\ell \alpha(y)$. Then the lexicographic egalitarian solution $L : \mathcal{C}_0^N \to \mathbb{R}^N$ assigns to each bargaining game S in $\mathcal{C}_0^N$ the unique point of S which is maximal with respect to $>^{\ell m}$. It can be checked that the procedure of the previous paragraph must lead to a maximizer of $>^{\ell m}$. So this implies existence of such a maximizer. Uniqueness follows from convexity of S.

It is obvious from section 4.1 that L does not satisfy strong monotonicity (SMON). Therefore, a weaker requirement will be imposed. In order to give the intuition for this requirement, suppose the players are involved in a division problem and have reached consensus on the division of a bundle of goods. By considerations of monotonicity, it seems reasonable that no player loses in case additional resources become available. On the other hand, the original agreement may have been "forced": some players had higher utilities at the agreed upon outcome only because the other players were satiated and there were no other goods available to compensate them. Additional resources might then be used for compensation purposes, even to the extent that some agents lose when compared with their situation at the original agreement. So in such a case, one might expect a violation of monotonicity. The following example further illustrates this idea.

Example 4.41 Consider a situation with two players and two commodities, bread and wine. Player 2 only cares for wine but not for more than 2 units: his utility function is $v(w, b) = \min\{2, w\}$. If there is no bread, player 1 can drink 1 unit of wine at the most. If there is also bread, player 1 derives additional utility from drinking wine. Specifically, player 1's utility function is $u(w, b) = \min\{1, w\} + \frac{1}{2}\min\{b, w\}$. Suppose at first there is no bread but only 3 units of wine to be divided. This leads to the bargaining game $S = \text{com}\{(1, 2)\}$. A reasonable outcome in S seems to be $(1, 2)$. If utilities are comparable and the players adhere to the egalitarian principle, then this outcome is "forced" since the egalitarian outcome $(1, 1)$ is not Pareto optimal: player 1 is satiated at $(1, 1)$ but there is still one unit of wine left.

Suppose next that there are, additionally, 3 units of bread to be divided between the players. This leads to the new bargaining game $T = \text{comv}\{(3/2, 2), (5/2, 0)\}$. The egalitarian outcome of T is $(5/3, 5/3)$ which is Pareto optimal. Note that player 2 loses when compared with S. The outcome in T can be reached by giving $5/3$ units of wine to player 2, and $4/3$ units of wine plus all the bread (or at least $4/3$ units) to player 1.

Suppose, finally, that there had only been $3/2$ units of wine available originally, leading to the bargaining game $S^* = \text{comv}\{(1, 1/2), (0, 3/2)\}$. Then the egalitarian outcome $(3/4, 3/4)$ would be Pareto optimal and "unforced". Three units of bread becoming available additionally would lead to be bargaining game $T^* = \text{comv}\{(7/4, 0), (3/2, 1/2), (0, 3/2)\}$ with egalitarian outcome $(9/10, 9/10)$, so both players gain when compared with S^*.

Example 4.41 suggests a way of formalizing the idea of "forcedness" of the solution outcome: if the solution outcome in the smaller (original) game is *not* an *interior* Pareto optimal point, then it may be "forced". In that case, we will not require monotonicity. In order to give a precise statement, we need some additional definitions. We say that z is an *interior Pareto optimal point* of $S \subset \mathcal{C}_0^N$ if z is in the relative (w.r.t. an $(n-1)$-dimensional subspace) interior of $P(S)$. For $M \subset N$ with $|M| > 1$, $S \in \mathcal{C}_0^N$ and $z \in P(S)$, we say that z is an *M-interior Pareto optimal point* of S if for every $\emptyset \neq Q \subsetneq M$ there exist $x, y \in P(S)$ with $x_Q > z_Q$ and $y_Q < z_Q$. Note that z is an interior Pareto optimal point if and only if it is an N-interior Pareto optimal point.

We can now define our monotonicity axiom, for a solution $\varphi : \mathcal{C}_0^N \to \mathbb{R}^N$.

Interior Monotonicity (IMON): For all $M \subset N$ with $|M| > 1$ and all $S, T \in \mathcal{C}_0^N$ with $S \subset T$, where

(i) $\varphi(S)$ is an M-interior Pareto optimal point of S, and

(ii) $\varphi_i(S) = \varphi_i(T)$ for all $i \notin M$,

we have $\varphi_M(T) \geq \varphi_M(S)$.

In words, if $\varphi(S)$ is an M-interior Pareto optimal point and in the larger bargaining game T every player outside M receives the same utility as in S, so that the additional "resources" represented by T can be divided among the players in M, then every player in M benefits.

The main result of this section is the following theorem.

Theorem 4.42 *The lexicographic egalitarian solution L is the unique solution on $\mathcal{C}_0^N$ satisfying Pareto optimality, anonymity, and interior monotonicity.*

We first show that the lexicographic egalitarian solution is interior monotonic.

Lemma 4.43 *L satisfies IMON.*

Proof Let $S, T \in \mathcal{C}_0^N$ and $M \subset N$ satisfy the conditions in the statement of IMON for $\varphi = L$. First note that $L_i(S) = L_j(S)$ for all $i, j \in M$. Otherwise, since $L(S)$ is by assumption an M-interior Pareto optimal point, the smallest coordinate(s) of $L(S)$ corresponding to players in M could be increased at the expense of the larger coordinates corresponding to players in M. If this increase is sufficiently small then (with α as in the definition of the lexicographic maximin ordering) we obtain a point x in S with $\alpha x = \pi x$ and $\alpha(L(S)) = \pi L(S)$ for the same permutation π of N and such that for the smallest index i with $\alpha_i(x) \neq \alpha_i(L(S))$ we have $\alpha_i(x) > \alpha_i(L(S))$. So this point x would dominate $L(S)$ in the lexicographic maximin ordering, which is a contradiction.

Finally, note that $L(T)$ must dominate $L(S)$ in the lexicographic maximin ordering, because $S \subset T$. Since, by assumption, $L_i(S) = L_i(T)$ for every i outside M, and by the first paragraph of the proof $L_i(S) = L_j(S)$ for all $i, j \in M$, this dominance can only hold if $L_i(T) \geq L_i(S)$ for every $i \in M$. $\square$

Proof of theorem 4.42 Observe that L satisfies PO and AN, and from lemma 4.43, IMON. Now let $\varphi : \mathcal{C}_0^N \to I\!\!R^N$ be a solution with these three properties. We show that $\varphi = L$. Let $S \in \mathcal{C}_0^N$.

Let the sequence $N = N^0, N^1, N^2, \ldots, N^k$ be defined as follows: N^k contains all players with the highest utilities at $L(S)$, N^{k-1} contains all players with the highest or second highest utilities at $L(S)$, etc. Note that $0 \leq k \leq n$. Denote $z := L(S)$. Let $z^1 \in S$ be the point with all coordinates equal to the lowest coordinate of $L(S)$, i.e., $z^1 = \varsigma e^N$ where $\varsigma := z_i$ for some (any) $i \in N \backslash N^1$. Take $0 < \varepsilon < \varsigma$ and let, for every $i \in N$, $x^i(\varepsilon)$ be the vector in $I\!\!R^N$ with i th coordinate $\varsigma - \varepsilon$ and the other coordinates equal to ς. Then $S^1(\varepsilon) := \mathrm{comv}\{x^i(\varepsilon) : i \in N\} \in \mathcal{C}_0^N$. By AN and PO, $\varphi(S^1(\varepsilon)) = (\varsigma - \varepsilon n^{-1})e^N$. Further $S^1(\varepsilon) \subset S$, $\varphi(S^1(\varepsilon))$ is an N-interior Pareto optimal point of $S^1(\varepsilon)$, and (ii) in the statement of IMON is trivially satisfied. So by IMON applied to $S^1(\varepsilon) \subset S$, $\varphi(S) \geq \varphi(S^1(\varepsilon))$. By letting ε approach 0, $\varphi(S) \geq z^1$. Now we claim $\varphi_i(S) = \varsigma = L_i(S)$ for every $i \in N \backslash N^1$. From the definitions of $L(S)$ and z^1 we have $L_i(S) = \varsigma$ for every $i \in N\backslash N^1$ and $L(S) \geq z^1$. Suppose by way of contradiction that $\varphi_i(S) \neq L_i(S)$ for some $i \in N\backslash N^1$. Since $\varphi(S) \geq z^1$, $\varphi_i(S) > L_i(S) = \varsigma$. Now for $0 < \lambda < 1$ the point $\lambda\varphi(S) + (1-\lambda)L(S)$ of S would dominate $L(S)$ in the lexicographic maximin ordering, an obvious impossibility.

Summarizing,

$$\varphi(S) \geq z^1, \ \varphi_i(S) = L_i(S) \text{ for every } i \in N\backslash N^1. \tag{4.18}$$

We proceed by induction. Let, for every $1 \leq \ell \leq k$, $z^\ell \in S$ be the point with i th coordinate equal to the i th coordinate of z if $i \in N\backslash N^\ell$ and with i th coordinate equal to the coordinates of the players in $N^{\ell-1}\backslash N^\ell$ otherwise. Note that $z = z^k$. We now fix ℓ with $1 \leq \ell < k$ and assume:

$$\varphi(S) \geq z^\ell, \ \varphi_i(S) = L_i(S) \text{ for every } i \in N\backslash N^\ell. \tag{4.19}$$

We will prove:

$$\varphi(S) \geq z^{\ell+1}, \ \varphi_i(S) = L_i(S) \text{ for every } i \in N\backslash N^{\ell+1}. \tag{4.20}$$

The proof of the theorem is then completed by induction using (4.18)–(4.20): if $|N^k| = 1$ we stop after $\varphi(S) \geq z^{k-1}$ and conclude $\varphi(S) = z^k = z = L(S)$ by PO and the fact that $L(S)$ is the only Pareto optimal point of S dominating z^{k-1}; otherwise we stop after $\varphi(S) \geq z^k = z = L(S)$, hence also $\varphi(S) = L(S)$.

We are left to prove (4.20). Let $\mu := z_j$ for some (any) $j \in N^\ell\backslash N^{\ell+1}$, i.e., μ is the highest coordinate of $z^{\ell+1}$, and let $0 < \delta < \mu$. Let, for every $i \in N^\ell$, $y^i(\delta) \in S$ be the vector with i th coordinate $\mu - \delta$ and j th coordinate equal to the j th coordinate of $z^{\ell+1}$ for every $j \neq i$. Then $S^{\ell+1}(\delta) := \text{comv}\{y^i(\delta): i \in N^\ell\} \in \mathcal{C}_0^N$. By PO and AN, $\varphi(S^{\ell+1}(\delta)) = \sum_{i\in N^\ell} |N^\ell|^{-1} y^i(\delta)$. Now $\varphi(S^{\ell+1}(\delta))$ is an N^ℓ-interior Pareto optimal point of $S^{\ell+1}(\delta)$, and, by (4.19), $\varphi_i(S^{\ell+1}(\delta)) = (z^{\ell+1})_i = L_i(S) = \varphi_i(S)$ for every $i \in N\backslash N^\ell$. By IMON, $\varphi_i(S) \geq \varphi_i(S^{\ell+1}(\delta))$ for every $i \in N^\ell$. By letting δ approach 0, $\varphi_i(S) \geq (z^{\ell+1})_i$ for every $i \in N^\ell$. With (4.19), this implies $\varphi(S) \geq z^{\ell+1}$. Moreover, by an argument similar to the one leading to the second statement in (4.18), $\varphi_i(S) = L_i(S)$ for every $i \in N\backslash N^{\ell+1}$. This completes the proof of (4.20), and of the theorem.   □

The approach in this section can also be applied to the lexicographic adaptation of the Raiffa-Kalai-Smorodinsky solution ρ (see sections 4.2, 4.3) on $\mathcal{C}_0^N$. Let us denote this solution by ρ^L and define it by $\rho^L(S) := u(S)L((u_1(S)^{-1}, \ldots, u_n(S)^{-1})S)$ for every $S \in \mathcal{C}_0^N$. That is, given a bargaining game S, first normalize it so that its utopia point is e^N, next apply L, and then transform back to S. As remarked at the beginning of this section, ρ^L was first characterized by Imai (1983). Let the axiom IMON' be defined by adding the following condition to conditions (i) and (ii) in the statement of IMON:

(iii) $u_M(T)$ is a positive multiple of $u_M(S)$, i.e., there exists on $\alpha > 0$ such that $u_i(T) = \alpha u_i(S)$ for every $i \in M$.

A proof of the following theorem can be given along the lines of the proof of theorem 4.42, and is omitted.

Theorem 4.44 *The lexicographic Raiffa-Kalai-Smorodinsky solution ρ^L is the unique solution on $\mathcal{C}_0^N$ satisfying PO, AN, STC, and IMON'.*

4.8   The lexicographic equal-loss solution

The equal-loss solution E^* discussed in section 4.6 equalizes the losses of the players relative to the utopia point $h(S, d)$ of a bargaining game (S, d). Remember that E^* has two drawbacks: it is only weakly Pareto optimal, and not individually rational. In the present section we provide a characterization of the so-called *lexicographic equal-loss solution* L^*, which is a modification of E^* satisfying Pareto optimality. Unfortunately, also L^* is not individually rational. However, at the end of this section we will discuss how the lexicographic equal-loss solution can be modified to satisfy both individual rationality and Pareto optimality. A characterization of this modified solution is not yet available.

The solution $L^* : C^N \to I\!\!R^N$ is defined as follows. For $(S, d) \in C^N$, let $t := h(S, d)$ and let $S^* := S - t$. Let x^* be the maximal element of S^* with respect to $>^{\ell m}$ (the lexicographic maximin ordering as defined in section 4.7). Then $L^*(S, d) := x^* + t$. (Recall that the lexicographic egalitarian solution L results if we set $t := d$ instead of $t := h(S, d)$.)

Alternatively, L^* may be defined by the following procedure. Let $(S, d) \in C_N$. First, *decrease* the utilities of the n players in $N^1 := N$ equally from $h(S, d)$, along $h(S, d) - \varsigma^1 e^{N^1}(\varsigma^1 \geq 0)$, until a boundary point is reached, say z^1. If $z^1 \in P(S)$, then set $z := z^1$. Otherwise, let $N^2 \subset N$ be the largest possible subset of players whose utilities can be equally *increased* in a nonnegative direction starting from z^1; i.e., go along the direction $z^1 + \varsigma^2 e^{N^2}(\varsigma^2 > 0)$. Let z^2 be the maximal point in this direction and still in S; if $z^2 \in P(S)$, then $z := z^2$, otherwise we continue along the direction $z^2 + \varsigma^3 e^{N^3}(\varsigma^3 > 0)$, where $N^3 \subset N^2$ is the largest possible subset of players for which *increase* along $z^2 + \varsigma^3 e^{N^3}$ is still possible. Etc. In this way we end up, after a finite number of steps, at a point $z \in P(S)$.

In order to characterize the lexicographic equal-loss solution, two additional axioms need to be defined. Let $\varphi : \mathcal{D}^N \to I\!\!R^N$ be a bargaining solution, where $\mathcal{D}^N \subset \tilde{\mathcal{B}}^N$. For $x \in I\!\!R^N$ and $i \in N$, let x_{-i} be the $(n-1)$-dimensional vector obtained after deleting the i th component of x. Also, for $(S, d) \in \mathcal{D}^N$, let $S_{d,-i} := \mathrm{cl}\{x_{-i} : x \in S, x \leq h(S, d)\}$.

Weak Monotonicity (WMON): For all $(S, d), (S', d) \in \mathcal{D}^N$, if $S \subset S'$ and $S_{d,-i} = S'_{d,-i}$ for all $i \in N$, then $\varphi(S', d) \geq \varphi(S, d)$.

If there are 2 players, this axiom is equivalent to the restricted monotonicity (RM) axiom defined in section 4.2, because then $S_{d,-i} = S'_{d,-i}$ is equivalent to $h_j(S, d) = h_j(S', d)$ for $j \neq i$. If $n > 2$, RM is stronger than WMON since $S_{d,-i} = S'_{d,-i}$ for all $i \in N$ implies $h(S, d) = h(S', d)$ but not the other way around. The weak monotonicity axiom was first introduced by Imai (1983).

Independence of Irrelevant Alternatives other than Utopia Point (IIA*): For all (S, d), $(S', d') \in \mathcal{D}^N$, if $S \subset S'$, $h(S, d) = h(S', d')$, and $\varphi(S', d') \in S$, then $\varphi(S, d) = \varphi(S', d')$.

The IIA* axiom is the analogon of IIA with, instead of equal disagreement points, equal utopia points. It was first introduced by Roth (1977c).

The main result of this section is the following theorem (Chun and Peters, 1991).

Theorem 4.45 *The lexicographic equal-loss solution L^* is the unique solution on C^N satisfying PO, AN, TC, WMON, and IIA*.*

It is not hard to check that L^* satisfies PO, AN, and TC. The two remaining properties are dealt with in the following lemmas.

Lemma 4.46 $L^* : C^N \to I\!\!R^N$ *satisfies IIA**.

Proof Let $(S,d), (S',d') \in C^N$ be two games satisfying the hypothesis of IIA*. Also, let $\{z^t\} \subset S$ be the sequence as defined in the process of finding $L^*(S,d) =: z^T$. Since $z^T \in S'$, $z^t \le z^T$ for all t, and S' is comprehensive, we have $z^t \in S'$ for all t. Now we construct the sequence $\{\overline{z}^t\} \subset S'$ to find $L^*(S',d')$. Since $S' \subset S$, $h(S',d') = h(S,d)$, and $z^t \in S'$ for all t, $\overline{z}^t = z^t$ for all t. Therefore, we conclude that $L^*(S',d') = z^T = L^*(S,d)$. $\square$

Lemma 4.47 $L^* : C^N \to I\!\!R^N$ *satisfies WMON*.

Proof Let $(S,d), (\overline{S},\overline{d}) \in C^N$ with $S \subset \overline{S}$, $d = \overline{d}$ and $S_{d,-i} = \overline{S}_{d,-i}$ for all i. Note that $S_{d,-i} = \overline{S}_{d.-i}$ for all i implies that $h(S,d) = h(\overline{S},d)$. Since L^* satisfies TC, we may assume that $h(S,d) = e^N$. The proof is done with the help of two claims which require the following additional notation. For $y \in S$, let $N(S,y) \subset N$ be defined by $N(S,y) := \{i \in N | y + \varsigma e^i \in S$ for some $\varsigma > 0\}$. $N(S,y)$ denotes the largest subset of players of N, whose utilities could be increased equally from y in S. Let ς^* be the minimal number such that for all $\varsigma > \varsigma^*$, $y + \varsigma e^{N(S,y)} \notin S$. Finally, let $z(S,y) := y + \varsigma e^{N(S,y)}$.

Claim 1. For all $y \in S$, if $N(S,y) \ne \emptyset$, then $N(S,y) = N(\overline{S},y)$.

Proof Since $S \subset \overline{S}$, it is clear that $N(S,y) \subset N(\overline{S},y)$. We will show that $N(\overline{S},y) \subset N(S,y)$. Suppose, by way of contradiction, that there exists $j \in N(\overline{S},y) \backslash N(S,y)$. Let $z := z(S,y)$ and $\overline{z} := (\overline{S},y)$. Clearly, $z \le \overline{z}$. Now pick $k \in N(S,y)$. Since $S_{d,-i} = \overline{S}_{d,-i}$ for all i, there exists $x \in S$ such that $x_{-k} = \overline{z}_{-k}$. By the convexity of S, for all $\lambda \in [0,1]$, $\lambda x + (1 - \lambda)z =: x^\lambda \in S$. Since $x_{-k} = \overline{z}_{-k} \ge y_{-k}$, $z_{-k} \ge y_{-k}$ and $z_k > y_k$, there exists $\lambda \in (0,1]$ such that $x^\lambda \ge y$. Since $\overline{z}_j > y_j = z_j$, $x_j^\lambda > y_j$. Altogether, we obtain $x_j^\lambda > y_j$, $x^\lambda \ge y$ and $x \in S$, which implies that $j \in N(S,y)$, a contradiction.

Claim 2. Let $T > 1$ be the final step in finding $L^*(S,d)$. Also, let $\{z^t\}$ and $\{\overline{z}^t\}$ be the two sequences as defined in the process of finding $L^*(S,d)$ and $L^*(\overline{S},d)$ respectively. Then, for all $t = 1, \ldots, T - 1$, $z^t = \overline{z}^t$.

Proof First, we will consider the case when $t = 1$. Since $S \subset \overline{S}$ and $h(S,d) = h(\overline{S},d)$, it is clear that $z^1 \le \overline{z}^1$. We need to show that $\overline{z}^1 \le z^1$. Suppose, by way of contradiction, that there exists $j \in N$ such that $\overline{z}_j^1 > z_j^1$. Since $\overline{z}^1$ and z^1 are points with equal coordinates, it follows that $\overline{z}^1 > z^1$. Since T is the final step, $z^1 \in W(S) \backslash P(S)$. Therefore, there exists $x \in S$ such that $x \ge z^1$, $x \ne z^1$. Let $k \in N$ be such that $x_k > z_k^1$. On the other hand, since $S_{d,-i} = \overline{S}_{d.-i}$ for all i, there exists $y \in S$ such that $y_{-k} = \overline{z}_{-k}^1$. By the convexity of S, for all $\lambda \in [0,1]$, $\lambda x + (1 - \lambda)y =: y^\lambda \in S$. Since $x \ge z^1$, $x \ne z^1$, $x_k > z_k^1$ and $y_{-k} = \overline{z}_{-k}^1 > z_{-k}^1$, there exists $\lambda \in (0,1)$ such that $y^\lambda > z^1$. This is a contradiction to $z^1 \in W(S)$.
The proofs for $t = 2, \ldots T - 1$, are analogous, using Claim 1, and are therefore omitted.

Finally, by combining the results of Claims 1 and 2, it follows that $z^T = L^*(S,d) \le \overline{z}^T \le L^*(\overline{S},d)$. Therefore, L^* satisfies WMON. $\square$

In the proof of theorem 4.45, we use the notation $H(p, p \cdot z) := \{x \in I\!\!R^N : p \cdot x \leq p \cdot z\}$ where $p, z \in I\!\!R^N$.

We sketch the main idea behind the proof before diving into the technicalities. The proof uses the procedure for finding $L^*(S, d)$ $((S, d) \in \mathcal{C}^N)$ described above. Note that we need to figure out $z^1, \ldots, z^T$ to obtain $L^*(S, d) = z^T$. First, by translation covariance, we may assume that the utopia point has all coordinates equal. The main step of the proof lies in the construction of sequences of games, whose solution outcome is z^t $(t = 1, \ldots, T)$. The first game of the sequence is symmetric, whence its solution outcome is determined to be z^1 by Pareto optimality and anonymity. In the induction argument, using WMON and IIA*, we obtain that the solution outcome for step t $(t = 2, \ldots, T)$ should be greater than or equal to the solution outcome for step $t - 1$, z^{t-1}. By Pareto optimality, we can conclude that it is equal to z^t.

Proof of theorem 4.45 Let φ be a solution satisfying the five axioms. Let $(\overline{S}, \overline{d}) \in \mathcal{C}^N$ be given. By TC we may assume that $h(\overline{S}, \overline{d}) = e^N$. Let $S := \{x \in \overline{S} : x \leq h(\overline{S}, \overline{d})\}$ and $d' \in \text{int}(S)$ be such that $d'_i = d'_j =: 1 - \delta$ for all $i, j \in N$ and $h(S, d') = e^N$. Equivalently, we may take, by TC, $d = 0$ and $h(S, d) = \delta e^N$. Note that $\delta > 0$. Now let $\{z^t\}_{t=1}^T$ and $\{N^t\}_{t=1}^T$ be the sequences as defined in the process of finding $L^*(S, d)$. We will show that $\varphi(S, d) = z^T$. Then, by IIA*, we have $\varphi(S, \overline{d}) = z^T$, and by WMON, we have $\varphi(\overline{S}, \overline{d}) = z^T = L^*(\overline{S}, \overline{d})$, which concludes the proof.

Now we construct auxiliary games. Let $M^t := N \backslash N^t$ and $p^t := e^{M^t}$ for $t = 1, \ldots, T$, (where $M^1 = \emptyset$ and $p^1 = 0$). Define

$$
\begin{aligned}
S^{1,t} &:= H(e^N, \sum z_i^t) \cap (\bigcap_{k=1}^{t} H(p^k, p^k \cdot z^k)) \cap (\delta e^N - I\!\!R_+^N) \\
&\qquad \text{for } t = 1, \ldots, T, \\
S^{2,t} &:= S^{1,t} \cap H(p^{t+1}, p^{t+1} \cdot z^{t+1}) \text{ for } t = 1, \ldots, T-1, \\
S^{3,t} &:= H(e^N, \sum z_i^t) \cap S \text{ for } t = 1, \ldots, T, \text{ and} \\
S^{4,t} &:= S^{1,t} \cap S \text{ for } t = 1, \ldots, T.
\end{aligned}
$$

Claim 1. $z^t \in S^{r,t}$ and $d \in \text{int}(S^{r,t})$ for all r and t.

Proof By definition of p^t, $p^t \cdot z^t = p^t \cdot z^{t+s}$ for all $t = 1, \ldots, T$ and for all $s = 1, \ldots, T-t$. Also, note that by definition of the sequence $\{z^t\}$, $z^t \leq z^{t+1}$, $z^t \neq z^{t+1}$, for all $t = 1, \ldots, T-1$. Now it follows immediately that $z^t \in S^{r,t}$ for all r and t. Since $d < z^1$ and S is comprehensive, $d \in \text{int}(S^{r,t})$ for all r and t. This proves the claim.

Claim 2. $h(S^{r,t}, d) = \delta e^N$ for all r and t.

Proof For all $i \in N$, let y^i be such that $y_i^i = \delta$ and $y_j^i = 0$ for all $j \neq i$. Since $h(S, d) = \delta e^N$ and S is comprehensive, $y^i \in S$ for all i. It is enough to show that all y^i's belong to the half-spaces defined above. For $t = 1$, $p^1 \cdot y^i = 0$ and trivially $y^i \in H(p^1, p^1 \cdot z^1)$ for all i.

Before we consider the case when $t > 1$, we first need to establish the following fact. Let m be such that $m = n$ if $T = 1$ and $m = |M^2|$ otherwise. We will show that $z^1 \geq (1/m)\delta e^N$. Since $z^1 \in W(S)$, there exists $p \in I\!\!R_+^N$ such that for all $z \in S$, $p \cdot z \leq p \cdot z^1$. Since $y^i \in S$,

$p \cdot y^i \leq p \cdot z^1$ for all i. Furthermore, if $i \in N^2$, $z^1 + \varsigma e^i \in S$ for some $\varsigma > 0$, and consequently $p_i = 0$, hence $p \cdot y^i = 0$. Therefore,

$$\sum_{i \in N} p \cdot y^i = \sum_{i \in N^2} p \cdot y^i + \sum_{i \in M^2} p \cdot y^i = \sum_{i \in M^2} p \cdot y^i \leq \sum_{i \in M^2} p \cdot z^1.$$

Since $|M^2| \leq m$, $p \cdot \sum y^i \leq mp \cdot z^1$. Equivalently, $(1/m)p \cdot \sum y^i \leq p \cdot z^1$. Since $\sum y^i = \delta e^N$, $p \cdot ((1/m)\delta e^N) \leq p \cdot z^1$. Using the fact that both $(1/m)\delta e^N$ and z^1 are points with equal coordinates, we obtain $(1/m)\delta e^N \leq z^1$.

Now we go back to the case when $t > 1$. Note that if $T > 1$, then $m \leq |M^t|$ for all $t = 2, \ldots, T$. Since $(1/m)\delta e^N \leq z^1 \leq z^t$,

$$p^t \cdot y^i \leq \delta \leq \frac{|M^t|}{m}\delta = p^t \cdot \left(\frac{1}{m}\delta e^N\right) \leq p^t \cdot z^1 \leq p^t \cdot z^t$$

for all $t = 2, \ldots T$. Therefore, $y^i \in H(p^t, p^t \cdot z^t)$ for all i and for all $t = 2, \ldots T$.

Also, $e^N \cdot y^i = \delta = e^N \cdot ((1/n) \sum y^i) \leq e^N \cdot z^1$. Therefore, $y^i \in H(e^N, \sum z_i^t)$ for all i and t. Altogether, we obtain the desired conclusion.

Claim 3. $S_{d,-i}^{1,t+1} = S_{d,-i}^{2,t}$ and $S_{d,-i}^{3,t+1} = S_{d,-i}^{3,t}$ for all $i = 1, \ldots, n$ and for all $t = 1, \ldots, T-1$.

Proof It is clear that $S_{d,-i}^{1,t+1} \supset S_{d,-i}^{2,t}$ for all $i = 1, \ldots, n$ and for all $t = 1, \ldots, T-1$. For the other inclusion, let $i \in N$ and $w \in S_{d,-i}^{1,t+1}$ be given. Then there exists $x \in S^{1,t+1}$ such that $x_{-i} = w$. If $e^N \cdot x \leq e^N \cdot z^t$, then we are done. Otherwise, let y be such that $y := x - (\sum x_j - \sum z_j^t) \cdot e^i$. By comprehensiveness of $S^{1,t+1}$, $y \in S^{1,t+1}$. Since $e^N \cdot y = \sum z_j^t = e^N \cdot z^t$ and $y_{-i} = x_{-i} = w$, $w \in S_{d,-i}^{2,t}$. Similarly, we can show that $S_{d,-i}^{3,t+1} = S_{d,-i}^{3,t}$ for all $i = 1, \ldots, n$ and for all $t = 1, \ldots, T-1$.

Claim 4. $\varphi(S^{r,1}, d) = z^1$ for all r.

Proof Note that $S^{1,1} := H(e^N, \sum z_i^1) \cap (\delta e^N - \mathbb{R}_+^N)$. Therefore, by PO and AN, $\varphi(S^{1,1}, d) = z^1$. By IIA* and Claim 2, $\varphi(S^{2,1}, d) = \varphi(S^{3,1}, d) = \varphi(S^{4,1}, d) = z^1$, as desired.

Claim 5. $\varphi(S^{r,t}, d) = z^t$ for all r and t.

Proof We use induction on t, based on Claim 4. Suppose, as induction hypothesis, that the conclusion of Claim 5 holds for all $t = 1, \ldots, h-1$. Now we consider the case when $t = h$. We will use Claims 2 and 3 several times, without explicit mentioning. By WMON applied between $(S^{2,h-1}, d)$ and $(S^{1,h}, d)$, $\varphi(S^{1,h}, d) \geq \varphi(S^{2,h-1}, d) = z^{h-1}$. Therefore, by PO and AN, $\varphi(S^{1,h}, d) = z^h$. By IIA* applied between $(S^{1,h}, d)$ and $(S^{4,h}, d)$, $\varphi(S^{4,h}, d) = \varphi(S^{1,h}, d) = z^h$. By WMON applied between $(S^{3,h-1}, d)$ and $(S^{3,h}, d)$, $\varphi(S^{3,h}, d) \geq \varphi(S^{3,h-1}, d) = z^{h-1}$. Note that $z \in S^{3,h}$ and $z \geq z^{h-1}$ imply that $z_i = z_i^{h-1}$ for all $i \in M^h$. Then $p^t \cdot z = p^t \cdot z^h = p^t \cdot z^t$ for all $t = 1, \ldots, h$ and consequently, $z \in S^{4,h}$. Since $\varphi(S^{3,h}, d) \geq z^{h-1}$, $\varphi(S^{3,h}, d) \in S^{4,h}$. Therefore, by IIA* applied between $(S^{3,h}, d)$ and $(S^{4,h}, d)$, $\varphi(S^{3,h}, d) = \varphi(S^{4,h}, d) = z^h$. Finally, by IIA* applied between $(S^{1,h}, d)$ and $(S^{2,h}, d)$, $\varphi(S^{2,h}, d) = z^h$ (this final step is not applicable when $h = T$). This completes the proof of Claim 5.

Claim 6. $\varphi(S,d) = L^*(S,d) = z^T$.

Proof From a proof similar to that of Claim 3, we can show that $S^{3,T}_{d,-i} = S_{d,-i}$ for all i. Therefore, by applying WMON between $(S^{3,T}, d)$ and (S, d), $\varphi(S,d) \geq \varphi(S^{3,T}, d) = z^T$, where the equality follows from Claim 5. Since $z^T \in P(S)$, $\varphi(S,d) = z^T$, as desired. $\square$

We conclude this section by indicating a possible modification $\overline{L^*}$ of L^* which is individually rational[3]. For $(S,d) \in \mathcal{C}^N$, recall that S_d denotes the comprehensive hull of the individually rational points of (S,d), that is, $S_d = \text{com}\{x \in S : x \geq d\}$. Let $\overline{L^*}(S,d) := L^*(S_d, d)$. Then $\overline{L^*}$ is both Pareto optimal and individually rational on $\mathcal{C}^N$. An axiomatic characterization is not yet available.

4.9   Further literature

Related work can be found at several places elsewhere in this book. In section 5.4 a characterization of proportional solutions based on an axiom of super-additivity is presented. In section 7.3 we give an axiomatization of the RKS solution based mainly on Thomson's population monotonicity axiom; characterizations of the egalitarian and lexicographic egalitarian solutions within the same variable population model are described in section 7.5. In section 8.2 we discuss an extension of the RKS solution as a multisolution, i.e., a correspondence. In section 8.5 the behavior of the RKS solution (and of the Nash solution) on certain economic environments (problems of fair division) is briefly considered. We obtain another characterization, related to a noncooperative implementation, of the RKS solution in section 9.6: this characterization is based on a so-called reduced game property. An extension of the proportional solutions to coalitional bargaining games (NTU games) is proposed and characterized by Kalai and Samet (1985); see section 10.5.

We conclude this chapter by mentioning some other related work not further discussed in this book. Butrim (1976, 1978) considers the RKS solution; the second paper proposes an extension to n-person bargaining games. A solution related to a lexicographic version of the RKS solution is the "Gauthier solution": see Klemisch-Ahlert (1988). Nielsen (1983) gives a characterization of the two-person lexicographic egalitarian solution. A (two-person) variation on the RKS solution is proposed and characterized by Salonen (1985). Myerson (1977) characterizes a class of two-person bargaining solutions; each solution in this class corresponds to a specific pair of order-preserving transformations of the axes (i.e., of the players' utility functions) so that by applying these transformations the solution outcome becomes egalitarian.

---

[3]This solution was suggested by Walter Bossert, private communication.

Chapter 5

Additivity properties

5.1 Introduction

Monotonicity properties and independence properties like independence of irrelevant alternatives describe the effect on the outcome assigned by a bargaining solution to a bargaining game of changing — expanding or shrinking — the feasible set. Additivity axioms contain statements concerning the outcomes assigned to specific *sums* of bargaining games.

At some places in the preceding chapters, additivity axioms are considered where the feasible set of a bargaining game is left unaltered, but sums of disagreement points are taken. Specifically, disagreement point convexity (DPC) and disagreement point linearity (DLIN), both introduced in section 2.5, are axioms of this kind. Further, the step-by-step negotiations axiom (SSN) used by Kalai to characterize the proportional solutions, was formulated as an additivity axiom due to the disagreement point being normalized to zero (see section 4.5).

The first explicit studies with regard to additivity properties of bargaining solutions were the articles by Perles and Maschler (1981) and Myerson (1981). The first two authors consider super-additive bargaining solutions on a domain of bargaining games of which the feasible sets contain only individually rational points. By adding some other axioms to the super-additivity axiom, they characterize a unique two-person bargaining solution. This result is reviewed in section 5.2.

In section 5.3, it is argued that it is not without loss of generality to consider only individually rational points. In the context of simultaneous bargaining over more than one issue a player may be better off receiving a bad (non-individually rational) payoff in one game in exchange for a very good payoff in another game. This intuition will be modelled by imposing certain additivity properties on bargaining solutions, leading to characterizations of proportional solutions (section 5.4) and nonsymmetric Nash bargaining solutions (section 5.5). A utility-theoretic foundation for the use of additivity axioms can be based on section 11.5; this is explained in section 5.3. The mentioned work by Myerson (1981) also characterizes proportional solutions by using the IIA axiom combined with an axiom of super-additivity.

The material in sections 5.3–5.5 is based on Peters (1986c).

5.2   The super-additive solution of Perles and Maschler

Perles and Maschler (1981) characterize a unique solution for a restricted domain of 2-person bargaining games by five axioms, one of which is super-additivity. Their results are reviewed here, partly based on Maschler and Perles (1981).

Perles and Maschler restrict their attention to the class $\overline{C}_* = \{S \in \overline{C}_0 : S = \text{com}(S \cap \mathbb{R}_{++}^{\{1,2\}})\}$ on two grounds[1]. The first ground is technical: the five axioms they propose (see below) are incompatible on the class $\overline{C}_0$. The second ground refers to an underlying bargaining process and is discussed in section 5.3.

Let φ be a solution on a class $\mathcal{D}^N \subset \tilde{\mathcal{B}}^N$.

Super-Additivity (SA): For all $(S,d),(T,e),(S+T,d+e) \in \mathcal{D}^N$, $\varphi(S+T,d+e) \geq \varphi(S,d) + \varphi(T,e)$.

The justification provided by Perles and Maschler to require the super-additivity axiom is based on the following observation. Suppose that φ is super-additive and homogeneous (HOM), let $(S,d),(T,e) \in \mathcal{D}^N$, and let $0 \leq \alpha \leq 1$ be such that $(\alpha S + (1 - \alpha)T, \alpha d + (1 - \alpha)e) =: (V,c)$, $(\alpha S, \alpha d)$, $((1 - \alpha)T,(1 - \alpha)e)$ are all in $\mathcal{D}^N$. Obviously, $\varphi(V,c) \geq \alpha \varphi(S,d) + (1 - \alpha)\varphi(T,e)$ by super-additivity and homogeneity. Regard α as a probability embodying the players' uncertainty about what the true bargaining game will be: (S,d) or (T,e). Then this observation implies that the players prefer the outcome of the expected bargaining game (V,c) to the outcome they expect to obtain by waiting until the uncertainty concerning the true bargaining game has been resolved. We cite Maschler and Perles (1981, p. 104): "The feasible set in a Nash bargaining game is a set in the utility space of the players. As such, its points often represent expectations of uncertain events. Nash's theory assumes that the players must reach an agreement before any of these uncertainties resolve, but in many real situations the players may have an option of delaying the time of reaching an agreement until more information is available concerning the true state of the world. Adherers of a solution concept that does not satisfy [super-additivity] may find themselves in situations where some players want to reach an agreement immediately and others at a later time [...]." This argument is closely related to the argument justifying the disagreement point concavity axiom (DCAV) in subsection 4.5.2.

Perles and Maschler (1981) derive theorem 5.1 below (the proof is not reproduced here). For $S \in \overline{C}_*$ and $0 \leq t \leq u_1(S)$, where $u(S)$ is the utopia point of S as usual, let $f^S(t) := \max\{s \in \mathbb{R} : (t,s) \in S\}$. The function f^S describes the boundary $W(S)$ of S, and is differentiable almost everywhere. The same holds for the function $g^S : [0, u_2(S)] \to \mathbb{R}_+$ defined by $g^S(s) := \max\{t \in \mathbb{R} : (t,s) \in S\}$ for every $0 \leq s \leq u_2(S)$.

Theorem 5.1 *There is a unique solution on* $\overline{C}_*$ *satisfying SA, PO, STC, SYM, and PCONT. This solution assigns to each game* $S \in \overline{C}_*$ *the unique point* $\overline{x}(S) \in P(S)$ *satisfying*

$$\int_0^{\overline{x}_1(S)} \sqrt{-\frac{df^S(t)}{dt}}\, dt = \int_0^{\overline{x}_2(S)} \sqrt{-\frac{dg^S(t)}{dt}}\, dt. \tag{5.1}$$

---

[1] Actually, Perles and Maschler consider only the nonnegative parts of these games.

A few remarks concerning the formulation of this theorem are in order. First, Perles and Maschler actually use a weaker continuity condition, but we take Pareto continuity in order to avoid another definition. Clearly, the solution defined in theorem 5.1 is not feasible set continuous (SCONT), since S may consist of just a line segment. Consider, for example, the set of bargaining games $\{\mathrm{conv}\{(0,0),(1,0),(0,s)\}\colon 0 \le s \le 1\}$. For $s \ne 0$, the solution outcome is $(\frac{1}{2},\frac{1}{2}s)$, but for $s = 0$ it is $(1,0)$. Second, the notation $d\ldots/dt$ in (5.1) is understood to apply whenever the corresponding derivatives exist; the integrals are well-defined because the functions f^S and g^S are absolutely continuous (see, e.g., Aliprantis and Burkinshaw, 1981, section 29).

Let us call the solution defined in theorem 5.1 the Perles-Maschler solution and denote it by φ^{PM}. For a bargaining game S, the solution outcome $\varphi^{PM}(S)$ can be approximated as follows. Construct small triangles of equal area below the boundary $W(S)$ of S, as in figure 5.1. There the areas of P_i and Q_i are equal for $i = 1,2,3,4$. P_4 and Q_4 meet at a

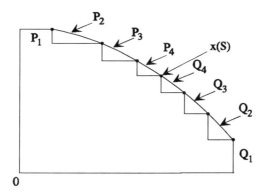

Figure 5.1: Construction of $\varphi^{PM}(S)$

point $x(S) \in W(S)$. By taking more and more triangles and letting their areas approach 0, the meeting point $x(S)$ approaches the point $\overline{x}(S) = \varphi^{PM}(S)$. This explains, roughly, how formula (5.1) is obtained. Observe that if we shift all triangles to the origin, the feasible S equals the sum of all shifted triangles, and the super-additivity axiom can be applied. In the proof of theorem 5.1, the triangles are proper triangles (S is assumed to be polygonal) on which the solution is determined by symmetry, scale transformation covariance, and Pareto optimality. For non-polygonal S, the Pareto continuity axiom is employed.

Another procedure to arrive at the solution outcome $\varphi^{PM}(S)$ is illustrated in figure 5.2. The curve starting at 0 and crossing through the point (v_1, w_2) is described by the differential equation $\mu'(v_1) = \sqrt{\lambda_1 \lambda_2}$ where $\lambda_1 = -df^S(v_1)/dx_1$ and $\lambda_2 = -df^S(w_1)/dx_1$, whenever these derivatives exist. It is assumed here that $P(S) = W(S)$; otherwise, the curve may start at a point larger than 0. The curve, i.e., the graph of μ, intersects $W(S)$ at $\varphi^{PM}(S)$. Moreover, any y on this curve taken as the disagreement point gives the same solution outcome; formally, $\varphi^{PM}(\mathrm{com}((S - y) \cap \mathbb{R}_+^2)) = \varphi^{PM}(S) - y$. For this reason, the graph of μ can be called the *disagreement point set* or *status quo curve*. In the present case of the Perles-Maschler solution the slope of this status quo curve is (almost everywhere)

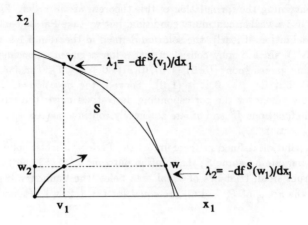

Figure 5.2: Disagreement point set of φ^{PM}

equal to the geometric mean of the slopes of the boundary $W(S)$ at the "momentary utopia points" (v and w in figure 5.2) of the players. These latter slopes, in turn, can be viewed as the utility exchange rates of the players. For formal proofs, see Perles and Maschler (1981, p. 178 ff.).

The five axioms in theorem 5.1 are independent. In particular, Perles and Maschler show the consequences of dropping Pareto continuity or symmetry. Nonsymmetric solutions are described by two parameters (see Maschler and Perles, 1981, p. 109). Christensen (1989) investigates the consequences of dropping the scale transformation covariance axiom. He shows that each solution satisfying the four remaining axioms is described by two nonnegative real-valued functions on the interval $[0, \frac{\pi}{2}]$.

For $n > 2$, the five axioms in theorem 5.1 are incompatible. More precisely, Perles (1982) shows that if $n = 3$ the axioms PO, STC, SYM, and SA are incompatible, even on the smaller class of bargaining games that are sums of nondegenerate simplices. So the impossibility is genuine and cannot be resolved, e.g., by dropping "pathological" games from the domain. One could, however, try to generalize the procedure based on the status quo curve described above to bargaining games with more than two players, but also this is still open. Of course, relaxing the axiomatic requirements will lead to possibilities as well. For instance, the egalitarian solution E is super-additive, symmetric, homogeneous and weakly Pareto optimal (see also section 5.4).

5.3   Simultaneity of issues and additivity in bargaining

Suppose two parties are facing several (separate) bargaining situations, on (possibly quite) different issues. Handling these situations one by one may yield both parties only small profits. Bargaining, however, over these issues simultaneously, may yield both parties larger total profits, thus reflecting more properly their perhaps strong interests in some of these issues. The following simple example illustrates this.

Mr. X and his wife each have a ticket for a magnificent movie, but, unfortunately, these tickets are not valid for the same show (there are two shows which take place on different evenings). Now, for each of the two shows for which one of the tickets is valid, there are three alternatives:

(a) the ticket-holder watches the movie leaving his/her partner at home, which gives him/her 6 units of utility and his/her partner -2 units;

(b) they both stay at home, but with the ticket-holder grudging the whole evening: 0 utility for both (the disagreement alternative);

(c) they both stay at home and play some card game: 0 utility for the ticket-holder and 1 unit of utility for the partner.

If we suppose for a moment that these utilities are additive, then Mr. X as well as his wife do very well by each one using his/her ticket and receiving a net utility of 4.

Modelling the above example with the aid of bargaining games, we may call Mr. X player 1 and Mrs. X player 2. There are two bargaining games to be played, corresponding to the two evenings on which the shows take place. If we suppose that Mr. X's ticket is valid for the first show, then on the first evening Mr. X and his wife play a bargaining game $S = \text{comv}\{(6,-2),(0,0),(0,1)\} \in \mathcal{C}_0$ where these three points correspond to the alternatives (a), (b), and (c) above and where we assume that lotteries between these alternatives are possible. Similarly, on the second evening they play $T = \text{comv}\{(-2,6),(0,0),(1,0)\}$. Suppose further that Mr. X and his wife agree to let some individually rational, Pareto optimal and symmetric bargaining solution $\varphi : \mathcal{C}_0 \to I\!R^2$ solve their conflicts. Then note that $\varphi_i(S) + \varphi_i(T) \le 3$ for $i \in \{1,2\}$, whereas $\varphi(\{s + t : s \in S,\ t \in T\}) = (4,4)$. So it is clearly advantageous for both players to play both games simultaneously, provided we can find a way to let $\{s + t : s \in S,\ t \in T\} \in \mathcal{C}_0$ represent the simultaneous bargaining game; to this end, we use the additive utility model of section 11.5 as follows.

Let $\mathcal{F}$ be a family of expected utility bargaining situations for $N = \{1,2\}$ (see subsection 1.3.1). For any $\Gamma = <A, \bar{a}, u^1, u^2>$ and $\Gamma' = <B, \bar{b}, v^1, v^2>$ in $\mathcal{F}$, assume that both players also have preferences over the lottery set $\mathcal{L}(A \times B)$ such that condition (11.11) (additive independence) and condition (11.13) with $\bar{a}$ and $\bar{b}$ in the roles of a^0 and b^0 hold, such that remark 11.15 applies, and such that these preferences over $\mathcal{L}(A \times B)$ are representable by vNM utility functions. Then theorem 11.14 and remark 11.15 imply that the preferences over $\mathcal{L}(A \times B)$ are representable by vNM utility functions w^i with $w^i(a,b) = u^i(a) + v^i(b)$ for all $i \in \{1,2\}$, $a \in A$, $b \in B$. Call $\Gamma \times \Gamma' :=< A \times B, (\bar{a},\bar{b}), w^1, w^2 >$ the corresponding *simultaneous bargaining situation*. Observe that $\Gamma \times \Gamma'$ can be considered as an expected utility bargaining situation for $\{1,2\}$. Assume, moreover, that for every $\Gamma \in \mathcal{F}$ the disagreement point utilities are normalized to 0. Consequently, S_Γ and $S_{\Gamma \times \Gamma'}$ are bargaining games in $\mathcal{C}_0$ for all $\Gamma, \Gamma' \in \mathcal{F}$. Let a bargaining solution $\varphi : \mathcal{C}_0 \to I\!R^2$ be given. The following condition expresses that simultaneous bargaining is (weakly) more profitable than separate bargaining for both players: For all $\ell \in \mathcal{L}(A)$, $\ell' \in \mathcal{L}(B)$, and $\ell'' \in \mathcal{L}(A \times B)$ with $u^i(\ell) = \varphi_i(S_\Gamma)$, $u^i(\ell') = \varphi_i(S_{\Gamma'})$, and $w^i(\ell'') = \varphi_i(S_{\Gamma \times \Gamma'})$ for $i = 1,2$, we have $(w^1(\ell''), w^2(\ell'')) \ge (u^1(\ell), u^2(\ell)) + (v^1(\ell'), v^2(\ell'))$. By the additivity of the utility functions w^i, this is equivalent to requiring

$$\varphi(S_\Gamma + S_{\Gamma'}) \ge \varphi(S_\Gamma) + \varphi(S_{\Gamma'})$$

which brings us back to the super-additivity property defined in the preceding section.

Remember that Perles and Maschler (1981) restrict their attention to games in the class $\overline{C}_*$ (section 5.2) where no player can commit himself to a (Pareto optimal) feasible outcome which is not individually rational for the other player, i.e., an outcome with at least one coordinate negative. Indeed, if one feels that one is actually dealing with noncooperative Nash bargaining games (Perles and Maschler, 1981, p. 167), then this restriction to C_* is justified. Recall the example of Mr. X and his wife at the beginning of this section. The outcome there of the subgame, $(4,4)$, can only be achieved by the sum $(6,-2)+(-2,6)$. This means that in one game player 1 can commit himself to $(6,-2)$, whereas in the other game player 2 can commit himself to $(-2,6)$. In a noncooperative setting, such commitments would be impossible: we are stuck in a prisoner's dilemma (cf. subsection 1.3.3). Yet in a cooperative setting, where binding agreements are possible, these commitments lead to a net utility profit of 4 both players. We shall assume such a cooperative setting. Perles and Maschler have already shown that their solution cannot be extended to C_0. This will also follow as a corollary of the results in the next section.

5.4   Partial super-additivity and proportional solutions

In this section we characterize the family of 2-person proportional solutions (see section 4.5) by the axioms of weak Pareto optimality, homogeneity, and the following axiom, formulated here for a solution φ on a subclass D^N of $\tilde{B}^N$.

Partial Super-Additivity (PSA): For all $(S,d),(T,e) \in D^N$, if $(S+T,d+e) \in D^N$, then $\varphi(S+T,d+e) \geq \varphi(S,d)$ and $\varphi(S+T,d+e) \geq \varphi(T,e)$.

Observe that this axiom can be viewed as a weakening of strong monotonicity (SMON). Consequently, the following theorem, which is the main result of this section, can be seen as a strengthening of theorem 4.30 in one direction (for 2 players).

Theorem 5.2 *Let $\varphi : C_0 \to \mathbb{R}^2$ be a bargaining solution. Then φ satisfies WPO, HOM, and PSA, if and only if it is proportional.*

The adjective "partial" is preferred to "weak" since PSA is not implied by SA alone. We have, however, the following lemma.

Lemma 5.3 *If the bargaining solution $\varphi : C_0 \to \mathbb{R}^2$ satisfies IR and SA, then it also satisfies PSA.*

Proof Straightforward.   □

The proof of theorem 5.2 will be based on the following three lemmas.

Lemma 5.4 *Let $\varphi : C_0 \to \mathbb{R}^2$ be a solution satisfying HOM and PSA, let $S \in C_0$, and let $r \in \mathbb{R}^2_{++}$. Then*

  (i) *if $r \in \text{int}(S)$, then $\varphi(S) \geq \varphi(\text{com}\{r\})$,*

  (ii) *$\varphi(\text{com}\{r\}) \geq 0$.*

Proof (i) $S = \text{com}\{r\} + \{x - r : x \in S\}$, so, if $r \in \text{int}(S)$, we have by PSA: $\varphi(S) \geq \varphi(\text{com}\{r\})$.

(ii) By HOM: $\varphi(\text{com}\{\frac{1}{2}r\}) = \frac{1}{2}\varphi(\text{com}\{r\})$, and, since $\frac{1}{2}r \in \text{int}(\text{com}\{r\})$, by (i): $\varphi(\text{com}\{r\}) \geq \varphi(\text{com}\{\frac{1}{2}r\})$. So $\varphi(\text{com}\{\frac{1}{2}r\}) \geq \frac{1}{2}\varphi(\text{com}\{\frac{1}{2}r\})$. Hence $\varphi(\text{com}\{r\}) = 2\varphi(\text{com}\{\frac{1}{2}r\}) \geq 0$.
□

Corollary 5.5 *Every homogeneous and partially super-additive bargaining solution: $C_0 \to \mathbb{R}^2$ is individually rational.*

Proof Follows immediately from lemma 5.4.
□

Let now L be the set $\{p \in \mathbb{R}^2_{++} : p_1 + p_2 = 1\}$.

Lemma 5.6 *Let $\varphi : C_0 \to \mathbb{R}^2$ be a solution satisfying HOM, PSA, and WPO. Then: Either (i) $\varphi(\text{com}\{p\}) = p$ for some $p \in L$, or (ii) $\varphi_2(\text{com}\{p\}) < p_2$ for all $p \in L$, or (iii) $\varphi_1(\text{com}\{p\}) < p_1$ for all $p \in L$.*

Proof Suppose (i) does not hold. Let $L^1 := \{p \in L : \varphi_1(\text{com}\{p\}) < p_1\}$, $L^2 := \{p \in L : \varphi_2(\text{com}\{p\}) < p_2\}$, and suppose that $L^1 \neq \emptyset$, $L^2 \neq \emptyset$. Let $p^1 \in L^1$, $p^2 \in L^2$. We show

$$p_1^1 \geq p_1^2. \tag{5.2}$$

Suppose (5.2) does not hold, i.e., $p_1^1 < p_1^2$ and $p_2^1 > p_2^2$. Let $q \in \mathbb{R}^2_{++}$ be defined by $q_1 := \frac{1}{2}(p_1^1 + \varphi_1(\text{com}\{p^1\}))$, $q_2 := \frac{1}{2}(p_2^2 + \varphi_2(\text{com}\{p^2\}))$. Then $q \in \text{int}(\text{com}\{p^1\})$, so by lemma 5.4 (i), $\varphi_1(\text{com}\{p^1\}) \geq \varphi_1(\text{com}\{q\})$. Similarly, $\varphi_2(\text{com}\{p^2\}) \geq \varphi_2(\text{com}\{q\})$. Altogether we obtain $q > \varphi(\text{com}\{q\})$, in contradiction with WPO. So (5.2) must hold.

From our assumptions: (i) does not hold, $L^1 \neq \emptyset$, $L^2 \neq \emptyset$, we conclude, with the aid of (5.2), that there exists a $\overline{p} \in L$ such that for all $p \in L$ with $p_1 < \overline{p}_1$ we have $p \in L^2$, and for all $p \in L$ with $p_1 > \overline{p}_1$ we have $p \in L^1$. The proof of the lemma is finished, by contradiction, if we show

$$\varphi(\text{com}\{\overline{p}\}) = \overline{p}. \tag{5.3}$$

For any $0 < x < \overline{p}$ with $x_1 x_2^{-1} < \overline{p}_1 \overline{p}_2^{-1}$, we have, by HOM, WPO, and the fact that $\alpha x \in L^2$ for some $\alpha > 0$, that $\varphi_1(\text{com}\{x\}) = x_1$. Similarly, $\varphi_2(\text{com}\{y\}) = y_2$ for any $0 < y < \overline{p}$ with $y_1 y_2^{-1} > \overline{p}_1 \overline{p}_2^{-1}$. So by lemma 5.4 (i) we conclude that (5.3) holds.
□

Lemma 5.7 *Let $\varphi : C_0 \to \mathbb{R}^2$ be a solution satisfying HOM, PSA, and WPO. Let $p \in L$ such that $\varphi(\text{com}\{p\}) = p$ if (i) in lemma 5.6 holds, let $p = (0,1)$ if (iii) there holds, and let $p = (1,0)$ if (ii) there holds. Then $\varphi = E^p$.*

Proof Let $S \in C_0$. First suppose $E^p(S) \in P(S)$. If $p > 0$, $\varphi(S) \geq \varphi(\text{com}\{(1-\varepsilon)E^p(S)\}) = (1-\varepsilon)E^p(S)$ for $1 > \varepsilon > 0$ by lemma 5.4 (i) and HOM, so the proof is finished by letting ε approach 0. If $p = (1,0)$, then take a sequence $r^1, r^2, \ldots$ in $\text{int}(S) \cap \mathbb{R}^2_{++}$ converging to $E^p(S)$. Then again $\varphi(S) \geq \varphi(\text{com}\{r^i\})$ for each $i = 1, 2, \ldots$, so $\varphi_1(S) \geq \varphi_1(\text{com}\{r^i\}) = r_1^i$ for each $i = 1, 2, \ldots$, hence $\varphi_1(S) \geq E_1^p(S)$. We conclude that $\varphi(S) = E^p(S)$. By a similar argument, $\varphi(S) = E^p(S)$ if $p = (0,1)$.

Suppose now that $E^p(S) \notin P(S)$. We assume (the other case is similar) that there exists $x \in P(S)$ with $x_1 = E_1^p(S)$. Given $\varepsilon > 0$, let $R^\varepsilon \in C_0$ be defined by $R^\varepsilon :=$

comv$\{(\varepsilon, E_2^p(S)-x_2), (0,\varepsilon)\}$. Let $T^\varepsilon := S + R^\varepsilon$. (See figure 5.3.) Note that $E^p(T^\varepsilon) \in P(T^\varepsilon)$. By the first part of this proof, $\varphi(T^\varepsilon) = E^p(T^\varepsilon)$. If ε approaches 0, $E^p(T^\varepsilon) = \varphi(T^\varepsilon)$ converges to $E^p(S)$, and by PSA, $\varphi(T^\varepsilon) \geq \varphi(S)$ for all ε, so $E^p(S) \geq \varphi(S)$. If $p = (1,0)$ the proof is complete. If $p > 0$, then also the proof is complete if we note that $\varphi(S) \geq E^p(S)$ by the argument in the third sentence of the proof. □

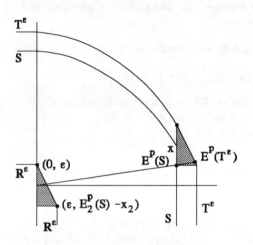

Figure 5.3: Proof of lemma 5.7

An immediate consequence of lemma 5.7 is that, if, for φ there, $\varphi(\text{com}\{p\}) = p$ for some $p \in L \cup \{(1,0),(0,1)\}$, then this p is unique. The proof of theorem 5.2 is now straightforward.

Proof of theorem 5.2 If φ satisfies the three properties in the theorem, then φ is proportional in view of lemma 5.7. It is straightforward to verify that a proportional solution has these properties. □

Note that partial super-additivity is implied by super-additivity and individual rationality combined (lemma 5.3), and that every proportional solution is super-additive. So the following corollary is immediate.

Corollary 5.8 Let $\varphi : C_0 \to \mathbb{R}^2$ be a 2-person bargaining solution. Then φ has the properties WPO, HOM, IR, and SA, if and only if φ is proportional.

A consequence of corollary 5.8 is that the five axioms imposed by Perles and Maschler (1981) — see the preceding section — are incompatible for individually rational solutions defined on C_0. It can be shown (and has been shown by Perles and Maschler) that they are incompatible even if we drop the individual rationality requirement. Another consequence is that there are only two solutions on C_0 satisfying, besides WPO, IR, and SA, scale transformation covariance (STC), namely the extreme solutions $E^{(1,0)}$ and $E^{(0,1)}$. In the next section, PO replaces WPO and super-additivity is weakened, leading to a characterization of 2-person nonsymmetric Nash solutions.

Yet another characterization of proportional solutions is obtained by Myerson (1981), who includes the independence of irrelevant alternatives axiom in the characterizing set of axioms.

5.5   Restricted additivity and nonsymmetric Nash solutions

Recall (see subsection 2.4.2) that an $S \subset I\!\!R^m$ is *smooth at* $x \in S$ if S has a unique supporting line at x. This smoothness condition plays an important role in the following axiom. For a discussion on this condition, see subsection 2.5.3. See also the end of this section. We formulate the following axiom for a solution φ on $\mathcal{D}^N \subset \tilde{\mathcal{B}}^N$.

Restricted Additivity (RA): For all $(S,d),(T,e) \in \mathcal{D}^N$ with $(S+T,d+e) \in \mathcal{D}^N$, if S and T are smooth at $\varphi(S,d)$ and $\varphi(T,e)$, respectively, and $\varphi(S,d) + \varphi(T,e) \in P(S+T)$, then $\varphi(S+T,d+e) = \varphi(S,d) + \varphi(T,e)$.

Observe that this axiom is implied by super-additivity (SA). The main result in this section is the following theorem.

Theorem 5.9 *A bargaining solution* $\varphi : C_0 \to I\!\!R^2$ *satisfies IR, PO, STC, PCONT, and RA, if and only if* $\varphi = \varphi^H$ *for some* $H \in \mathcal{H}^{\{1,2\}}$.

The solutions φ^H were defined in section 2.3, after lemma 2.15. For $H = <N,\omega>$, $\varphi^H(S)$ is the point of $S \cap I\!\!R^2_+$ where the product $x_1^{\omega_1} x_2^{\omega_2}$ is maximized. For $H = <\{1\},\{2\},(1,1)>$, $\varphi^H(S)$ is the point of $P(S) \cap I\!\!R^2_+$ with maximal first coordinate. For $H = <\{2\},\{1\},(1,1)>$, $\varphi^H(S)$ is the point of $P(S) \cap I\!\!R^2_+$ with maximal second coordinate.

Theorem 5.9 follows from the following two propositions.

Proposition 5.10 *For every* $H \in \mathcal{H}^{\{1,2\}}$, *the solution* φ^H *on* C_0 *satisfies IR, PO, STC, PCONT, and RA.*

Proposition 5.11 *Let* $\varphi : C_0 \to I\!\!R^2$ *be a bargaining solution satisfying IR, PO, STC, PCONT, and RA. Let* $t \in [0,1]$ *be such that* $\varphi(\Delta) = (t, 1-t)$. *If* $t = 1$ *then* $\varphi = \varphi^{<\{1\},\{2\},(1,1)>}$; *if* $t = 0$ *then* $\varphi = \varphi^{<\{2\},\{1\},(1,1)>}$; $\varphi = \varphi^{<N,(t,1-t)>}$ *otherwise.*

(Recall that $\Delta = \Delta^{\{1,2\}} = \mathrm{comv}\{(1,0),(0,1)\}$.)

In the proof of proposition 5.10 we use the following lemma, which characterizes Pareto optimality of sums of points with the aid of parallel supporting lines.

Lemma 5.12 *Let* $S,T \in C_0$ *and* $z = x + y \in P(S+T)$ *where* $x \in S$, $y \in T$. *Then:*

(i) $x \in P(S)$, $y \in P(T)$,

(ii) if ℓ *is a supporting line of* $S + T$ *at* z, *then there exist supporting lines* ℓ' *and* ℓ'' *of* S *and* T *at* x *and* y *respectively, such that* ℓ, ℓ' *and* ℓ'' *are parallel,*

(iii) if S *and* T *are smooth at* x *and* y *respectively, then* ℓ, ℓ' *and* ℓ'' *in (ii) are unique (and* $S + T$ *is smooth at* z).

Proof (i) is straightforward by the definition of a Pareto optimal subset, and (iii) by (ii). To prove (ii), let ℓ be such a supporting line with a normal vector λ, then $\lambda \geq 0$, and $\lambda \cdot z = \max\{\lambda \cdot (s+t): s \in S, t \in T\} = \max\{\lambda \cdot s: s \in S\} + \max\{\lambda \cdot t: t \in T\}$, hence $\lambda \cdot x = \max\{\lambda \cdot s: s \in S\}$ and $\lambda \cdot y = \max\{\lambda \cdot t: t \in T\}$, from which (ii) follows immediately. $\qquad\square$

For convenience we introduce the following notations: $N^t := \varphi^{<\{1,2\},(t,1-t)>}$ for $0 < t < 1$, $D^1 := \varphi^{<\{1\},\{2\},(1,1)>}$, and $D^2 := \varphi^{<\{2\},\{1\},(1,1)>}$.

Proof of proposition 5.10 Let $\varphi = \varphi^H$ for some $H \in \mathcal{H}^{\{1,2\}}$. We only show that φ satisfies RA; the other axioms are left to the reader (see also proposition 2.16). First, let $\varphi = N^t$ for some $t \in (0,1)$. Let $S, T \in \mathcal{C}_0$ such that S and T are smooth at $x := N^t(S)$ and $y := N^t(T)$ respectively, and $x + y \in P(S+T)$. From lemma 5.12 (iii) it follows that there exists a vector $\lambda \geq 0$, unique up to multiplication with a positive scalar, such that $\lambda \cdot x = \max\{\lambda \cdot s: s \in S\}$, $\lambda \cdot y = \max\{\lambda \cdot t: t \in T\}$, $\lambda \cdot (x+y) = \max\{\lambda \cdot v: v \in S+T\}$. From lemma 2.20, it follows that $x = \gamma y$ for some $\gamma > 0$, hence $x + y = (1+\gamma)y$. By applying lemma 2.20 again, we obtain $N^t(S+T) = x + y$.

Second, let $\varphi = D^1$, and S and T in $\mathcal{C}_0$ such that S and T are smooth at $D^1(S)$ and $D^1(T)$, respectively, and $D^1(S) + D^1(T) \in P(S+T)$. If $D^1_2(S) = D^1_2(T) = 0$, then $D^1_2(S) + D^1_2(T) = 0$, and so $D^1(S+T) = D^1(S) + D^1(T)$ since $D^1(S) + D^1(T) \in P(S)$. Otherwise, in view of lemma 5.12 (iii), the unique supporting lines of S, T, and $S + T$, at $D^1(S)$, $D^1(T)$ and $D^1(S) + D^1(T)$ are the straight lines with equations $x_1 = D^1_1(S)$, $x_1 = D^1_1(T)$, and $x_1 = D^1_1(S+T)$, respectively. So $D^1(S+T) = D^1(S) + D^1(T)$ since $D^1(S) + D^1(T) \in P(S+T)$.

The third case, $\varphi = D^2$, is similar to the second one. $\qquad\square$

In the proof of proposition 5.11 we use the following two lemmas.

Lemma 5.13 Let $\varphi : \mathcal{C}_0 \to \mathbb{R}^2$ be a bargaining solution satisfying IR, PO, and PCONT. Let $S \in \mathcal{C}_0$ such that S is smooth everywhere, i.e., at every point of $P(S)$, and such that the line of support of S at $\varphi(S)$ has a normal vector with one coordinate equal to 0. Let $z \in P(S)$, $z \neq \varphi(S)$. Then there exists an everywhere smooth $S' \in \mathcal{C}_0$ with $S' \subset S$ and $z \in S'$ such that $\varphi(S') \neq z$ and such that the line of support of S' at $\varphi(S')$ has a strictly positive normal vector.

Proof First note that $\varphi(S) = D^1(S)$ or $\varphi(S) = D^2(S)$. Assume $\varphi(S) = D^2(S)$ (the other case is similar). If $\varphi_1(S) = 0$, then an S' as in the lemma can easily be found by cutting off a suitable neighborhood of $\varphi(S)$ in S in a smooth way. Suppose now, that $\varphi_1(S) > 0$. First, choose $\bar{x} \in P(S)$ with $\varphi_2(S) > \bar{x}_2 > z_2$ and such that $\varphi_2(T) > z_2$ where T consists of all points of S except those strictly above the straight line through $\bar{x}$ and $\varphi(S)$. Such a point $\bar{x}$ exists in view of PCONT. The proof is complete if $\varphi(T) \neq \varphi(S)$ for then we can take, for S', the game T smoothed off at $\varphi(S)$ and $\bar{x}$, in view of PCONT. Now suppose $\varphi(T) = \varphi(S)$. For every ε with $0 \leq \varepsilon \leq \varphi_1(S)$, let $S^\varepsilon \in \mathcal{C}_0$ be the game consisting of all points of S except those strictly above the straight line through $\bar{x}$ and the point $(\varphi_1(S) - \varepsilon, \varphi_2(S))$. Note that $S^0 = T$, so $\varphi(S^0) = \varphi(T) = \varphi(S) = D^2(S) = D^2(S^0)$. Now let $\bar{\varepsilon} := \sup\{\varepsilon \in [0, \varphi_1(S)]: \varphi(S^\varepsilon) = D^2(S^\varepsilon)\}$. By PCONT, $\varphi(S^{\bar{\varepsilon}}) = D^2(S^{\bar{\varepsilon}})$. If

$\bar{\varepsilon} = \varphi_1(S)$, then we are back in the case of the first paragraph of the proof (where we assumed $\varphi_1(S) = 0$). Otherwise, $0 \leq \bar{\varepsilon} < \varphi_1(S)$. Then take η with $\bar{\varepsilon} < \eta < \varphi_1(S)$ small enough to have $(D_2^2(S^\eta) >)\varphi_2(S^\eta) > z_2$. Take for S' the game S^η smoothed off at $D^2(S^\eta)$ and $\bar{x}$. $\qquad\square$

Lemma 5.14 *Let $\varphi : \mathcal{C}_0 \to I\!\!R^2$ be a 2-person bargaining solution with the properties IR, PO, STC, PCONT, and RA. Let $\mu \in \{\varphi^H : H \in \mathcal{H}^{\{1,2\}}\}$ be such that $\varphi(\Delta) = \mu(\Delta)$. Let $T \in \mathcal{C}_0$ be such that $P(T) \supset \text{conv}\{v, w\}$ where $v, w \in I\!\!R^2$ satisfy $v_1 + v_2 = w_1 + w_2 = \alpha > 0$, $v_2 < 0$, $w_1 < 0$. Then $\varphi(T) = \mu(T)$.*

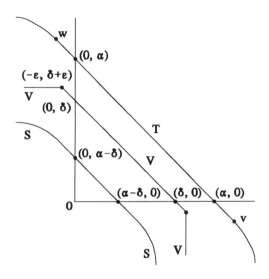

Figure 5.4: Proof of lemma 5.14

Proof (See figure 5.4.) By STC, $\varphi(\delta\Delta) = \mu(\delta\Delta)$ for every $\delta \in (0, \infty)$. Fix $\delta \in (0, \alpha)$. Fix $0 < \varepsilon < \min\{v_1 - \delta, w_2 - \delta, -v_2, -w_1\}$. Let $S \in \mathcal{C}_0$ be given by the following constraints:

$$\{x \in W(S) : x_1 \leq 0\} = \{(x_1 + \varepsilon, x_2 - \delta - \varepsilon) : x \in W(T), x_1 \leq -\varepsilon\},$$
$$\{x \in W(S) : x \geq 0\} = \{x \geq 0 : x_1 + x_2 = \alpha - \delta\},$$
$$\{x \in W(S) : x_2 \leq 0\} = \{(x_1 - \delta - \varepsilon, x_2 + \varepsilon) : x \in W(T), x_2 \leq -\varepsilon\}.$$

Let $V \in \mathcal{C}_0$ be given by $V := \text{comv}\{(\delta + \varepsilon, -\varepsilon), (-\varepsilon, \delta + \varepsilon)\}$. Then $V + S = T$. Note that V and S are smooth at every $x \in P(V) \cap I\!\!R_+^2$ and $y \in P(S) \cap I\!\!R_+^2$, and that all supporting lines at these points are parallel, with a normal vector $\lambda = (1, 1)$. In particular, $x + y \in P(T)$ for every $x \in P(V) \cap I\!\!R_+^2$, $y \in P(S) \cap I\!\!R_+^2$. So by PO, IR, and RA, $\varphi(T) = \varphi(S) + \varphi(V)$, hence $\varphi_1(V) \leq \varphi_1(T) \leq \varphi_1(V) + \alpha - \delta$ and $\varphi_2(V) \leq \varphi_2(T) \leq \varphi_2(V) + \alpha - \delta$. Letting ε approach 0 gives, by PCONT and the fact that $\varphi(\delta\Delta) = \mu(\delta\Delta)$, $\mu_1(\delta\Delta) \leq \varphi_1(T) \leq \mu_1(\delta\Delta) + \alpha - \delta$, $\mu_2(\delta\Delta) \leq \varphi_2(T) \leq \mu_2(\delta\Delta) + \alpha - \delta$. Letting δ approach α, we obtain $\varphi(T) = \mu(\alpha\Delta)$; hence, since by definition of $\mu : \mu(\alpha\Delta) = \mu(T)$, we have $\varphi(T) = \mu(T)$. $\qquad\square$

Proof of proposition 5.11 (See figure 5.5.) Let $\mu \in \{\varphi^H : H \in \mathcal{H}^{\{1,2\}}\}$ be the solution such that $\mu(\Delta) = \varphi(\Delta) = (t, 1-t)$. Suppose there exists an $S \in \mathcal{C}_0$ such that

$$\varphi(S) \neq \mu(S). \tag{5.4}$$

By PCONT of φ and μ we may suppose that S is smooth everywhere, and by lemma 5.13 (with $\mu(S)$ in the role of z), that the supporting line of S at $\varphi(S)$ has a strictly positive normal vector λ. By STC, we may further suppose that $\lambda = (1,1)$ and $\varphi_1(S) + \varphi_2(S) = 1$. Then, by lemma 2.20 and (5.4),

$$\varphi(S) \neq (t, 1-t). \tag{5.5}$$

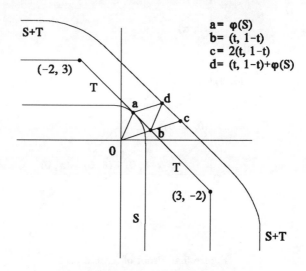

Figure 5.5: Proof of proposition 5.11

Let $T := \mathrm{comv}\{(3, -2), (-2, 3)\}$, then, by lemma 5.14 and $\mu(T) = (t, 1-t)$, we have

$$\varphi(T) = (t, 1-t). \tag{5.6}$$

Further, STC and lemma 5.14 applied to $S + T$, give

$$\varphi(S + T) = 2(t, 1-t). \tag{5.7}$$

On the other hand, since S is smooth at $\varphi(S)$, T is smooth at $(t, 1-t)$, and $\varphi(S) + (t, 1-t) \in P(S+T)$, we have by RA and (5.6)

$$\varphi(S + T) = \varphi(S) + (t, 1-t). \tag{5.8}$$

By combining (5.7) and (5.8) we obtain $\varphi(S) = (t, 1-t)$, in contradiction with (5.5). Hence (5.4) must be false, so $\varphi(S) = \mu(S)$ for all $S \in \mathcal{C}_0$. $\square$

With the proof of proposition 5.11 also the proof of theorem 5.9 is completed.

The following example shows that we cannot dispense with the Pareto continuity property in this theorem.

Example 5.15 We construct a solution $\varphi : \mathcal{C}_0 \to I\!\!R^2$ by first defining it for all games S with $h(S) = (1,1)$. By applying the appropriate scale transformations, the definition is then extended to $\mathcal{C}_0$,which guarantees that φ satisfies STC. So let $S \in \mathcal{C}_0$ with $h(S) = (1,1)$. We define $\varphi(S)$ as follows. If S is smooth at $\nu(S)$, then $\varphi(S) := \nu(S)$. If S is not smooth at $\nu(S)$, then also $\varphi(S) := \nu(S)$ except for the case that there exists exactly one other point $x \in P(S) \cap I\!\!R_+^2$ such that S is not smooth at x; in that case, $\varphi(S) := x$. It can be verified that this φ, besides STC, satisfies IR, PO, and RA, but not PCO. (Recall, that ν denotes the symmetric Nash bargaining solution: $\nu = N^{\frac{1}{2}} = \varphi^{<\{1,2\},(\frac{1}{2},\frac{1}{2})>}$.)

The smoothness condition in the definition of restrictive additivity cannot be dispensed with, either.

Example 5.16 Let $S := \text{com}\{(2,1)\}$. Then $\nu(\Delta + S) = (2,2) \neq (\frac{1}{2},\frac{1}{2}) + (2,1) = \nu(\Delta) + \nu(S) \in P(\Delta + S)$. Here Δ is smooth at $\nu(\Delta)$, but S is not smooth at $\nu(S)$.

As to the other axioms in theorem 5.9: without IR the solution assigning to each $S \in \mathcal{C}_0$ the Pareto optimal point with maximal first coordinate becomes possible, without PO the solution $E^{(1,0)}$, and without STC the lexicographic egalitarian solution L.

We conclude with two remarks.

Remark 5.17 The following link exists between the results in this section and those in section 5.4. For a solution $\varphi : \mathcal{C}_0 \to I\!\!R^2$ and $S, T \in \mathcal{C}_0$, say that RA *applies to* φ, S, *and* T if S and T are smooth at $\varphi(S)$ and $\varphi(T)$ respectively, and $\varphi(S) + \varphi(T) \in P(S + T)$. Then, as a consequence of lemmas 2.20 and 5.12, for every $0 < t < 1$, if RA applies to N^t, S, and T, we have $N^t(S) = E^p(S)$, $N^t(T) = E^p(T)$, and $N^t(S + T) = E^p(S + T)$ for some $p > 0$. In this sense, Nash solutions offer a compromise between proportional principles and utilitarian principles, where the latter refer to the maximization of weighted utilities expressed by lemma 2.20.

Remark 5.18 The main result of this section is related to the main result in Aumann (1985a), where an axiomatic characterization of the so-called Non-Transferable Utility value is given (cf. Shapley, 1969). Aumann uses a Conditional Additivity axiom, which is stronger than restricted additivity, in the sense that it does not require smoothness. However, Aumann restricts attention to smooth games where here we have the Pareto continuity property to take care of non-smoothness. See also chapter 10, in particular section 10.3.

Chapter 6

Risk properties

6.1 Introduction

Suppose a player in a bargaining game is replaced by a more risk averse player. Intuitively, in many situations one would expect this to be advantageous for the other players. Also, one might expect the more risk averse player to envy his (less risk averse) predecessor, because that player would probably get more out of the bargaining process. It is nevertheless surprising that bargaining solutions almost generically seem to confirm this intuition.

Replacing a player by a more risk averse player will be modelled by replacing that player's utility function in an underlying expected bargaining situation by a nondecreasing concave transformation of that utility function. This is based on theorem 11.11. For the behavior of bargaining solutions it makes an essential difference whether the solution outcome is obtained by an alternative in the set of riskless alternatives (usually denoted by A) or by a lottery in the lottery set $\mathcal{L}(A)$. Therefore, explicit consideration of expected utility bargaining situations (definition 1.2) is needed.

Axioms and preliminary results are given in section 6.2. The most regular behavior of solutions is observed when alternatives sustaining the solution outcome are always riskless, i.e., no proper lotteries. Some results for the opposite ("risky") case are discussed in section 6.4, the "riskless" case is treated in section 6.3. To some extent it is paradoxical that bargaining solutions are sensitive to risk even if solution outcomes are always sustained by riskless alternatives: this "paradox" and some related issues of strategic playing are discussed in section 6.5. Section 6.6 deals with a few special relations between risk behavior of a solution and other properties of that solution for a class of 2-person games.

6.2 Risk properties of bargaining solutions

Recall that an expected utility bargaining situation for the player set N is an $(n+2)$-tuple $\Gamma = < A, \bar{a}, u^1, \ldots, u^n >$ as defined in definition 1.2. Let $\mathcal{C}S^N$ denote the family of all such expected utility bargaining situations. As defined in section 1.3, with each $\Gamma \in \mathcal{C}S^N$ a bargaining game $(S_\Gamma, d_\Gamma) \in \mathcal{C}^N$ is associated. Throughout this chapter d_Γ will be assumed to be normalized to zero. Therefore, let $\mathcal{C}S_0^N$ denote the family of expected utility bargaining situations Γ as above with $u^i(\bar{a}) = 0$ for every $i \in N$. For $\Gamma \in \mathcal{C}S_0^N$, $S_\Gamma \in \mathcal{C}_0^N$.

For $\Gamma = <A, \overline{a}, u^1, \ldots, u^n> \in CS_0^N$ and $i \in N$, let $C^i(\Gamma)$ denote the family of all continuous nondecreasing concave functions $k : u^i(A) \to I\!R$ with $k(0) = 0$ and $k(\lambda) > 0$ for some $\lambda \in u^i(A)$. For $k^i \in C^i(\Gamma)$, the expected utility bargaining situation

$$k^i(\Gamma) := <A, \overline{a}, u^1, u^2, \ldots, u^{i-1}, k^i \circ u^i, u^{i+1}, \ldots, u^n>$$

is an element of CS_0^N. In view of theorem 11.11, we say that $k^i(\Gamma)$ arises from Γ by the replacement of player i by a more risk averse player.

What will be the effect on the outcome assigned by a bargaining solution if a player in an expected utility bargaining situation is replaced by a more risk averse player? Two possible effects are described in definitions 6.1 and 6.2 for a solution φ defined on a subclass $\mathcal{D}^N$ of $\mathcal{C}_0^N$. For $\Gamma = <A, \overline{a}, u^1, \ldots, u^n> \in CS_0^N$ we use the notation

$$\text{alt}(\varphi, \Gamma) := \{\ell \in \mathcal{L}(A) : Eu(\ell) = \varphi(S_\Gamma)\}$$

for the *set of φ-alternatives* of Γ. Recall from section 1.3 that $Eu(\ell)$ denotes the expected utility of the lottery ℓ under the n-tuple of utility functions $u = (u^1, u^2, \ldots, u^n)$.

Definition 6.1 Let $\varphi : \mathcal{D}^N \to I\!R^N$ be a solution and let $\mathcal{D}S^N \subset CS_0^N$ with $S_\Gamma \in \mathcal{D}^N$ for every $\Gamma \in \mathcal{D}S^N$. The solution φ is called *risk sensitive* (RS) *on* $\mathcal{D}S^N$ if, for each $i \in N$, $\Gamma \in \mathcal{D}S^N$, $k^i \in C^i(\Gamma)$ with $k^i(\Gamma) \in \mathcal{D}S^N$, we have $\varphi_j(S_{k^i(\Gamma)}) \geq \varphi_j(S_\Gamma)$ for all $j \in N\backslash\{i\}$.

If a solution is risk sensitive on a class of expected utility bargaining situations, then it is (weakly) advantageous for all opponents if a player in a bargaining situation in that class is replaced by a more risk averse player. Risk sensitivity was introduced by Kihlstrom, Roth, and Schmeidler (1981)[1].

Definition 6.2 Let $\varphi : \mathcal{D}^N \to I\!R^N$ be a solution and let $\mathcal{D}S^N \subset CS_0^N$ with $S_\Gamma \in \mathcal{D}^N$ for every $\Gamma \in \mathcal{D}S^N$. The solution φ has the *worse alternative property* (WA) *on* $\mathcal{D}S^N$ if, for each $i \in N$, $\Gamma \in \mathcal{D}S^N$, $k^i \in C^i(\Gamma)$ with $k^i(\Gamma) \in \mathcal{D}S^N$, $\ell \in \text{alt}(\varphi, \Gamma)$, $m \in \text{alt}(\varphi, k^i(\Gamma))$, we have $Eu^i(\ell) \geq Eu^i(m)$.

The worse alternative property claims that a bargainer does not prefer an alternative giving rise to the solution outcome of the game played by his more risk averse substitute to an alternative leading to the solution outcome of the game played by himself.

As remarked in the introductory section, the risk behavior of a solution depends heavily on whether or not the solution outcome may be sustained by a proper lottery in the underlying expected utility bargaining situation. Generally speaking, this behavior is more regular if the solution outcome can always be obtained by a riskless outcome. The subclass $\mathcal{P}S_0^N$ of CS_0^N ("$\mathcal{P}$" from "pure") is defined as

$$\mathcal{P}S_0^N := \{\Gamma = <A, \overline{a}, u^1, \ldots, u^n> \in CS_0^N : \text{ for every } x \in P(S_\Gamma)$$
$$\text{there is an } a \in A \text{ with } x = u(a)\}.$$

In order to illustrate concepts introduced so far, we proceed with two examples.

---

[1]Kannai (1977) already observed that the two-person Nash bargaining solution is risk sensitive.

Example 6.3 Let $\Gamma = < A, \bar{a}, u^1, u^2 > \in CS_0$ with $A = \{(1,0), (0,1), (0,0)\}$, $\bar{a} = (0,0)$, $u^1(\bar{a}) = u^2(\bar{a}) = 0$, $u^1((0,1)) = u^2((1,0)) = 0$, and $u^1((1,0)) = u^2((0,1)) = 1$. This may describe a situation where two players bargain over who gets the one unit of an indivisible good, say a closed bottle of wine. Note that $\Gamma \notin PS_0$. Let $k^2 \in C^2(\Gamma)$, $k^2(t) := \sqrt{t}$ for all $t \in u^2(A)$. Then $S_\Gamma = S_{k^2(\Gamma)} = \text{comv}\{(0,0), (1,0), (0,1)\}$, $\varphi_1(S_\Gamma) = \varphi_1(S_{k^2(\Gamma)})$, $\text{alt}(\varphi, \Gamma) = \text{alt}(\varphi, k^2(\Gamma))$, $Eu^1(\ell) = Eu^1(m)$ for all $\ell, m \in \text{alt}(\varphi, \Gamma)$; all of this holds for any bargaining solution $\varphi : C_0 \to I\!R^2$.

Example 6.4 Let $\Gamma = < A, \bar{a}, u^1, u^2 > \in CS_0$ with $A = \{(0,0)\} \cup \{(x, 1-x) : 0 \le x \le 1\}$, $\bar{a} = (0,0)$, $u^1(\bar{a}) = u^2(\bar{a}) = 0$, and $u^1((x, 1-x)) = u^2((1-x, x)) = x$ for every $0 \le x \le 1$. This corresponds to a situation in which two bargainers have to agree on the division of one unit of a perfectly divisible good, say an open bottle of wine. Now $\Gamma \in PS_0$. Let $k^2 \in C^2(\Gamma)$, $k^2(t) := \sqrt{t}$ for all $t \in u^2(A)$. Then $S_\Gamma = \text{comv}\{(1-t, t) : 0 \le t \le 1\}$ and $S_{k^2(\Gamma)} = \text{comv}\{(1-\lambda, \sqrt{\lambda}): 0 \le \lambda \le 1\}$. Let $\rho : C_0 \to I\!R^2$ be the Raiffa-Kalai-Smorodinsky solution, then $\rho(S_\Gamma) = (\frac{1}{2}, \frac{1}{2})$, $\rho(S_{k^2(\Gamma)}) = (\frac{1}{2}\sqrt{5} - \frac{1}{2}, \frac{1}{2}\sqrt{5} - \frac{1}{2})$, $\text{alt}(\rho, k^2(\Gamma)) = \{(\frac{1}{2}\sqrt{5} - \frac{1}{2}, \frac{3}{2} - \frac{1}{2}\sqrt{5})\}$. So $\rho_1(S_\Gamma) < \rho_1(S_{k^2(\Gamma)})$, $\frac{1}{2} = Eu^2(\ell) > \frac{3}{2} - \frac{1}{2}\sqrt{5} = u^2((\frac{1}{2}\sqrt{5} - \frac{1}{2}, \frac{3}{2} - \frac{1}{2}\sqrt{5}))$ for all $\ell \in \text{alt}(\rho, \Gamma)$. Also note that $(\frac{1}{2}; (1,0), \frac{1}{2}; (0,1)) \in \text{alt}(\rho, \Gamma)$, and $E(k^2 \circ u^2)((\frac{1}{2}; (1,0), \frac{1}{2}; (0,1))) = \frac{1}{2} < \frac{1}{2}\sqrt{5} - \frac{1}{2} = k^2 \circ u^2((\frac{1}{2}\sqrt{5} - \frac{1}{2}, \frac{3}{2} - \frac{1}{2}\sqrt{5}))$; that is, the more risk averse player 2, in $k^2(\Gamma)$, prefers the alternative obtained by him (the unique element of $\text{alt}(\rho, k^2(\Gamma))$), to at least one element of $\text{alt}(\rho, \Gamma)$, which is the set of alternatives giving rise to the solution outcome obtained by the less risk averse player 2 in Γ.

These examples indicate, first, that it makes all the difference which bargaining situation is though to underlay a specific bargaining game when we study risk properties of bargaining solutions; second, that a property similar to the WA property formulated for the more risk averse player would not always be satisfied. As to the latter remark: it may from the point of view of the more risk averse player actually be advantageous to be — openly — more risk averse, depending on which alternative will be picked out to realize the solution outcome. Section 6.5 deals with some related questions of a strategical nature.

The following lemma states that bargaining situations in PS_0^N "behave nicely" under transformations k^i in $C^i(\Gamma)$.

Lemma 6.5 *Let* $\Gamma = < A, \bar{a}, u^1, \ldots, u^n > \in PS_0^N$, $i \in N$, $k^i \in C^i(\Gamma)$. *For* $x \in P(S_\Gamma)$ *let* $\hat{x}$ *denote the point with i th coordinate equal to $k^i(x_i)$ and j th coordinate equal to x_j for all $j \ne i$. Let* $\hat{P} := \{\hat{x} : x \in P(S_\Gamma)\}$. *Then* $S_{k^i(\Gamma)} = \text{com}(\hat{P})$ *and* $P(S_{k^i(\Gamma)}) \subset \hat{P}$.

Proof The equality follows from the inclusion. To prove the inclusion, let $x \in P(S_{k^i(\Gamma)})$, say $i = 1$ and $x = (Ek^1 \circ u^1(\ell), Eu^2(\ell), \ldots, Eu^n(\ell))$ where $\ell \in \mathcal{L}(A)$. Since $\Gamma \in PS_0^N$ there exists an $a \in A$ with $u(a) \in P(S_\Gamma)$ and $u^i(a) \ge Eu^i(\ell)$ for all $i \in N$. As a consequence of theorem 11.6, $k^1 \circ u^1(a) \ge Ek^1 \circ u^1(\ell)$. Hence $x \le (k^1 \circ u^1(a), u^2(a), \ldots, u^n(a))$. Because $x \in P(S_{k^i(\Gamma)})$, this implies $x = (k^1 \circ u^1(a), u^2(a), \ldots, u^n(a)) \in \hat{P}$. □

The remainder of this section is devoted to establishing some relations between risk properties of bargaining solutions in general. The first result states that risk sensitivity implies the worse alternative property for Pareto optimal solutions.

Lemma 6.6 *Let $\mathcal{D}^N \subset \mathcal{C}_0^N$, φ a solution on $\mathcal{D}^N$, and $\mathcal{D}S^N \subset \mathcal{C}S_0^N$ with $S_\Gamma \in \mathcal{D}^N$ for every $\Gamma \in \mathcal{D}S^N$. Let φ be Pareto optimal and risk sensitive on $\mathcal{D}S^N$. Then φ has the worse alternative property on $\mathcal{D}S^N$.*

Proof Let $\Gamma = < A, \bar{a}, u^1, \ldots, u^n > \in \mathcal{D}S^N$, $i \in N$, $k^i \in C^i(\Gamma)$ with $k^i(\Gamma) \in \mathcal{D}S^N$, $\ell \in \mathrm{alt}(\varphi, \Gamma)$, $m \in \mathrm{alt}(\varphi, k^i(\Gamma))$. By RS, $Eu^j(m) \geq Eu^j(\ell)$ for all $j \neq i$. So by PO of φ, $Eu^i(\ell) \geq Eu^i(m)$. $\qquad\square$

The converse of lemma 6.6 in general does not hold. For instance, for $n > 2$, the symmetric Nash bargaining solution ν has the worse alternative property on $\mathcal{P}S_0^N$ but is not risk sensitive on that class; see section 6.3, in particular example 6.13.

If we do not restrict attention to $\mathcal{P}S_0^N$, then no "reasonable" bargaining solution exists which is risk sensitive or has the worse alternative property. Specifically, we have the following theorem.

Theorem 6.7 *Let $\varphi : \mathcal{C}_0^N \to I\!\!R^N$ be a bargaining solution. If φ is weakly Pareto optimal and individually rational then φ is not risk sensitive and does not have the worse alternative property on $\mathcal{C}S_0^N$.*

Proof Let φ satisfy the conditions of the theorem. Define $\Gamma = < A, \bar{a}, u^1, \ldots, u^n >$ as follows: $A := \{a^1, a^2, \ldots, a^n\}$; $u^i(\bar{a}) := 0$ for all $i \in N$; $u^i(a^j) := -1$ for all $i \neq j \in N$; $u^i(a^i) := n$ for all $i \in N$. For all $i, j \in N$ define $x_j^i := u^i(a^j)$. Then $\Gamma \in \mathcal{C}S_0^N$, $d_\Gamma = 0$, $S_\Gamma = \mathrm{comv}\{x^i : i \in N\}$, $P(S_\Gamma) = W(S_\Gamma) = \mathrm{conv}\{x^i : i \in N\}$. Suppose φ is risk sensitive. Let $\ell \in N$. We will prove that $\varphi(S_\Gamma) = e^\ell$. Suppose not, then IR implies that there exists some $h \in N$, $h \neq \ell$, such that $\varphi_h(S_\Gamma) =: \alpha > 0$. Let $k^\ell \in C^\ell(\Gamma)$ be defined by:

$$k^\ell(t) := t \text{ for all } t \in (-\infty, o], \quad k^\ell(n) := \frac{2n - 2 + \alpha}{4 - \alpha},$$

k^ℓ is linear on $[0, \infty)$.

Observe that k^ℓ is concave since $\alpha \leq 1$. Then $d_{k^\ell(\Gamma)} = 0$, $S_{k^\ell(\Gamma)} = \mathrm{comv}\{y^i : i \in N\}$ and $W(S_{k^\ell(\Gamma)}) = P(S_{k^\ell(\Gamma)}) = \mathrm{conv}\{y^i : i \in N\}$ where $y^i := x^i$ if $i \neq \ell$, $y_j^i := -1$ if $j \neq \ell$, $y_\ell^\ell = (2n - 2 + \alpha)/(4 - \alpha)$. The hyperplane containing $W(S_{k^\ell(\Gamma)})$ is given by the equation

$$2 \sum_{j \neq \ell} z_j + (4 - \alpha) z_\ell = \alpha.$$

This implies that points in $W(S_{k^\ell(\Gamma)}) \cap I\!\!R_+^N$ have maximal h [th] coordinate equal to $\frac{1}{2}\alpha$. In particular, $\varphi_h(S_{k^\ell(\Gamma)}) \leq \frac{1}{2}\alpha$. On the other hand, risk sensitivity of φ implies $\varphi_h(S_{k^\ell(\Gamma)}) \geq \varphi_h(S_\Gamma) = \alpha > \frac{1}{2}\alpha$. This contradiction implies $\varphi(S_\Gamma) = e^\ell$. Since $\ell \in N$ was chosen arbitrarily, $\varphi(S_\Gamma) = e^i$ for every $i \in N$, an obvious impossibility. Therefore φ cannot be risk sensitive. The same example can be used to show that φ does not have the worse alternative property. $\qquad\square$

Because of this "impossibility result", in the remainder of this section attention is confined to the class $\mathcal{P}S_0^N$. The next theorem characterizes the worse alternative property. Recall from section 2.3 the notation

$$(T, \varphi)_M := \{x_M : x \in T, \ x_{N \setminus M} = \varphi_{N \setminus M}(T)\},$$

for a bargaining game T and a solution φ.

Theorem 6.8 *Let* $\varphi : C_0^N \to I\!\!R^N$ *be a Pareto optimal bargaining solution. Then the following two statements are equivalent.*

(i) φ *has the worse alternative property on* PS_0^N.

(ii) *For every* $\Gamma \in PS_0^N$, $i \in N$, $k^i \in C^i(\Gamma)$:

$$(S_\Gamma, \varphi)_{N \setminus \{i\}} \subset (S_{k^i(\Gamma)}, \varphi)_{N \setminus \{i\}}.$$

Proof Suppose φ satisfies WA on PS_0^N. Let $\Gamma = \langle A, \bar{a}, u^1, \ldots, u^n \rangle \in PS_0^N$, $i \in N$, $k^i \in C^i(\Gamma)$, and take $a, b \in A$ with $a \in \mathrm{alt}(\varphi, \Gamma)$, $b \in \mathrm{alt}(\varphi, k^i(\Gamma))$. Such a and b exist since $\Gamma \in PS_0^N$, φ is Pareto optimal, and by lemma 6.5. By WA, $u^i(a) \geq u^i(b)$. By PO of φ and lemma 6.5, $u(a)$ and $u(b)$ are both in $P(S_\Gamma)$. Therefore, $(S_\Gamma, \varphi)_{N \setminus \{i\}} = \{x_{N \setminus \{i\}} : x \in S_\Gamma, x_i = u^i(a)\} \subset \{x_{N \setminus \{i\}} : x \in S_\Gamma, x_i = u^i(b)\} = (S_{k^i(\Gamma)}, \varphi)_{N \setminus \{i\}}$. The implication (ii) $\Rightarrow$ (i) follows by reversing this argument. $\square$

The following definition is inspired by the equivalence in theorem 6.8.

Definition 6.9 Let $\varphi : D^N \to I\!\!R^N$ be a solution and let $DS^N \subset CS_0^N$ with $S_\Gamma \in D^N$ for every $\Gamma \in DS^N$. The solution φ has the *risk profit opportunity property* (RPO) *on* DS^N if, for each $i \in N$, $\Gamma \in DS^N$, $k^i \in C^i(\Gamma)$ with $k^i(\Gamma) \in DS^N$, we have $(S_\Gamma, \varphi)_{N \setminus \{i\}} \subset (S_{k^i(\Gamma)}, \varphi)_{N \setminus \{i\}}$.

Thus, if a solution has the risk profit opportunity property, then the set of utility $(n-1)$-tuples in an n-person bargaining game S, available for the players $j \neq i$ if player i receives $\varphi_i(S)$, does not decrease if player i is replaced by a more risk averse player. A further explanation of the expression "risk profit opportunity" is given by the observation that (with notations as in definition 6.9), if φ is Pareto optimal, then $(S_\Gamma, \varphi)_{N \setminus \{i\}} \subset (S_{k^i(\Gamma)}, \varphi)_{N \setminus \{i\}}$ implies either $\varphi_j(S_\Gamma) = \varphi_j(S_{k^i(\Gamma)})$ for all $j \neq i$, or $\varphi_j(S_\Gamma) < \varphi_j(S_{k^i(\Gamma)})$ for at least one $j \neq i$.

An immediate consequence of theorem 6.8 for Pareto optimal solutions is that on $PS_0^{\{1,2\}}$ the worse alternative and risk profit opportunity properties are equivalent to risk sensitivity.

This section is concluded by a theorem showing that for a Pareto optimal and consistent solution the risk profit opportunity (or worse alternative) property on PS_0^N implies scale transformation covariance. The consistency axiom (CONS) was introduced in section 2.3; for $n = 2$, it is implied by Pareto optimality. For that case, the following theorem was proved by Kihlstrom, Roth, and Schmeidler (1981). For the general case, it corresponds to Theorem 1.2 in Peters and Tijs (1985b).

Theorem 6.10 *Let* $\varphi : C_0^N \to I\!\!R^N$ *be a consistent and Pareto optimal bargaining solution which has the risk profit opportunity property on* PS_0^N. *Then* φ *is scale transformation covariant.*

Proof Let $S \in C_0^N$, $k \in I\!\!R_{++}^N$. Let $\Gamma := \langle S, 0, \mathrm{pr}^1, \ldots, \mathrm{pr}^n \rangle$, cf. subsection 1.3.1. Then $\Gamma \in PS_0^N$, $S = S_\Gamma$. Denote by $k^i \in C^i(\Gamma)$ multiplication by k_i. Since also the inverse function of k^i, i.e., dividing by k_i, is in $C^i(\Gamma)$, we have by double application of RPO:

$$(S_\Gamma, \varphi)_{N \setminus \{i\}} = (S_{k^i(\Gamma)}, \varphi)_{N \setminus \{i\}} \text{ for every } i \in N. \tag{6.1}$$

The linearity of k^i, (6.1), and PO imply $[k_i \varphi_i(S_\Gamma) =] k^i(\varphi_i(S_\Gamma)) = \varphi_i(S_{k^i(\Gamma)})$ for every $i \in N$, hence

$$k_i \varphi_i(S_\Gamma) = \varphi_i((1, \ldots, 1, k_i, 1, \ldots, 1)S_\Gamma) \text{ for every } i \in N. \tag{6.2}$$

From (6.1), (6.2), and CONS of φ, we obtain $k_1 \varphi_1(S_\Gamma) = \varphi_1((k_1, 1, \ldots, 1)S_\Gamma)$ and $\varphi_j(S_\Gamma) = \varphi_j((k_1, 1, \ldots, 1)S_\Gamma)$ for all $j \neq 1$. Repeating this argument $(n-1)$ times, it follows that $k\varphi(S) = k\varphi(S_\Gamma) = \varphi(kS_\Gamma) = \varphi(kS)$, thus proving STC of φ. $\quad\square$

Remark 6.11 By a small modification of the proof of theorem 6.10, it follows that CONS and RPO may be replaced by one property: risk sensitivity.

6.3   Risk properties, independence of irrelevant alternatives, individual monotonicity

This section deals with the risk behavior of bargaining solutions possessing special properties, viz. independence of irrelevant alternatives or individual monotonicity. This will enable us to draw conclusions concerning the risk behavior of many solutions studied hitherto, in particular in chapters 2 and 4. Attention is restricted to the "riskless" case, i.e., expected utility bargaining situations in $\mathcal{P}S_0^N$.

We start with the following theorem concerning IIA solutions.

Theorem 6.12 *Let* $\varphi : C_0^N \to \mathbb{R}^N$ *be a bargaining solution satisfying IR, PO, STC, and IIA. Then* φ *has the risk profit opportunity property on* $\mathcal{P}S_0^N$.

Proof Let $\Gamma \in \mathcal{P}S_0^N$, $i \in N$, $k^i \in C^i(\Gamma)$. Let $z := \varphi(S_\Gamma), \hat{z} := \varphi(S_{k^i(\Gamma)})$. We will prove

$$(S_\Gamma, \varphi)_{N \setminus \{i\}} \subset (S_{k^i(\Gamma)}, \varphi)_{N \setminus \{i\}}. \tag{6.3}$$

First suppose that $\hat{z}_i = 0$. Then $(S_{k^i(\Gamma)}, \varphi)_{N \setminus \{i\}} = \{x_{N \setminus \{i\}} \in \mathbb{R}^{N \setminus \{i\}} : x \in S_\Gamma \text{ with } x_i = 0\}$ by lemma 6.5, so (6.3) follows. Next suppose $\hat{z}_i > 0$. By lemma 6.5 there is a (unique) point y in $P(S_\Gamma)$ with $y_j = \hat{z}_j$ for every $j \in N \setminus \{i\}$. By STC we may suppose

$$\hat{z}_i = k^i(y_i) = y_i, \quad \hat{z} = y. \tag{6.4}$$

The concavity of k^i, (6.4), and $k^i(0) = 0$ imply for all λ in the domain of k^i:

$$k^i(\lambda) \geq \lambda \text{ if } \lambda \in [0, y_i], \quad k^i(\lambda) \leq \lambda \text{ if } \lambda \geq y_i. \tag{6.5}$$

Suppose that $\hat{z}_i > z_i (\geq 0)$ and let $T := \text{comv}\{z, \hat{z}, \alpha e^N\}$ where $\alpha \in \mathbb{R}_{++}$ is so small that $\alpha e^N \in S_\Gamma \cap S_{k^i(\Gamma)}$. Then $T \in C_0^N$, $T \subset S_\Gamma$ since $\hat{z} \in S_\Gamma$ by (6.4), $T \subset S_{k^i(\Gamma)}$ since $z \in S_{k^i(\Gamma)}$ by (6.5). So by IIA, $\varphi(T) = z = \hat{z}$, contradicting our assumption $\hat{z}_i > z_i$. Hence, $\hat{z}_i \leq z_i$. Together with (6.4) and lemma 6.5 this implies (6.3). $\quad\square$

This result applies in particular to all solutions φ^H for some weighted hierarchy $H \in \mathcal{H}^N$, see theorem 2.32. So all solutions φ^H have the risk profit opportunity property and therefore (theorem 6.8) the worse alternative property on $\mathcal{P}S_0^N$; that is, for expected utility bargaining situations where all Pareto optimal points can be obtained by riskless alternatives. If $n = 2$ then the solutions φ^H are also risk sensitive on $\mathcal{P}S_0^N$, cf. the remark following definition 6.9. For $n > 2$, this is no longer true, as the following example shows.

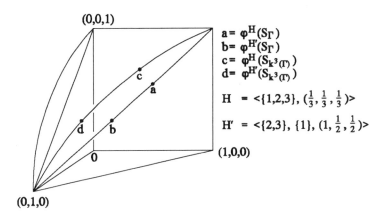

$$a = \varphi^H(S_\Gamma)$$
$$b = \varphi^{H'}(S_\Gamma)$$
$$c = \varphi^H(S_{k^3(\Gamma)})$$
$$d = \varphi^{H'}(S_{k^3(\Gamma)})$$

$$H = <\{1,2,3\}, (\tfrac{1}{3}, \tfrac{1}{3}, \tfrac{1}{3})>$$

$$H' = <\{2,3\}, \{1\}, (1, \tfrac{1}{2}, \tfrac{1}{2})>$$

Figure 6.1: Example 6.13

Example 6.13 (See figure 6.1.) Let $N = \{1,2,3\}$ and $\Gamma \in \mathcal{P}S_0^N$ be such that $S_\Gamma = S$ where

$$S := \text{comv}\{(1,0,0),(0,1,0),(0,0,1),(1,0,1)\}.$$

Then $P(S) = \text{conv}\{(0,1,0),(1,0,1)\}$. Let $k^3 \in C^3(\Gamma)$ be defined by $k^3(\lambda) = \sqrt{\lambda}$ for all $\lambda \in [0,1]$. Then $P(S_{k^3(\Gamma)}) = \{(\alpha, 1-\alpha, \sqrt{\alpha}) : \alpha \in [0,1]\}$.

(i) Let $H = < \{1,2,3\}, \omega > \in \mathcal{H}^N$. Straightforward calculations show: $\omega_1 + \omega_3 = \varphi_1^H(S_\Gamma) > \varphi_1^H(S_{k^3(\Gamma)}) = (2\omega_1 + \omega_3)(2 - \omega_3)^{-1}$, so φ^H is not risk sensitive on $\mathcal{P}S_0^N$.

(ii) Let $H' = < \{2,3\}, \{1\}, \omega > \in \mathcal{H}^N$, so $\omega > 0$, $\omega_2 + \omega_3 = 1$, $\omega_1 = 1$. Again, straightforward calculations show: $\omega_3 = \varphi_1^{H'}(S_\Gamma) > \varphi_1^{H'}(S_{k^3(\Gamma)}) = \omega_3(1 + \omega_2)^{-1}$, so also $\varphi^{H'}$ is not risk sensitive on $\mathcal{P}S_0^N$.

Example 6.13 is used in the proof of the following theorem, which characterizes the solutions φ^H that are risk sensitive on $\mathcal{P}S_0^N$.

Theorem 6.14 *Let* $H \in \mathcal{H}^N$. *The following two statements are equivalent.*

(i) φ^H *is risk sensitive on* $\mathcal{P}S_0^N$.

(ii) There is a permutation π *of* N *such that either*

$$H = < \{\pi(1)\}, \{\pi(2)\}, \dots, \{\pi(n)\}, e^N >$$

or

$$H = < \{\pi(1)\}, \{\pi(2)\}, \dots, \{\pi(n-2)\}, \{\pi(n-1), \pi(n)\}, \omega >.$$

Proof We first show the implication (ii) $\Rightarrow$ (i). Let $\Gamma \in \mathcal{P}S_0^N$. Let π be a permutation of N. If $H = < \{\pi(1)\}, \{\pi(2)\}, \dots, \{\pi(n)\}, e^N >$, then, if a player (say) $\pi(i)$ for $i \in N$, is replaced by a more risk averse player, by definition of φ^H the solution changes only (possibly) for player $\pi(i)$. So φ^H is risk sensitive on $\mathcal{P}S_0^N$. If $H = < \{\pi(1)\}, \dots, \{\pi(n-2)\}, \{\pi(n-$

$1), \pi(n)\}, \omega >$, then, if a player $\pi(i)$ with $i \leq n - 2$ is replaced by a more risk averse player then the solution outcome assigned by φ^H changes only (possibly) for player $\pi(i)$. If player $\pi(n-1)$ $[\pi(n)]$ is replaced by a more risk averse player, then the solution outcome does not change for all players $\pi(j)$ with $j \leq n - 2$, and changes for player $\pi(n)$ $[\pi(n-1)]$ only to that player's advantage. This last fact is a consequence of the risk sensitivity of 2-person nonsymmetric Nash solutions, see the remark before example 6.13. So also this φ^H is risk sensitive on PS_0^N.

Next, we prove the implication (i) $\Rightarrow$ (ii). Suppose that H is not as in (ii). Let $H = < N^1, N^2, \ldots, N^\ell, \omega >$. The assumption that H is not as in (ii) implies that either

Case 1: Some class N^h $(1 \leq h \leq \ell)$ contains at least three players

or

Case 2: Each class contains at most two players, and some class N^h $(1 \leq h < \ell)$ contains exactly two players.

First, suppose that H is as in case 1. We may suppose w.l.o.g. that 1, 2, and 3 are in N^h. Let S, Γ and k^3 be as in example 6.13, and let $T := \text{com}(E^N(S))$. Then $P(T) = \{E^N(z) : z \in P(S)\}$. The same calculation as in example 6.13 (i) shows that $\varphi_1^H(T) > \varphi_1^H(\text{com}(E^N(S_{k^3(\Gamma)})))$, which can be seen to imply that φ^H is not risk sensitive on PS_0^N, e.g., by looking at underlying expected utility bargaining situations as described following definition 1.2. Similarly, example 6.13 (ii) can be used to show that also in case 2, φ^H is not risk sensitive on PS_0^N.   □

Nielsen (1984) shows that the 3-person (symmetric) Nash bargaining solution (the solution φ^H with $H = < \{1,2,3\}, (\frac{1}{3}, \frac{1}{3}, \frac{1}{3}) >$) is not risk sensitive on PS_0^N but does have some property like the worse alternative property. He also shows that the n-person Raiffa-Kalai-Smorodinsky solution ρ (sections 4.2, 4.3) is risk sensitive on $\{\Gamma \in PS_0^N : S_\Gamma \in I^N\}$. We will show, more generally, that every Pareto optimal, scale transformation covariant and individually monotonic solution on I^N as characterized in theorem 4.12 is risk sensitive on $\{\Gamma \in PS_0^N : S_\Gamma \in I^N\}$.

Theorem 6.15 Let $\varphi : I^N \to \mathbb{R}^N$ be a bargaining solution satisfying PO, STC, and IM. Then φ is risk sensitive on $\{\Gamma \in PS_0^N : S_\Gamma \in I^N\}$.

Proof Let $\Gamma \in PS_0^N$ with $S_\Gamma \in I^N$, and (say) $k^1 \in C^1(\Gamma)$. By STC and lemma 6.5 it is without loss of generality to assume that $k^1(h_1(S_\Gamma)) = h_1(S_\Gamma)$. The concavity of k^1 and $k^1(0) = 0$ imply that $k^1(t) \geq t$ for all $t \in [0, h_1(S_\Gamma)]$. By lemmas 4.6 and 6.5, $h(S_\Gamma) = h(S_{k^1(\Gamma)})$, and IM, we obtain $\varphi(S_\Gamma) \leq \varphi(S_{k^1(\Gamma)})$, implying RS of φ.   □

Of the main other solutions occurring in the first five chapters, the Perles-Maschler solution defined in section 5.2 is risk sensitive on the class $\{\Gamma \in PS_0^N : S_\Gamma \in C_*\}$, as was shown by Kihlstrom, Roth, and Schmeidler (1981). As to the proportional solutions E^p (e.g., theorem 4.30), except for the "extreme" elements $E^{e^i}(i \in N)$ these solutions are not risk sensitive and do not have the worse alternative or risk profit opportunity property on PS_0^N. We leave this for the reader to prove. In light of theorem 6.10 and remark 6.11, the mentioned observations are not surprising — although in their forms as stated this theorem and remark do not apply directly. In other words, scale transformation noncovariant solutions do in general not behave regularly under changes in the risk attitudes of the players.

6.4   Risk behavior in "risky" situations

If not all Pareto optimal outcomes in a bargaining game derived from a specific expected utility bargaining situation correspond to riskless alternatives, then the effects on a bargaining solution outcome caused by the changing risk attitude of a player may be quite irregular. This is already suggested by theorem 6.7, and for this reason until now attention has been restricted to bargaining situations in PS_0^N, the class of expected utility bargaining situations where all Pareto optimal outcomes in the corresponding games can be obtained by riskless alternatives. To some extent it seems paradoxical that the intuitively expected effects of a changing risk attitude are observed if the "physical" alternative sustaining the utility outcome is riskless; the next section contains a more extensive discussion of this "paradox".

In this section a few results are reviewed pertaining to situations where solution outcome alternatives may be risky. The first result is due to Wakker *et al.* (1985) and holds for the 2-person case. It says, roughly, that if all Pareto optimal outcomes are nonnegative (i.e., weakly dominate the disagreement outcome) then it does not matter much whether the underlying alternatives are riskless or risky. In order to state this result in a precise way, denote by C_+S_0 the family $\{\Gamma \in CS_0^{\{1,2\}} : P(S_\Gamma) \subset I\!R_+^2\}$.

Theorem 6.16 *Let* $\varphi : \{S_\Gamma : \Gamma \in C_+S_0\} \to I\!R^2$ *be risk sensitive on* $PS_0 \cap C_+S_0$. *Then* φ *is risk sensitive on* C_+S_0.

The proof of this theorem is a bit technical; the reader is referred to Wakker *et al.* (1985). In combination with the theorems of the preceding section some results for IIA and IM solutions can be derived.

The second result is based on Roth and Rothblum (1982). Let $\Gamma =< A, \overline{a}, u^1, u^2 > \in CS_0^{\{1,2\}}$. Call $x \in S_\Gamma$ *u-supported* by $a^1, a^2 \in A$ if $x = \hat{t}u(a^1) + (1 - \hat{t})u(a^2)$ for some $0 < \hat{t} < 1$ and for no $0 < t < 1$ there is an $a \in A$ with $u(a) = tu(a^1) + (1 - t)u(a^2)$, $u(a) \neq u(a^1)$. In other words, x is the pair of expected utilities corresponding to some lottery $(t; a^1, (1 - t); a^2)$ and it cannot be achieved by lotteries between riskless alternatives which are "closer". If $x \in S_\Gamma$ is u-supported by a^1 and a^2, it is called *favorably u-supported for player i* if $u^i(a^1) \geq 0$ and $u^i(a^2) \geq 0$; otherwise, it is called *unfavorably u-supported*. Roth and Rothblum obtain the following result for the (symmetric, 2-person) Nash bargaining solution ν.

Theorem 6.17 *Let* $\Gamma =< A, \overline{a}, u^1, u^2 > \in CS_0^{\{1,2\}}$, *and let* $k^2 \in C^2(\Gamma)$.

(i) If $\nu(S_\Gamma)$ *is favorably u-supported for player 2, then* $\nu_1(S_\Gamma) \leq \nu_1(S_{k^2(\Gamma)})$.

(ii) If $\nu(S_{k^2(\Gamma)})$ *is unfavorably u-supported for player 2, then* $\nu_1(S_\Gamma) > \nu_1(S_{k^2(\Gamma)})$.

Part (i) of this theorem (for the proof of which we refer to the article of Roth and Rothblum) is what we would obtain if ν were risk sensitive. Part (ii) goes in the opposite direction.

Observe that the theorem is not exhaustive since the condition in (i) refers to the situation with the less risk averse player 2 and the condition in (ii) to the situation with the more risk averse player 2. Also note that in case (ii) player 1 is worse off when bargaining against a more risk averse opponent. Roth and Rothblum (1982, p. 639) explain this as follows: "Intuitively, for bargaining games in which potential agreements involve lotteries having a positive probability of leaving one of the bargainers worse off than if a disagreement had occurred, the more risk averse a player, the better the terms of the agreement which he must be offered in order to induce him to reach an agreement". Of course, with such an explanation one should keep in mind that no explicit bargaining procedure is specified.

We finally mention the article by Safra *et al.* (1990). This work is concerned with the behavior of the Nash bargaining solution in situations where the disagreement outcome $\bar{a}$ itself may be risky, i.e., a nontrivial lottery. Like in the Roth-Rothblum result, what happens depends on the relative positions of the riskless alternatives supporting the relevant lotteries, i.e., the solution lottery and the disagreement lottery. For details see the mentioned article.

6.5 Improvement sensitivity of bargaining solutions

Suppose φ is a 2-person bargaining solution which has the worse alternative property on PS_0, the class of 2-person expected utility bargaining situations where all Pareto optimal points in the corresponding bargaining games can be sustained by riskless alternatives. Suppose furthermore that a solution outcome is always achieved by a riskless alternative, even if nontrivial lotteries are available for this. In that case, both a bargainer and his more risk averse substitute prefer a solution alternative obtained by that bargainer to the alternative obtained by his more risk averse substitute. This follows from the worse alternative property and the fact that both players (the original bargainer and the more risk averse substitute) order the riskless alternatives in the same way. Thus, it is paradoxical that this effect should occur even if there is no real risk involved.

The question arises whether this effect can be explained in a different way. In this section we propose such a way based on the "improving faster than" criterion which is developed in section 11.4. Let A be a nonempty set of alternatives, and let u, v be real-valued functions on A. We assume u and v to be value functions representing strength of preference relations and preference relations as in section 11.4. The function v is *improving faster than* u (*v* IF *u*) if and only if $u(c) - u(d) \geq u(a) - u(b)$ implies $v(c) - v(d) \geq v(a) - v(b)$ for all $a, b, c, d \in A$ with $u(a) \geq u(b) \geq u(c) \geq u(d)$, cf. formula (11.8). In other words, for v compared to u, marginal values are relatively higher for lower preferred alternatives and lower for higher preferred alternatives. In theorem 11.13 it is proved that, if $u(A)$ is an interval, then v is improving faster than u if and only if there exists a nondecreasing concave function $k : u(A) \rightarrow I\!\!R$ with $v = k \circ u$. Thus, the improving-faster-than criterion parallels the more-risk-averse-than criterion. Intuitively, one may expect a player with a fastly improving value function to be more easily satisfied and therefore perhaps less persistent at the bargaining table. In order to formalize this intuition, define a *value function bargaining situation for N* as an $(n + 2)$-tuple.

$$\Gamma := <A, \bar{a}, u^1, u^2, \ldots, u^n>$$

where A is a nonempty compact and convex subset of $I\!\!R^k$ for some natural number k;

$\overline{a} \in A$; for each $i \in N$, $u^i : A \to I\!\!R$ is a concave, continuous function with $u^i(\overline{a}) = 0$; and there is an $a \in A$ with $u^i(a) > 0$ for each $i \in N$. Denote the class of all such situations by $\mathcal{V}S_0^N$. For $\Gamma \in \mathcal{V}S_0^N$ as above, let

$$S_\Gamma := \{x \in I\!\!R^N : x \leq u(a) \text{ for some } a \in A\}$$

where $u(a) := (u^1(a), \dots, u^n(a))$. Then $S_\Gamma \in C_0^N$. Also, for every $S \in C_0^N$ there is a $\Gamma \in \mathcal{V}S_0^N$ with $S = S_\Gamma$; this can be shown in a similar fashion as in subsection 1.3.1 for expected utility bargaining situations.

Definition 6.18 Let $\mathcal{D}^N \subset C_0^N$, and let $\varphi : \mathcal{D}^N \to I\!\!R^N$ be a solution. Let $\mathcal{D}S^N \subset \mathcal{V}S_0^N$ with $S_\Gamma \in \mathcal{D}^N$ for every $\Gamma \in \mathcal{D}S^N$. The solution φ is called *improvement sensitive* (IS) on $\mathcal{D}S^N$ if, for each $i \in N$, $\Gamma \in \mathcal{D}S^N$, $k^i \in C^i(\Gamma)$ with $k^i(\Gamma) \in \mathcal{D}S^N$, $a \in \text{alt}(\varphi, \Gamma)$, $b \in \text{alt}(\varphi, k^i(\Gamma))$, we have $u^i(a) \geq u^i(b)$.

Observe that, under the conditions in this definition, also $k^i \circ u^i(a) \geq k^i \circ u^i(b)$. Improvement sensitivity parallels the worse alternative property and therefore many of the results in the preceding sections concerning the worse alternative property hold true for the IS property in the context of value function bargaining situations. Adaptation of the corresponding proofs is straightforward.

Example 6.19 Let $\Gamma :=< \{(x,y) : x, y \geq 0, \ x + y \leq 1\}, (0,0), u^1, u^2 >$ with $u^1(x,y) = x$, $u^2(x,y) = y$. Let $k^2(t) := \sqrt{t}$ for $0 \leq t \leq 1$. Γ may be interpreted as a division problem in which one unit of a perfectly divisible good must be divided between two players. $k^2(\Gamma)$ arises by substituting for player 2 in Γ a player with a faster improving value function. Then $S_\Gamma = \text{comv}\{(1,0),(0,1)\}$ and $S_{k^2(\Gamma)} = \text{comv}\{(x,y) : 0 \leq x \leq 1, \ y = \sqrt{1-x}\}$. So $\nu(S_\Gamma) = (\frac{1}{2}, \frac{1}{2})$, $\text{alt}(\nu, \Gamma) = \{(\frac{1}{2}, \frac{1}{2})\}$, $\nu(S_{k^2(\Gamma)}) = (\frac{2}{3}, \frac{1}{3}\sqrt{3})$, $\text{alt}(\nu, k^2(\Gamma)) = \{(\frac{2}{3}, \frac{1}{3})\}$. So the improvement sensitivity condition is satisfied as expected. Suppose that Γ had been an expected utility bargaining situation. Then $(\frac{1}{2}, \frac{1}{2}) = \nu(S_\Gamma)$ could also be obtained by a lottery that gives each player a 50% chance of obtaining all of the good. If we denote this lottery by ℓ then clearly $Eu^2(\ell) = \frac{1}{2} > \frac{1}{3} = u^2(\frac{2}{3}, \frac{1}{3})$, but $Ek \circ u^2(\ell) = \frac{1}{2} < \frac{1}{3}\sqrt{3} = k \circ u^2(\frac{2}{3}, \frac{1}{3})$. As in example 6.4, the more risk averse player 2 prefers his own solution alternative to at least one of the solution alternatives in the situation with the original player 2.

The IS property may be desirable as a property which an appealing solution should have, but it has some other consequences. Crawford and Varian (1979) consider the problem in which an arbitrator has to divide one unit of a perfectly divisible good between two players. The value function of each player is of the form $u : [0,1] \to [0,1]$ with $u(x)$ denoting the value of receiving x, and with u increasing, continuous and concave, $u(0) = 0$, $u(1) = 1$. The precise shape of his value function u^i is private information of player i and, in particular, unknown to the arbitrator. The players may report to the arbitrator any value function they like, as long as it has the aforementioned properties. This problem can be modelled as the bargaining situation Γ in example 6.19, with u^1 and u^2 given by the players' reports. The arbitrator uses a bargaining solution φ to determine the final value allocation and hence physical distribution of the good. The players know φ before reporting. If the arbitrator announces the use of an IS solution, then it follows that for each player i, regardless of his opponent's report, it is optimal to report the linear value function $u^i = \overline{u}$ with $\overline{u}$ assigning the value x to an allocation giving a player x units of the good. Any other report must be an increasing concave transformation of $\overline{u}$, and thus can never give a better alternative. In other words, each player pretends to have a least fastly improving value function, if he knows that φ allocates more to such players.

We argue not only that Crawford and Varian's result is well explained by referring to the IF criterion and the corresponding IS property, but also that an explanation in terms of risk aversion is not convincing. This latter explanation would say that pretending to be as least risk averse as allowed pays in case the solution is sensitive to it. However, there is no explicit risk involved in the above model (see also Binmore *et al.*, 1986, p. 179). Second, even if one allows lotteries and regards the presence of lotteries as an adequate modelling of risk in this problem, then the least one should allow is the final physical distribution of the good to be achieved by a lottery. However, this is precisely a case where Crawford and Varian's result does not hold (see example 6.19). Similar instances of "loose modelling" are mentioned in Drèze (1982).

Concave transformations of utility functions may have attractive interpretations in terms of risk aversion or changing marginal utilities, but applied to bargaining games they just lead to very specific ways of changing the feasible set. The extent to which accompanying changes in solution outcomes depend on the specificity of these feasible set changes is investigated in the following section, where a geometric characterization of risk sensitivity for a class of two-person bargaining games is derived.

6.6   Risk sensitivity, twist sensitivity, and the slice property

In this section we present a "geometric" characterization of the risk sensitivity property of bargaining solutions defined on the subclass C_* of $C_0^{\{1,2\}}$. Attention is limited to this subclass mainly to serve convenience of presentation. Recall that

$$C_* = \{S \in C_0^{\{1,2\}} : S = \mathrm{com}(S \cap I\!R_+^2)\}.$$

For $S \in C_*$ and $i \in \{1,2\}$ let $C^i(S)$ denote the family of all continuous nondecreasing nonconstant concave functions $k^i : [0, h_i(S)] \rightarrow I\!R$ with $k^i(0) = 0$. For $k^i \in C^i(S)$ let $k^i(S)$ denote the comprehensive hull of the set of points obtained by applying k^i to the i th coordinates of the points in $S \cap I\!R_+^2$. In view of lemma 6.5 the following observation is straightforward, and it will be used throughout this section as an alternative definition of risk sensitivity.

Lemma 6.20 *A bargaining solution* $\varphi : C_* \rightarrow I\!R^2$ *is risk sensitive on* $\{\Gamma \in PS_0 : S_\Gamma \in C_*\}$ *if and only if* $\varphi_j(k^i(S)) \geq \varphi_j(S)$ *for all* $S \in C_*$, $i, j \in \{1, 2\}$ *with* $i \neq j$, $k^i \in C^i(S)$.

We introduce two properties for a bargaining solution $\varphi : C_* \rightarrow I\!R^2$ and prove that these are related to risk sensitivity of φ on $\{\Gamma \in PS_0 : S_\Gamma \in C_*\}$. By-products of this result are alternative proofs of the risk sensitivity of solutions that are independent of irrelevant alternatives or individually monotonic because — as will be seen — all these solutions satisfy twist sensitivity: this is one of the two properties announced a few lines earlier.

Let $S, T \in C_*$, $i \in \{1, 2\}$, $\alpha_i \in [0, h_i(S)]$. We say that T is a *favorable twist of S or S an unfavorable twist of T for player i at level α_i* if

$$x_i > \alpha_i \text{ for all } x \in T \backslash S \qquad (6.6)$$

$$x_i < \alpha_i \text{ for all } x \in S \backslash T. \qquad (6.7)$$

Definition 6.21 A bargaining solution $\varphi : C_* \in I\!\!R^2$ is called *twist sensitive* (TS) if for all S and T in C_* with $\varphi(S) \in P(T)$, we have for each $i \in \{1, 2\}$:

$$\varphi_i(T) \geq \varphi_i(S) \text{ if } T \text{ is a favorable twist of } S \text{ for player } i \text{ at level } \varphi_i(S). \qquad (6.8)$$

Lemma 6.22 *Let $\varphi : C_* \to I\!\!R^2$ satisfy TS and PO. Let $S, T \in C_*$ with $\varphi(S) \in P(T)$, $i \in \{1, 2\}$, and suppose that T is an unfavorable twist of S for player i at level $\varphi_i(S)$. Then $\varphi_i(T) \leq \varphi_i(S)$.*

Proof For all $x \in S \backslash T$, we have $x_i > \varphi_i(S)$, hence $x_j < \varphi_j(S)$ for $j \neq i$ since $\varphi(S) \in P(S)$. For all $x \in T \backslash S$ we have $x_i < \varphi_i(S)$, hence $x_j > \varphi_j(S)$ for $j \neq i$ since $\varphi(S) \in S$. So T is a favorable twist of S for player $j \neq i$ at level $\varphi_j(S)$. By TS : $\varphi_j(T) \geq \varphi_j(S)$; because $\varphi(S) \in P(T)$, this implies $\varphi_i(T) \leq \varphi_i(S)$. $\qquad \square$

For Pareto optimal solutions, TS is equal to the twisting property Tw (for $n = 2$), introduced in Thomson and Myerson (1980, p. 39). In general (for $n = 2$), Tw $\Rightarrow$ TS.

The following theorem is one of the main results of this section.

Theorem 6.23 *Let $\varphi : C_* \to I\!\!R^2$ satisfy PO and STC. Let φ be twist sensitive. Then φ is risk sensitive on $\{\Gamma \in PS_0 : S_\Gamma \in C_*\}$.*

Proof Let $S \in C_*$, and, say, $k^2 \in C^2(S)$. We have to prove that

$$\varphi_1(k^2(S)) \geq \varphi_1(S). \qquad (6.9)$$

If $\varphi_2(k^2(S)) = 0$ then by PO, we have $\varphi_1(k^2(S)) = h_1(k^2(S)) = h_1(S) \geq \varphi_1(S)$, and (6.9) holds. Suppose now that $\varphi_2(k^2(S)) > 0$. Since φ satisfies STC it is no loss of generality to suppose that, for $q = (q_1, q_2) \in P(S)$ with $q_1 = \varphi_1(k^2(S))$, we have

$$k^2(q_2) = q_2. \qquad (6.10)$$

By the concavity of k^2 we then have

$$k^2(\lambda) \geq \lambda \text{ for all } \lambda \in [0, q_2], \ k^2(\lambda) \leq \lambda \text{ for all } \lambda \in [q_2, h_2(S)]. \qquad (6.11)$$

From (6.10) and (6.11) it follows that S is an unfavorable twist of $k^2(S)$ for player 1 at level $\varphi_1(k^2(S))$. From lemma 6.22 we may conclude that (6.9) holds. $\qquad \square$

The converse of theorem 6.23 does not hold as example 6.27 below shows. We introduce now another property for 2-person bargaining solutions on C_*.

Definition 6.24 A bargaining solution $\varphi : C_* \to I\!\!R^2$ is said to have the *slice property* (SL) if, for all $S, T \in C_*$ with $h(S) = h(T)$ and $T \subset S$, we have:

(SL$_1$) $\varphi_1(T) \geq \varphi_1(S)$ if $x_2 > \varphi_2(S)$ for all $x \in S \backslash T$

(SL$_2$) $\varphi_2(T) \geq \varphi_2(S)$ if $x_1 > \varphi_1(S)$ for all $x \in S \backslash T$.

An SL solution φ favors the opponent of a player i when a piece of the outcome set S, preferred by i over $\varphi(S)$, is sliced off, the utopia point remaining the same. The slice property resembles the Cutting axiom of Thomson and Myerson (1980), for $n = 2$. The difference (for Pareto optimal solutions) is, that in the Cutting axiom there is no condition on the utopia point, which makes SL weaker than Cutting.

Theorem 6.25 *Let $\varphi : \mathcal{C}_* \to I\!\!R^2$ satisfy PO. Let φ be twist sensitive. Then φ has the slice property.*

Proof We only prove that (SL$_1$) holds. Let $S, T \in \mathcal{C}_*$ with $h(S) = h(T)$, $T \subset S$, and $x_2 > \varphi_2(S)$ for all $x \in S \backslash T$. We have to show that

$$\varphi_1(T) \geq \varphi_1(S). \tag{6.12}$$

Note that $\varphi(S) \in P(T)$ and $x_1 < \varphi_1(S)$ for all $x \in S \backslash T$ because $\varphi(S) \in P(S)$. Since $T \backslash S = \emptyset$, we may conclude that T is a favorable twist of S for player 1 at level $\varphi_1(S)$. So (6.12) follows from (6.8) for $i = 1$. $\square$

Example 6.28 shows that the converse of theorem 6.25 does not hold. In the following theorem a characterization of twist/risk sensitivity is given.

Theorem 6.26 *Let $\varphi : \mathcal{C}_* \to I\!\!R^2$ satisfy PO and STC. Then φ is twist sensitive if and only if it has the slice property and is risk sensitive on $\{\Gamma \in PS_0 : S_\Gamma \in \mathcal{C}_*\}$.*

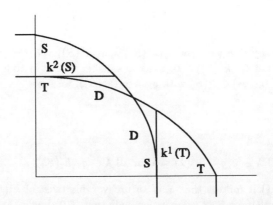

Figure 6.2: Proof of theorem 6.26

Proof (See figure 6.2.) The "only if" part follows from theorems 6.23 and 6.25. For the "if" part, let φ satisfy SL and RS on $\{\Gamma \in PS_0 : S_\Gamma \in \mathcal{C}_*\}$. Let $S, T \in \mathcal{C}_*$ with $\varphi(S) \in P(T)$, such that

$$x_1 > \varphi_1(S) \text{ for all } x \in T\backslash S \tag{6.13}$$

and

$$x_1 < \varphi_1(S) \text{ for all } x \in S\backslash T. \tag{6.14}$$

Suppose, contrary to what we want to prove, that

$$\varphi_1(T) < \varphi_1(S). \tag{6.15}$$

We derive a contradiction which will complete the proof. Let $k^1 \in C^1(T)$ be defined by: $k^1(t) = t$ if $0 \le t \le h_1(S)$, $k^1(t) = h_1(S)$ if $h_1(S) \le t \le h_1(T)$. Then $k^1(T) = \{x \in T : x_1 \le h_1(S)\}$, and by RS of φ we have $\varphi_2(k^1(T)) \ge \varphi_2(T)$, hence, since $\varphi(T) \in P(T)$:

$$\varphi_1(k^1(T)) \le \varphi_1(T). \tag{6.16}$$

By a similar argument we obtain for $k^2(S) := \{x \in S : x_2 \le h_2(T)\}$:

$$\varphi_1(k^2(S)) \ge \varphi_1(S). \tag{6.17}$$

Let $D := S \cap T \in C_*$. Then $h(D) = (h_1(S), h_2(T)) = h(k^1(T)) = h(k^2(S))$. If $x \in k^1(T)\backslash D$, then $x \in T\backslash S$, so by (6.13), (6.15), and (6.16), we have $x_1 > \varphi_1(S) > \varphi_1(T) \ge \varphi_1(k^1(T))$. By (SL$_2$) applied to $D \subset k^1(T)$, we then obtain $\varphi_2(D) \ge \varphi_2(k^1(T))$ hence by PO:

$$\varphi_1(D) \le \varphi_1(k^1(T)). \tag{6.18}$$

By a similar argument we have $\varphi_1(D) \ge \varphi_1(k^2(S))$, which combined with (6.18), (6.16), and (6.17), gives $\varphi_1(S) \le \varphi_1(T)$. This contradicts (6.15). $\square$

The slice property is a very weak property which is satisfied by most solutions occurring in the bargaining literature (see, however, example 6.27). Thus, theorem 6.26 may be read as follows: under the "standard" assumptions of Pareto optimality, scale transformation covariance and the slice property, risk sensitivity on the class in theorem 6.26 is equivalent to twist sensitivity. Intuitively, however, twist sensitivity involves more general changes in the feasible set.

The following four examples concern the three properties which are central in this section.

Example 6.27 The super-additive solution of Perles and Maschler (section 5.2) is risk sensitive on $\{\Gamma \in PS_0 : S_\Gamma \in C_*\}$ but not twist sensitive and does not have the slice property. See Counter-Example 7.1, p. 189, in Perles and Maschler (1981).

Example 6.28 Let the Pareto optimal, scale transformation covariant solution $\varphi : C_* \to \mathbb{R}^2$ be defined by: for all $S \in C_*$ with $h(S) = (1,1)$, $\varphi(S)$ is the point of intersection of $P(S)$ with γ which has maximal second coordinate, where γ is the curve depicted in figure 6.3, and described as follows. Let $\alpha := \frac{3}{2} - \frac{1}{2}\sqrt{3}$, then between $(1,1)$ and (α, α), $\gamma := \text{conv}\{(1,1), (\alpha, \alpha)\}$, and between (α, α), and $(1,1)$, γ is an arc of the circle $(x_1 - 2)^2 + (x_2 - 1)^2 = 2$. By STC, φ is uniquely determined for all $S \in C_*$. It is easy to see that φ has the slice property. However, φ is not twist sensitive. Let $S := \text{comv}\{(1,0), (\alpha, \alpha), (0,1)\}$ and $T := \text{comv}\{(1,0), (0, \alpha(1-\alpha)^{-1})\}$. Then T is an unfavorable twist of S for player 1 at level $\alpha = \varphi_1(S)$, but $\varphi_1(T) = 1 > \alpha = \varphi_1(S)$, so by lemma 6.22, φ is not twist sensitive.

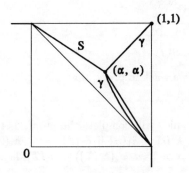

Figure 6.3: Example 6.28

Example 6.29 We give another example of a (continuous) solution which has the slice property but is not twist sensitive (and hence, not risk sensitive). Let this solution φ : $C_* \rightarrow I\!\!R^2$ be defined by: for all $S \in C_*$, $\varphi(S)$ maximizes the product $(x_1 + h_1(S))(x_2 + h_2(S))$ on $S \cap I\!\!R_+^2$. (So $\varphi(S)$ is obtained by calculating the Nash solution with $-h(S)$ as disagreement outcome.) It is easy to see that φ satisfies PO, STC, and SL. However, φ is not twist sensitive. Let $S := \text{comv}\{(1,0),(0,1)\}$, then $\varphi(S) = (\frac{1}{2},\frac{1}{2})$. Let $T := \text{comv}\{(1,0),(1/4,3/4)\}$, then T is a favorable twist of S for player 1 at level $\varphi_1(S) = \frac{1}{2}$. Now $\varphi(T) = (3/8,5/8)$, so $\varphi_1(T) < \varphi_1(S)$. Hence, φ is not twist sensitive.

Example 6.30 Let $\alpha : C_* \rightarrow I\!\!R^2$ be the *equal area split solution*, that is, for every $S \in C_*$, $\alpha(S)$ is that point of $P(S)$ such that the area in $S \cap I\!\!R_+^2$ lying above the straight line through 0 and $\alpha(S)$ equals half the area of $S \cap I\!\!R_+^2$. Then α satisfies PO and STC, is twist sensitive, and consequently is also risk sensitive and slice sensitive.

This section is concluded by two results which together with theorem 6.26 can be used to give alternative proofs of theorems 6.12 and 6.15 for the 2-person case. Note that for the solutions to which these theorems apply the restriction to the class C_* is without loss of generality. Further, on the class PS_0 the risk profit opportunity property and risk sensitivity are equivalent for Pareto optimal solutions (theorem 6.8 and the second paragraph following definition 6.9).

Theorem 6.31 Let $\varphi : C_* \rightarrow I\!\!R^2$ be a solution satisfying PO, STC, and IIA. Then φ is *twist sensitive*.

Proof Let $S,T \in C_*$ with $\varphi(S) \in P(T)$ and with T a favorable twist of S for player 1 at level $\varphi_1(S)$, i.e.

$$x_1 > \varphi_1(S) \text{ for all } x \in T\backslash S, \ x_1 < \varphi_1(S) \text{ for all } x \in S\backslash T. \qquad (6.19)$$

We have to prove that

$$\varphi_1(T) \geq \varphi_1(S). \qquad (6.20)$$

Let $D := S \cap T$. Since $D \subset S$ and $\varphi(S) \in T$, we have by IIA

$$\varphi(D) = \varphi(S). \tag{6.21}$$

Since $D \subset T$ the IIA property implies $\varphi(D) = \varphi(T)$ or $\varphi(T) \notin D$. In the first case, we have $\varphi(T) = \varphi(S)$ in view of (6.21), so (6.20) holds. If $\varphi(T) \notin D$, then $\varphi(T) \in T \backslash S$, and then (6.20) follows from (6.19). □

The proof of theorem 6.31 is related to the proof of lemma 5 in Thomson and Myerson (1980). As to the following theorem: Thomson and Myerson (1980, lemma 9 for $n = 2$) show that their property WM (which is somewhat stronger than IM) together with WPO implies Tw.

Theorem 6.32 *Let $\varphi : C_* \to \mathbb{R}^2$ be a solution satisfying PO, STC, and IM. Then φ is twist sensitive.*

Proof Let $S, T \in C_*$ with $\varphi(S) \in P(T)$ and suppose (6.19) holds. We have to show that (6.20) holds. Let $D := S \cap T$. Since $D \subset S$ and $h_1(D) = h_1(S)$ by (6.19), by IM $\varphi_2(S) \geq \varphi_2(D)$. Since $\varphi(S) \in D$ and $\varphi(D) \in P(D)$, $\varphi_2(S) \geq \varphi_2(D)$ implies that

$$\varphi_1(S) \leq \varphi_1(D). \tag{6.22}$$

From $D \subset T$, $h_2(D) = h_2(T)$ and IM we may conclude $\varphi_1(D) \leq \varphi_1(T)$ which, together with (6.22), implies (6.20). □

The results of this section were published in Tijs and Peters (1985).

Chapter 7

Bargaining with a variable number of players

7.1 Introduction

With the exception of the replication models for nonsymmetric Nash and Raiffa-Kalai-Smorodinsky bargaining solutions (subsection 2.4.4 and section 4.3) hitherto the number of players in a bargaining game was assumed to be fixed. In Thomson and Lensberg (1989) axiomatic characterizations of bargaining solutions are collected where the number of players may vary. The book shows that axioms based on such a variable population of players have proved to be powerful tools in axiomatic bargaining, leading to new characterizations of well-known solutions like the Nash, Raiffa-Kalai-Smorodinsky, and egalitarian solutions.

Roughly, two — closely related — kinds of variable population axioms may be distinguished: monotonicity and stability axioms.

An example of a monotonicity axiom is the *population monotonicity axiom* introduced under a different name by Thomson (1983a). The interpretation of this axiom is that if a player is added while the amount of available "resources" remains the same, all other players should lose in order to give something to the newcomer. The Raiffa-Kalai-Smorodinsky solution can be characterized based on this axiom: see section 7.3. This axiom has its counterpart in the theory of cooperative games with sidepayments, where so-called population monotonic allocation schemes are considered; see Sprumont (1990), Moulin (1990), Derks (1991, p. 50).

An example of a stability axiom is the one used by Lensberg (1988) to characterize the symmetric Nash bargaining solution. This axiom states that a utility vector can be the solution outcome to a particular n-person bargaining game only if it agrees with the solution outcomes to all subgames obtained from the original one by keeping the utility levels to some players constant at the original solution outcome. The axiom belongs to a category of axioms in cooperative game theory usually referred to as consistency axioms or reduced game properties. In spirit, also the consistency axiom CONS introduced in chapter 2 belongs to this category. See Driessen (1991) for a survey of consistency properties in cooperative game theory. Lensberg's characterization of the symmetric Nash bargaining solution is reviewed in section 7.4.

There is a natural relation between variable population models of bargaining and extensive game procedures to implement bargain solutions. This is due to the fact that also in extensive games players "leave the scene" after they have made their moves. See Krishna and Serrano (1990), Moulin (1984), Peters *et al.* (1991); some of this literature is discussed in chapter 9.

The next section introduces the variable population bargaining model and the main axioms. Sections 7.3 and 7.4 present the mentioned characterizations of the Raiffa-Kalai-Smorodinsky and Nash bargaining solutions, respectively. Section 7.5 reviews characterizations of the egalitarian solution based on population monotonicity or (weak) stability; that the egalitarian solution satisfies both axioms is not too surprising in view of the fact that also for a fixed number of players it satisfies independence of irrelevant alternatives as well as individual or strong monotonicity.

As mentioned earlier, a comprehensive survey of the work on bargaining with a varying number of players is given by Thomson and Lensberg (1989).

7.2   The variable population bargaining model

In the variable population bargaining model there is a pool I of "potential players". I may be finite (e.g., the player set N considered hitherto), but unless stated otherwise we assume it to be infinite, and identified with the natural numbers $I\!N$. The class of all finite subsets of I is denoted by $\mathcal{N}$, and typical elements of $\mathcal{N}$ by $M, N, \ldots$. For each $N \in \mathcal{N}$ the class C_*^N of bargaining games for N is defined by

$$C_*^N = \{S \in C_0^N : S = \text{com}(S \cap I\!R_+^N)\}.$$

(This notation is consistent with earlier notations.)

Thus, C_*^N consists of bargaining games for the player set N which have convex comprehensive feasible sets, contain strictly positive points, have disagreement points equal to 0 and all Pareto optimal points nonnegative.

Let $C^* := \bigcup_{N \in \mathcal{N}} C_*^N$ denote the class of all possible bargaining games for finite subsets of I. A *variable population solution* or (if no confusion can arise) a *solution* is a map φ on C^* such that $\varphi(S) \in S$ for every $S \in C^*$. A solution defined for games with fixed sets of players is extended to a variable population solution in the obvious way. Thus, the Nash solution ν, the Raiffa-Kalai-Smorodinsky solution ρ, and the egalitarian solution E are well-defined as variable population solutions.

Also, most of the axioms defined hitherto extend in an obvious way for variable population solutions. In particular, the axioms of Pareto optimality (PO), weak Pareto optimality (WPO), independence of irrelevant alternatives (IIA), scale transformation covariance (STC), symmetry (SYM), and feasible set continuity (SCONT) will play a role in what follows. The variable population version of the anonymity axiom (AN, see section 4.3) is somewhat different. Let φ be a solution on C^*.

Population Anonymity (PAN): For all $N, N' \in \mathcal{N}$ with $|N| = |N'|$, for all bijections $\pi : N \to N'$, for all $S \in C_*^N$ and $S' \in C_*^{N'}$, if $S' = \pi S$ then $\varphi(S') = \pi \varphi(S)$.

Here, the definitions of πx and πS are analogous to the corresponding definitions when

$N = N'$, see subsection 2.4.5. Population anonymity requires that two bargaining games which cannot be distinguished geometrically should have the same (geometrical) solution outcome. In other words, all relevant information is contained in the description of the bargaining game, and in particular the names of the players do not matter.

7.3 Population monotonicity and the Raiffa-Kalai-Smorodinsky solution

Under a different name, the following axiom was introduced in Thomson (1983a). Let φ be a solution on C^*.

Population Monotonicity (PMON): For all $M, N \in \mathcal{N}$ with $M \subset N$, all $S \in C_*^M$, $T \in C_*^N$, if $S = T_M$ then $\varphi(S) \geq \varphi_M(T)$.

Suppose the players in M have already arrived to play the bargaining game T. If the players in $N \backslash M$ would not show up, M would play $T_M = S$ and reach an agreement $\varphi(S)$. If the players in $N \backslash M$ show up afterwards, play starts anew and no player in M should be better off, i.e., $\varphi_M(T) \leq \varphi(S)$.

Proposition 7.1 *The Raiffa-Kalai-Smorodinsky solution ρ satisfies WPO, PAN, STC, SCONT, and PMON.*

Proof We only prove PMON for ρ. Let M, N, S, and T be as in the statement of PMON. Then $h(S) = h(T_M)$, therefore $\rho_M(T)$ is on the line segment joining 0 and $h(S)$. In particular, $\rho_M(T) \leq \rho(S)$. $\square$

It will be shown that the solution ρ is actually characterized by these five axioms. The main part of the proof of this result is established by the following proposition.

Proposition 7.2 *Let φ satisfy WPO, PAN, STC, and PMON. Then $\varphi(S) \geq \rho(S)$ for all $M \in \mathcal{N}$ and $S \in C_*^M$.*

Proof Let $M \in \mathcal{N}$ and $S \in C_*^M$. By STC, we may assume $h(S) = e^M$. Let $x := \rho(S)$, say $x = \alpha e^M$, where $0 < \alpha \leq 1$. Let $y := \varphi(S)$ and suppose by way of contradiction that $\varphi_i(S) < \alpha$ for some $i \in N$. Let $\beta := \varphi_i(S)$.
Without loss of generality, assume $M = \{1, 2, \ldots, m\}$, and $i = 1$.
Let $N := \{1, 2, \ldots, m, m+1\}$. Define $S^1, S^2, \ldots, S^{m+1}$ by

$$S^k := \{y \in \mathbb{R}^{N \backslash \{k\}} : \left(y_{(k+1)\bmod(m+1)}, y_{(k+2)\bmod(m+1)}, \cdots, y_{(k+m)\bmod(m+1)}\right) \in S\}$$

for every $k \in N$. Thus, S^k is a replica of S with player set $N \backslash \{k\}$ where player $(k+1)\bmod(m+1)$ plays the role of player 1 in S, $(k+2)\bmod(m+1)$ plays the role of player 2 in S, etc. Here, player $(m+1)\bmod(m+1)$ is taken to be player $m+1$. Note that $S^{m+1} = S$. See figure 7.1 for an illustration of the case $m = 2$. Let

$$T := \text{comv}\{O^N(S^1), \ldots, O^N(S^{m+1}), \alpha e^N\}.$$

Then $T \in C_*^N$, and $T_{N \backslash \{k\}} = S^k \in C_*^{N \backslash \{k\}}$ for every $k \in N$. By PMON, $\varphi_{N \backslash \{k\}}(T) \leq \varphi(S^k)$ for every $k \in N$. By PAN,

$$\varphi_{(k+1)\bmod(m+1)}(T) \le \varphi_{(k+1)\bmod(m+1)}(S^k) = \varphi_1(S) = \beta$$

for every $k \in N$. Hence, $\varphi(T) \le \beta e^N < \alpha e^N \in T$, contradicting WPO.   □

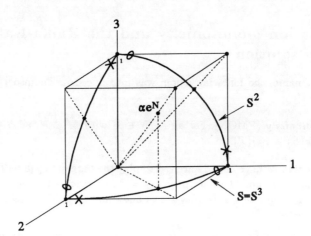

Figure 7.1: Proof of proposition 7.2 for $m = 2$

Remark 7.3 The proof of proposition 7.2 is an extension of Thomson's proof for the 2-person case. For the general case, Thomson has a different proof.

Theorem 7.4 *A solution on C^* satisfies WPO, PAN, STC, SCONT, and PMON, if and only if it is the Raiffa-Kalai-Smorodinsky solution.*

Proof The "if" part is proposition 7.1. The "only if" part follows from proposition 7.2, SCONT, and the fact that every $S \in C_*^M$ can be approximated by a sequence of bargaining games where the Raiffa-Kalai-Smorodinsky outcomes are in the Pareto optimal subsets. □

It is obvious that if attention is restricted to bargaining games $S \in C_*^N$ with $W(S) \cap \mathbb{R}_+^N = P(S)$ then the continuity axiom can be omitted from theorem 7.4. In general, however, none of the axioms can be omitted. See Thomson (1983a) for details.

If the set of potential agents I is finite, then theorem 7.4 and in particular proposition 7.2 are no longer valid. E.g., let $I := \{1, 2, \ldots, n\}$ and let $\varphi(S) := \rho(S)$ for all $M \subset I$, $M \ne I$, $S \in C_*^M$. For $S \in C_*^I$ let $\varphi(S)$ maximize the product $x_1 x_2 \ldots x_n$ over the subset of $S \cap \mathbb{R}_+^I$ determined by the inequalities required by population monotonicity. It is easily verified that this solution φ satisfies the five axioms in theorem 7.4.

In Peters *et al.* (1991) a related axiomatic characterization of the RKS solution is obtained. Since this characterization is closely linked to a noncooperative procedure, it is presented in chapter 9.

7.4 Stability and the Nash solution

This section is based on Lensberg (1988), who characterizes the Nash bargaining solution with the aid of a stability axiom. Two versions of stability play a role. The first version is the weaker one. It was first introduced by Harsanyi (1959, 1963). Let φ be a solution on C^*.

Bilateral Stability (BSTAB): For all $M, N \in \mathcal{N}$ with $M \subset N$ and $|M| = 2$, for all $S \in C_*^M$ and $T \in C_*^N$, if $S = (T, \varphi)_M$, then $\varphi(S) = \varphi_M(T)$.

Loosely speaking bilateral stability states that a utility vector can be the solution outcome to a particular bargaining game only if it agrees with the solution outcome for all 2-person subgames obtained from the original game. To quote Lensberg (1988, p. 333):

> "... a rational player i will not accept a tentative agreement x for the $|N|$-person bargaining game T if he has reason to believe that he may successfully threaten some other player j to make a concession in his favor. If i does not simultaneously challenge any of the other players for concessions, then i can base his beliefs concerning j's willingness to concede on what i and j know about solving 2-person bargaining games. Since the situation is similar for all members of N, the solution outcome of T has to agree with the solution outcomes of all 2-person subgames obtained from T by keeping the payoffs of the other $|N| - 2$ players constant at the solution outcome in T."

This idea can be extended to all subgames of a game T, leading to the following strengthening of BSTAB.

Multilateral Stability (MSTAB): For all $M, N \in \mathcal{N}$ with $M \subset N$, for all $S \in C_*^N$ and $T \in C_*^N$, if $S = (T, \varphi)_M$, then $\varphi(S) = \varphi_M(T)$.

Harsanyi (1959) proves the following result.

Theorem 7.5 *If φ is a solution on C^* satisfying SCONT and BSTAB and $\varphi(S) = \nu(S)$ for all $S \in C_*^M$ with $|M| = 2$, then φ is the Nash solution ν.*

Lensberg (1988) gives a characterization of the Nash solution based on the multilateral stability axiom, and three other axioms.

Proposition 7.6 *The Nash solution satisfies PO, PAN, STC, and MSTAB.*

Proof As in proposition 2.3, verification of PO, PAN, and STC for ν is left to the reader. Let M, N, S, and T be as in the statement of MSTAB with ν instead of φ. Since $\nu(T)$ maximizes the product $\prod_{i \in N} x_i$ on $T \cap \mathbb{R}_+^N$, it certainly maximizes this product on $\{y \in T : y_{N \setminus M} = \nu_{N \setminus M}(T), y \geq 0\}$. Therefore, $\nu_M(T)$ maximizes the product $\prod_{i \in M} x_i$ on $S \cap \mathbb{R}_+^N$. So $\nu_M(T) = \nu(S)$. $\qquad\square$

Lensberg shows that the converse of this proposition also holds. His proof will be presented below. Unfortunately, theorem 2.32 cannot be used for this; although CONS there can be derived from MSTAB, there is no apparent easy way to derive IIA from the four axioms in proposition 7.6.

The proof of the converse of proposition 7.6 is based on the following lemma.

Lemma 7.7 *Let φ satisfy PO, PAN, and BSTAB. Let $S \in \mathcal{C}_*^{\{1,2\}}$ with $\nu_1(S) = \nu_2(S) = 1$ and such that* $\mathrm{conv}\{(1+\delta, 1-\delta), (1-\delta, 1+\delta)\} \subset P(S)$ *for some $\delta > 0$. Then $\varphi(S) = \nu(S)$.*

Proof If $\delta = 1$ then $S = \mathrm{comv}\{(1,0),(0,1)\}$ and the desired conclusion follows from PO and PAN. Otherwise, let $n \in I\!N$ be such that $n \geq 1+\frac{1}{\delta}$, let $N := \{1, \ldots, n\}$ and $M := \{3, \ldots, n\}$. For each $j \in N$, let $S^j := \{x \in I\!R_+^N : (x_j, x_{(j+1) \bmod n}) \in S, \ x_k = 1 \text{ otherwise}\}$. (Here, $n \bmod n := n$.) Let $T := \mathrm{comv}\{S^j : j \in N\}$. Let $\overline{S} := \{x \in I\!R_+^2 : x_1 + x_2 \leq 2\}$, and for every $j \in N$, let $\overline{S}^j := \{x \in I\!R_+^N : (x_j, x_{(j+1) \bmod n}) \in S, \ x_k = 1 \text{ otherwise}\}$. Let $\overline{T} := \mathrm{comv}\{S^1 \cup \overline{S}^j : j \in N \backslash \{1\}\}$. Then $T \subset \overline{T}$ since $S \subset \mathrm{com}(\overline{S})$.

Claim (i): $\varphi(T) = e^N$. Since S is supported at $(1,1)$ by the hyperplane $\{x \in I\!R^2 : x_1 + x_2 = 2\}$, it follows that each S^j is supported at e^N by the hyperplane $\{x \in I\!R^N : \sum_{i \in N} x_i = n\}$. So this hyperplane also supports T at e^N. By PAN, $\varphi_i(T) = \varphi_j(T)$ for all $i, j \in N$. Therefore, because $e^N \in P(T)$, $\varphi(T) = e^N$.

Claim (ii): $S = (T, \varphi)_{\{1,2\}}$. By construction of T, $S \subset (T, \varphi)_{\{1,2\}}$. Since $T \subset \overline{T}$ it suffices to show that $(\overline{T}, e^N)_{\{1,2\}} \subset S$. Let $x \in \overline{T}$ with $x_M = e^M$. We have to show that $(x_1, x_2) \in S$. There exist $z^1 \in P(S^1)$ and, for $j = 2, \ldots, n$, $z^j \in P(\overline{S}^j)$, and $\alpha_1, \ldots, \alpha_n \geq 0$ with $\sum \alpha_j = 1$ such that $x \leq \sum_{j=1}^n \alpha_j z^j$. Since $z^1 \in S^1$, $z_M^1 = e^M$. For all $j \in N \backslash \{1\}$, since $z^j \in P(\overline{S}^j)$, we have $z^j = e^N + \beta_j(e^{(j+1) \bmod n} - e^j)$ for some $-1 \leq \beta_j \leq 1$. The system $x \leq \sum_{j=1}^n \alpha_j z^j$ may be written more explicitly as follows:

(1) $\quad x_1 \ \leq \ 1 + (z_1^1 - 1)\alpha_1 \hspace{5cm} + \alpha_n \beta_n$

(2) $\quad x_2 \ \leq \ 1 + (z_2^1 - 1)\alpha_1 - \alpha_2 \beta_2$

(3) $\quad 0 \ \leq \hspace{3.5cm} \alpha_2 \beta_2 - \alpha_3 \beta_3$

$\qquad \vdots$

(n) $\quad 0 \ \leq \hspace{3.5cm} \alpha_{n-1} \beta_{n-1} - \alpha_n \beta_n$

Let $\gamma := (n-1)^{-1} \sum_{j=2}^n \alpha_j \beta_j$. From $-1 \leq \beta_j \leq 1$, $\sum_{j=2}^n \alpha_j = 1-\alpha_1$, and $n \geq 1+\frac{1}{\delta}$ it follows that $-\delta(1-\alpha_1) \leq \gamma \leq \delta(1-\alpha_1)$. From inequalities (3)–(n) it follows that $\alpha_2 \beta_2 \geq \alpha_3 \beta_3 \geq \ldots \geq \alpha_n \beta_n$, so by definition of γ, $\alpha_n \beta_n \leq \gamma$ and $-\alpha_2 \beta_2 \leq -\gamma$. Therefore, by (1) and (2), $(x_1, x_2) \leq \alpha_1 z_{\{1,2\}}^1 + (1-\alpha_1)e^{\{1,2\}} + (\gamma, -\gamma)$, which since $-\delta(1-\alpha_1) \leq \gamma \leq \delta(1-\alpha_1)$ implies $(x_1, x_2) \leq \alpha_1 z_{\{1,2\}}^1 + (1-\alpha_1)v$ with v some vector in $\mathrm{conv}\{(1+\delta, 1-\delta), (1-\delta, 1+\delta)\} \subset S$. Since $z_{\{1,2\}}^1, v \in S$, also $(x_1, x_2) \in S$. This completes the proof of claim 2.

Claims (i), (ii) and BSTAB imply $\varphi(S) = (1,1) = \nu(S)$. $\qquad \square$

The dependence of n on δ in the proof of lemma 7.7 is really needed. In particular, taking $n = 3$ does not work if δ is (too) small; more precisely, claim (ii) in the proof no longer holds. The reader may verify this by applying the construction of the proof to $S := \mathrm{comv}\{(2,0), (1-\delta, 1+\delta)\}$ for δ small, say $\delta = \frac{1}{4}$. Then $S \neq (T, \varphi)_{\{1,2\}}$, see also p. 102–103 in Thomson and Lensberg (1989).

Proposition 7.8 *Let the solution φ satisfy PO, PAN, STC, and MSTAB. Then φ is the Nash solution ν.*

Proof Let $M \in \mathcal{N}$ and $S \in \mathcal{C}_*^M$. By STC, we may assume $\nu(S) = e^M$. Let $k \in I$, $k \notin M$, and let $M' := M \cup \{k\}$. Let $|M| =: m$. We construct a bargaining game $T \in \mathcal{C}_*^{M'}$ with $\varphi(T) = e^{M'}$ and $S = (T, \varphi)_M$; then MSTAB implies $\varphi(S) = e^M = \nu(S)$.

Let $S^1 := S + e^k$, $H := \{x \in \mathbb{R}_+^{M'} : \sum_{i \in M'} x_i = m + 1, \, x_k \leq 1\}$. For $\varepsilon > 0$, let C^ε be the cone with vertex $(1 + \varepsilon)e^k$ spanned by S^1 (see figure 7.2 for a case with $m = 2$). Choose ε small enough such that $ne^i \in \text{int}(C^\varepsilon)$ for all $i \in M$. Let $T := C^\varepsilon \cap \text{comv}(H)$. Then $T \in \mathcal{C}_*^{M'}$ and the relative interiors σ^i of $\text{conv}\{e^{M'}, ne^i\}$ are subsets of the relative interior of $H \cap P(T)$, for all $i \in M$. Moreover, $(T, e^{M'})_M = S$. It remains to show that $\varphi(T) = e^{M'}$. Two cases will be distinguished.

Case (i): $m = 2$. Suppose, by way of contradiction, that $\varphi(T) \neq e^{M'}$. Since $\max\{x_k : x \in T\} = 1$, PO implies that $\varphi_j(T) > 1$ for some $j \in M$. Assume first that $\varphi_j(T) < 3$. Let $M = \{i, j\}$ and let $S' := (T, \varphi)_{\{i,k\}}$. Since $3 > \varphi_j(T) > 1$ there is a point $w \in \sigma^j$ with $(w_i, w_k) \in S'$. Since σ^j is a subset of the relative interior of $H \cap P(T)$, $P(S')$ contains a nondegenerate line segment normal to $e^{\{i,k\}}$ centered at w. By STC, PAN, MSTAB, and lemma 7.7, we have $\varphi(S') = \nu(S')$. By BSTAB, $\varphi_i(T) = \varphi_k(T)$. Thus, $\varphi(T) \in \sigma^j$ and $\varphi_k(T) < 1$. One can prove similarly that $(T, \varphi)_{\{i,j\}}$ satisfies the conditions of lemma 7.7, so that $\varphi_i(T) = \varphi_j(T) = \varphi_k(T) < 1$, in contradiction with PO.

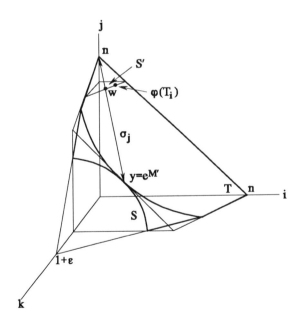

Figure 7.2: Proof of proposition 7.8

The case $\varphi_j(T) = 3$ cannot occur; then, $(T, \varphi)_M$ would be the comprehensive hull of a symmetric triangle and via BSTAB we would have a contradiction with PAN.

Case (ii): $m > 2$. Observe first that for all $i \in M$ and $z \in T$, the point x with $x_k := 0$, $x_i := z_i + z_k$, and $x_j := z_j$ for all $j \in M\backslash\{i\}$ is also in T. The next step is to show that $\varphi_i(T) \geq \varphi_k(T)$ for all $i \in M$. Take $i \in M$ and let $V := (T, \varphi)_{\{i,k\}}$. Then the segment $\sigma := \text{conv}\{(\varphi_i(T), \varphi_k(T)), (\varphi_i(T) + \varphi_k(T), 0)\}$ is a subset of V. By case (i) and BSTAB, $\varphi(V) = \nu(V) = (\varphi_i(T), \varphi_k(V))$. So $\varphi_i(T)\varphi_k(V) \geq x_i x_k$ for all $(x_i, x_k) \in \sigma$. In particular, for all $0 \leq \alpha \leq 1 : \varphi_i(T)\varphi_k(T) \geq [\alpha\varphi_i(T) + (1 - \alpha)(\varphi_i(T) + \varphi_k(T))][\alpha\varphi_k(T) + (1 - \alpha)0]$, i.e., $(1 - \alpha)\varphi_i(T) \geq \alpha(1 - \alpha)\varphi_k(T)$. By taking α arbitrarily close to 1, it follows that $\varphi_i(T) \geq \varphi_k(T)$.

Since $\varphi_i(T) \geq \varphi_k(T)$ for all $i \in M$, PO implies that $\varphi(T) \in A := \text{conv}\{e^{M'}, (m+1)e^i : i \in M\} \subset H \cap P(T)$. Further, for all $P \subset M'$ with $|P| = 2$ and $(T, \varphi(T))_P \in \mathcal{C}_*^P$ we have

$$\varphi_P(T) = \nu((T, \varphi(T))_P). \tag{7.1}$$

This follows from BSTAB and case (i) above. To show that $\varphi(T) = e^{M'}$, suppose by way of contradiction that $\varphi(T) \neq e^{M'}$. Then $\varphi_k(T) < 1$ since $\varphi(T) \in A$. So $\varphi(T)$ is in the relative interior of A. Therefore, by (7.1), for all $P \subset M'$ with $|P| = 2$ and $(T, \varphi(T))_P \in \mathcal{C}_*^P$, we have

$$\varphi_P(T) = \nu((\overline{T}, \varphi(T))_P) \tag{7.2}$$

where $\overline{T} := \text{com}(H)$. However, it is easy to see that $e^{M'}$ is the only point of $\overline{T}$ for which (7.2) holds; consequently, $\varphi(T) = e^{M'}$, contrary to what we assumed. □

From propositions 7.6 and 7.8 the following characterization of the Nash bargaining solution ν results.

Theorem 7.9 *A solution on $\mathcal{C}^*$ satisfies PO, PAN, STC, and MSTAB, if and only if it is the Nash solution.*

We conclude this section with a discussion of the domain and the axioms. If I is finite, then theorem 7.9 in its present form no longer holds. The case $|I| = 2$ is trivial since then MSTAB is then implied by PO. For the case $|I| \geq 3$, consider the following example (cf. example 2.33). Let $M := \{1, 2\} \subset I$ and let $\overline{T} \in \mathcal{C}_*^I$ be defined by $\overline{T} := \text{comv}\{e^I, \frac{3}{2}e^M\}$. Set $\varphi(\overline{T}) := \frac{1}{2}e^I + \frac{3}{4}e^M$. For any $T \in \mathcal{C}_*^I$ that is related with $\overline{T}$ through the conditions in PAN or STC, define $\varphi(T)$ accordingly. For any other $S \in \mathcal{C}_*^N$ with $N \subset I$, let $\varphi(S) := \nu(S)$. It is easy to verify that this solution φ satisfies the four axioms in theorem 7.9.

An elaborate study of the consequences of omitting Pareto optimality is Lensberg and Thomson (1988). See also chapter 8 in Thomson and Lensberg (1989). One interesting result is the following theorem.

Theorem 7.10 *A solution on $\mathcal{C}^*$ satisfies PAN, STC, BSTAB, and SCONT, if and only if it is either the Nash solution or the disagreement point solution.*

Compare this result (which is Theorem 8.1 in Thomson and Lensberg, 1989) with theorem 2.7, and with Roth (1977a).

As to population anonymity: solutions defined like the solutions φ^H in section 2.3 for some given ordering of I satisfy PO, STC, and MSTAB. Further details concerning this axiom and the remaining axioms can be found in chapter 7 of Thomson and Lensberg (1989). Another characterization of the Nash bargaining solution within the framework of a variable number of players can be found in Young (1988).

7.5   The egalitarian solution, weak stability and population monotonicity

The egalitarian solution E (section 4.5) assigns to each bargaining game the maximal point with equal coordinates. It involves interpersonal comparisons of utilities and obviously does not satisfy scale transformation covariance. It is not Pareto optimal but only weakly Pareto optimal. On $\mathcal{C}_0^N$, the egalitarian solution is the only one to satisfy the combination of strong monotonicity, weak Pareto optimality, and symmetry (theorem 4.31); on $\mathcal{C}^N$, it is the unique solution satisfying weak Pareto optimality, symmetry, independence of non-individually rational outcomes, feasible set continuity, and disagreement point concavity, as follows from theorem 4.33. Further, theorem 5.2 implies that E is the unique 2-person bargaining solution (on $\mathcal{C}_0$) satisfying weak Pareto optimality, symmetry, homogeneity, and (partial) super-additivity. Yet other characterizations of the egalitarian solution can be derived from or are given by theorem 4.32 (based on the step-by-step negotiations axiom), theorem 4.38 (based on the strong transfer responsiveness axiom, which concerns the disagreement point), or Myerson (1981), who uses among other conditions the independence of irrelevant alternatives axiom. This recapitulation shows that, at the price of failing to satisfy Pareto optimality and scale transformation covariance, the egalitarian solution offers a compromise between many other properties discussed so far. The question we address in this section is, how it can be characterized in the variable population model. The first characterization is due to Thomson (1983b; see also chapter 4 in Thomson and Lensberg, 1989) and, like the other results in this section, is reproduced here without a proof.

Theorem 7.11 *The solution φ on C^* satisfies WPO, SYM, IIA, PMON, and SCONT, if and only if it is the egalitarian solution.*

Apparently, the egalitarian solution satisfies variable population monotonicity — and this is not hard to check either. As the following example shows, E does not satisfy BSTAB (and, consequently, also not MSTAB). The remainder of this section is based on Thomson (1983b), see also Thomson and Lensberg (1989, chapter 10).

Example 7.12 Let $N : \{1,2,3\}$, $M := \{2,3\}$, and $T := \text{comv}\{(1,2,2)\}$. Then $E(T) = (1,1,1)$, and $(T,E)_M = \text{comv}\{(2,2)\}$. So $E((T,E)_M) = (2,2) \neq (1,1) = E(T)_M$.

This example indicates that, from a strategic point of view, the egalitarian solution is not very convincing: given that player 1 is satisfied with 1, why should not players 2 and 3 renegotiate their part of the outcome in order to obtain $(2,2)$? Indeed, this would lead to the outcome $(1,2,2)$ assigned by the lexicographic egalitarian solution L as defined and characterized in section 4.7. Thomson and Lensberg (1989, chapter 9) give the following characterization of the solution L, which includes the individual monotonicity axiom (IM).

Theorem 7.13 *The solution φ on C^* satisfies PO, PAN, IM, and MSTAB, if and only if it is the lexicographic egalitarian solution.*

Here, we further concentrate on the egalitarian solution. It does satisfy the following weakening of multilateral stability. Let φ be a solution on C^*.

Weak Stability (WSTAB): For all $M, N \in \mathcal{N}$ with $M \subset N$, for all $S \in C_*^M$ and $T \in C_*^N$, if $S = (T, \varphi)_M$, then $\varphi(S) \geq \varphi_M(T)$.

The term "weak stability" is based on the consideration that this axiom is weaker than multilateral stability. WSTAB cannot really be defended as a condition leading to a "stable" grand coalition since it does not preclude renegotiations by subgroups. A possible interpretation is as follows: in order to form the grand coalition all members of a subgroup have to pay. In this respect, it is related to variable population monotonicity but now taking the solution outcome as a starting point. More globally, if the egalitarian outcome is regarded as just, then all members of any subgroup should pay in order to satisfy this principle of justice.

We have the following theorem.

Theorem 7.14 *The solution φ on C^* satisfies WPO, SYM, SCONT, PMON, and WSTAB, if and only if it is the egalitarian solution.*

The proof of the "only if" part of theorem 7.14 is, roughly, as follows. Let $M \in \mathcal{N}$ and $S \in C_*^M$. By SCONT, it is without loss of generality to assume that $W(S) \cap \mathbb{R}_+^M = P(S)$. Then, by WSTAB, we are done if we know that $\varphi = E$ for all bargaining games with less players than there are in M. Therefore, a proof by induction can be based on the fact $\varphi = E$ whenever there are two players. The proof of this fact, however, is not straightforward and involves the laborious construction of 3-player bargaining games based on a given 2-player game. See Lemma 10.1 in Thomson and Lensberg (1989). Further, it can be shown that the axioms in this theorem are independent. The requirement that I be infinite is not needed, however; this is clear from the above outline of the proof.

Chapter 8

Alternative models and solution concepts

8.1 Introduction

In this chapter some alternative models of axiomatic bargaining theory are collected. In section 8.2 we consider multivalued solutions, which assign to a bargaining game a subset of feasible outcomes rather than a unique outcome. Section 8.3 deals with probabilistic solutions, which assign to each bargaining game a probability measure on the feasible set. In section 8.4 we discuss some extensions of existing solution concepts to bargaining with possibly nonconvex feasible sets. Certain applications and implications of axiomatic bargaining game theory for specific economic models are considered in section 8.5. Section 8.6 reviews a few (axiomatic) models where time is involved. Sections 8.7 and 8.8 very briefly discuss ordinally covariant solutions and continuity, respectively.

8.2 Multivalued solutions

Multivalued solution concepts are common practice in game theory; e.g. the core for side-payment and nonsidepayment games, the set of Nash equilibria or refinements thereof for noncooperative games. In this book until now only single-valued (bargaining) solutions were considered, but in this section as well as in section 8.4 on nonconvex bargaining games and in chapter 10 on nonsidepayment games multi-valued solutions will be studied. The present section is based on Peters *et al.* (1983). Attention is restricted to the class $\mathcal{C}_0$ of 2-person bargaining games with convex comprehensive feasible sets, disagreement points normalized to 0, and containing strictly positive feasible outcomes.

Definition 8.1 A *multisolution* $\varphi : \mathcal{C}_0 \to I\!\!R^2$ is a correspondence assigning to each $S \in \mathcal{C}_0$ a nonempty subset $\varphi(S)$ of S.

With every bargaining solution $\varphi : \mathcal{C}_0 \to I\!\!R^2$ we can associate a multisolution $\tilde{\varphi} : \mathcal{C}_0 \to I\!\!R^2$ by $\tilde{\varphi}(S) := \{\varphi(S)\}$ for every $S \in \mathcal{C}_0$. We write φ instead of $\tilde{\varphi}$. Also, we often omit the braces in case of one-point sets.

The purpose of this section is to characterize multisolutions with the aid of generalizations of properties of bargaining solutions. We give a list of the properties which play a role in this section, for a multisolution $\varphi : C_0 \to I\!\!R^2$.

Definition 8.2   (i) *Individual rationality* (IR): $\varphi(S) \subset I\!\!R_+^2$ for every $S \in C_0$.

(ii) *[Weak] Pareto optimality* ([W]PO): $\varphi(S) \subset P(S)$ [$W(S)$] for every $S \in C_0$.

(iii) *Scale transformation covariance* (STC): $\varphi(aS) = a\varphi(S)$ for every scale transformation $a \in I\!\!R_{++}^2$ and every $S \in C_0$.

(iv) *Independence of irrelevant alternatives* (IIA): $\varphi(S) = \varphi(T) \cap S$ for all S and T in C_0 with $S \subset T$ and $\varphi(T) \cap S \neq \emptyset$.

(v) *Restricted monotonicity* (RM): $\varphi(S) \subset \varphi(T) - I\!\!R_+^2$ and $\varphi(T) \subset \varphi(S) + I\!\!R_+^2$ for all S and T in C_0 with $S \subset T$ and $h(S) = h(T)$.

Note that for bargaining solutions all these properties coincide with the existing properties with the same names, which justifies the use of these same names.

The IIA property as formulated here, can also be found in Kaneko (1980); see section 8.4. Aumann (1985a) propose the following "IIA" property for a multisolution $\varphi : C_0 \to I\!\!R^2$: for all S and T in C_0 with $S \subset T$ and $\varphi(T) \cap S \neq \emptyset$, $\varphi(S) \supset \varphi(T) \cap S$. For bargaining solutions, both versions coincide. Note however, that the multisolution given by $S \mapsto P(S)$ for every $S \in C_0$ satisfies Aumann's "IIA" but not our IIA: "IIA" is strictly weaker than IIA. See further section 10.3.

The remainder of this section consists of two parts. In the first part, subsection 8.2.1, we describe the family of all multisolutions satisfying IR, WPO, STC, and IIA. Notice that, apart from considering multisolutions instead of bargaining solutions, we also generalize corollary 2.24 by replacing PO by WPO. In subsection 8.2.2 we describe the family of all closed-valued multisolutions satisfying PO, STC, and RM. (We use RM instead of a multisolution version of IM merely for convenience.) Thus, the second part provides a generalization of corollary 4.14.

8.2.1   Independence of irrelevant alternatives

We start with a few notations.

Definition 8.3 For $S \in C_0$, let $\overline{p}(S)$ and $\underline{p}(S)$ be the points of $P(S) \cap I\!\!R_+^2$ with maximal second and first coordinate, respectively. Let $\overline{w}(S)$ and $\underline{w}(S)$ denote the points of $W(S)$ with first and second coordinate 0, respectively. Let $\overline{W}(S) := \mathrm{conv}\{\overline{w}(S), \overline{p}(S)\}$ and $\underline{W}(S) := \mathrm{conv}\{\underline{w}(S), \underline{p}(S)\}$. Finally, by $\overline{M}(S)$ we denote $(\overline{W}(S)\backslash\{\overline{w}(S)\}) \cup \{\overline{p}(S)\}$, and by $\underline{M}(S)$ the set $(\underline{W}(S)\backslash\{\underline{w}(S)\}) \cup \{\underline{p}(S)\}$.

Note that $\overline{p} = \varphi^H$ with $H = <\{2\}, \{1\}, (1,1) > \in \mathcal{H}^{\{1,2\}}$; $\underline{p} = \varphi^H$ with $H = <\{1\}, \{2\}, (1,1) >$, $\overline{w} = E^{(0,1)}$, $\underline{w} = E^{(1,0)}$. The purpose of this subsection is to prove the following theorem.

Theorem 8.4 $\{\varphi^H : H \in \mathcal{H}^{\{1,2\}}\} \cup \{\overline{w}, \underline{w}\} \cup \{\overline{W}, \underline{W}, \overline{M}, \underline{M}\}$ *is the family of all multisolutions which have the properties IR, WPO, STC, and IIA.*

We leave it to the reader to verify that all the mentioned multisolutions have the mentioned properties. The other part of the theorem will be proved with the aid of a string of lemmas. We frequently use the notation $U = U^{\{1,2\}} = \text{com}\{(1,1)\}$ (cf. section 4.2) and $S_0 = \text{com}(S \cap \mathbb{R}^2_+)$ (cf. subsection 2.5.2) for $S \in \mathcal{C}_0$.

Remark 8.5 In Peters *et al.* (1983), compactness instead of comprehensiveness of bargaining games is assumed. A consequence is that, there, four additional multisolutions are found to satisfy the four properties of theorem 8.4. See the mentioned reference for details.

Lemma 8.6 *Let $\varphi : \mathcal{C}_0 \to \mathbb{R}^2$ be a multisolution satisfying IR, STC, and IIA. Then:*

(i) *If $\varphi(U) = (0,1)$, then $\varphi = \overline{w}$.*

(ii) *If $\varphi(U) = (1,0)$, then $\varphi = \underline{w}$.*

Proof We only show (i). Let $\varphi(U) = (0,1)$ and $S \in \mathcal{C}_0$, then by STC: $\varphi(h(S)U) = \overline{w}(S)$. So by IIA applied to $S_0 \subset h(S)U$, we have $\varphi(S_0) = \overline{w}(S)$. Finally, by IR and IIA applied to $S_0 \subset S$, we obtain $\varphi(S) = \overline{w}(S)$. □

The following lemma can be proved in the same way as lemma 8.6. Details are omitted.

Lemma 8.7 *Let $\varphi : \mathcal{C}_0 \to \mathbb{R}^2$ be a multisolution with the properties IR, STC, and IIA. Then:*

(i) *If $\varphi(U) = \overline{W}(U)$, then $\varphi = \overline{W}$.*

(ii) *If $\varphi(U) = \underline{W}(U)$, then $\varphi = \underline{W}$.*

We need four more lemmas before we can prove theorem 8.4.

Lemma 8.8 *Let $\varphi : \mathcal{C}_0 \to \mathbb{R}^2$ be a multisolution satisfying IR, WPO, STC, and IIA. Suppose $a, b \in \varphi(S)$ with $a \neq b$, for some $S \in \mathcal{C}_0$. Then $a_1 = b_1$ or $a_2 = b_2$.*

Proof Suppose that $a_1 \neq b_1$ and $a_2 \neq b_2$, say $a_1 < b_1$ and $a_2 > b_2$ (noting that φ satisfies WPO). In view of IR, we distinguish two cases: (i) $a_1 = 0$, (ii) $a_1 > 0$. In case (i), let $T := \text{comv}\{a, b\}$. Then $(\frac{1}{2}, 1)T \subset T$, and $a \in (\frac{1}{2}, 1)T \cap \varphi(T) \neq \emptyset$ since $\varphi(T) = \varphi(S) \cap T \supset \{a, b\}$ by IIA; so, also by IIA, $\varphi((\frac{1}{2}, 1)T) = \varphi(T) \cap (\frac{1}{2}, 1)T$. By STC, $(\frac{1}{2}b_1, b_2) \in \varphi((\frac{1}{2}, 1)T)$, hence $(\frac{1}{2}b_1, b_2) \in \varphi(T)$, in contradiction with WPO. So in case (i): $a_1 = b_1$ or $a_2 = b_2$. For case (ii), let $c := (a_1(\frac{1}{2}a_1 + \frac{1}{2}b_1)^{-1}, a_2(\frac{1}{2}a_2 + \frac{1}{2}b_2)^{-1}) \in \mathbb{R}^2_{++}$, T as above, and $E := \text{comv}\{b, \frac{1}{2}(a + b)\}$. (See figure 8.1.) Then an elementary calculation shows that $cE \subset T$ and $cb \notin W(T)$. Since $a = c(\frac{1}{2}(a + b)) \in cE \cap \varphi(T)$, by IIA: $\varphi(cE) = \varphi(T) \cap cE$. Since, by IIA, $b \in \varphi(E)$, by STC: $cb \in \varphi(cE)$. So $cb \in \varphi(T)$, a contradiction since $cb \notin W(T)$. Hence also in case (ii): $a_1 = b_1$ or $a_2 = b_2$. □

Lemma 8.9 *Let $\varphi : \mathcal{C}_0 \to \mathbb{R}^2$ be a multisolution satisfying IR, WPO, STC, and IIA. Then:*

(i) *If $(\alpha, 1) \in \varphi(U)$ for some $\alpha \in (0,1)$, and $\varphi \neq \overline{W}$, then $\varphi = \overline{M}$.*

(ii) *If $(1, \alpha) \in \varphi(U)$ for some $\alpha \in (0,1)$, and $\varphi \neq \underline{W}$, then $\varphi = \underline{M}$.*

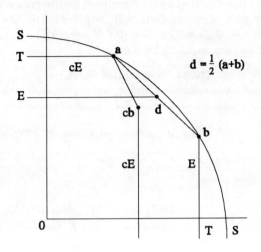

Figure 8.1: Proof of lemma 8.8

Proof We only show (i). Let $(\alpha, 1) \in \varphi(U)$ for some $\alpha \in (0,1)$, and $\varphi \neq \overline{W}$. Then, by IIA, $(\alpha, 1) \in \varphi(\text{comv}\{(\alpha, 1)\}) = \varphi((\alpha, 1)U)$, so by STC, $(1,1) \in \varphi(U)$. Let $\alpha \leq \beta \leq 1$, then, since $(\alpha, 1) \in \varphi(U) \cap (\beta, 1)U$, we have by IIA: $\varphi((\beta, 1)U) = (\beta, 1)U \cap \varphi(U)$, so because $(\beta, 1) \in \varphi((\beta, 1)U)$ by STC and $(1,1) \in \varphi(U)$, we have $(\beta, 1) \in \varphi(U)$. We have shown:

$$(\beta, 1) \in \varphi(U) \text{ for all } \beta \in [\alpha, 1]. \tag{8.1}$$

By (8.1) and IIA applied to $(\alpha, 1)U \subset U$, we obtain $\varphi((\alpha, 1)U) = (\alpha, 1)U \cap \varphi(U)$, hence by (8.1) and STC: $(\beta, 1) \in \varphi(U)$ for all $\beta \in [\alpha^2, 1]$. So, since $\lim_{n \to \infty} \alpha^n = 0$, we have $\overline{M}(U) \subset \varphi(U)$. By lemma 8.8, IR, and lemma 8.7(i) we then have: $\varphi(U) = \overline{M}(U)$.

Let $S \in \mathcal{C}_0$. If $\overline{p}_1(S) > 0$, then $\varphi(S) = \overline{M}(S)$ by a proof analogous to the proof of lemma 8.6. Otherwise, let $x \in W(S)$, $x \geq 0$, $x_1 > 0$. Take $y \in S$ such that $0 < y_1 < x_1$ and $y_2 > x_2$. Then $x \notin \overline{M}(\text{comv}\{x, y\}) = \varphi(\text{comv}\{x, y\})$, so by IIA applied to $\text{comv}\{x, y\} \subset S$, we have $x \notin \varphi(S)$. So $\varphi(S) = \{\overline{p}(S)\} = \overline{M}(S)$, also in this case.   □

Lemma 8.10 *Let $\varphi : \mathcal{C}_0 \to \mathbb{R}^2$ be a multisolution satisfying IR, WPO, STC, and IIA. Then:*

(i) If $(0,1), (1,1) \in \varphi(U)$, then $\varphi = \overline{W}$.

(ii) If $(1,0), (1,1) \in \varphi(U)$, then $\varphi = \underline{W}$.

Proof We only show (i). Suppose $(0,1), (1,1) \in \varphi(U)$. Take $0 < \beta < 1$. By IIA: $\varphi((\beta, 1)U) = \varphi(U) \cap (\beta, 1)U$, hence $(\beta, 1) \in \varphi(U)$, since $(\beta, 1) \in \varphi((\beta, 1)U)$ by STC. Since β was arbitrary, we have $\varphi(U) = \overline{W}(U)$, and hence $\varphi = \overline{W}$, by lemma 8.7(i).   □

Lemma 8.11 *Let $\varphi : \mathcal{C}_0 \to \mathbb{R}^2$ be multisolution satisfying IR, WPO, STC, and IIA. If $\varphi(U) = (1,1)$, then $\varphi \in \{\varphi^H : H \in \mathcal{H}^{\{1,2\}}\}$.*

Proof Assume $\varphi(U) = (1,1)$. Suppose $\varphi(S)\backslash P(S) \neq \emptyset$ for some $S \in \mathcal{C}_0$. Say $x \in \varphi(S)\backslash P(S)$, then $y \in W(S)$ exists with $y \geq x$, $y \neq x$. By STC: $\varphi(yU) = y$. By IIA: $x \in \varphi(yU)$. So we have a contradiction from which we conclude that φ satisfies PO. Hence, in view of lemma 8.8, φ is a bargaining solution. Now the proof is complete by corollary 2.24.   □

Proof of theorem 8.4 As noted before, the proof of the fact that the mentioned multi-solutions satisfy the mentioned properties, is left to the reader. Now let $\varphi : \mathcal{C}_0 \to I\!\!R^2$ be a multisolution satisfying IR, WPO, STC, and IIA. We distinguish a few cases.

(i) $\varphi(U) = (1,1)$. Then $\varphi \in \{\varphi^H : H \in \mathcal{H}^{\{1,2\}}\}$ by lemma 8.11.

(ii) $\varphi(U) \cap \overline{W}(U)\backslash\{(1,1)\} \neq \emptyset$. Then, by lemma 8.8, $\varphi(U) \subset \overline{W}(U)$. If $\varphi(U) = \overline{W}(U)$, then $\varphi = \overline{W}$ by lemma 8.7(i). If $\varphi \neq \overline{W}$ and $(\alpha,1) \in \varphi(U)$ for some $\alpha \in (0,1)$, then $\varphi = \overline{M}$ by lemma 8.9(i). Otherwise $\varphi(U) \subset \{(0,1),(1,1)\}$, hence $\varphi(U) = (0,1)$ by lemma 8.10(i), so $\varphi = \overline{w}$ by lemma 8.6(i).

(iii) $\varphi(U) \cap \underline{W}(U)\backslash\{(1,1)\} \neq \emptyset$. Analogous to (ii), left to the reader.   □

8.2.2 Restricted monotonicity

We start by introducing an extension of the concept of a monotonic curve of section 4.2.

Definition 8.12 A *monotonic multicurve* is a multifunction $\mu : [1,2] \to \nabla$, where $\nabla :=$ conv$\{(1,1),(1,0),(0,1)\}$, with the following properties:

For every $t \in [1,2]$, $\mu(t)$ is a non-empty closed subset of $\{x \in \nabla : x_1 + x_2 = t\}$.   (8.2)

For all $s,t \in [1,2]$ with $s \leq t$: $\mu(t) \subset \mu(s) + I\!\!R_+^2$, $\mu(s) \subset \mu(t) - I\!\!R_+^2$.   (8.3)

The family of all monotonic multicurves is denoted by M.

We will see that to monotonic multicurves correspond closed-valued RM multisolutions. A multisolution φ is called *closed-valued* if $\varphi(S)$ is closed for every $S \in \mathcal{C}_0$. We first take a closer look at monotonic multicurves. For $\mu \in M$, let $D(\mu) := \bigcup_{t\in[1,2]} \mu(t)$. Further, recall that a correspondence $F : X \to Y$ (with X and Y topological spaces) is called *upper semicontinuous* if for every open $U \subset Y$ the set $F^+(U) := \{x \in X : F(x) \subset U\}$ is open in X; and *lower semicontinuous* if for every open $U \subset Y$ the set $F^-(U) := \{x \in X : F(x) \cap U \neq \emptyset\}$ is open in X.

Lemma 8.13 *Let $\mu \in M$. Then μ is upper and lower semicontinuous and $D(\mu)$ is a closed subset of ∇.*

Proof (i) First we prove that μ is upper semicontinuous. Let U be an open subset of ∇ (where ∇ is provided with the relative topology). We show that $\mu^+(U)$ is open in $[1,2]$. This is true if $\mu^+(U) = \emptyset$. Suppose $t^\circ \in \mu^+(U)$. Then $\mu(t^\circ)$ is a compact subset of U. So we can take an $\varepsilon > 0$ such that $T := \{x \in \nabla : ||x - y||_1 < \varepsilon \text{ for some } y \in \mu(t^\circ)\} \subset U$. Let $t \in [1,2]$, with $t^\circ - \varepsilon < t \leq t^\circ$. By (8.3), for each $x \in \mu(t)$ there is an $y \in \mu(t^\circ)$ with $x \leq y$. Then (by (8.2)) $||y - x||_1 = (y_1 - x_1) + (y_2 - x_2) = (y_1 + y_2) - (x_1 + x_2) = t^\circ - t < \varepsilon$, so

$x \in T \subset U$. Hence $\mu(t) \subset U$, $t \in \mu^+(U)$. If $t \in [1,2]$ with $t° \leq t < t° + \varepsilon$, then there is, for each $x \in \mu(t)$, a $z \in \mu(t°)$ with $z \leq x$. We then find, similarly, $\mu(t) \subset U$, $t \in \mu^+(U)$.

(ii) Next, we prove that μ is lower semicontinuous. Let U again be an open subset of $\bigtriangledown$. We show that $\mu^-(U)$ is open in $[1,2]$. Suppose $t^1 \in \mu^-(U)$ and $x \in \mu(t^1) \cap U$. There is a $\delta > 0$ with $\{y \in \bigtriangledown : \|y - x\|_1 < \delta\} \subset U$. Let $s \in [t^1, t^1 + \delta) \cap [1,2]$. Then $u \geq x$ for some $u \in \mu(s)$. Then $\|u - x\|_1 < \delta$, so $u \in U$, $s \in u^-(U)$. Similarly for $s \in (t^1 - \delta, t^1] \cap [1,2]$.

(iii) Finally, we show that $D(\mu)$ is a closed subset of $\bigtriangledown$. Let $H(\mu) := \{(t,x) : t \in [1,2], x \in \mu(t)\}$ be the graph of μ. Then, since μ is upper semicontinuous, $H(\mu)$ is a closed subset of $[1,2] \times \bigtriangledown$ (see Hildenbrand and Kirman (1976, p. 194)). So $H(\mu)$ is compact, and also $D(\mu) = \pi(H(\mu))$ is compact where $\pi : [1,2] \times \bigtriangledown \rightarrow \bigtriangledown$ is the continuous function with $\pi(t,x) = x$ for all $(t,x) \in [1,2] \times \bigtriangledown$.   □

Lemma 8.14 *Let* $S \in \mathcal{C}_0$ *with* $h(S) = (1,1)$, *and* $\mu \in M$.

  (i) *If* $a \in D(\mu)$ *and* $(a - I\!R_+^2) \cap P(S) \neq \emptyset$, *then* $(a - I\!R_+^2) \cap P(S) \cap D(\mu) \neq \emptyset$.

  (ii) *If* $b \in D(\mu)$ *and* $(b + I\!R_+^2) \cap P(S) \neq \emptyset$, *then* $(b + I\!R_+^2) \cap P(S) \cap D(\mu) \neq \emptyset$.

Proof We only prove (ii). If $b \in P(S)$ or $(1,1) \in P(S)$, then there is nothing to prove. So, suppose $b \notin P(S)$ and $(1,1) \notin P(S)$. Let $K := \{x \in \bigtriangledown : b \leq x \leq (1,1)\}$ and let $\beta := b_1 + b_2$. Let $\overline{\mu} : [\beta, 2] \rightarrow \bigtriangledown$ be the multifunction with $\overline{\mu}(s) = \mu(s) \cap K$ for all $s \in [\beta, 2]$. In view of (8.3), $\overline{\mu}(s) \neq \emptyset$ for each $s \in [\beta, 2]$, and $\overline{\mu}$ is upper and lower semicontinuous in view of lemma 8.13 and the fact that $\overline{\mu}$ is the restriction to $[\beta, 2]$ of a monotonic multicurve. Now let

$$
\begin{aligned}
V &:= \{x \in K : x \notin P(S), (x - I\!R_+^2) \cap P(S) \neq \emptyset\}, \\
I_1 &:= \{t \in [\beta, 2] : \overline{\mu}(t) \subset V\}, \\
W &:= \{x \in K : x \notin P(S), (x + I\!R_+^2) \cap P(S) \neq \emptyset\}, \\
I_2 &:= \{t \in [\beta, 2] : \overline{\mu}(t) \cap W \neq \emptyset\}.
\end{aligned}
$$

Note that $2 \in I_1$, that $\beta \in I_2$ because $b \in \overline{\mu}(\beta)$, and that $I_1 \cap I_2 = \emptyset$. Since V and W are open subsets of K (in the relative topology) it follows from the upper and lower semicontinuity of the multifunction $\overline{\mu}$, that I_1 and I_2 are open subsets of $[\beta, 2]$. Now $I_1 \cup I_2 = [\beta, 2]$ if $(b + I\!R_+^2) \cap P(S) \cap D(\mu) = \emptyset$ and that is in contradiction with the connectedness of $[\beta, 2]$. Hence $(b + I\!R_+^2) \cap P(S) \cap D(\mu) \neq \emptyset$.   □

We now associate with each $\mu \in M$ a multifunction $\pi^\mu : \mathcal{C}_0 \rightarrow I\!R^2$. Let $S \in \mathcal{C}_0$. If $h(S) = (1,1)$ then let $\pi^\mu(S) := D(\mu) \cap P(S)$. In general, let $\pi^\mu(S) := h(S)\pi^\mu((h_1(S)^{-1}, h_2(S)^{-1})S)$.

Proposition 8.15 *Let* $\mu \in M$. *Then* π^μ *is a closed-valued multisolution satisfying PO, STC, and RM.*

Proof By lemma 8.14, $\pi^\mu(S) \neq \emptyset$ for each $S \in \mathcal{C}_0$. Since $D(\mu)$ is closed in view of lemma 8.13 and also $P(S)$ is closed, we have $\pi^\mu(S)$ closed for each $S \in \mathcal{C}_0$. Further, it is obvious that π^μ satisfies PO and STC. To prove that π^μ satisfies the RM property, let S and T in $\mathcal{C}_0$ with $h(S) = h(T) = (1,1)$ and $S \subset T$. Take $a \in \pi^\mu(T)$. Then $(a - I\!R_+^2) \cap P(S) \neq \emptyset$. By lemma 8.14(i): $\emptyset \neq (a - I\!R_+^2) \cap P(S) \cap D(\mu) = (a - I\!R_+^2) \cap \pi^\mu(S)$. This implies that $\pi^\mu(T) \subset \pi^\mu(S) + I\!R_+^2$. Analogously, it follows with lemma 8.14(ii) that $\pi^\mu(S) \subset \pi^\mu(T) - I\!R_+^2$.   □

Lemma 8.16 *Let* $\varphi : \mathcal{C}_0 \to I\!\!R^2$ *be a multisolution satisfying PO and RM. Let* $S, T \in \mathcal{C}_0$ *with* $h(S) = h(T)$. *Then* $\varphi(S) \cap P(T) \subset \varphi(T)$.

Proof Let $D := S \cap T \in \mathcal{C}_0$. Then $h(D) = h(S) = h(T)$. Take $y \in \varphi(S) \cap P(T)$. Then $y \in P(D)$. By RM, $x \leq y$ for some $x \in \varphi(D)$. Since also $x \in P(D)$ by PO, we have $x = y$, so $y \in \varphi(D)$. By RM again, there is a $z \in \varphi(T)$ with $y \leq z$. Since $y, z \in P(T)$ we have $y = z \in \varphi(T)$. Hence, $\varphi(S) \cap P(T) \subset \varphi(T)$. □

Lemma 8.17 *Let* $\varphi : \mathcal{C}_0 \to I\!\!R^2$ *be a multisolution satisfying PO and RM. Let* $S \in \mathcal{C}_0$. *Then:*

(i) $\varphi(S) = \varphi(S_0)$,

(ii) φ *is individually rational.*

Proof (ii) follows from (i) and PO, and (i) from PO and RM. □

Proposition 8.18 *Let* $\varphi : \mathcal{C}_0 \to I\!\!R^2$ *be a closed-valued multisolutions satisfying PO, STC, and RM. Then* $\varphi = \pi^\mu$ *for some* $\mu \in M$.

Proof Let $V(t) := \text{comv}\{(1,0), (1, t-1), (t-1, 1), (0,1)\}$ for each $t \in [1,2]$. Define the multifunction $\mu : [1,2] \to I\!\!R^2$ by $\mu(t) := \varphi(V(t))$ for all $t \in [1,2]$. Then $\mu(t)$ is a non-empty closed subset of $P(V(t)) = \{x \in \triangledown : x_1 + x_2 = t\}$ and for $1 \leq s \leq t \leq 2$ we have by RM of φ:

$$\mu(t) = \varphi(V(t)) \subset \varphi(V(s)) + I\!\!R_+^2 = \mu(s) + I\!\!R_+^2,$$
$$\mu(s) = \varphi(V(s)) \subset \varphi(V(t)) - I\!\!R_+^2 = \mu(t) - I\!\!R_+^2.$$

Hence, $\mu \in M$. We want to show that $\varphi = \pi^\mu$. In view of STC, it is sufficient to show that $\varphi(S) = \pi^\mu(S)$ where $S \in \mathcal{C}_0$ with $h(S) = (1,1)$. Note that $\varphi(V(t)) = \pi^\mu(V(t))$ for all $t \in [1,2]$. Take $x \in \pi^\mu(S)$. Let $s := x_1 + x_2$. Then, by applying lemma 8.16 we obtain:

$$x \in \pi^\mu(S) \cap P(V(s)) \Rightarrow x \in \pi^\mu(V(s)) = \varphi(V(s)),$$
$$x \in \varphi(V(s)) \cap P(S) \Rightarrow x \in \varphi(S).$$

Hence, $\pi^\mu(S) \subset \varphi(S)$. For the converse, take an $y \in \varphi(S)$ and let $t := y_1 + y_2$ (note that $y \in \triangledown$ in view of PO of φ and lemma 8.17(ii)). Then, by applying lemma 8.16 again:

$$y \in \varphi(S) \cap P(V(t)) \Rightarrow y \in \varphi(V(t)) = \pi^\mu(V(t)),$$
$$y \in \pi^\mu(V(t)) \cap P(S) \Rightarrow y \in \pi^\mu(S).$$

So $\varphi(S) \subset \pi^\mu(S)$. We have proved that $\varphi(S) = \pi^\mu(S)$. □

The main result of this part of the section follows from propositions 8.15 and 8.18.

Theorem 8.19 $\{\pi^\mu : \mu \in M\}$ *is the family of all closed-valued multisolutions:* $\mathcal{C}_0 \to I\!\!R^2$ *which satisfy PO, STC, and RM.*

In Peters *et al.* (1983), it is shown that PO in theorem 8.19 can be relaxed to WPO if a class of not necessarily comprehensive bargaining games is considered, instead of $\mathcal{C}_0$. In the present theorem 8.19 however, PO cannot be replaced by WPO, as the following example shows.

Example 8.20 All following multisolutions $\varphi : \mathcal{C}_0 \to I\!\!R^2$ satisfy WPO, STC, RM, but not PO. For every $S \in \mathcal{C}_0$:

(i) $\varphi(S) = W(S)$,

(ii) $\varphi(S) = W(S) \cap I\!\!R_+^2$,

(iii) $\varphi(S) = h(S)(D(\mu) \cap W((h_1(S)^{-1}, h_2(S)^{-1})S))$ for a fixed arbitrary $\mu \in M$,

(iv) $\varphi(S) = \{([\bar{p}_1(S)]^2, \bar{p}_2(S)), ([\bar{p}_1(S)]^3, \bar{p}_2(S))\}$ if $h(S) = (1,1)$ and
$\varphi(S) = h(S)\varphi((h_1(S)^{-1}, h_2(S)^{-1})S)$ otherwise.

8.3 Probabilistic solutions

Whereas a bargaining solution assigns exactly one point to a bargaining game, and a multisolution a set of points, a so-called probabilistic solution assigns a probability distribution (measure) to each bargaining game. We will see that (multi)solutions can be related to probabilistic solutions, study "probabilistic" versions of the independence of irrelevant alternatives property, and characterize families of probabilistic solutions with the aid of such properties. Thereby, like in the previous section, results of section 2.3 are extended. Attention is again restricted to the class $\mathcal{C}_0$ of 2-person bargaining games.

For $S \in \mathcal{C}_0$, we denote by $\sigma(S)$ the Borel σ-algebra of S. A *probability measure on* S is a map $\varphi_S : \sigma(S) \to [0,1]$ such that $\varphi_S(S) = 1$ and such that φ_S is σ-additive, i.e. $\varphi_S(\bigcup_i E_i) = \sum_i \varphi_S(E_i)$ if $E_1, E_2 \dots$ is a sequence of pairwise disjoint elements in $\sigma(S)$. The *support of* φ_S, denoted $\text{supp}(\varphi_S)$, is defined by

$$\text{supp}(\varphi_S) := \{x \in S : \varphi_S(E) \neq 0 \text{ for all open } E \text{ in } S \text{ with } x \in E\}.$$

$M(S)$ denotes the family of all probability measures on S and $F(S) \subset M(S)$ the family of all probability measures with finite support.

A *probabilistic solution* is a map φ assigning to each $S \in \mathcal{C}_0$ an element φ_S in $M(S)$. For $S \in \mathcal{C}_0$ and $E \in \sigma(S)$, $\varphi_S(E)$ can be interpreted as the probability that the final agreement between the players in the bargaining game S will be in E.

With a bargaining solution $\varphi : \mathcal{C}_0 \to I\!\!R^2$ we associate a probabilistic solution $\tilde{\varphi}$ by $\tilde{\varphi}_S(\{\varphi(S)\}) = 1$ for every $S \in \mathcal{C}_0$. $\tilde{\varphi}$ is the *probabilistic solution corresponding to* φ, and we write φ instead of $\tilde{\varphi}$. As in the previous section, we omit braces in case of one-point sets.

Further, the (multi)solution $\tilde{\varphi} : \mathcal{C}_0 \to I\!\!R^2$ *supports* the probabilistic solution φ if $\tilde{\varphi}(S) = \text{supp}(\varphi_S)$ for every $S \in \mathcal{C}_0$.

In the remainder of this section, we use the abbreviation "p-solution" for "probabilistic solution". Many properties for bargaining solutions can be translated in an obvious way for a probabilistic solution φ, as in the following definition.

Definition 8.21

(i) *Individual rationality* (IR): $\varphi_S(S \cap I\!\!R_+^2) = 1$ for all $S \in \mathcal{C}_0$.

(ii) *[Weak] Pareto optimality* ([W]PO): $\varphi_S(P(S)) = 1$ $[\varphi_S(W(S)) = 1]$ for all $S \in \mathcal{C}_0$.

(iii) *Scale transformation covariance* (STC): $\varphi_{aS}(aE) = \varphi_S(E)$ for all $S \in \mathcal{C}_0$, $E \in \sigma(S)$, and $a \in I\!\!R_{++}^2$.

We propose the following "probabilistic" version of the IIA property, for a p-solution φ. For solutions, this property coincides with the IIA property.

Definition 8.22 φ is *independent of irrelevant alternatives* (IIA) if, for all S and T in $\mathcal{C}_0$ with $S \subset T$, and every E in $\sigma(S)$, we have $\varphi_S(E) \geq \varphi_T(E)$.

This IIA property may be interpreted as follows. If the set of feasible outcomes in a bargaining game is decreased, then every still available (Borel) subset of outcomes should have at least as large a probability of containing the final agreement of the game as it originally had. Two preliminary results with respect to this property are in order. Recall the notation $S_0 = \text{com}(S \cap \mathbb{R}_+^2)$ for $S \in \mathcal{C}_0$.

Lemma 8.23 *Let φ be a p-solution satisfying IR and IIA. Then:*

(i) $\varphi_S(E) = \varphi_{S_0}(E)$ for every $S \in \mathcal{C}_0$ and $E \in \sigma(S_0)$.

(ii) For all $S, T \in \mathcal{C}_0$ with $S_0 \subset T_0$, we have $\varphi_S(E) \geq \varphi_T(E)$ for every $E \in \sigma(S)$.

Proof Let $S \in \mathcal{C}_0$. Then by IR and IIA, $\varphi_{S_0}(E) = \varphi_{S_0}(E \cap \mathbb{R}_+^2) \geq \varphi_S(E \cap \mathbb{R}_+^2) = \varphi_S(E)$ and $\varphi_{S_0}((S \cap \mathbb{R}_+^2) \backslash E) \geq \varphi_S((S \cap \mathbb{R}_+^2) \backslash E)$, hence $\varphi_{S_0}(E) = \varphi_S(E)$ since otherwise $\varphi_{S_0}(S \cap \mathbb{R}_+^2) > 1$. This proves (i). Let $T \in \mathcal{C}_0$ with $S_0 \subset T_0$. Let $E' \in \sigma(S)$. Then $\varphi_S(E') = \varphi_S(E' \cap \mathbb{R}_+^2) = \varphi_{S_0}(E' \cap \mathbb{R}_+^2) \geq \varphi_{T_0}(E' \cap \mathbb{R}_+^2) = \varphi_T(E' \cap \mathbb{R}_+^2) = \varphi_T(E')$, by IR, IIA, and (i). This proves (ii).   □

Lemma 8.24 *Let $S \in \mathcal{C}_0$ and let φ be a p-solution with the properties IR, STC, and IIA. Then $x \notin \mathbb{R}_+^2 \cap P(S) \cup \{0, \underline{w}(S), \overline{w}(S)\}$ implies $\varphi_S(x) = 0$.*

Proof Let $x \in S$. If $x \notin \mathbb{R}_+^2$, then $\varphi_S(x) = 0$ by IR. Suppose $x \in \mathbb{R}_+^2$, and suppose there exists a set $S_x \subset S$ such that $y \geq x$ for all $y \in S_x$, S_x is countably infinite, and for every $y \in S_x$ there exists an $a \in \mathbb{R}_{++}^2$ with $ay = x$. By STC and IIA, if $y \in S_x$ and $ay = x$ for some $a \in \mathbb{R}_{++}^2$, then $\varphi_S(y) = \varphi_{aS}(x) \geq \varphi_S(x)$ since $a \leq (1,1)$. If $\varphi_S(x) > 0$, then summing for all $y \in S_x$ would yield $\infty = \varphi_S(S_x)$, an impossibility. So $\varphi_S(x) = 0$. The proof is complete by the observation that such a set S_x exists for every $x \in S \cap \mathbb{R}_+^2$ with $x \notin P(S) \cap \{0, \underline{w}(S), \overline{w}(S)\}$.   □

The remainder of this section consists of two parts. In subsection 8.3.1, we characterize a family of finite p-solutions with the aid of the IIA property; we call a p-solution *finite* if $\varphi_S \in F(S)$ for every $S \in \mathcal{C}_0$. In subsection 8.3.2, we characterize a family of p-solutions with the aid of the so-called "conditional" IIA property, which is strictly weaker than IIA.

8.3.1   Finite probabilistic solutions with the IIA property

In order to formulate the main result of this subsection, some additional notation is needed. For every $k \in \mathbb{N}$, let

$$Q^k := \{x \in \mathbb{R}_+^k : \sum_{i=1}^{k} x_i = 1\}$$

denote the set of probability vectors of length k. Let Υ denote the family of p-solutions $\{\varphi^H :$ $H \in \mathcal{H}^{\{1,2\}}\} \cup \{\underline{w}, \overline{w}, \delta\}$, where $\underline{w}$ and $\overline{w}$ were defined in section 8.2, and we use δ to denote the disagreement point solution (see section 2.2). For $q \in Q^k$ and $v = (v^1, v^2, \ldots, v^k) \in \Upsilon^k$ let the finite p-solution $q \cdot v$ be defined by $q \cdot v_S(E) := \sum_{i=1}^{k} q_i v_S^i(E)$ for every $S \in \mathcal{C}_0$ and $E \in \sigma(S)$. In words, $q \cdot v$ is a lottery over k p-solutions of the family Υ. The main result in this subsection is the following theorem.

Theorem 8.25 φ *is a finite p-solution satisfying IR, STC, and IIA, if and only if $\varphi = q \cdot v$ for some $q \in Q^k$ and $v \in \Upsilon^k$.*

Observe that corollary 2.24 follows from theorem 8.25. The "if part" of this theorem is the following proposition.

Proposition 8.26 *For every $k \in \mathbb{N}$, $q \in Q^k$, and $v \in \Upsilon^k$, the p-solution $q \cdot v$ is finite and satisfies IR, STC, and IIA.*

Proof Follows from the fact that every solution in Υ has the mentioned properties. □

The "only if" part of theorem 8.25 is based on a string of lemmas. Let $S \in \mathcal{C}_0$. As in section 5.2, $f^S : [0, h_1(S)] \to \mathbb{R}$ has $\overline{W}(S) \cup P(S) \cap \mathbb{R}_+^2$ as its graph, and $g^S : [0, h_2(S)] \to \mathbb{R}$ has $\underline{W}(S) \cup P(S) \cap \mathbb{R}_+^2$ as its graph (see section 8.2 for the definition of $\underline{W}(S)$ and $\overline{W}(S)$). Both f^S and g^S are nonincreasing and concave. Further, it will be convenient to write N^t instead of φ^H with $H < \{1,2\}, <t, 1-t>$, N^0 instead of $\overline{p}$, and N^1 instead of $\underline{p}$ (cf. section 5.5).

Lemma 8.27 *Let $S \in \mathcal{C}_0$. Then:*

(i) *There are at most countably many points in the domains of f^S and g^S where these functions are not differentiable.*

(ii) *For every $x \in P(S) \cap \mathbb{R}_+^2$ there is a $\varphi \in \{N^t : 0 \leq t \leq 1\}$ with $\varphi(S) = x$; if $x > 0$, $x \neq \overline{p}(S)$ then this φ is unique if and only if g^S is differentiable at x_2; if $x > 0$, $x \neq \underline{p}(S)$, then this φ is unique if and only if f^S is differentiable at x_1.*

(iii) *For every $x \in P(S) \cap \mathbb{R}_+^2$, there is a closed interval J_x in $[0,1]$ such that, for all $\varphi \in \{N^t : 0 \leq t \leq 1\}$, $\varphi(S) = x$ if and only if $\varphi = N^t$ for some $t \in J_x$.*

(iv) *If $x, y \in P(S) \cap \mathbb{R}_+^2$, then $\alpha \leq \beta$ for all $\alpha \in J_x$, $\beta \in J_y$ if and only if $x_1 \leq y_1$.*

Proof (i) E.g. Theorem 25.3 in Rockafellar (1970). (ii) Let $x \in P(S) \cap \mathbb{R}_+^2$. If $x \neq \overline{p}(S)$ and $x \neq \underline{p}(S)$ then there is a supporting line of S at x (e.g. Theorem 11.6 in Rockafellar (1970)) with a strictly positive normal vector, say $(tx_1^{-1}, (1-t)x_2^{-1})$ for some $t \in (0,1)$. Then $x = N^t(S)$ by lemma 2.20. Now let $x > 0$, $x \neq \overline{p}(S)$. If $(g^S)'(x_2)$ exists then either $(g^S)'(x_2) = 0$ implying $\varphi(S) = x \iff \varphi = \underline{p}$ for all $\varphi \in \{N^t : 0 \leq t \leq 1\}$ by lemma 2.20, or $(g^S)'(x_2) < 0$ implying $\varphi(S) = x \iff \varphi = N^s$ for all $\varphi \in \{N^t : 0 \leq t \leq 1\}$ and some unique $s \in (0,1)$, by lemma 2.20 again. If g^S is not differentiable at x_2, then $N^t(S) = x$ for infinitely many $t \in (0,1)$, by lemma 2.20 again. The final statement in (ii) can be proved analogously. Also (iii) and (iv) can be proved mainly with the aid of lemma 2.20. We only note: if $x = \overline{p}(S) = \overline{w}(S)$, then $J_x = \{0\}$; if $x = \overline{p}(S) \neq \overline{w}(S)$ then $J_x = [0,t]$ for some $t \in [0,1]$; if $x \in P(S)$ with $\overline{p}_1(S) < x_1 < \underline{p}_1(S)$ then $J_x = [s,t]$ for some $s,t \in (0,1)$ with

$s \leq t$; if $x = \underline{p}(S) \neq \underline{w}(S)$, then $J_x = [t, 1]$ for some $t \in [0, 1]$; and if $x = \underline{p}(S) = \underline{w}(S)$, then $J_x = \{1\}$. The proof of these facts is left to the reader. $\square$

If φ is a p-solution with $\varphi = q \cdot v$ for some $q \in Q^k$ and $v \in \Upsilon^k$ then according to lemma 8.27 the values of k, q, and v could be determined by considering φ_S for an $S \in \mathcal{C}_0$ with only positive Pareto optimal points and with the functions f^S and g^S differentiable everywhere on the interiors of their domains; e.g., the comprehensive hull of the ball in $I\!\!R^2$ with center $(1, 1)$ and radius 1. For proof-technical reasons, however, it is more convenient to look at the games $\Delta = \text{comv}\{(1, 0), (0, 1)\}$ and $U = \text{com}\{(1, 1)\}$.

Lemma 8.28 *Let φ be a finite p-solution satisfying IR, STC, and IIA. Then:*

(i) $\varphi_\Delta(0) = \varphi_U(0)$,

(ii) $\varphi_U((1, 1)) = \varphi_\Delta(P(\Delta)) - \varphi_U((1, 0)) - \varphi_U((0, 1))$,

(iii) $\varphi_\Delta((1, 0)) \geq \varphi_U((0, 1))$, $\varphi_\Delta((0, 1)) \geq \varphi_U((0, 1))$.

Proof By IIA, $\varphi_\Delta(0) \geq \varphi_U(0)$, and by IIA and STC, $\varphi_U(0) = \varphi_{\frac{1}{2}U}(0) \geq \varphi_\Delta(0)$, hence (i) is proved. (iii) follows by IIA. In view of lemma 8.24 and (i), $\varphi_\Delta(P(\Delta)) = 1 - \varphi_\Delta(0) = 1 - \varphi_U(0) = \varphi_U((1, 1)) + \varphi_U((1, 0)) + \varphi_U((0, 1))$, hence (ii) is proved. $\square$

For an arbitrary fixed p-solution φ, we define the following numbers in $[0, 1]$:
$q_\delta := \varphi_U(0)$, $q_{\underline{w}} := \varphi_U((1, 0))$, $q_{\overline{w}} := \varphi_U((0, 1))$, $q_1 := \varphi_\Delta((1, 0)) - \varphi_U((1, 0))$, $q_0 := \varphi_\Delta((0, 1)) - \varphi_U((0, 1))$, $q_t := \varphi_\Delta((t, 1 - t))$ for every $t \in (0, 1)$. If φ is a finite p-solution satisfying IR, STC, and IIA, then, by lemma 8.28 and lemma 8.24, we know:

$$\varphi_S(E) = q_\delta \delta_S(E) + q_{\underline{w}} \underline{w}_S(E) + q_{\overline{w}} \overline{w}_S(E) + \sum_{t \in [0, 1]} q_t N_S^t(E) \text{ for each } E \in \sigma(S) \quad (8.4)$$

holds for $S = U$ and $S = \Delta$. Until further notice, φ will be this arbitrary but fixed finite p-solution satisfying IR, STC, and IIA. We want to show that φ satisfies (8.4) for every $S \in \mathcal{C}_0$.

Lemma 8.29 *Let $S \in \mathcal{C}_0$. Then:*

(i) $\varphi_S(N^t(S)) \geq q_t$ *for every* $0 \leq t \leq 1$,

(ii) $\varphi_S(0) \geq q_\delta$,

(iii) $\varphi_S(\underline{w}(S)) \geq q_{\underline{w}}$,

(iv) $\varphi_S(\overline{w}(S)) \geq q_{\overline{w}}$,

(v) $\varphi_S(N^t(S)) \geq q_1$,

(vi) $\varphi_S(N^0(S)) \geq q_0$.

Proof (ii), (iii), and (iv), follow, with the aid of lemma 8.23 (ii) from applying STC and IIA to S and $h(S)U$. (i) follows, with the aid of lemma 8.23 (ii) and lemma 2.20, from applying, for each $t \in (0, 1)$, STC, and IIA to S and $(t^{-1}N_1^t(S), (1 - t)^{-1}N_2^t(S))\Delta$. Of (v) and (vi), we prove (vi). If $S = U$, then (vi) holds since (8.4) holds for $S = U$. Now suppose $S \neq U$. Since $\varphi_S \in F(S)$, there is a point $z \in P(S)$, $z \neq N^0(S)$ such that $\varphi_S(x) = 0$ for all

$x \in P(S)$ with $N_1^0(S) < x_1 \le z_1$. Let the straight line through $\overline{w}(S)$ and z contain $(\alpha, 0)$ where $\alpha > 0$, and let $T := \text{comv}\{\overline{w}(S), (\alpha, 0)\}$. Let $V := S \cap T$. By STC, $\varphi_T(\overline{w}(S)) = q_0 + q_{\overline{w}}$, hence by IIA, $\varphi_V(\overline{w}(S)) \ge q_0 + q_{\overline{w}}$. We now distinguish two cases. First, suppose $\overline{w}(S) \ne N^0(S)$. By the choice of z and lemma 8.24, $\varphi_S(V) = 1 - \varphi_S(N^0(S))$. Further, $\varphi_S(V) = \varphi_S(\overline{w}(S)) + \varphi_S(V \backslash \{\overline{w}(S)\})$, so $\varphi_S(\overline{w}(S)) = 1 - \varphi_S(N^0(S)) = \varphi_S(V \backslash \{\overline{w}(S)\}) \ge 1 - \varphi_S(N^0(S)) - \varphi_V(V) + \varphi_V(\overline{w}(S)) \ge q_{\overline{w}} + q_0 - \varphi_S(N^0(S))$. Further, STC, and IIA give $q_{\overline{w}} = \varphi_{aU}(\overline{w}(S)) \ge \varphi_S(\overline{w}(S))$ where $a = N^0(S)$. We conclude, for this case, that $\varphi_S(N^0(S)) \ge q_0$. Second, if $\overline{w}(S) = N^0(S)$ then $1 - \varphi_S(N^0(S)) = \varphi_S(V \backslash \{\overline{w}(S)\}) \le \varphi_V(V \backslash \{\overline{w}(S)\}) \le 1 - q_0 - q_{\overline{w}}$. So also in this case: $\varphi_S(N^0(S)) \ge q_0$. □

If $S \in \mathcal{C}_0$ is such that the set $\{\overline{w}(S), \underline{w}(S)\} \cup \{N^t(S) : q_t > 0\}$ contains exactly $2 + |\{t \in [0,1] : q_t > 0\}|$ elements, then φ satisfies (8.4) for such an S, in view of lemma 8.29, since the sum of all probabilities $(q_\delta, q_{\underline{w}}, \dots)$ equals 1. The following two lemmas take care of games S where this is not the case.

Lemma 8.30 *Let $S \in \mathcal{C}_0$.*

   (i) *If $\overline{w}(S) = N^0(S)$, then $\varphi_S(\overline{w}(S)) \ge q_{\overline{w}} + q_0$.*

   (ii) *If $\underline{w}(S) = N^1(S)$, then $\varphi_S(\underline{w}(S)) \ge q_{\underline{w}} + q_1$.*

Proof We only prove (i). Let $\overline{w}(S) = N^0(S)$. Choose $z > 0$ as in the proof of lemma 8.29. Let $V := \{x \in S : x_2 \le z_2\}$. Then, by IIA, $\varphi_V(V \backslash \{z, (0, z_2)\}) \ge \varphi_S(V \backslash \{z, (0, z_2)\}) = \varphi_S(S \backslash \{\overline{w}(S)\}) = 1 - \varphi_S(\overline{w}(S))$. So $1 = \varphi_V(V) \ge 1 - \varphi_S(\overline{w}(S)) + \varphi_V(\{z, (0, z_2)\}) \ge 1 - \varphi_S(\overline{w}(S)) + q_0 + q_{\overline{w}}$, where the last inequality follows from lemma 8.29, (iv) and (vi). We conclude that $\varphi_S(\overline{w}(S)) \ge q_{\overline{w}} + q_0$. □

Lemma 8.31 *Let $S \in \mathcal{C}_0$, $z \in P(S)$, $z > 0$. Then: $\varphi_S(z) \ge \sum_{t:N^t(S)=z} q_t$.*

Proof Let $I := \{N^t : N^t(S) = z, q_t > 0\}$. If $|I| = 1$, then the proof is complete in view of lemma 8.27, (i), (v), and (vi). If $N^0, N^1 \in I$, then $S = h(S)U$ (e.g., lemma 2.7 (iii)), and the proof is complete again. We are left with the case: $|I| \ge 2$ and $\{N^0, N^1\} \not\subset I$, and we will give a proof by induction on $|I|$. So we suppose the lemma holds for $|I| < k$, where $k \in \mathbb{N}$, $k \ge 2$. Then let $|I| = k$, $I \not\supset \{N^0, N^1\}$. Let J_z be the closed interval in $[0,1]$ as in lemma 8.27 (iii). There is an $r \in \text{int}(J_z)$ such that $t' < r < t''$, with $t', t'' \in J_z$ and $N^{t'}, N^{t''} \in I$. By lemma 2.20, there is a supporting line ℓ of S at z with equation $rz_2 x_1 + (1 - r) z_1 x_2 = z_1 z_2$. Since $r \in \text{int}(J_z)$, $\ell \cap S = \{z\}$. Let $\varepsilon > 0$, $\varepsilon < z_1 z_2$. Then:

$$S^\varepsilon := S \cap \{x \in \mathbb{R}^2 : rz_2 x_1 + (1 - r) z_1 x_2 \le z_1 z_2 - \varepsilon\} \in \mathcal{C}_0.$$

By lemma 2.20, $N^r(S^\varepsilon) = (z_1 z_2 - \varepsilon)(z_1 z_2)^{-1} z$. Since $z > N^r(S^\varepsilon)$, we have $N^r(S^\varepsilon) \notin P(S)$, so, in particular, g^{S^ε} is differentiable at $N_2^r(S^\varepsilon)$. Hence, it follows by lemma 8.27, (ii)–(iv), that:

$$N_1^t(S^\varepsilon) < [>] N_1^r(S^\varepsilon) \text{ if } N^t \in I \text{ with } t < [>]r,$$
$$N_1^1(S^\varepsilon) > N_1^r(S^\varepsilon), N_1^0(S^\varepsilon) < N_1^r(S^\varepsilon). \tag{8.5}$$

Because $\ell \cap S = \{z\}$ and φ is a finite p-solution, there is an $\eta \in (0, z_1 z_2)$ so small that

$$\varphi_S(S \backslash \{z\}) = \varphi_S(S^\eta) = \varphi_S(S^\eta \backslash A) \tag{8.6}$$

where $A := \{x \in S^{\eta} : rz_2x_1 + (1-r)z_1x_2 = z_1z_2 - \eta\}$. By definition of S^{η}, we have $\psi(S^{\eta}) \in A$ for all $\psi \in I$. By the choice of r, (8.5), and the induction hypothesis, we obtain:

$$\varphi_{S^{\eta}}(A) \geq \alpha := \sum_{N^t \in I} q_t. \tag{8.7}$$

By (8.7) we have: $1 = \varphi_{S^{\eta}}(S^{\eta}) = \varphi_{S^{\eta}}(S^{\eta}\backslash A) + \varphi_{S^{\eta}}(A) \geq \alpha + \varphi_{S^{\eta}}(S^{\eta}\backslash A)$.

So by (8.6): $\varphi_S(S\backslash\{z\}) \leq 1 - \alpha$, hence: $\varphi_S(z) \geq \alpha$, which proves the lemma. $\quad\square$

Proof of theorem 8.25 The "if" part of the theorem is proposition 8.26. For the "only if" part, let φ be a finite p-solution with the properties IR, STC, and IIA. We want to show: $\varphi = q \cdot v$ for some $k \in I\!N$, $q \in Q^k$, $v \in \Upsilon^k$. Let $q_\delta, q_{\overline{w}}, q_{\underline{w}}, q_t$, be the numbers defined before lemma 8.29. Among these numbers there are only finitely many positive ones, say k, and these sum to 1, in view of lemma 8.28. These positive numbers can be arranged to constitute a vector $q \in Q^k$, and the corresponding solutions constitute an element $v \in \Upsilon^k$. Lemmas 8.29–8.31 show that φ satisfies (8.4) for every $S \in \mathcal{C}_0$. Hence, $\varphi = q \cdot v$. $\quad\square$

We conclude this part of section 8.3 by noting that corollary 2.24 can be derived from theorem 8.25 by considering p-solutions corresponding to bargaining solutions; recall that corollary 2.24 provides a characterization of the family of bargaining solutions $\{\varphi^H : H \in \mathcal{H}^{\{1,2\}}\}$, i.e., the family $\{N^t : 0 \leq t \leq 1\}$ in the notation introduced above.

8.3.2 Conditional independence of irrelevant alternatives

This subsection is concerned with a variation on theorem 8.25. A p-solution φ is no longer required to be finite, but IIA is replaced by the following, stronger property. This property bears close resemblance to the so-called Choice Axiom in Luce (1979).

Definition 8.32 The p-solution φ is called *conditionally independent of irrelevant alternatives* (CIIA) if for all $S, T \in \mathcal{C}_0$ with $S \subset T$ and every E in $\sigma(S)$, we have $\varphi_S(E)\varphi_T(S) = \varphi_T(E)$.

An equivalent way to formulate CIIA is: For all S and T in $\mathcal{C}_0$ with $S \subset T$, and for all $E \in \sigma(S)$, if $\varphi_T(S) \neq 0$, then $\varphi_S(E) = \varphi_T(E)\varphi_T(S)^{-1}$. So $\varphi_S(E)$ is equal to the conditional probability of E given S under φ_T. This explains the use of the expression "conditional" IIA.

Note that, for S and T in $\mathcal{C}_0$ with $S \subset T$, and $E \in \sigma(S)$, IIA only requires $\varphi_S(E) \geq \varphi_T(E)$. If $\varphi_T(T\backslash S) \neq 0$, then this remaining "probability mass" has to be distributed over S. The CIIA property describes one way to do this. Thus, IIA is weaker than CIIA; in the sequel, it will turn out that IIA is strictly weaker, even in the presence of the conditions of PO, IR, and STC.

The p-solutions described in the following definition all satisfy IR, STC, and CIIA. The *indicator function* of a set E is denoted by 1_E, i.e., $1_E(x) = 0$ if $x \notin E$, $1_E(x) = 1$ if $x \in E$.

Definition 8.33 For every $t \in (0, \infty)$, the solutions $\underline{\delta}^t, \overline{\delta}^t, \underline{W}^t, \overline{W}^t$, are defined as follows. For $S \in \mathcal{C}_0$ and $E \in \sigma(S)$,

$$\underline{\delta}_S^t(E) := \underline{w}_1(S)^{-t} \int_{[0,\underline{w}_1(S)]} 1_{\{x \in E : x_2 = 0\}}(x) dx_1^t,$$

$$\overline{\delta}^t_S(E) \ := \ \overline{w}_2(S)^{-t} \int_{[0,\overline{w}_2(S)]} 1_{\{x\in E: x_1=0\}}(x)dx^t_2,$$

$$\underline{W}^t_S(E) \ := \ \begin{cases} \underline{p}_2(S)^{-t} \int_{[0,\underline{p}_2(S)]} 1_{\{x\in E: x_1=\underline{p}_1(S)\}}(x)dx^t_2 \text{ if } \underline{p}_2(S) > 0 \\ \underline{w}_S(E) \text{ if } \underline{p}_2(S) = 0, \end{cases}$$

$$\overline{W}^t_S(E) \ := \ \begin{cases} \overline{p}_1(S)^{-t} \int_{[0,\overline{p}_1(S)]} 1_{\{x\in E: x_2=\overline{p}_2(S)\}}(x)dx^t_1 \text{ if } \overline{p}_1(S) > 0 \\ \overline{w}_S(E) \text{ if } \overline{p}_1(S) = 0. \end{cases}$$

For all $t,s \in (0,\infty)$, the solutions $h^{t,s}$ are defined as follows. For $S \in \mathcal{C}_0$, $E \in \sigma(S)$:

$$h^{t,s}_S(E) := \alpha \iint_{\mathbb{R}^2_+} 1_E(x)dx^t_1 dx^s_2 \text{ where } \alpha := \left(\iint_{\mathbb{R}^2_+} 1_S(x)dx^t_1 dx^s_2 \right)^{-1}.$$

Thus, for $S \in \mathcal{C}_0$, $\underline{\delta}^t_S$ and $\overline{\delta}^t_S$ are nonatomic probability measures with supports $\mathrm{conv}\{0,\underline{w}(S)\}$ and $\mathrm{conv}\{0,\overline{w}(S)\}$ respectively, and $\underline{W}^t_S$ and $\overline{W}^t_S$ are nonatomic probability measures with supports $\underline{W}(S)$ and $\overline{W}(S)$ (if $\underline{W}(S) \neq \{\underline{w}(S)\}$, $\overline{W}(S) \neq \{\overline{w}(S)\}$), respectively, and $h^{t,s}_S$ is a nonatomic probability measure with support $S \cap \mathbb{R}^2_+$.

The proof of the following proposition is left to the reader.

Proposition 8.34 *If* $\varphi \in \Upsilon$ *or* $\varphi \in \{\underline{\delta}^t,\overline{\delta}^t,\underline{W}^t,\overline{W}^t,h^{t,s} : t,s \in (0,\infty)\}$, *then* φ *satisfies IR, STC, and CIIA.*

We show that the converse of this proposition also holds. The proof is based on a string of lemmas. In these lemmas, φ is an arbitrary but fixed p-solution satisfying IR, STC, and CIIA.

Lemma 8.35 *Let* $E \in \sigma(U)$, $E \subset \mathbb{R}^2_+$, *and let* $a^1,a^2,\ldots \in \mathbb{R}^2_{++}$ *with* $(1,1) \geq a^1 \geq a^2 \geq \ldots$ *Let* $a^n E = E$ *for every* $n \in \mathbb{N}$, *and* $E = (\lim_{n\to\infty} a^n)U \cap \mathbb{R}^2_+$. *If* $\varphi_U(E) > 0$, *then* $\varphi_U(E) = 1$.

Proof Let $\varphi_U(E) =: \varepsilon > 0$. By STC and CIIA, for every $n \in \mathbb{N}$, $\varepsilon = \varphi_U(E) = \varphi_{a^n U}(E)\varphi_U(a^n U) = \varepsilon\varphi_U(a^n U)$, hence $\varphi_U(a^n U) = 1$. So $\lim_{n\to\infty} \varphi_U(a^n U) = 1$, which implies, by σ-additivity of φ_U, that $\varphi_U(E) = 1$. $\qquad\square$

Lemma 8.36

(i) $\varphi_U(0) > 0 \Rightarrow \varphi_U(0) = 1$,

(ii) $\varphi_U((1,0)) > 0 \Rightarrow \varphi_U((1,0)) = 1$,

(iii) $\varphi_U((0,1)) > 0 \Rightarrow \varphi_U((0,1)) = 1$,

(iv) $\varphi_U((1,1)) > 0 \Rightarrow \varphi_U((1,1)) = 1$.

Proof (i) Apply lemma 8.35 with $E = \{0\}$ and $a^n = (n^{-1},n^{-1})$ for every $n \in \mathbb{N}$.

(ii) Suppose $0 < \varepsilon = \varphi_U((1,0))$. Let $0 < a < (1,1)$. By STC, CIIA, and lemma 8.24, $0 = \varphi_U((a_1,0)) = \varphi_U(aU)\varphi_{aU}((a_1,0)) = \varepsilon\varphi_U(aU)$, hence $\varphi_U(aU) = 0$. From this we may conclude $\varphi_U(\mathrm{conv}\{(0,0),(1,0)\}\backslash\{(1,0)\}) = 0$. Now apply lemma 8.35 with $E = \mathrm{conv}\{(0,0),(1,0)\}$ and $a^n = (1,n^{-1})$ for every $n \in \mathbb{N}$. This gives $\varphi_U(\mathrm{conv}\{(0,0),(1,0)\}) = 1$, hence $\varphi_U((1,0)) = 1$.

(iii) Analogous to (ii).   (iv) Analogously as in (ii), one proves $\varphi_U(aU) = 0$ for every $a \in I\!\!R_{++}^2$ with $a \leq (1,0)$, $a \neq (1,1)$. Hence, $\varphi_U(U\backslash\{(1,0)\}) = \varphi_U(\cup_{a \in A}aU) = 0$ where $A := \{a \in I\!\!Q_{++}^2 : a \leq (1,1), a \neq (1,1)\}$. So $\varphi_U((1,1)) = 1$. $\square$

For every $S \in \mathcal{C}_0$, we denote $\underline{\delta}(S) := \text{conv}\{(0,0), \underline{w}(S)\}$, and $\overline{\delta}(S) := \text{conv}\{(0,0), \overline{w}(S)\}$. ($\underline{\delta}, \overline{\delta} : \mathcal{C}_0 \to I\!\!R^2$ are multisolutions.)

Lemma 8.37

(i) $\varphi_U(\text{relint}(\underline{\delta}(U))) = \varepsilon > 0 \Rightarrow \varepsilon = 1$.

(ii) $\varphi_U(\text{relint}(\overline{\delta}(U))) = \varepsilon > 0 \Rightarrow \varepsilon = 1$.

Proof (i) Suppose $0 < \varepsilon = \varphi_U(\text{relint}(\underline{\delta}(U)))$. By lemma 8.35 with $E = \underline{\delta}(U)$ and $a^n = (1, n^{-1})$ for every $n \in I\!\!N$, we have $\varphi_U(\underline{\delta}(U)) = 1$. Since $\varepsilon > 0$ we have in view of lemma 8.36 (i), (ii): $\varepsilon = 1$.   (ii) Analogous to (i). $\square$

Lemma 8.38

(i) $\varphi_U(\text{relint}(\underline{W}(U))) = \varepsilon > 0 \Rightarrow \varepsilon > 1$.

(ii) $\varphi_U(\text{relint}(\overline{W}(U))) = \varepsilon > 0 \Rightarrow \varepsilon = 1$.

(iii) $\varphi_U(\text{int}(U \cap I\!\!R_+^2)) = \varepsilon > 0 \Rightarrow \varepsilon = 1$.

Proof (i) Suppose $0 < \varepsilon < 1$. In view of lemma 8.36 (ii), (iv), there must exist $\alpha, \delta > 0$ with $\alpha < 1$ such that $\varphi_U((\beta,1)U) \geq \delta$ for every β with $\alpha \leq \beta < 1$. Hence, for every such β, we obtain by STC and CIIA: $\varphi_U(\text{relint}(\underline{W}((\beta,1)U))) \geq \varepsilon\delta$. From this: $1 = \varphi_U(U) \geq \sum_{\alpha < \beta < 1, \beta \in I\!\!Q} \varepsilon\delta = \infty$, an impossibility. So $\varepsilon = 1$.
(ii) Analogous to (i).
(iii) Follows from (i), (ii), and lemmas 8.36, 8.37. $\square$

So far, we have examined $\text{supp}(\varphi_U)$. Next we consider φ_Δ.

Lemma 8.39 $\varphi_U((1,1)) = 1 \Rightarrow \varphi_\Delta((t, 1-t)) = 1$ *for some* $t \in [0,1]$.

Proof Let $a \in I\!\!R_{++}^2$ with $a_1 + a_2 < 1$. By STC, CIIA, and lemma 8.24, $0 = \varphi_\Delta(a) = \varphi_{aU}(a)\varphi_\Delta(aU) = \varphi_\Delta(aU)$ because by assumption $\varphi_U((1,1)) = 1$. Then $1 = \varphi_\Delta(\Delta) = \varphi_\Delta(\Delta\backslash P(\Delta)) + \varphi_\Delta(P(\Delta)) = \varphi_\Delta(\cup_{b \in A}aU) + \varphi_\Delta(P(\Delta)) = \varphi_\Delta(P(\Delta))$, where $A := \{b \in I\!\!Q_{++}^2 : b_1 + b_2 < 1\}$. So $\varphi_\Delta(P(\Delta)) = 1$.

Suppose $\varphi_\Delta((t, 1-t)) \neq 1$ for every $t \in [0,1]$. Then we can find $s, u \in [0,1]$ with $s < u$ such that $\varphi_\Delta(\{x \in P(\Delta) : x_1 \leq s\}) \neq 0$, $\varphi_\Delta(\{x \in P(\Delta) : x_1 \geq u\}) \neq 0$. (See figure 8.2.)

Take $r \in (s, u)$. Take $\eta \in (r, 1)$ close enough to 1 to guarantee that $b_2(1 - u) < 1 - r$ where $(b_1, b_2) \in I\!\!R_{++}^2$ such that $b\Delta = \Delta^\eta$, where Δ^η is the convex comprehensive hull of $(\eta, 0)$ and the point with first coordinate 0 on the straight line through $(\eta, 0)$ and $(r, 1-r)$. Further, let $T := \Delta \cap \Delta^\eta$, so $T = \text{comv}\{(0,1), (r, 1-r), (\eta, 0)\}$. Since $\varphi_\Delta(P(\Delta)) = 1$, we have $\varphi_\Delta(T) = \varphi_\Delta(\text{conv}\{(0,1), (r, 1-r)\})$. By CIIA: $\varphi_T(\text{conv}\{(0,1), (r, 1-r)\})\varphi_\Delta(T) = \varphi_\Delta(\text{conv}\{(0,1), (r, 1-r)\}) \geq \varphi_\Delta(\text{conv}\{(0,1), (s, 1-s)\}) \neq 0$, hence $\varphi_T(\text{conv}\{(0,1), (r, 1-r)\}) = 1$. From this, we obtain: $\varphi_T(b\{x \in P(\Delta) : x_1 \geq u\}) = 0$, in view of the choice of η. On the other hand, by CIIA and STC, we have $\varphi_T(b\{x \in P(\Delta) : x_1 \geq u\})\varphi_{\Delta^\eta}(T) = \varphi_{\Delta^\eta}(b\{x \in P(\Delta) : x_1 \geq u\}) = \varphi_\Delta(\{x \in P(\Delta) : x_1 \geq u\}) \neq 0$, hence $\varphi_T(b\{x \in P(\Delta) :$

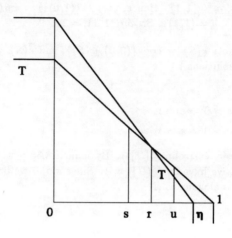

Figure 8.2: Proof of lemma 8.39

$x_1 \geq u\}) \neq 0$. We have a contradiction and may conclude that $\varphi_\Delta((t, 1-t)) = 1$ for some $t \in [0,1]$. $\square$

Before proceeding, we need an elementary result in real analysis. The result may be derived from, e.g., Theorem 2.6.3 in Eichhorn (1978).

Lemma 8.40 *For the function $f : [0,1] \to [0,1]$, the following two statements are equivalent:*

(i) *There exists $t \in (0, \infty)$ with $f(x) = x^t$ for all $x \in [0,1]$.*

(ii) *The function f has the following properties: (a) $f(x) = 0$ if and only if $x = 0$, for all $x \in [0,1]$ (b) f is continuous at 0 and 1, and f is bounded (c) $f(xy) = f(x)f(y)$ for all $x, y \in [0,1]$.*

We take up again the string of lemmas which will lead to the converse of proposition 8.34. As before φ is a solution satisfying IR, STC, and CIIA.

Lemma 8.41

(i) *If $\varphi_U(\text{relint}(\underline{\delta}(U))) = 1$, then there is a $t > 0$ such that $\varphi_U(\text{conv}\{(0,0), (\lambda, 0)\}) = \lambda^t$ for all $\lambda \in [0,1]$.*

(ii) *If $\varphi_U(\text{relint}(\overline{\delta}(U))) = 1$, then there is a $t > 0$ such that $\varphi_U(\text{conv}\{(0,0), (0, \lambda)\}) = \lambda^t$ for all $\lambda \in [0,1]$.*

(iii) *If $\varphi_U(\text{relint}(\underline{W}(U))) = 1$, then there is a $t > 0$ such that $\varphi_U(\text{conv}\{(1,0), (1, \lambda)\}) = \lambda^t$ for all $\lambda \in [0,1]$.*

(iv) *If $\varphi_U(\text{relint}(\overline{W}(U))) = 1$, then there is a $t > 0$ such that $\varphi_U(\text{conv}\{(0,1), (\lambda, 1)\}) = \lambda^t$ for all $\lambda \in [0,1]$.*

Proof We only prove (i). The proofs of (ii), (iii), and (iv) are similar.
Suppose $\varphi_U(\text{relint}(\underline{\delta}\ (U))) = 1$. Let $f : [0,1] \to [0,1]$ be defined by $f(\lambda) = \varphi_U(\text{conv}\{(0,0),$ $(\lambda,0)\})$ for all $\lambda \in [0,1]$. The proof is complete if we show that f satisfies (ii) of lemma 8.40. Obviously, $f(0) = 0$ and $f(1) = 1 > 0$. Hence, (a) is partly proved.

Next, let $\eta, \lambda \in [0,1]$. If $\eta \in \{0,1\}$ or $\lambda \in \{0,1\}$, then $f(\eta\lambda) = f(\eta)f(\lambda)$. Suppose $0 < \lambda \leq \eta < 1$. Then, by CIIA and STI, $f(\lambda\eta) = \varphi_U((\eta,1)U)\varphi_{(\eta,1)U}(\text{conv}\{(0,0),(\lambda\eta,0)\}) = f(\eta)f(\lambda)$. So (c) holds. Now let $\hat{\lambda} := \inf\{\lambda \in [0,1] :\ f(\lambda) > 0\}$. Then obviously $\hat{\lambda} < 1$. Suppose that $\hat{\lambda} > 0$. Take $\eta \in (\hat{\lambda}, 1)$ such that $\eta^2 < \hat{\lambda}$. Then $f(\eta^2) = 0$ and $f(\eta) > 0$, in contradiction with $f(\eta^2) = f(\eta)^2$. So $\hat{\lambda} = 0$, and (a) is proved completely.

Since f is nondecreasing and $\varphi_U((1,1)) = 0$, it follows that f is continuous in 1. Further, if λ decreases to 0, then $f(\lambda)$ decreases to $\varphi_U(0) = 0 = f(0)$, so f is continuous in 0. Noting that f is bounded, we have proved (b). $\qquad\square$

Lemma 8.42 *Suppose $\varphi_U(\text{int}(U \cap I\!\!R_+^2)) = 1$. Then there exist $t, s \in (0,\infty)$ such that $\varphi_U(E) = \iint_{I\!\!R_+^2} 1_E(\varsigma,\eta)d\varsigma^t d\eta^s$ for every $E \in \sigma(U)$.*

Proof Let the functions $f, g : [0,1] \to [0,1]$ be defined by $f(\varsigma) = \varphi_U((\varsigma,1)U)$ and $g(\eta) = \varphi_U((1,\eta)U)$ for all $\varsigma, \eta \in [0,1]$. Similarly as in the proof of lemma 8.41, one verifies that f and g satisfy (ii) of lemma 8.40, so there exist $s, t \in (0,\infty)$ such that $f(\varsigma) = \varsigma^t$ and $g(\eta) = \eta^s$ for all $\varsigma, \eta \in [0,1]$. Now let the probability measures μ_1, μ_2 on the σ-algebra $\sigma([0,1])$ be defined by $\mu_1(C) = \int_C d\varsigma^t$ and $\mu_2(C) = \int_C d\eta^s$ for all $C \in \sigma([0,1])$. Let $\hat{\varsigma}, \hat{\eta} \in (0,1]$. Then, by CIIA and STC, we have

$$\varphi_U((\hat{\varsigma},\hat{\eta})U) = \varphi_U((1,\hat{\eta})U)\varphi_{(1,\hat{\eta})U}((\hat{\varsigma},\hat{\eta})U) = g(\hat{\eta})f(\hat{\varsigma}) =$$
$$= \int_{[0,\hat{\eta}]} d\eta^s \int_{[0,\hat{\varsigma}]} d\varsigma^t = \mu_1([0,\hat{\varsigma}])\mu_2([0,\hat{\eta}]).$$

Hence, because $\sigma(U \cap I\!\!R_+^2) = \sigma([0,1]) \times \sigma([0,1])$, $\varphi_U = \mu_1 \times \mu_2$ is the product measure of μ_1 and μ_2.
By Fubini's theorem, we have for every $E \in \sigma(U)$: $\varphi_U(E) = \iint_{I\!\!R_+^2} 1_E(\varsigma,\eta)d\varsigma^t d\eta^s$. $\qquad\square$

We are now sufficiently equipped to show:

Proposition 8.43 $\varphi \in \Upsilon \cup \{\overline{\delta}^t, \underline{\delta}^t, \overline{W}^t, \underline{W}^t, h^{t,s} :\ t, s \in (0,\infty)\}$.

Proof We distinguish several cases.
(i) $\varphi_U(0) \neq 0$. Then $\varphi_U(0) = 1$ by lemma 8.36 (i). Let $S \in \mathcal{C}_0$. By IR and CIIA, $\varphi_S(E) = \varphi_{S_0}(E)$ for every $E \in \sigma(S_0)$. By STC and CIIA, $1 = \varphi_U(0) = \varphi_{h(s)U}(0) = \varphi_{h(s)U}(S_0)\varphi_{S_0}(0) = \varphi_S(0)$. So $\varphi = \delta$.

(ii) $\varphi_U((1,0)) \neq 0$. Similarly as in (i), $\varphi = \underline{w}$, with the aid of lemma 8.36 (ii).

(iii) $\varphi_U((0,1)) \neq 0$. Similarly as in (i), $\varphi = \overline{w}$, with the aid of lemma 8.36 (iii).

(iv) $\varphi_U(\text{relint}(\underline{\delta}(U))) \neq 0$. Similarly as in (i), $\varphi = \underline{\delta}^t$ for some $t > 0$, with the aid of lemma 8.37 (i) and lemma 8.41 (i).

(v) $\varphi_U(\text{relint}(\overline{\delta}(U))) \neq 0$. Similarly as in (i), $\varphi = \overline{\delta}^t$ for some $t > 0$, with the aid of lemma 8.37 (ii) and lemma 8.41 (ii).

(vi) $\varphi_U(\text{relint}(\underline{W}(U))) \neq 0$. Then $\varphi_U(\text{relint}(\underline{W}(U))) = 1$ by lemma 8.38 (i).

Let $S \in \mathcal{C}_0$. We distinguish two subcases.

(vi.a) $\underline{p}(S) \neq \underline{w}(S)$. Similarly as in (i), $\varphi_S = \underline{W}_S^t$, for $t > 0$ with $\varphi_U = \underline{W}_U^t$, with the aid of lemma 8.41 (iii).

(vi.b) $\underline{p}(S) = \underline{w}(S)$. Suppose $\varphi_S(\underline{p}(S)) \neq 1$. Then there exists $z \in P(S)$, $z > 0$, such that for all $y \in P(S)$ with $z_1 \leq y_1 < \underline{p}_1(S)$, we have $\varphi_S(S_y) \geq \varphi_S(S_z) > 0$ where $S_y := \{x \in S : x_1 \leq y_1\}$. By (vi.a), $\varphi_S(S_y) = \varphi_S(\underline{W}(S_y))$, and because $y \neq y' \Rightarrow \underline{W}(S_y) \cap \underline{W}(S_{y'}) = \emptyset$ for all y, y' with $z_1 \leq y_1$, $y_1' < \underline{p}_1(S)$, we obtain $\varphi_S(S) \geq \sum_{y \in A} \varphi_S(S_y) = \infty$, where $A := \{y \in \mathcal{Q}_{++}^2 : y \in P(S), z_1 \leq y_1 < \underline{p}_1(S)\}$. From this impossibility we conclude $\varphi_S(\underline{p}(S)) = 1$.

By (vi.a) and (vi.b) we conclude: $\varphi = \underline{W}^t$, for t as in (vi.a).

(vii) $\varphi_U(\text{relint}(\overline{W}(U))) \neq 0$. Similarly as in (vi), $\varphi = \overline{W}^t$ for some $t > 0$, with the aid of lemma 8.38 (ii) and lemma 8.41 (iv).

(viii) $\varphi_U(\text{int}(U \cap I\!\!R_+^2)) \neq 0$. Similarly as in (i), $\varphi = h^{t,s}$ for some $t, s > 0$, with the aid of lemma 8.38 (iii) and lemma 8.42.

(ix) and final case: $\varphi_U((1,1)) \neq 0$. Then $\varphi_U((1,1)) = 1$ by lemma 8.36 (iv), so $\varphi_\Delta((t, 1 - t)) = 1$ for some $t \in [0,1]$ by lemma 8.39. In this case $\varphi = N^t$ for some $t \in [0,1]$ by a modification of (the proof of) corollary 2.24.   □

The following theorem combines propositions 8.34 and 8.43, and is the main result of this subsection.

Theorem 8.44 *A probabilistic solution φ satisfies IR, STC, and CIIA, if and only if $\varphi \in \Upsilon \cup \{\underline{\delta}^t, \overline{\delta}^t, \underline{W}^t, \overline{W}^t, h^{t,s} : t, s \in (0, \infty)\}$.*

The material in section 8.3 is based on Peters and Tijs (1983).

8.4   Nonconvex bargaining games

Convexity of feasible sets of bargaining games may be derived from several assumptions concerning underlying bargaining situations. Bargaining games may be derived from expected utility bargaining situations (cf. subsection 1.3.1) or from noncooperative games (subsection 1.3.3); the possibility of randomization between alternatives in these examples implies convexity of the feasible sets of the corresponding bargaining games. Or the bargaining games may concern the division of a commodity bundle, as in subsection 1.3.2, where convexity is a consequence of concavity of the utility functions. Also the wage-employment bargaining model of subsection 1.3.4 leads to a convex feasible set in the corresponding bargaining game. In general, however, economic situations may lead to nonconvex feasible sets. Take, for instance, the division of a bundle of commodities between individuals with nonconcave utility functions. Then, the question arises if and how the various solution concepts and their axiomatic characterizations extend to bargaining games with possibly nonconvex feasible sets.

In many cases, such extensions are straightforward. For instance, most results in the literature concerning the Raiffa-Kalai-Smorodinsky solution are easily adapted to the nonconvex case. E.g., the characterization in theorem 7.4 using the population monotonicity axiom can easily be modified to hold for a general class of bargaining games including non-convex games as well (see Thomson and Lensberg, 1989, p. 39). In light of these remarks, it is not surprising that the bargaining literature on nonconvex games is very limited. More-over, most of this work concerns the Nash bargaining solution, the extension of which to nonconvex games is not obvious. Also in this section, attention will be confined to the Nash solution. In the first two subsections the extensions of Kaneko (1980) and Herrero (1989) are discussed.

Both these authors consider multisolutions and obtain extensions of the Nash bargaining solution that are multivalued. The multisolution proposed by Kaneko assigns to each bargaining game the set of all points that maximize the (symmetric) Nash product. It is characterized by strong individual rationality, Pareto optimality, scale transformation co-variance, anonymity, independence of irrelevant alternatives (the same as in section 8.2), and a continuity axiom (actually, upper semicontinuity). If the solution is single-valued and restricted to convex games, then in particular continuity is redundant in this charac-terization (cf. theorem 2.5).

Whereas (broadly speaking) Kaneko's extension is obtained by "extending" the Nash axioms (and adding continuity), the extended solution proposed by Herrero (1989) is based on a geometric property of the Nash bargaining solution in the 2-person case. Let $S \in \mathcal{C}_0$ be a 2-person bargaining game with convex feasible set, then $z \in P(S)$ is the Nash bargaining solution outcome if and only if z cuts the (or a) maximal line segment in $\mathbb{R}^2_+$ supporting S at z into two pieces of equal length. This characterization is a consequence of lemma 2.2. Herrero's extension of the Nash bargaining solution assigns to each nonconvex bargaining game the set of all Pareto optimal points which have a geometric property as described (replace "supporting" by "tangential"). It follows that, for 2-person games where Herrero's extension is defined, the solution set always contains the Kaneko solution set. Although the Herrero extension is also characterized axiomatically, it derives its main justification from the fact that the solution outcomes correspond exactly to the payoffs attainable by the stationary subgame perfect equilibria in a corresponding Rubinstein alternating offers model. See section 9.4 for details.

Maschler *et al.* (1988) study so-called Nash points of (possibly nonconvex) n-person bargaining games. For the 2-person case, these Nash points coincide precisely with the Herrero extension; thus, they extend the multisolution proposed by Herrero to n-person games. Further, Nash points are characterized as limit points of an appropriately chosen dynamic adjustment process. In this way, another motivation for the Herrero extension is obtained. Nash points are also closely related to the so-called Shapley NTU values (Shapley, 1969), which are discussed in chapter 10, see in particular sections 10.2 and 10.3.

Subsections 8.4.1, 8.4.2, and 8.4.3, discuss the approaches by Kaneko (1980), Herrero (1989), and Maschler *et al.* (1988), respectively.

8.4.1 An axiomatic extension of the Nash solution

This subsection is based on Kaneko (1980). Consider the class $\mathcal{B}_0^N$ of n-person bargain-ing games with comprehensive but not necessarily convex feasible sets containing strictly positive outcomes and with disagreement points normalized to 0. As in section 8.2, a *mul-tisolution* $\varphi : \mathcal{B}_0^N \to \mathbb{R}^N$ assigns to each $S \subset \mathcal{B}_0^N$ a nonempty subset $\varphi(S)$ of S. The axioms of Pareto optimality (PO), scale transformation covariance (STC), and independence of irrelevant alternatives (IIA) are defined completely analogous to their versions for a multisolution on C_0; see definition 8.2 (ii), (iii), and (iv), respectively. The multisolution φ is *strongly individually rational* (SIR) if $x > 0$ for all $S \in B_0^N$ and all $x \in \varphi(S)$. The multisolution φ is *anonymous* (AN) if for every $S \in B_0^N$ and every permutation π of N we have $\varphi(\pi S) = \{z \in \pi S : z = \pi x \text{ for some } x \in \varphi(S)\}$. Obviously, for (single-valued) solutions SIR and AN reduce to the axioms defined earlier, which justifies the use of the same names. Also the following continuity axiom reduces to the axiom with the same name for single-valued solutions.

Feasible set continuity (SCONT): Let $S, S^1, S^2, \ldots \in B_0^N$ with $S^k \to S$ in the Hausdorff metric. Let $x, x^1, x^2, \ldots \in \mathbb{R}_+^N$ with $x^k \in \varphi(S^k)$ for every $k \in \mathbb{N}$ and with $x^k \to x$. Then $x \in \varphi(S)$.

Note that this axiom characterizes upper semicontinuity of the multisolution, see for instance Hildenbrand and Kirman (1976, p. 188 ff.). Together with IIA for correspondences it was included in an informal note on utility theory by Nash, dated August 8, 1950; see also Shubik (1982, pp. 420–421).

For a *multisolution* φ restricted to the class C_0^N of convex bargaining games the axioms SIR, PO, STC, AN, and IIA actually characterize the (single-valued!) Nash bargaining solution ν, as is shown by the following theorem. This is in accordance with theorem 8.4, and implies that the Kaneko extension below extends not only the Nash bargaining solution, but also its axiomatic characterization.

Theorem 8.45 *Let φ be a multisolution on C_0^N satisfying SIR, PO, STC, AN, and IIA. Then $\varphi(S) = \{\nu(S)\}$ for every $S \in C_0^N$.*

Proof The proof is analogous to the proof of proposition 2.4. The only thing to verify is that $\varphi(T) = \{(1, 1, \ldots, 1)\}$, T as defined there, that is:

$$T := \{x \in \mathbb{R}^N : \sum_{i \in N} x_i \leq n, \ x \leq (K, K, \ldots, K)\}$$

for some large number $K > 0$, say $K \geq n$. By AN, it suffices to show that $|\varphi(T)| = 1$. Suppose to the contrary that there are $a, b \in \varphi(T)$ with $a \neq b$. We proceed similarly as in the proof of lemma 8.8. Define, for each $i \in N$, c_i by $c_i := a_i(\frac{1}{2}a_i + \frac{1}{2}b_i)^{-1}$. Then $c \in \mathbb{R}_{++}^N$, $c(\frac{1}{2}a + \frac{1}{2}b) = a$, and $(cb)_i < \frac{1}{2}a_i + \frac{1}{2}b_i$ whenever $a_i \neq b_i$. Let $E := \text{comv}\{a, b\}$, then $a \in cE \subset T$ and $cb \notin P(T)$. By IIA, $\varphi(cE) = \varphi(T) \cap cE$. Also by IIA, $b \in \varphi(E)$, hence by STC: $cb \in \varphi(cE)$. So $cb \in \varphi(T) \subset P(T)$, which is the desired contradiction. □

The Kaneko extension of the Nash bargaining solution is the multisolution $\nu^K : B_0^N \to \mathbb{R}^N$ defined by

$$\nu^K(S) := \{x \in S : x \geq 0, \ x_1 x_2 \ldots x_n \geq y_1 y_2 \ldots y_n \text{ for all } y \in S, y \geq 0\}$$

for all $S \in B_0^N$.

It is obvious that ν^K satisfies PO, SIR, AN, STC, and IIA. The next lemma shows that ν^K is also feasible set continuous.

Lemma 8.46 ν^K *satisfies SCONT.*

Proof Let $S, S^1, S^2, \ldots$ and $x, x^1, x^2, \ldots$ be as in the premise of SCONT for $\varphi = \nu^K$. Let $y \in S$ arbitrary. Construct a sequence $y^k \in S^k$ $(k \geq 1)$ with $y^k \to y$. (This can be done, for instance, by taking for y^k a point of S^k with minimal Euclidean distance to y.) Because $\Pi_{i \in N} y_i^k \leq \Pi_{i \in N} x_i^k$ for all $k \geq 1$, also $\Pi_{i \in N} y_i \leq \Pi_{i \in N} x_i$. Since $y \in S$ was arbitrary, $x \in \nu^K(S)$. $\qquad\square$

The main result of this subsection is the following theorem.

Theorem 8.47 *Let* $\varphi : \mathcal{B}_0^N \to \mathbb{R}^N$ *be a multisolution. Then* φ *satisfies SIR, PO, STC, AN, IIA, and SCONT, if and only if* $\varphi = \nu^K$.

The proof of the "only if" part of theorem 8.47 is based on a revealed preference argument, as in chapter 3. The present context, however, is different because φ is a multisolution instead of a single-valued solution, and because here "choice situations" may be nonconvex. In what follows, φ is assumed to have the properties mentioned in theorem 8.47.

We define a binary relation on $\mathbb{R}^N_{++}$ by

$$x \succeq y \text{ if and only if } x \in \varphi(\text{com}\{x, y\}). \tag{8.8}$$

Lemma 8.48 *The binary relation* $\succeq$ *defined by (8.8) is complete and transitive.*

Proof Completeness of $\succeq$ (i.e., $x \succeq y$ or $y \succeq x$ for all $x, y \in \mathbb{R}^N_+$) follows from Pareto optimality of φ and the fact that, by definition, $\varphi(S) \neq \emptyset$ for every $S \in \mathcal{B}_0^N$. In order to prove transitivity of φ, suppose $x \succeq y$, $y \succeq z$ and $x \not\succeq z$ for some $x, y, z \in \mathbb{R}^N_+$. This is equivalent to

$$x \in \varphi(\text{com}\{x, y\}), \ y \in \varphi(\text{com}\{y, z\}), \ \{z\} = \varphi(\text{com}\{x, z\}).$$

Let $T := \text{com}\{x, y, z\} \in \mathcal{B}_0^N$. If $x \in \varphi(T)$ then by IIA $x \in \varphi(\text{com}\{x, z\})$, a contradiction. If $y \in \varphi(T)$ then by IIA and $x \in \varphi(\text{com}\{x, y\})$ also $x \in \varphi(T)$, which was seen to be impossible. Therefore, $\{z\} = \varphi(T)$ but this contradicts $y \in \varphi(\text{com}\{y, z\})$ by IIA. Apparently, $x \succeq z$, which proves the lemma. $\qquad\square$

The previous lemma showed that $\succeq$ is a weak ordering on $\mathbb{R}^N_{++}$. The next lemma collects some properties of $\succeq$. We write $x \succ y$ if $x \succeq y$ and not $y \succeq x$, and $x \sim y$ if $x \succeq y$ and $y \succeq x$.

Lemma 8.49 *For all* $x, y, z, a \in \mathbb{R}^N_{++}$:

(i) $x \succeq y$ *if and only if* $ax \succeq ay$,

(ii) If $x \geq y$ *and* $x \neq y$ *then* $x \succ y$,

(iii) If $x \succ y \succ z$ *then there exists a* $\bar{\lambda}$, $0 < \bar{\lambda} < 1$, *with* $\bar{\lambda}x + (1 - \bar{\lambda})z \sim y$,

(iv) For every permutation π *of* N *with* $\pi = \pi^{-1}$, $x \sim \pi x$.

Proof (i) and (ii) follow from STC and PO of φ, respectively. For (iv), let π be a permutation with $\pi = \pi^{-1}$, and let $x \in \mathbb{R}^N_{++}$. Then $\text{com}\{x, \pi x\} = \text{com}\{\pi^{-1}x, x\} = \pi^{-1}\text{com}\{x, \pi x\}$, so that, by AN, $\varphi(\text{com}\{x, \pi x\}) = \{x, \pi x\}$. This implies $x \sim \pi x$.

For (iii), suppose $x \succ y \succ z$ and let $L_1 := \{\lambda \in [0,1]: \lambda x + (1 - \lambda)z \succeq y\} \neq \emptyset$ and $L_2 := \{\lambda \in [0,1]: y \succ \lambda x + (1 - \lambda)z\} \neq \emptyset$. Let $\overline{\lambda} := \sup L_2$, and let $\{\lambda^k\}$ be a sequence in L_2 with $\lambda^k \to \overline{\lambda}$. Then $y \in \varphi(\text{com}\{y, \lambda^k x + (1 - \lambda^k)z\})$ for all $k \geq 1$, so by SCONT, $y \in \varphi(\text{com}\{y, \overline{\lambda}x + (1 - \overline{\lambda})z\})$. Let $\{\mu^k\}$ be a sequence in L_1 with $\mu^k \to \overline{\lambda}$. Then $\mu^k x + (1 - \mu^k)z \in \varphi(\text{com}\{\mu^k x + (1 - \mu^k)z, y\})$ for all $k \geq 1$, so by SCONT, $\overline{\lambda}x + (1 - \overline{\lambda})z \in \varphi(\text{com}\{\overline{\lambda}x + (1 - \overline{\lambda})z, y\})$. Thus, $\overline{\lambda}x + (1 - \overline{\lambda})z \sim y$. Obviously, $0 < \overline{\lambda} < 1$. □

Because of (ii) and (iii) of lemma 8.49, there exists a real-valued function G on $I\!\!R_{++}^N$ representing the weak ordering $\succeq$, i.e.,

$$G(x) \geq G(y) \Longleftrightarrow x \succeq y \tag{8.9}$$

for all $x, y \in I\!\!R_{++}^N$. This is a standard result from utility theory, see Debreu (1959), or Varian (1984). In view of (i) and (ii) of lemma 8.49 there exist constants $\omega_i \in I\!\!R_{++}$ $(i \in N)$ such that G can be represented as

$$G(x) = V\left(\Pi_{i \in N} x_i^{\omega_i}\right) \tag{8.10}$$

for all $x \in I\!\!R_{++}^N$, where V is a monotonically strictly increasing function on $I\!\!R_{++}$. This follows from Osborne (1976, Lemma 3.1).

Proof of theorem 8.47 The "if" part follows from lemma 8.46 and the paragraph preceding that lemma. For the "only if" part, lemma 8.49 (iv) implies $\omega_1 = \omega_2 = \ldots = \omega_n$ for ω_i as in (8.10). Then (8.8)–(8.10) imply

$$\varphi(\text{com}\{x, y\}) = \{z \in \{x, y\} : \Pi_{i \in N} z_i = \max(\Pi_{i \in N} x_i, \Pi_{i \in N} y_i)\} \tag{8.11}$$

for all $x, y \in I\!\!R_{++}^N$. Let now $S \in \mathcal{B}_0^N$ be arbitrary, and $\overline{x} \in \varphi(S)$. Then, for all $y \in S$, by IIA applied to $\text{com}\{\overline{x}, y\} \subset S$ and (8.11), $\Pi_{i \in N}\overline{x}_i \geq \Pi_{i \in N} y_i$. So $\overline{x} \in \nu^K(S)$. Conversely, let $\overline{z} \in \nu^K(S)$. Take $\overline{y} \in \varphi(S) \subset \nu^K(S)$, then (8.11) and IIA imply $\{\overline{z}, \overline{y}\} = \varphi(\text{com}\{\overline{z}, \overline{y}\}) = \varphi(S) \cap \text{com}\{\overline{z}, \overline{y}\}$. Hence, $\overline{z} \in \varphi(S)$. Thus, $\varphi(S) = \nu^K(S)$. □

We conjecture that in theorem 8.45 the strong individual rationality requirement can be weakened to individual rationality or even be dropped. It is not clear whether this is also true for theorem 8.47.

8.4.2 A geometric extension of the Nash solution

Let S be a (convex) bargaining game in $\mathcal{C}_0$. It follows from lemma 2.2 that the Nash solution $\nu(S)$ is the (unique) point of $P(S) \cap I\!\!R_+^2$ with the following property: there exists a supporting line of S at $\nu(S)$ such that $\nu(S)$ is the midpoint of the intersection of this supporting line with $I\!\!R_+^2$. Herrero (1989) proposes an extension of the Nash bargaining solution to 2-person bargaining games with possibly nonconvex feasible sets based on this geometric property. The definition of this extension and an axiomatic characterization are presented in this subsection. The main motivation for this particular extension comes from its relation with a noncooperative Rubinstein type alternating offers model; for details, the reader is referred to section 9.4. Furthermore, there is a very close relationship with the concept of a Nash point, discussed in subsection 8.4.3 below.

The Herrero extension ν^H is defined for bargaining games in $\mathcal{B}_0$, i.e., $\mathcal{B}_0^N$ with $N = \{1,2\}$. For $S \in \mathcal{B}_0$, let f^S be the function on $[0, h_1(S)]$ defined by $x_1 \mapsto \max\{x_2 : (x_1, x_2) \in S\}$, cf. sections 5.2 and 8.3. Note that this function is upper semicontinuous but not necessarily continuous. Also, it is (not necessarily strictly) monotonically decreasing. At each $x_1 \in [0, h_1(S)]$ the left and right derivates (with possibly value $-\infty$) are denoted by $(f^S)'_-(x_1)$ and $(f^S)'_+(x_1)$, respectively. At a point of discontinuity, $(f^S)'_+(x_1) = -\infty$, as is easily established. Define the *subdifferential of* f^S at x_1, denoted by $(f^S)'(x_1)$, as the interval with left and right derivates of f^S at x_1 as endpoints. For $z \in P(S)$, $z > 0$, if $-\infty < \alpha < 0$ and $\alpha \in (f^S)'(z_1)$, then let $P^\alpha(z)$ $[Q^\alpha(z)]$ be the point on the straight line ℓ through z with slope α and with first [second] coordinate equal to 0. The line ℓ is called *subtangential to S at z*. We are now in a position to define ν^H.[1]

Definition 8.50 For every $S \in \mathcal{B}_0$, $z \in \nu^H(S)$ if and only if $z \in P(S)$, $z > 0$, and there is an $\alpha \in (f^S)'(z_1) \cap (-\infty, 0)$ such that $z = \frac{1}{2}(P^\alpha(z) + Q^\alpha(z))$.

Note that, for $S \in \mathcal{C}_0$, $\nu^H(S) = \{\nu(S)\}$. This can be derived from lemma 2.2. Thus, ν^H extends the symmetric Nash bargaining solution ν to nonconvex bargaining games. Also, $\nu^K(S) \subset \nu^H(S)$, again by lemma 2.2.

An axiomatic characterization of ν^H is now briefly outlined. Apart from SIR, PO, and STC, this characterization uses the three axioms formulated in the following definition. We will just refer to these axioms as H.1, H.2, and H.3, respectively[2].

Definition 8.51 Let $\varphi : \mathcal{B}_0 \to I\!\!R^2$ be a multisolution.

Axiom H.1: If $S \in \mathcal{C}_0$ and S is symmetric, then $x_1 = x_2$ for all $x \in \varphi(S)$.

Axiom H.2: For all $S \in \mathcal{B}_0$ and all $x \in \varphi(S)$, $x \geq 0$, if $\#(f^S)'(x_1) > 1$, then there exist sequences $\{x^k\}$ and $\{S^k\}$ with $S^k \in \mathcal{B}_0$, $x^k \in \varphi(S^k)$, $x^k \geq 0$, and $\#(f^{S^k})'(x_1^k) = 1$ for all k such that $S^k \to S$ and $x^k \to x$.

Axiom H.3: For all $S, T \in \mathcal{B}_0$ and $x \in \varphi(S) \cap P(T) \cap I\!\!R_+^2$, if $\#(f^S)'(x_1) = 1$ and $(f^S)'(x_1) \subset (f^T)'(x_1)$, then $x \in \varphi(T)$.

Axiom H.1 says that the restriction of φ to $\mathcal{C}_0$ is symmetric; together with Pareto optimality this would imply that the solution is single-valued on convex symmetric bargaining games. Axiom H.2 is a continuity condition which will enable us to approach a bargaining game with a solution outcome where the feasible set is nonsmooth, by games with smooth boundaries at solution outcomes converging to the outcome of the given game. Axiom H.3 is a quite strong variation on IIA. Herrero's (1989) characterization of ν^H is as follows.

Theorem 8.52 *Let* $\varphi : \mathcal{B}_0 \to I\!\!R^2$ *be a multisolution. Then* φ *satisfies SIR, PO, STC, and H.1–H.3, if and only if* $\varphi = \nu^H$.

---

[1]Actually, Herrero's formal definition is different from definition 8.50. However, the multisolution ν^H introduced in definition 8.50 is the one characterized by the axioms below. It contains exactly all stationary points of the Nash product with respect to a given feasible set S, cf. corollary 8.55. In H.2 and H.3, $\#$ denotes cardinality.

[2]In Herrero (1989) these axioms are called *symmetry, lower semi-continuity*, and *independence of locally irrelevant alternatives*, respectively. In H.2 and H.3, $\#$ denotes cardinality.

Proof The proof is rather straightforward and will merely be outlined. That ν^H satisfies the six axioms is not hard to prove and left to the reader. Let now φ be a multisolution satisfying the six axioms. By PO and H.1, $\varphi(\Delta) = \{(\frac{1}{2},\frac{1}{2})\}$ where $\Delta = \text{comv}\{(1,0),(0,1)\}$ as before. In particular, $\varphi(\Delta) = \nu^H(\Delta)$. Take $S \in \mathcal{B}_0$ arbitrary, and let $x \in \varphi(S)$. By PO and SIR, $x > 0$ and $x_2 = f^S(x_1)$.

First, suppose $\#(f^S)'(x_1) = 1$, say $\{\alpha\} = (f^S)'(x_1)$. By H.3, $x \in \varphi(\text{comv}\{P^\alpha(x), Q^\alpha(x)\})$. By STC and $\varphi(\Delta) = \nu^H(\Delta) = \{(\frac{1}{2},\frac{1}{2})\}$, $x = \frac{1}{2}(P^\alpha(x) + Q^\alpha(x))$. Therefore, $x \in \nu^H(S)$.

Next, if $\#(f^S)'(x_1) > 1$, the same argument can be applied to sequences as in axiom H.2, and the proof is completed by invoking a limiting argument. So altogether, we have $\varphi(S) \subset \nu^H(S)$.

Finally, suppose $z \in \nu^H(S)$, say $z = \frac{1}{2}(P^\beta(z) + Q^\beta(z))$ for some $\beta \in (f^S)'(z_1)$. Then $\{z\} = \varphi(\text{comv}\{P^\beta(z), Q^\beta(z)\})$ by STC and $\varphi(\Delta) = \nu^H(\Delta) = \{(\frac{1}{2},\frac{1}{2})\}$. Now $z \in \varphi(S)$ by H.3. Thus, $\nu^H(S) \subset \varphi(S)$. $\square$

Axiom H.3 resembles the axiom of localization (LOC) for (single-valued) bargaining solutions introduced in subsection 2.5.2. It seems to be stronger in the sense that the premise of LOC is stronger: bargaining games are required to coincide in a neighborhood of the (a) solution outcome.

The multisolution ν^H does *not* satisfy IIA. For instance, let $S := \text{com}\{x \in I\!\!R_+^2 : x_2 \leq \max(2 - 2x_1, 1 - \frac{1}{2}x_1)\}$, and let $T := \text{com}\{x \in I\!\!R_+^2 : x_2 \leq 2 - 2x_1\}$. Then $T \subset S$, $(\frac{2}{3},\frac{2}{3}) \in \nu^H(S) \cap T$ but $(\frac{2}{3},\frac{2}{3}) \notin \nu^H(T) = \{(\frac{1}{2},1)\}$. If, however, V and W are games in $\mathcal{B}_0$ with $V \subset W$, $x \in \nu^H(W) \cap V$, and $\#(f^W)'(x_1) = 1$, then $x \in \nu^H(V)$. Thus, smoothness of the boundary at a solution outcome plays an important role.

As mentioned before, the main justification for considering the extension ν^H of the Nash bargaining solution to nonconvex games is given by its close relationship with the noncooperative Rubinstein bargaining model. For details, the reader is referred to section 9.4. Another justification is provided by the dynamic model proposed by Maschler *et al.* (1988). This is the subject of the next subsection.

8.4.3 Nash points and dynamics

In the previous subsection, a point x was defined to belong to the Herrero extension $\nu^H(S)$ of a game $S \in \mathcal{B}_0^{\{1,2\}}$ if and only if x was the midpoint of a (one-dimensional) simplex determined by a line ℓ (sub)tangential to S at x with positive normal. In chapter 10 (section 10.2) we will see that this is precisely the idea underlying the Shapley NTU-value (Shapley, 1969). In the present subsection, this idea will be extended to n-person bargaining games, and it will be related to a dynamic system, which might describe a possible negotiation process between the players. This system is based on the assumption that the subtangential line ℓ, or, in the differentiable case, the partial derivatives of the function describing the boundary of the feasible set, reflect the "just" or "natural" rates of exchange between the utilities of the players. The material in this subsection is based on Maschler *et al.* (1988).

We consider the subclass $\hat{\mathcal{B}}_0^N$ of $\mathcal{B}_0^N$ consisting of bargaining games S which satisfy the following additional property: there exists a C^1 function G such that $W(S) = \{x \in$

$I\!\!R^N : G(x) = 0\}$ and such that the partial derivatives $\partial G(x)/\partial x_i$ $(i \in N)$ are positive on $W(S) \cap I\!\!R^N_+$.

The existence of such a function G amounts to requiring the boundary of S to be sufficiently smooth. In particular, (sub)tangent hyperplanes are unique[3]. The requirement that the partial derivatives do not vanish mainly serves mathematical convenience. It implies that $W(S) \cap I\!\!R^N_+ \subset P(S)$, as is not hard to verify. The converse of this statement is not true, e.g., consider $T \in \mathcal{B}_0^{\{1,2\}}$ defined by $T := \text{com}\{x \in I\!\!R^2_+ : (x_1 - 1)^3 + x_2 - 1 \leq 0\}$; the point $(1,1)$ on the boundary of T is a point of inflection.

A *Nash point* of S is a point $x > 0$ of $W(S)$ where the Nash product $V(x) := x_1 x_2 \ldots x_n$ is stationary.

Theorem 8.53 *Let $S \in \hat{\mathcal{B}}_0^N$ and $\hat{x} \in W(S)$, $\hat{x} > 0$. Let $H(\hat{x})$ be the tangent hyperplane to $W(S)$ at $\hat{x}$. Then $\hat{x}$ is a Nash point of S if and only if $\hat{x}$ is the barycenter of the simplex $H(\hat{x}) \cap I\!\!R^N_+$.*

Proof By definition, $\hat{x}$ is a Nash point of S if and only if $\hat{x}$ is a solution to the system

$$\frac{\partial}{\partial x_i}(x_1 x_2 \ldots x_n - \lambda G(x)) = 0 \text{ for all } i \in N, \ G(x) = 0, \ x \in I\!\!R^N_{++}, \tag{8.12}$$

where λ is the Lagrange multiplier. This can be written as

$$\frac{V(x)}{x_i} - \lambda \frac{\partial G(x)}{\partial x_i} = 0 \text{ for all } i \in N, \ G(x) = 0, \ x \in I\!\!R^N_{++}. \tag{8.13}$$

Therefore, $\hat{x}$ is a Nash point of S if and only if it is a solution of

$$x_1 \frac{\partial G(x)}{\partial x_1} = x_2 \frac{\partial G(x)}{\partial x_2} = \ldots = x_n \frac{\partial G(x)}{\partial x_n}, \ x \in W(S) \cap I\!\!R^N_{++}. \tag{8.14}$$

The hyperplane $H(\hat{x})$ is the set $\{x \in I\!\!R^N : \nabla G(\hat{x}) \cdot x = \nabla G(\hat{x}) \cdot \hat{x}\}$, where $\nabla G(\hat{x})$ is the gradient vector $(\partial G(\hat{x})/\partial x_1, \ldots, \partial G(\hat{x})/\partial x_n)$, so the vertices of $H(\hat{x}) \cap I\!\!R^N_+$ are the points $(\nabla G(\hat{x}) \cdot \hat{x})/(\partial G(\hat{x})/\partial x_i)e^i$, $i \in N$. By (8.14), x is a Nash point of S if and only if x can be written as a convex combination of these vertices with weights equal to n^{-1}. $\square$

Observe that nonvanishingness of the partial derivatives of G is not used in the proof of this theorem, but follows from (8.13). The proof also implies the following corollary.

Corollary 8.54 *Let $S \in \hat{\mathcal{B}}_0^N$. Then $\hat{x}$ is a Nash point of S if and only if $\hat{x}$ is a solution to (8.14).*

Definition 8.50 and theorem 8.53 imply the following characterization of the Herrero extension ν^H.

Corollary 8.55 *Let $S \in \hat{\mathcal{B}}_0^{\{1,2\}}$. Then $\hat{x} \in \nu^H(S)$ if and only if $\hat{x}$ is a Nash point of S.*

---

[3]For convex games the problem posed by nonsmoothness of the boundary could presumably be overcome by representing the dynamic system below by a system of differential inclusions. For nonconvex games, it is not clear how one should proceed. Cf. Maschler *et al.* (1988, p. 322).

Corollary 8.55 in combination with theorem 8.53 suggests a natural way of extending the multisolution ν^H to games with more than two players. The exact formulation is left to the reader.

We proceed by introducing the announced dynamic system. Let $S \in \hat{B}_0^N$ be fixed, and let $x \in S$. The dynamic system, described by the autonomous system of first-order ordinary differential equations in (8.15) below, is motivated as follows. Consider a pair i, j of players for which (say) $x_i \partial G(x)/\partial x_i < x_j \partial G(x)/\partial x_j$. These players may reason as follows. At x there is a natural rate of exchange between the utilities given by the partial derivatives. Thus, in "common" units, player j is receiving $x_j \partial G(x)/\partial x_j$ which is more than what player i receives in the same units, namely $x_i \partial G(x)/\partial x_i$. Player i therefore claims that j should transfer (in the common units) an amount of ε times the difference, where ε is some small positive number. Since the same argument holds between any pair of players, player i demands, in total, a transfer of ε times the sum of the differences with all players $j \neq i$. In order to stay on the boundary of S, ε must be infinitesimally small, and we are thus led to the system of differential equations

$$\dot{x}_i \partial G(x)/\partial x_i = \sum_{j \in N \setminus \{i\}} (x_j \partial G(x)/\partial x_j - x_i \partial G(x)/\partial x_i), \ i \in N, \tag{8.15}$$

where dot denotes time derivative. Observe that $\sum_{i \in N} \dot{x}_i \partial G(x)/\partial x_i = 0$, so that solutions starting on $W(S)$ stay there. Further, from the assumption that the partial derivatives of G are continuous and do not vanish on $W(S) \cap \mathbb{R}_+^N$ it follows that through each point of this set passes at least one trajectory.

From corollary 8.54 follows for a point $x \in W(S)$, $x > 0$, that it is a Nash point of S if and only if it is a critical point of the system (8.15), i.e., a point where all dot derivatives vanish.

A point $\hat{x} \in S$ is called an *accumulation point* of a solution $x = \psi(t)$ of (8.15) if there exists a sequence $\{t_k\}$ with $t_k \to \infty$ and $\psi(t_k) \to \hat{x}$. Because every Nash point of S is a critical point of (8.15), it is obvious that it is an accumulation of some solution $\psi(t)$ (in particular, a solution starting in a Nash point will stay there forever). The following theorem shows that also the converse of this is true.

Theorem 8.56 *Let $x = \psi(t)$ be a solution of (8.15) that at some time passes through $W(S) \cap \mathbb{R}_+^N$. Then ψ has an accumulation point; and each such accumulation point is a Nash point.*

Proof Suppose, w.l.o.g., that $\psi(0) \in W(S) \cap \mathbb{R}_+^N$. If, say, $\psi_i(0) = 0$ it follows from (8.15) that $\dot{\psi}_i(0) > 0$, because $\psi(0) \neq 0$ and all partial derivatives are positive by assumption. Thus, it is without loss of generality to assume $\psi(0) > 0$. It will follow, below, that $\psi(t) > 0$ for all $t \geq 0$.

Define the (Lyapunov) function L by

$$L : x \mapsto \ln V(x) = \sum_{j=1}^n \ln x_j, \ x \in W(S) \cap \mathbb{R}_{++}^N. \tag{8.16}$$

We study its behavior on the path $x = \psi(t)$ as long as $\psi(t) > 0$. Clearly, $\dot{L}(x) = \sum_{j \in N} \dot{x}_j/x_j$. By (8.15),

$$\dot{x}_j \partial G(x)/\partial x_j = \sum_{k=1}^{n} x_k \partial G(x)/\partial x_k - n x_j \partial G(x)/\partial x_j, \qquad (8.17)$$

therefore,

$$\frac{\dot{x}_j}{x_j} = \frac{1}{x_j \partial G(x)/\partial x_j} \sum_{k=1}^{n} x_k \partial G(x)/\partial x_k - n,$$

so that

$$\dot{L}(x) = \sum_{j=1}^{n} \frac{1}{x_j \partial G(x)/\partial x_j} \cdot \sum_{k=1}^{n} x_k \partial G(x)/\partial x_k - n^2.$$

Let $M(x)$ and $A(x)$ denote the harmonic and arithmetic means of the $x_k \partial G(x)/\partial x_k$'s, respectively. Then we can write

$$\dot{L}(x) = \frac{n}{M(x)} n A(x) - n^2 = n^2 \left(\frac{A(x)}{M(x)} - 1 \right).$$

As is well-known (or easy to prove by induction), $A(x) \geq M(x)$, with equality holding if and only if all $x_k \partial G(x)/\partial x_k$'s are equal, i.e., if and only if x is a Nash point. It follows that, for $x = \psi(t)$, $L(x(t))$, and therefore $V(x(t))$, strictly increases at all times unless a Nash point has been reached. Because $\psi(0) > 0$ by assumption and in view of the definition of V, this implies that $\psi(t) \in W(S) \cap \mathbb{R}_{++}^N$ for all $t \geq 0$. In particular, $\{\psi(t)\}$ is a subset of the compact set $W(S) \cap \mathbb{R}_+^N$ and therefore must have accumulation points.

Let z be such an accumulation point. It remains to show that z is a Nash point. Suppose not. If $z_i = 0$ for some i then, because $z \neq 0$ and $\partial G(z)/\partial z_k > 0$ for all $k \in N$, z does not satisfy all equalities in (8.14). If $z > 0$, then z does not satisfy all these equalities in view of corollary 8.54. Thus, not all the $x_k \partial G(x)/\partial x_k$'s are equal and so $A(x) > M(x)$. Consequently, $\dot{L}(z) > 0$, say $\dot{L}(z) = \varepsilon > 0$. By continuity, there exists $r > 0$ such that $\dot{L}(x) \geq \varepsilon/2$ whenever $x \in U := \{x \in W(S) : \|x - z\| \leq r\}$. Let

$$h := \max_{x \in U} \sqrt{ \sum_{j \in N} \left\{ \frac{1}{\partial G(x)/\partial x_j} \sum_{k \in N} (x_k \partial G(x)/\partial x_k - x_j \partial G(x)/\partial x_j) \right\}^2 }.$$

The max exists by compactness of U. By (8.17),

$$\sum_{j \in N} \dot{x}_j^2(t) \leq h^2 \text{ if } x = \psi(t) \in U. \qquad (8.18)$$

Expression (8.18) implies that any solution $x = \psi(t)$ that enters U moves there at a speed of at most h, as long as it stays in U.

Let $U' := \{x \in W(S) : \|x - z\| < r/2\}$. Because z is an accumulation point of $x = \psi(t)$, we can take a sequence $\{t_k\}$ with $t^k \to \infty$, $x(t_k) \in U'$, and $t_{k+1} \geq t_k + r/2h$, for all $k \geq 1$.

If $\psi(t) \in U$ during the time period $[t_k, t_{k+1}]$, then $L(\psi(t))$ has increased at a rate of at least $\varepsilon/2$ by definition of U, so that

$$L(\varphi(t_{k+1})) \geq L(\varphi(t_k)) + \frac{\varepsilon}{2}(t_{k+1} - t_k) \geq L(\varphi(t_k)) + \frac{\varepsilon r}{4h}. \qquad (8.19)$$

If $\psi(t)$ is not in U all the time between t_k and t_{k+1}, then there is a last moment $t' \in [t_k, t_{k+1}]$ in which $\psi(t)$ enters U. Then

$$\|\psi(t_{k+1}) - \psi(t')\| \geq \|z - \psi(t')\| - \|z - \psi(t_{k+1})\| > r - \frac{r}{2} = \frac{r}{2}.$$

Because, by (8.18), $x = \psi(t)$ moves with speed at most h while in U, it takes at least $r/2h$ to reach $\psi(t_{k+1})$ from $\psi(t')$, so that $t_{k+1} \geq t' + r/2h$, and therefore $L(\psi(t_{k+1})) \geq L(\psi(t')) + \varepsilon r/4h$. By the monotonicity of $L(\psi(t))$, (8.19) follows also for this case. This, however, implies that $L(\psi(t))$ is unbounded, so that the Nash product V is unbounded on $W(S) \cap I\!\!R^N_{++}$. This is impossible, so z must be a Nash point. $\square$

Thus, it has been shown that (on $W(S) \cap I\!\!R^N_+$) the accumulation points of solutions of the dynamic system (8.15) are precisely the Nash points of S — and precisely the critical points of (8.15). The remainder of this subsection is concerned with convergence properties. First, we have the following lemma.

Lemma 8.57 *Suppose $x^* \in W(S)$, $x^* > 0$, is an isolated accumulation point of the solution $x = \psi(t)$ of (8.15). Then $\psi(t) \to x^*$ as $t \to \infty$.*

Proof Take $r > 0$ such that $\{x \in W(S) : \|x - x^*\| < r\}$ contains no accumulation point of ψ other than x^*. Suppose $\psi(t) \not\to x^*$ as $t \to \infty$. Then, by compactness, there must be some other accumulation point z, and $\|z - x^*\| \geq r$. Let $W := \{x : r/4 \leq \|x - x^*\| \leq 3r/4\}$. W is compact and contains no accumulation point. Since both x^* and z are accumulation points, the trajectory $\psi(t)$ must cross W infinitely many times. Therefore, there exists a sequence $\{t_k\}$ with $t_k \to \infty$ and $\psi(t_k) \in W$ for all $k \geq 1$. But then W must contain an accumulation point of ψ as well. This contradiction shows that $\psi(t) \to x^*$ as $t \to \infty$. $\square$

Lemma 8.57 and theorem 8.56 imply the following corollary.

Corollary 8.58 *If all Nash points are isolated, then each solution of the dynamic system (8.15) that passes through $W(S) \cap I\!\!R^N_+$ converges to a Nash point.*

The final question addressed in this subsection is that of (local) asymptotic stability of critical points of (8.15), i.e., of Nash points. A Nash point is asymptotically stable if every solution that enters a small enough neighborhood of the Nash point converges to it. Clearly, such a Nash point has to be isolated. The following theorems characterize the set of asymptotically stable Nash points.

Theorem 8.59 *Let x^* be an isolated Nash point at which the Nash product $V(x^*)$ is a local maximum. Then x^* is asymptotically stable with respect to the dynamic system (8.15).*

Proof Let U be a neighborhood of x^* relative to $W(S)$ which is so small that x^* is the only Nash point contained in the closure $\mathrm{cl}(U)$. This implies that $V(x) < V(x^*)$ for all $x \in \mathrm{cl}(U)$, $x \neq x^*$. Let r be the maximum of V on the boundary of U. Clearly, $r < V(x^*)$. Now the set $U' := \{x \in U : V(x) > (V(x^*) + r)/2\}$ is also a neighborhood of x^*. From the proof of theorem 8.56 we know that $V(x)$ increases along solutions $x = \psi(t)$. Therefore, a solution that enters U' at a certain time will never leave U. Consequently, x^* is stable with respect to the system (8.15). Also, all accumulation points of such a solution must be in U, and therefore must coincide with x^*, in view of theorem 8.56. Hence, any solution that enters U' converges to x^*. Thus, x^* is not only stable but also asymptotically stable. $\square$

Theorem 8.60 *Let x^* be an isolated Nash point such that $V(x^*)$ is not a local maximum. Then x^* is not asymptotically stable with respect to the system (8.15).*

Proof Let U be a neighborhood of x^* such that x^* is the only Nash point in some open neighborhood $\tilde{U}$ of $cl(U)$. Let U' be an arbitrary neighborhood of x^*. Let $x^\circ \in U'$ with $V(x^\circ) > V(x^*)$. Any solution $x = \psi(t)$ of (8.15) that at some time t_0 passes through x° must have $V(\psi(t)) > V(\psi(t_0))$ for $t > t_0$ (see the proof of theorem 8.56). Therefore, x^* cannot be an accumulation point of ψ. But ψ has accumulation points, and in view of theorem 8.56 these are all outside $\tilde{U}$. Consequently, ψ must leave U at some time. This shows that x^* is not stable, hence not asymptotically stable, with respect to (8.15). $\quad\Box$

Because only isolated Nash points may be asymptotically stable, we have the following corollary of theorems 8.59 and 8.60.

Corollary 8.61 *Let $x^* \in W(S)$, $x > 0$. Then x^* is an asymptotically stable critical point of the dynamic system (8.15), if and only if x^* is an isolated Nash point at which the Nash product $V(x)$ has a local maximum.*

8.5 Bargaining on economic environments

This book is concerned mainly with bargaining games defined in utility space, although, sometimes, underlying bargaining situations are considered to justify the use of certain axioms; in particular, see chapters 5 and 6.

If specific economic environments — for instance division problems — are studied, then the corresponding more detailed information may lead to more specific results concerning the behavior of bargaining solutions. In two subsections below, we briefly discuss two examples: monotonicity properties of solutions applied to economic problems of fair division as studied by Chun and Thomson (1988), and axiomatizations of solutions on economic exchange problems as investigated in Roemer (1988).

In a third subsection, we briefly review work of Crawford and Varian (1979), Sobel (1981), and Peters (1992) on strategic bargaining on economic environments.

8.5.1   Monotonicity properties and fair division

Chun and Thomson (1988) define, for $n \geq 2$ and $\ell \geq 1$, an *ℓ-commodity n-person problem of fair division* to be a pair (u, Ω) of a utility profile $u = (u^1, \ldots, u^n)$, where for each i, $u^i : I\!R_+^\ell \to I\!R$ is *agent i's utility function*[4], and of an *aggregate endowment* $\Omega \in I\!R_+^\ell$. Let $E(\ell, n)$ be the class of all problems (u, Ω) such that, for each i, u^i is continuous, concave, non-constant, and nondecreasing (i.e., if $x, y \in I\!R_+^\ell$ with $x \geq y$, then $u^i(x) \geq u^i(y)$) and satisfies $u^i(0) = 0$. With (u, Ω) an n-person bargaining game $S \in \mathcal{C}_0^N$ can be associated by defining $S := \{\bar{u} \in I\!R^N : \bar{u} \leq (u^1(x^1), \ldots, u^n(x^n))\}$ for some $x^1, \ldots, x^n \in I\!R_+^\ell$ with $\sum x^i \leq \Omega\}$. Consequently, well-known bargaining solutions like the Nash solution ν and the Raiffa-Kalai-Smorodinsky solution ρ can be applied to problems in $E(\ell, n)$ without difficulty, by applying them to the associated bargaining games. Call a solution φ on $E(\ell, n)$ *resource monotonic* (RMON) whenever an increase of the aggregate endowment

---

[4]In economic contexts, often the expression "agent" instead of "player" is used.

implies that no agent is worse off at the outcome assigned by φ. We summarize some of the results of Chun and Thomson (1988) in the following theorem, which we state here without a proof.

Theorem 8.62 *(a) The Nash solution ν is resource monotonic on $E(1,n)$ for all n.*
(b) The Nash solution ν is not resource monotonic on $E(\ell,n)$ for any $(\ell,n) \geq (2,2)$.
(c) The Raiffa-Kalai-Smorodinsky solution ρ is resource monotonic on $E(1,2)$. (d) The solution ρ is not resource monotonic on $E(\ell,n)$ whenever $(\ell,n) \neq (1,2)$.

A surprising consequence of this theorem is that the RKS solution ρ — which was proposed in view of a certain lack of monotonicity of the Nash solution, see sections 4.1, 4.2 — performs worse than the Nash solution when it comes to being monotonic on problems of fair division; even if there is only one good, the solution ρ fails to satisfy RMON if there are more than 2 agents!

As a final remark, observe that in order to establish a theorem like theorem 8.62 one only needs to consider problems of fair division and their associated bargaining games, and not bargaining games in $\mathcal{C}_0^N$ in general[5].

8.5.2 Axiomatic bargaining on economic environments

As indicated by theorem 8.62, if bargaining solutions are restricted to specific economic environments and axioms are redefined accordingly, then, generally speaking, these axioms become less demanding; they apply to "less" instances of the class of economic problems under consideration. For example, we know that the Nash bargaining solution ν is not strongly monotonic (SMON) on the subclass of $\mathcal{C}_0$ $(n = 2)$ consisting of those games S for which $P(S) = W(S) \cap \mathbb{R}_+^2$. It is, however, also easy to verify that any such bargaining game is the image in utility space of a fair division problem from the class $E(1,2)$; according to theorem 8.62(a), the Nash solution is resource monotonic on $E(1,2)$. A similar story holds for the Raiffa-Kalai-Smorodinsky solution ρ, based on theorem 8.62(c).

In the same spirit is the fact, observed by Roemer (1988), that the usual axiomatizations of bargaining solutions no longer hold if attention is restricted to specific economic problems and the axioms are redefined accordingly, in economic terms. Roemer considers the class $E(2) := \bigcup_{\ell=1}^{\infty} E(\ell,2)$ of 2-person fair division problems with any arbitrary finite number of commodities. The image in utility space of any member of $E(2)$ is again a bargaining game in $\mathcal{C}_0$, and a bargaining solution φ may be applied. An *allocation mechanism* is a map F assigning to each $(u,\Omega) \in E(2)$ a complete set of feasible allocations generating the same utilities; i.e., for all (x^1, x^2), $(y^1, y^2) \in F(u,\Omega)$, we have $x^1 + x^2 \leq \Omega$, $u^1(x^1) = u^1(y^1)$, $u^2(x^2) = u^2(y^2)$, and if (z^1, z^2) satisfies $z^1 + z^2 \leq \Omega$ and $u^1(z^1) = u^1(x^1)$, $u^2(z^2) = u^2(x^2)$, then $(z^1, z^2) \in F(u,\Omega)$. Bargaining solutions on $\mathcal{C}_0$ give rise to allocation mechanisms in the obvious way. Axioms for bargaining solutions may be reformulated for allocation mechanisms. For instance, the "Kalai-Smorodinsky axioms" for an allocation mechanism F may be formulated as follows:

(i) Pareto optimality: The allocations in $F(u,\Omega)$ are Pareto optimal in the corresponding bargaining game, for every $(u,\Omega) \in E(2)$.

---

[5]Billera and Bixby (1973) establish conditions under which a bargaining game is the image in utility space of a fair division problem.

(ii) Scale transformation covariance: $F(u,\Omega) = F(au,\Omega)$ for any $a \in I\!\!R^2_{++}$ and $(u,\Omega) \in E(2)$, where $au = (a_1u^1, a_2u^2)$.

(iii) Symmetry: For any $(u,\Omega) \in E(2)$ with $u^1 = u^2$, we have $(\Omega/2, \Omega/2) \in F(u,\Omega)$.

(iv) Individual monotonicity: For all $\ell \geq 1$ and all $(u,\Omega), (u,\Omega') \in E(\ell,2)$ with $\Omega' \geq \Omega$ and $\Omega'_j > \Omega_j$ only for commodities j not liked by the first [resp. second] agent, we have $u^2(x^2) \geq u^2(y^2)$ [resp. $u^1(x^1) \geq u^1(y^1)$] for all $(x^1, x^2) \in F(u,\Omega')$, $(y^1, y^2) \in F(u,\Omega)$.

(An agent is said *not to like* commodity j if an increase in the level of commodity j never increases his utility.) Recall that the corresponding four axioms for bargaining solutions characterize the RKS solution ρ, see section 4.2. Consider the allocation mechanism F defined as follows. If $(u,\Omega) \in E(2)$ such that $\alpha u^1 = \beta u^2$ for some $\alpha, \beta > 0$, then let $(\Omega/2, \Omega/2) \in F(u,\Omega)$; by definition of an allocation mechanism, this completely determines F for the "symmetric" case. Otherwise, let F assign those feasible allocations that lead to the Pareto optimal point with highest second coordinate in the corresponding bargaining game. The allocation mechanism F thus defined can be seen to satisfy the four axioms formulated above. Now let $\ell = 1$, $\Omega = 1$, $u^1 : x \mapsto x$, $u^2 : x \mapsto \sqrt{1 - (1-x)^2}$, $v^1 : x \mapsto \sqrt{x}$, $v^2 : x \mapsto \sqrt{x}$. Then $F(u,\Omega) = \{(0,1)\}$ and $F(v,\Omega) = \{(\frac{1}{2}, \frac{1}{2})\}$. The corresponding outcomes in utility space are $(0,1)$ and $(\frac{1}{2}\sqrt{2}, \frac{1}{2}\sqrt{2})$, respectively; the corresponding bargaining games, however, are both equal to $\text{com}\{(x_1, x_2) \in I\!\!R^2 : x_1^2 + x_2^2 = 1\}$. Thus, not only do the axioms not characterize the allocation mechanism corresponding to the RKS bargaining solution, but even do they not necessarily generate a bargaining solution, because the following basic axiom is violated.

Welfarism: Whenever two problems of fair division generate the same bargaining game in utility space, the allocations assigned by the allocation mechanism generate the same point in this game.

Roemer (1988) retrieves the welfarism property by adding (for instance, to the four axioms above) an axiom called Consistency of Resource Allocation across Dimension (CONRAD); this axiom for an allocation mechanism relates fair division problems with different numbers of commodities. In order for it to have sufficient power, the potential number of commodities must be unbounded. Adding CONRAD to the four axioms above yields an axiomatization of the "RKS" allocation mechanism; and similar results concerning other bargaining solutions can be established (see Roemer, 1988, for details).

The welfarist assumption is appropriate if one feels that all relevant information is included in the utility outcomes generated by a specific economic problem — which seems to be a defendable position. Otherwise — if other information is considered relevant instead, or as well — obviously the results of bargaining theory do not carry over automatically, and additional conditions like CONRAD may have to be required.

8.5.3   Strategic bargaining on economic environments

Suppose, in a fair division problem $(u,\Omega) \in E(\ell,2)$, the utility functions of the agents are private knowledge, i.e., only known to these agents themselves. An arbitrator or mediator announces to use some allocation mechanism F and asks the agents to privately and confidentially report their preferences, i.e., their utility functions. In general, it will be in the agents' interest to lie; depending, of course, on their true utility functions and on the allocation mechanism to be applied. The reported utility functions must satisfy the usual requirements, listed in subsection 8.5.1. Crawford and Varian (1979) show that in the case of one commodity $(\ell = 1)$ it is a dominant strategy to report a linear utility function for allocation mechanisms derived from well known bargaining solutions like the Nash or the RKS solution; this is an immediate consequence of the fact that such solutions are risk sensitive (RS), so that it pays to pretend to be as least risk averse as possible, i.e., to have a linear utility function[6]. These results are extended by Sobel (1981) who shows that for the mentioned mechanisms there may be Nash equilibria in reported utility functions that lead to inefficient (not Pareto optimal) allocations judged by the true utility functions; this can be avoided by restricting the reported utility functions to be linear, in which case Nash equilibria correspond to so-called "equal income competitive equilibria", which are always efficient. Another way to obtain efficiency is to put an additional constraint on the reported utility functions called "self-optimality": the reported utility functions should be best replies given that they were the true utility functions. For details see Peters (1992).

The results of Crawford and Varian (1979) and Sobel (1981) as well as the results in chapter 6 on risk properties, show that under mild conditions bargaining solutions favor less risk averse players. Therefore, axiomatic bargaining game theory is less suited to handle social choice problems of the kind where one wishes a solution to favor a poor man when "playing" against a rich man; also poverty is usually modelled by assuming the utility functions to be more concave, see Luce and Raiffa (1957, p. 130) and Aumann and Kurz (1977). These statements are worked out in detail for the Nash bargaining solution in Klemisch-Ahlert (1991, p. 90 ff.)

It should be noted that in the above mentioned work by Sobel (1981) and Peters (1992) the fair division problem is modelled as a game with *complete information*. In fact, for the equilibria in these models to make sense, it should be assumed that there is complete information on the part of the players; they should know each other's utility functions. There is only a limited amount of work involving *incomplete information* and related to cooperative, axiomatic bargaining. We mention Harsanyi and Selten (1972) and Myerson (1979, 1984).

8.6   Axiomatic bargaining over time

In this section we discuss two ideas which both involve a time — or duration — aspect. Contrary to the Rubinstein model, which will be discussed in section 9.4, the models presented below are dealt with axiomatically.

8.6.1   Continuation of bargaining solutions

Consider a two-person bargaining problem (S, d) in, say, $\overline{C}$; observe that $(S, x) \in \overline{C}$ for every $x \in S$. Let φ be a bargaining solution on $\overline{C}$. Define $\varphi^S : S \to I\!\!R^2$ by $\varphi^S(x) := \varphi(S, x) - x$, and observe that φ^S is actually a *vector field* defined on S. Under standard conditions, integral curves of φ^S, i.e., of the system

---

[6]See also section 6.5.

$\dot{x}_i = \varphi_i^S(x)$ for $i = 1, 2$

exist through all points of S (see Hirsch and Smale, 1974). Suppose that through each point x of S or of $\mathrm{int}(S)$ there is a unique integral curve, which intersects the Pareto boundary $P(S)$ in a point $C\varphi(S, x)$. Then $C\varphi$ is again a bargaining solution called the *continuation of* φ. (The definition of continuation for $n > 2$ is analogous.)

The Nash bargaining solution ν has the disagreement point linearity property DLIN (see section 2.5) and therefore is equal to its continuation: $\nu = C\nu$. The continuation of the Raiffa-Kalai-Smorodinsky solution ρ was already introduced by Raiffa (1953); $C\rho$ can be interpreted as reflecting an idea of bargaining over time where the disagreement point changes gradually towards the Pareto optimal boundary in the direction of the corresponding utopia point, which changes accordingly. Axiomatic characterizations of $C\rho$ were given by Livne (1989a) and Peters and van Damme (1991); see also Livne (1989b), which solves a technical problem associated with the definition of $C\rho$.

Furth (1990) presents a detailed study of the continuation idea. It is investigated, in particular, which properties of bargaining solutions are inherited by their continuations (a lot of well known properties are). In this area, there are still many interesting open questions; the reader is referred to Furth's paper.

8.6.2 Axiomatic bargaining over shrinking pies

Bargaining over a shrinking pie — as a metaphor for bargaining over time with discounting — is usually modelled as a noncooperative game in extensive form (see chapter 9). An axiomatic approach to the problem can be found in Livne (1987). A *bargaining chain* is a sequence of pure bargaining games in (say) $\overline{C} = \overline{C}^{\{1,2\}}$ in discrete or continuous time, say $\{(S^t, d^t) \in \overline{C} \colon t \in \{0, 1, \dots, \overline{t}\}\}$ or $\{(S^t, d^t) \in \overline{C} \colon 0 \le t \le \overline{t}\}$, for which $d^t \le d^s$ and $S^t \subset S^s$ whenever $s \le t$. In words, as time passes on, the bargaining game moves to the southwest; the available outcomes deteriorate for both players. Given a bargaining solution φ on $\overline{C}$, a derived solution g^φ for bargaining chains is obtained as follows. First suppose the chain is finite and calculate the solution for the last game in the chain, that is, calculate $\varphi(S^{\overline{t}}, d^{\overline{t}}) =: z^{\overline{t}}$; then calculate $\varphi(S^{\overline{t}-1}, z^{\overline{t}}) =: z^{\overline{t}-1}$, etc.; g^φ assigns to the chain the point z^0. If the chain is infinite (discrete or continuous) then approach it by finite chains and let the solution g^φ assign the limit (if it exists) of the solution outcomes of the finite chains. Under standard conditions on φ — WPO, STC, SYM, PCONT and an axiom called Adding, see Thomson and Myerson, 1980 — the solution g^φ for chains is well-defined. Furthermore, Livne shows that such a solution inherits some of the properties of the bargaining solution on which it is based, redefined for chains in an appropriate manner.

8.7 Ordinal bargaining

In axiomatic bargaining the usual assumption is that the players have cardinal utility functions — of von Neumann-Morgenstern or other type, see chapter 11. Such utility functions are unique up to positive affine transformations, which justifies the widespread use of the scale transformation covariance axiom (STC), or the weaker homogeneity axiom (HOM) in case we do not want to exclude interpersonal comparisons of utility. In economic models, however, like in the fair division problems discussed in section 8.5, utility functions are often assumed to be of ordinal type. The accompanying axiom would require a bargaining solution to be covariant with any monotonic transformations of the utility functions, and the obvious question is whether such solutions exist.

This question was first addressed by Shapley (1969), who showed that for the two-person case such solutions in general do not exist. For instance, take the triangular game $\text{comv}\{(1,0),(0,1)\}$ in $\mathcal{C}_0$, and suppose the solution assigns an outcome $(\alpha, 1-\alpha)$ with $0 < \alpha < 1$. Apply the transformation $x \mapsto 2x - x^2$ $(x \leq 1)$, $x \mapsto 1$ $(x \geq 1)$ to player 1's utilities; the solution assigned to the transformed game should be the outcome $(2\alpha - \alpha^2, 1 - \alpha)$. Next, apply the transformation $y \mapsto y^2$ $(y \geq 0)$, $y \mapsto y$ $(y \leq 0)$ to the utilities of player 2. The solution outcome should be transformed to $(2\alpha - \alpha^2, (1-\alpha)^2)$; the new game, however, is equal to the original triangular game and therefore has $(\alpha, 1-\alpha)$ as its solution outcome.

For higher dimensions it is in general not possible to map a Pareto surface onto itself as in the above two dimensional example, see Bradley and Shubik (1974). Therefore, solutions that are covariant with monotonic transformations can be constructed. For instance, let S be a game in $\mathcal{C}_0^{\{1,2,3\}}$. There is a unique triple of points in $W(S) \cap I\!R_+^{\{1,2,3\}}$ of the form $(x_1^1, x_2^1, 0), (x_1^1, 0, x_3^1), (0, x_2^1, x_3^1)$. Next, there is a unique triple in $W(S) \cap I\!R_+^{\{1,2,3\}}$ of the form $(x_1^2, x_2^2, x_3^1), (x_1^2, x_2^1, x_3^2), (x_1^1, x_2^2, x_3^2)$, and so on. In this way we create a sequence of points $x^1, x^2, \ldots$ which alternately lie above and below the surface $W(S)$; this sequence is covariant with monotonic transformations — we might restrict attention to transformations that keep a game within the class $\mathcal{C}_0^{\{1,2,3\}}$ — and so is its limit point, which we take as the bargaining solution outcome. The given construction was proposed by Shubik (1982, p. 96).

8.8 Continuity of bargaining solutions

In this book several continuity properties are used: disagreement point continuity (DCONT), feasible set continuity (SCONT), Pareto continuity (PCONT). The latter two are based on the so-called Hausdorff distance, which can be defined in terms of the Euclidean distance d_E on $I\!R^n$ as follows. Let $S, T \subset I\!R^n$ be nonempty closed sets. For $x \in I\!R^n$ let $d_E(x, S) := \min_{y \in S} d_E(x, y)$; then let the Hausdorff distance between S and T be defined by

$$d_H(S, T) := \sup_{x \in S, y \in T} \{d_E(x, T), d_E(y, S)\}.$$

Note that we allow $d_H(S, T) = \infty$.[7] A sequence of closed sets $S^1, S^2, \ldots$ converges to a closed set S if $d_H(S^k, S) \to 0$ as $k \to \infty$.

A comprehensive study of continuity properties (SCONT) of bargaining solutions is Jansen and Tijs (1983).

---

[7]So, strictly speaking, d_H is not a distance function.

Chapter 9

Noncooperative models for bargaining solutions

9.1 Introduction

Axiomatic bargaining theory started with Nash's seminal paper "The Bargaining Problem", which appeared in 1950. This paper is still the most important paper in the field; it introduces and axiomatically characterizes the Nash bargaining solution. In his 1951 paper, Nash proposes his equilibrium concept for noncooperative games. Also this contribution to game theory is pathbreaking. Nash's 1953 paper on bargaining tries to combine both the cooperative and the noncooperative approach. Nash designs a noncooperative demand game of which the, in a certain sense unique, Nash equilibrium leads to the payoffs prescribed by the Nash bargaining solution. Although the argument laid out in the last paper is formally incomplete and somewhat *ad hoc*, it has plotted a course for what some authors have termed the *Nash program* (Binmore and Dasgupta, 1987). This "program" aims at constructing bargaining procedures that have an axiomatic as well as a noncooperative justification. See also the quotation from Nash (1953) in section 9.3.

One of the most important papers in noncooperative bargaining is Rubinstein (1982). Surprisingly, the unique payoffs corresponding to a perfect equilibrium of Rubinstein's bargaining procedure with discounting turned out to be related to the Nash bargaining solution outcome. Thus, Rubinstein's contribution fits well within the Nash program.

Earlier Zeuthen (1930), *avant la lettre*, derived the Nash bargaining solution by means of describing a negotiation process. This fact was first recognized by Harsanyi (1956).

The purpose of this chapter is to give an overview of noncooperative models of bargaining that bear a relation to cooperative, axiomatic models. For surveys on noncooperative bargaining models in general, the reader is referred to Sutton (1985) and Osborne and Rubinstein (1990).

We start, in section 9.2 with the Harsanyi-Zeuthen model of bargaining. Section 9.3 reviews Nash's demand game, and section 9.4 discusses the Rubinstein approach in the context of the Nash demand game. Extensions to nonconvex games and to n-person games are also indicated, based on Herrero (1989) and Krishna and Serrano (1990). In section 9.5 a simple model by Anbar and Kalai (1978) and some related work will be reviewed. A strategic model for the Raiffa-Kalai-Smorodinsky solution, related to an axiomatic characterization, is presented in section 9.6; the material there is based on Moulin (1984) and Peters *et al.* (1991). Van Damme (1986) proposes a noncooperative game to compare different bargaining solutions; this model is reviewed in section 9.7. Section 9.8 discusses so-called arbitration games or threat games, which were first introduced by Nash (1953).

9.2   The Harsanyi-Zeuthen procedure

Zeuthen, in Chapter IV of his *Problems of Monopoly and Economic Warfare*, described a bargaining process, which was recognized by Harsanyi (1956) as leading to the outcome predicted by the Nash bargaining solution. Zeuthen's book appeared in 1930, more than a decade before von Neumann and Morgenstern's *Theory of Games and Economic Behavior*, and more than two decades before Nash's articles on the bargaining problem. This section presents Harsanyi's account of the relation between the Nash bargaining solution and Zeuthen's negotiation procedure. Following Harsanyi, the flavor of the argument is presented rather than a rigorous game-theoretic formalism.

The setting is a 2-person bargaining game $S \in C_0$. In the first round of bargaining, the players independently and simultaneously make proposals as to how to solve the game; say players 1 and 2 propose x and y, respectively, with $x, y \in P(S) \cap \mathbb{R}^2_{++}$. The interesting case is where these proposals are incompatible, so $x_1 > y_1$ and (consequently) $x_2 > y_2$. Zeuthen's presumption was that, in a next round, one of the players has to make a concession; if not, that is, if both players stick to their previous proposals, the game ends in conflict, with the disagreement payoff of 0 for each. First consider player 1. Will he accept y or insist on obtaining x? This will obviously depend on player 1's view of the probability that player 2 would definitely reject x, and that his own insistence on x would lead to a conflict.

Let p_2 be the probability, as estimated by player 1, that player 2 would finally reject x. Then, if player 1 accepts y he will obtain y_1 with certainty, while if he rejects y and insists on x he will have the probability $(1 - p_2)$ of obtaining x_1 and the probability p_2 of obtaining 0. Therefore, on the assumption that player 1 tries to maximize his expected utility, he will accept y if $y_1 > (1 - p_2)x_1$, that is, if $p_2 > (x_1 - y_1)/x_1$, and insist on x otherwise. Consequently, the utility quotient $(x_1 - y_1)/x_1$ expresses the maximum risk (maximum probability of conflict) that player 1 is prepared to face in order to secure the better outcome x instead of the less favorable y. Analogously, the utility quotient $(y_2 - x_2)/y_2$ is the maximum risk player 2 is willing to take in order to achieve the outcome y.

At this point Zeuthen introduces the further assumption that each party will make a concession to his opponent once he finds that the latter's determination is firmer (i.e., the latter's readiness to risk a conflict is greater) than his own. Thus, player 1 will always make a further concession if

$$\frac{x_1 - y_1}{x_1} < \frac{y_2 - x_2}{y_2}, \tag{9.1}$$

while player 2 will always make a concession in the opposite case. A concession must be large enough to reverse the inequality sign. Furthermore, a concession must have a certain minimal size, in accordance with the indivisibility of the smallest monetary unit and other technical or psychological indivisibilities. It is easy to see that this negotiation process will converge to the Nash bargaining solution outcome if the minimal size of admissible concessions goes to zero, as follows. Formula (9.1) can be rewritten as

$$x_1 x_2 < y_1 y_2,$$

that is, the player for which the product of the coordinates of his proposal is smaller always has to make a concession so as to increase this product.

This is in essence Zeuthen's negotiation model as described by Harsanyi. The *crux* of the Zeuthen model is the assumption that the player with the lower risk limit will make a concession. Harsanyi (1956) attempts to derive this assumption from more basic postulates. The interested reader is referred to his original article. Another way to interpret formula (9.1) is to assume that the player with the lower relative loss of accepting the proposal of his opponent, will make the concession. Both interpretations — in terms of maximum probability of conflict, or relative loss from accepting a worse proposal — lead to intuitive though not necessary assumptions about the bargaining process. Consequently, they increase the plausibility and attractiveness of the Nash bargaining solution without pushing it forward as the only reasonable, or necessary, solution.

An extension of Zeuthen's model to obtain outcomes corresponding to nonsymmetric Nash bargaining solutions using the replication method proposed by Kalai (1977a) — see section 2.4.4 — is given in Peters (1987). Batinelli *et al.* (1986) give a critical discussion of the Harsanyi-Zeuthen principle.

9.3   The Nash demand game

In his 1950 Nash paper dealt with the bargaining problem as a 2-person cooperative game. Nash (1951) introduced the well-known Nash equilibrium concept for noncooperative games. In a third paper, Nash tried to combine both approaches; in Nash's own words (Nash, 1953, p. 129): "We give two independent derivations of our solution of the two-person cooperative game. In the first, the cooperative game is reduced to a noncooperative game. To do this, one makes the players' steps of negotiation in the cooperative game become moves in the non-cooperative model. Of course, one cannot represent all possible bargaining devices as moves in the non-cooperative game. The negotiation process must be formalized and restricted, but in such a way that each participant is still able to utilize all the essential strengths of his position.

The second approach is by the axiomatic method. One states as axioms several properties that it would seem natural for the solution to have and then discovers that the axioms actually determine the solution uniquely. The two approaches to the problem, via the negotiation model or via the axioms, are complementary; each helps to justify and clarify the other."

Nash's negotiation model consists of two moves; it is a two-stage noncooperative game. Let some feasible set S be given. At the first stage the players simultaneously and independently choose their *threats* t_1 and t_2. These threats are strategies in some underlying noncooperative game, and are carried out in case of disagreement in the demand game which constitutes the second stage of Nash's negotiation model, described in the next paragraph.

The implicit assumption is that the feasible set S results as the payoff space corresponding to the underlying noncooperative game. The payoffs corresponding to the threats t_1 and t_2 determine the disagreement point $d \in S$. Given that the players would agree on letting the Nash bargaining solution or some other Pareto optimal solution φ determine the final outcome of the game, $\varphi(S, d)$, this first stage would result in a new noncooperative game with payoffs transformed by φ and having a zerosum-like character due to the Pareto optimality of the solution. This game is usually called the *threat game* or *arbitration game*, see also section 9.8. Instead of assuming that the players agree on using the Nash bargaining solution to determine the final outcome given their threats, Nash derived this by proposing a *demand game* as the second stage of the negotiation game. This demand game can be analyzed separately for a given disagreement point (or pair of threat payoffs) $d \in S$. From now on, assume $S \in \mathcal{C}_0$, so that the disagreement point has been normalized to 0, and, for convenience, assume $W(S) \cap I\!R_+^2 \subset P(S)$.

The demand game is played as follows. The players simultaneously and independently make demands $x_1 \geq 0$, $x_2 \geq 0$. If $x \in S$, then the resulting payoffs are x_1 and x_2 for player 1 and 2, respectively. Otherwise, the payoffs are given by the disagreement point $(0,0)$. A *Nash equilibrium* (Nash (1951)) for this game is a pair of demands (x_1^*, x_2^*) with $K_1(x_1, x_2^*) \leq K_1(x_1^*, x_2^*)$ and $K_2(x_1^*, x_2) \leq K_2(x_1^*, x_2^*)$ for all $x_1, x_2 \geq 0$, where K_1 and K_2 are the payoff functions described above. That is, a Nash equilibrium has a certain stability property: no player can gain by a unilateral deviation. It is straightforward to check that the set of Nash equilibria of this demand game is

$$\{x \geq 0 : \ x \in P(S) \text{ or } x \geq h(S)\}.$$

Nash's ambition was to derive the Nash bargaining solution outcome as an in some sense unique equilibrium of the demand game. Confronted with the multiplicity of equilibria of the above demand game, he proposed (Nash, 1953, p. 132) to "*smooth* the game to obtain a continuous payoff function and then study the limiting behavior of the equilibrium points of the smoothed game as the amount of smoothing approaches zero." In order to "smooth" the game Nash considers continuous functions $h : I\!R_+^2 \to I\!R$ with $h(x) = 1$ if $x \in S$ and which "taper[s] off rapidly towards zero as (x_1, x_2) moves away from S, without ever actually reaching zero." The payoff functions of the smoothed games are $K_1^h(x_1, x_2) = x_1 h(x_1, x_2)$ and $K_2^h(x_1, x_2) = x_2 h(x_1, x_2)$. The functions h "should be thought of as representing uncertainties in the information structure of the game, the utility scales etc." If $x^* \in I\!R_+^2$ is a point where the product $x_1 x_2 h(x_1, x_2)$ is maximized — and such a point exists if h "tapers off rapidly towards zero" — then x^* must be a Nash equilibrium of the smoothed game. Indeed, suppose player 1 could deviate profitably: $x_1 h(x_1, x_2^*) > x_1^* h(x^*)$ for some $x_1 > 0$. Then, because $x^* > 0$, also $x_1 x_2^* h(x_1, x_2^*) > x_1^* x_2^* h(x^*)$, a contradiction. Next, if "the amount of smoothing approaches zero", i.e., the smoothing functions h converge pointwise to the (discontinuous) indicator function of S, then these Nash equilibria converge to the Nash bargaining solution outcome of S. Thus, the Nash outcome can be obtained as the limit of Nash equilibria of a general class of smoothed demand games. Furthermore, Nash (1953, p. 132) remarks that "if h varies regularly there will be only one equilibrium point, coinciding with a unique maximum of $x_1 x_2 h$". Since Nash aims at deriving the Nash bargaining solution outcome as the only *necessary* limit of equilibrium points of smoothed games, it is sufficient to produce *one* example of a sequence of "regularly varying" smoothing functions h so that the Nash bargaining solution outcome is the unique limit of equilibrium points. Nash, however, does not give such an example; only later has his argument been completed, see Binmore and Dasgupta (1987, p. 65 ff.) or van Damme (1987, p. 144 ff.). The example presented below is based on the latter reference.

For convenience, we assume that the part $W(S) \cap R_+^2 \subset P(S)$ of the boundary is smooth, meaning that the function f^S on $[0, h_1(S)]$ describing the boundary is differentiable. We write f instead of f^S, and let

$$\gamma(x) := \min\{\gamma : x \in \gamma S\}, \quad x \in R_+^2,$$

denote the *gauge* of S (Rockafellar, 1970, p. 28). This function is convex, as is not hard to prove, and differentiable by smoothness of the boundary of S. If $x \neq 0$, $\gamma(x)^{-1}x \in P(S)$, hence $f(\gamma(x)^{-1}x_1) = \gamma(x)^{-1}x_2$. Writing γ for $\gamma(x)$, this simplifies to $f(\gamma^{-1}x_1) = \gamma^{-1}x_2$ for all $x \in R_+^2$, $x \neq 0$. By differentiating both sides with respect to x_1 and x_2, we obtain

$$f'(\gamma^{-1}x_1)(\gamma - x_1\gamma_1) = x_2\gamma_1, \quad -f'(\gamma^{-1}x_1)x_1\gamma_2 = \gamma - x_2\gamma_2, \tag{9.2}$$

where γ_i denotes the partial derivative of γ at x with respect to the i th coordinate. Combining the two equalities in (9.2) gives $(\gamma - x_1\gamma_1)(\gamma - x_2\gamma_2) = x_1x_2\gamma_1\gamma_2$ or equivalently

$$\gamma = x_1\gamma_1 + x_2\gamma_2, \quad x \in R_+^2, \ x \neq 0, \tag{9.3}$$

an identity which will be useful below. For every $\varepsilon > 0$ define the smoothing function h^ε by

$$h^\varepsilon(x) := \begin{cases} 1 & \text{if } x \in S \\ \exp(-(\gamma - 1)^2/\varepsilon) & \text{if } x \notin S. \end{cases}$$

We will show that the demand game with payoff functions $K_1^\varepsilon(x_1, x_2) = x_1 h^\varepsilon(x_1, x_2)$ and $K_2^\varepsilon(x_1, x_2) = x_2 h^\varepsilon(x_1, x_2)$ has a *unique* equilibrium x^ε; as can be expected from the foregoing, x^ε maximizes $x_1x_2 h^\varepsilon(x)$, and converges to the Nash bargaining solution outcome of S.

Obviously, interior points of S cannot be equilibria. For $x \notin S$, $x > 0$, we have, for $i = 1, 2$:

$$\frac{\partial}{\partial x_i} K_i^\varepsilon(x) = h^\varepsilon(x)[1 - 2x_i\gamma_i(\gamma - 1)/\varepsilon] \tag{9.4}$$

and if we interpret this partial derivative as the right derivate (approaching from outside of S), it holds also on $P(S)$. Thus, for $x^* \in P(S)$, $\partial(K_i^\varepsilon(x^*))/\partial x_i = 1$ because $\gamma(x^*) = 1$. This implies that $x^* \in P(S) \cap R_+^2$ cannot be an equilibrium; both players could gain by demanding slightly more. Therefore, if x is an equilibrium, then $x \notin S$ and consequently $\partial K_1^\varepsilon(x)/\partial x_1 = \partial K_2^\varepsilon(x)/\partial x_2 = 0$. By (9.4) this implies

$$\varepsilon = 2x_1\gamma_1(\gamma - 1) = 2x_2\gamma_2(\gamma - 1), \tag{9.5}$$

so that $x_1\gamma_1 = x_2\gamma_2$. With (9.3), this implies

$$x_1\gamma_1 = x_2\gamma_2 = \gamma/2. \tag{9.6}$$

Substitution of (9.6) into (9.5) gives

$$\gamma = (1 + \sqrt{1 + 4\varepsilon})/2, \tag{9.7}$$

so $\gamma \downarrow 1$ as $\varepsilon \downarrow 0$. By substitution of (9.6) into the first equality of (9.2), one obtains $f'(\gamma^{-1}x_1) = -x_2 x_1^{-1} = -\gamma^{-1}x_2/\gamma^{-1}x_1$. By lemma 2.2, this can be seen to imply that $\gamma^{-1}x$ is the Nash bargaining solution outcome of S, i.e., $\nu(S) = \gamma^{-1}x$. This uniquely determines the equilibrium $x = x^\varepsilon$ of the demand game with smoothing function h^ε, and shows (indeed) that $x^\varepsilon \to \nu(S)$ as $\varepsilon \to 0$.

Following van Damme (1987), we can state the obtained result formally in the following way. Let $H := \bigcup_{\delta > 0} H^\delta$ where H^δ is the class of continuous functions $h : I\!\!R_+^2 \to (0, 1]$ with $h(x) = 1$ if $x \in S$ and $\max\{h(x), x_1 x_2 h(x)\} < \delta$ if the Euclidean distance between x and S is larger than δ. Note that $h^\varepsilon \in H^{\delta(\varepsilon)}$ for $\varepsilon > 0$ and $\delta(\varepsilon)$ small enough (where the functions $h(\varepsilon)$ are as introduced above). Call an equilibrium x of the demand game H-essential if associated with every sequence $\{g^\delta\}_{\delta \downarrow 0}$ with $g^\delta \in H^\delta$ there is a sequence $\{y^\delta\}_{\delta \downarrow 0}$ such that y^δ is an equilibrium of the g^δ-smoothed demand game and such that y^δ converges to x as δ approaches 0. The above reasoning is summarized by the following theorem.

Theorem 9.1 *The Nash bargaining solution outcome is the unique H-essential equilibrium of the demand game associated with S.*

It is interesting to remark that, apparently, Nash was the first to *refine* the Nash equilibrium concept.

9.4 Perfect equilibrium in an alternating Nash demand game

An elegant implementation of the Nash bargaining solution can be obtained by employing the Rubinstein (1982) alternating offers bargaining game. This section reviews the essentials of Rubinstein's results with the Nash demand game as a starting point. An extension to nonconvex games is provided by Herrero (1989, see also subsection 8.4.2), and to n-person games by Krishna and Serrano (1990); also these will be briefly discussed.

Let $S \in C_0$ be a 2-person bargaining game. For presentational convenience assume $W(S) \cap I\!\!R_+^2 \subset P(S)$. Rubinstein's alternating demand game is defined as follows. In the first round $(t = 1)$ player 1 proposes an outcome $x \in S$, $x \geq 0$, and player 2 either accepts or rejects this outcome. If player 2 accepts, the game ends with the outcome x. If he rejects, the game continues with round 2 $(t = 2)$ where it is player 2's turn to propose an outcome $x \in S$, $x \geq 0$, which player 1 can either accept or reject. Etc. If an agreement is reached in round t on a proposal $x \in S$, then player 1's payoff equals $\delta_1^{t-1}x_1$, whereas 2's payoff is $\delta_2^{t-1}x_2$. Here, $0 < \delta_1, \delta_2 < 1$ are the discount factors of players 1 and 2, respectively. Because we are mainly interested in the symmetric Nash bargaining solution, until further notice we assume $\delta_1 = \delta_2$ and write δ instead. The description of the game is completed by the assumption that, if no player ever accepts, the final payoffs are the disagreement payoffs $(0, 0)$.

A *strategy* for a player is a prescription which tells that player what to do at every moment $t = 1, 2, \ldots$ At each moment, the action prescribed by the strategy may depend on the whole history until that moment, possibly including a proposal of the opponent at the same moment. For instance, for player 1, if t is odd then a strategy describes a proposal to be made by player 1, which may depend on everything that happened before moment t. If t is even, then the strategy tells player 1 whether to accept or reject player 2's last proposal; acceptance or rejection may depend, not only on 2's last proposal, but also on the whole history before moment t. A *Nash equilibrium* is a pair of strategies such that, for every player $i \in \{1, 2\}$, unilaterally deviating to a different strategy yields a final payoff which is *at most* equal to i's payoff when he does not deviate.

The first observation is that any point $x \in P(S)$, $x \geq 0$, can be supported by a Nash equilibrium pair of strategies, as follows. Player 1 proposes always x and rejects any proposal y of player 2 for which $y_1 < x_1$. Player 2 also proposes x always, and rejects any proposal y of player 1 for which $y_2 < x_2$. All other proposals are accepted. These strategies lead to payoffs x_1 and x_2 for players 1 and 2, respectively, and agreement is reached in the first round. It is straightforward to check that this pair of strategies constitutes a Nash equilibrium.

Rubinstein next observed that these kinds of Nash equilibria are, in general, not very convincing. For suppose player 1 slightly deviates from his strategy — by mistake or on purpose. Say, in the first round, instead of x he proposes $y \in P(S)$, $y \geq 0$, with y_1 slightly larger than x_1 and, consequently, y_2 slightly smaller than x_2, say $y_2 = x_2 - \varepsilon$ for some small $\varepsilon > 0$. If, from that point on, both players stick to their original strategies, then player 2 rejects y and in the second round proposes x, which is accepted by player 1 and leads to payoffs of δx_1 and δx_2 for the respective players. However, if player 2 thinks that 1 made a mistake and probably will not deviate any more, then it might be better for him to also deviate in the first round and accept y. This gives him a payoff of y_2; if ε is so small that $\varepsilon < (1 - \delta)x_2$ then, indeed, $y_2 = x_2 - \varepsilon > \delta x_2$. Player 1, knowing this, thus has an incentive to deviate.

This kind of behavior can be ruled out by requiring a Nash equilibrium to be *subgame perfect* (Selten (1965)). A Nash equilibrium pair of strategies is called subgame perfect if for any possible *subgame* reached, the strategies restricted to that subgame still constitute a Nash equilibrium. In the game under consideration, this means the following. Consider any history in the game, that is, any sequence of proposals and rejections starting at $t = 1$. So either, one of the players has to make a proposal, or one of the players has to accept or reject the proposal that ended the history. The given pair of strategies still prescribe all actions to be taken during the remainder of the game, the so-called subgame. If, in this subgame, the given pair of strategies still constitutes a Nash equilibrium, and if this is true for any history in the game, then it is called *subgame perfect*. Note that requiring subgame perfectness has implications only if there is a deviation from the equilibrium path generated by playing according to the given pair of strategies. Clearly, the example of the previous paragraph shows that the pair of strategies considered there is not subgame perfect: by the original deviation of player 1, a subgame is reached where player 2 gains by a unilateral deviation, namely accepting y instead of rejecting it and proposing x at the next round.

Rubinstein shows that in the alternating offer game described above there is a unique pair of payoffs supported by a subgame perfect Nash equilibrium. Let $x^*, y^* \geq 0$ be points of $P(S)$ satisfying the equations

$$x_2 = \delta y_2, \quad y_1 = \delta x_1. \tag{9.8}$$

Consider the following strategies. Player 1 always proposes x^* and rejects a proposal y of player 2 if and only if $y_1 < \delta x_1^*$. Player 2 always proposes y^* and rejects a proposal x of player 1 if and only if $x_2 < \delta y_2^*$. These strategies constitute a Nash equilibrium leading to the payoffs (x_1^*, x_2^*). Furthermore, this Nash equilibrium is subgame perfect: in view of (9.8) deviating, in particular by offering your opponent slightly less, never makes you better off because your opponent is not better off accepting your proposal and hence it will be rejected. So the existence of a pair of payoffs corresponding to a subgame perfect Nash equilibrium is established, once it is shown that (9.8) has a solution. This is demonstrated by means of a geometrical argument which also clarifies the relation with the Nash bargaining solution.

Let $z := \nu(S)$ be the Nash bargaining solution outcome, i.e., z maximizes the product $x_1 x_2$ on $\{x \in S : x \geq 0\}$. Let $\overline{\alpha} := z_1 z_2$. For any $0 < \alpha < \overline{\alpha}$ there are exactly two different points $x^\alpha, y^\alpha \in P(S)$ with $x_1^\alpha x_2^\alpha = y_1^\alpha y_2^\alpha = \alpha$ (assume $x_1^\alpha > y_1^\alpha$, see figure 9.1). Observe that

$$\frac{y_1^\alpha}{x_1^\alpha} = \frac{x_2^\alpha}{y_2^\alpha}$$

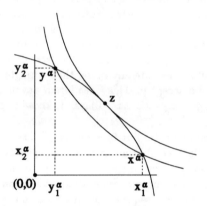

Figure 9.1: Alternating proposals and the Nash bargaining solution

for every $0 < \alpha < \overline{\alpha}$. Furthermore, the function $g : (0, \overline{\alpha}) \to (0, 1)$ defined by

$$g(\alpha) := \frac{y_1^\alpha}{x_1^\alpha}$$

is a continuous strictly increasing function with as range the interval $(0, 1)$. In particular, there is a unique α^* with

$$g(\alpha^*) = \frac{y_1^{\alpha^*}}{x_1^{\alpha^*}} = \frac{x_2^{\alpha^*}}{y_2^{\alpha^*}} = \delta$$

which implies that the pair $x^{\alpha^*}, y^{\alpha^*}$ is a (unique) solution to (9.8). Furthermore, if the discount factor δ approaches 1, then the points x^{α^*} and y^{α^*} both converge to the point z, which is the Nash bargaining solution outcome. Thus, these particular payoffs corresponding to subgame perfect Nash equilibria of the alternating demand game converge to the payoffs prescribed by the Nash bargaining solution outcome as the discount factor approaches 1, i.e., the situation without discounting. This observation would be interesting but not more than that if there would be many — more than one — pair of payoffs corresponding to subgame perfect Nash equilibria. Rubinstein showed that this is not the case. Instead of his proof, the simpler argument by Shaked and Sutton (1984) is reproduced here. See also Sutton (1985).

Let M denote the (undiscounted) supremum player 1 can obtain in any subgame perfect equilibrium. Consider the subgame starting at $t = 3$, when player 1 has to make a proposal. Since this subgame is essentially the same game as the original one starting at $t = 1$, M is still the supremum that player 1 can get in any subgame perfect equilibrium. Now consider the subgame starting at $t = 2$ with a proposal by player 2. Any proposal y of player 2 with $y_1 > \delta M$ would certainly be accepted by player 1, since in the subgame starting at $t = 3$ player 1 can obtain at most M, and δM is the discounted value. So player 2 obtains at least $f^S(\delta M)$: this represents the infimum of what player 2 can obtain in any subgame perfect equilibrium. Here, as before $f^S : [0, h_1(S)] \to [0, h_2(S)]$ is the concave decreasing function describing $W(S) \cap \mathbb{R}_+^2$, see figure 9.2. Next, consider 1's proposal at time $t = 1$, the beginning of the game.

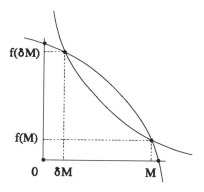

Figure 9.2: Uniqueness of subgame perfect equilibrium payoffs

Any proposal x with $x_2 < \delta f^S(\delta M)$ will certainly be rejected by player 2, since $\delta f^S(\delta M)$ is the discounted value of what player 2 at least gets in the subgame starting at $t = 2$. Therefore, player 1 will obtain at most $(f^S)^{-1}(\delta f^S(\delta M))$. It follows that $M = (f^S)^{-1}(\delta f^S(\delta M))$, which implies that $f^S(M) = \delta f^S(\delta M)$, so $x := (M, f^S(M))$ and $y := (\delta M, f^S(\delta M))$ solve (9.8). Since (9.8) has a unique solution, it follows that $x^* = (M, f^S(M))$ and $y^* = (\delta M, f^S(\delta M))$. By a similar story for M being the infimum rather than the supremum of what player 1 can obtain in any subgame perfect equilibrium, it can be shown that also in that case $x^* = (M, f^S(M))$, $y^* = (\delta M, f^S(\delta M))$. This proves that the payoffs corresponding to a subgame perfect Nash equilibrium are unique indeed.

Different discount factors: asymmetric solutions

If the players have different discount factors δ_1 and δ_2 then, by similar arguments, it can be shown that the unique subgame perfect equilibrium payoffs in the Rubinstein alternating demand game converge to the nonsymmetric Nash bargaining solution maximizing the product $x_1^t x_2^{1-t}$ on $S \cap I\!\!R_+^2$, where $t := (\ln \delta_2)(\ln \delta_1 \delta_2)^{-1}$, as δ_1 and δ_2 approach 1 such that t is being held constant.

Nonconvex feasible sets

If the feasible set is not convex, then subgame perfect equilibrium payoffs no longer need to be unique. Binmore (1987b) provides a complete characterization of the set of subgame perfect equilibria for that case. Herrero (1989) offers a characterization of all stationary subgame perfect equilibria. A *stationary* subgame perfect equilibrium can be described by a pair (x, y) where player 1 [2] always proposes x [y] and accepts a proposal z if and only if $z_1 \geq y_1$ [$z_2 \geq x_2$]. Obviously, the subgame perfect equilibrium found for the convex case above is stationary.

Due to the stationarity requirement, the nonconvex case is similar to the convex case. It is easy to show that a pair (x, y) is a stationary subgame perfect equilibrium for the alternating Nash demand game based on $S \in \mathcal{B}_0$ if and only if $x, y \geq 0$, $x, y \in P(S)$, and x, y satisfy formula (9.8) again. (The proof is easy since by stationarity the form of the strategies is already known.) Since S does not need to be convex there may be more than one pair satisfying (9.8). See figure 9.3 for an illustration.

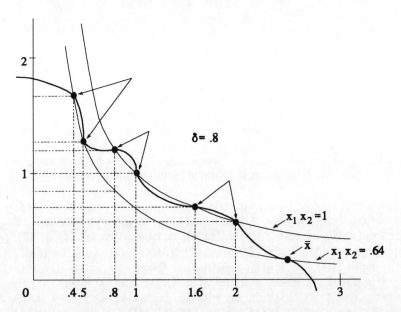

Figure 9.3: An example of (at least) three stationary subgame perfect equilibria

Let (for S fixed) $E(\delta)$ denote the set of all $x \in S$ such that, for some $y \in S$, (x, y) is a stationary subgame perfect equilibrium of the alternating demand game with common discount factor δ. Let $\{(x^\delta, y^\delta)\}_{\delta \uparrow 1}$ be a sequence of stationary subgame perfect equilibria with $x^\delta \in E(\delta)$ for every δ, and with $(x^\delta, y^\delta) \to z \in P(S)$ as $\delta \to 1$. From (9.8) and the definition of ν^H, it follows that $z \in \nu^H(S)$. Hence, $E(\delta)$ converges to a subset of $\nu^H(S)$ as $\delta \to 1$. However, not every $x \in \nu^H(S)$ needs to be the limit of a sequence of stationary subgame perfect equilibria for the common discount factor approaching to 1. For instance, take an $S \in \mathcal{B}_0$ and an $\overline{x} > 0$, $\overline{x} \in P(S)$ such that $\overline{x}$ is a stationary point of the Nash product — hence, an element of $\nu^H(S)$, see subsection 8.4.3 — and such that in some neighborhood B of $\overline{x}$ the following holds: if $y \in P(S) \cap B$ with $y_1 < \overline{x}_1$ then $y_1 y_2 > \overline{x}_1 \overline{x}_2$, if $y \in P(S) \cap B$ with $y_1 > \overline{x}_1$ then $y_1 y_2 < \overline{x}_1 \overline{x}_2$ (see figure 9.3). Such an $\overline{x}$ cannot be the limit of stationary subgame perfect equilibria since the proposals $(\hat{x}, \hat{y})$ in any stationary subgame perfect equilibrium have equal Nash products, $\hat{x}_1 \hat{x}_2 = \hat{y}_1 \hat{y}_2$, in view of (9.8)[1].

Bargaining games with more than two players

An at first sight natural extension of the alternating offers game to bargaining games $S \in \mathcal{C}_0^N$ with $|n| > 2$ would be the following. Player 1 starts by making a proposal. If all other players accept, the game is over. Otherwise, player 2 makes a proposal. If all other players accept, the game is over. Otherwise ... etc. Unfortunately, this game has many subgame perfect equilibria (see Osborne and Rubinstein, 1990).

An extension in which the uniqueness of subgame perfect equilibrium is maintained, is given by Krishna and Serrano (1990). Their alternating offers game is defined as follows. Let $S \in \mathcal{C}_0^N$, $N = \{1, 2, \ldots, n\}$ with $n \geq 2$. Player 1 starts by making a proposal, say $x \in S$. All other players simultaneously respond to this proposal by accepting or rejecting it. If all players in $N \backslash \{1\}$ accept x, the game is over and each player j receives x_j. If a proper subset $M \subset N \backslash \{1\}$ accepts the proposal x, then each player $j \in M$ receives x_j and leaves the game. The game continues with $N^1 := N \backslash M$ as player set and $(S, x)_{N^1} \in \mathcal{C}_0^{N^1}$ as bargaining game. In this reduced bargaining game player j makes a proposal where j is the smallest index in N^1 larger than 1 (in general, j is the smallest index in the remaining player set larger than i, if i was the last player to make a proposal, and j is the smallest index in this set if i happens to be the largest index). This procedure continues until there is no player left; if the game continues forever, the remaining players receive their disagreement payoffs 0. Observe that this game reduces to the Rubinstein game if $n = 2$.

Krishna and Serrano (1990) show hat there is a unique outcome $x^* \in P(S)$ that can be obtained by a subgame perfect equilibrium of the game above. The proposals of the players in such a subgame perfect equilibrium are related in a way similar to the equalities in formula (9.8). Furthermore, they show that as the common discount factor approaches 1 the subgame perfect equilibrium outcome converges to the symmetric Nash bargaining solution outcome of the game S. For further details the reader is referred to their paper.

An attractive feature of this model is the close link with Lensberg's (1988) axiomatic characterization based on the multilateral stability axiom (MSTAB); see section 7.4. The subgames occurring in the noncooperative extensive game model above correspond to the "subgames" or "reduced games" occurring in the definition of MSTAB. The multilateral stability requirement in the cooperative, axiomatic approach is closely related to the sub-

---

[1]The multisolution defined in D.1 in Herrero (1989) contains exactly the points which can be obtained as the limit of stationary subgame perfect equilibria. This multisolution, however, is not the one characterized by the axioms. See also footnote 1 in chapter 8.

game perfectness requirement in the noncooperative solution.

A similar relation between a cooperative and a noncooperative approach is established in section 9.6 for the Raiffa-Kalai-Smorodinsky solution.

9.5 A one-shot bargaining problem

A very simple bargaining model leading to the Nash bargaining solution outcome was proposed by Anbar and Kalai (1978). Let $S \in \mathcal{C}_0$ be a 2-person bargaining game. For simplicity suppose $W(S) \cap I\!R_+^2 \subset P(S)$, and $h(S) = (1,1)$. Players 1 and 2 play the Nash demand game, that is, player 1 demands $x_1 \in [0,1]$, player 2 demands $x_2 \in [0,1]$, and the payoffs are (x_1, x_2) if $(x_1, x_2) \in S$, $(0,0)$ otherwise. Suppose player 1 expects player 2 to demand some x_2 according to the uniform distribution on $[0,1]$. His expected utility from demanding x_1 is then equal to $x_1 \Pr[x_2 \leq f^S(x_1)] + 0\Pr[x_2 > f^S(x_1)]$. Here, f^S describes the boundary $P(S)$ as a function of $x_1 \in [0, h_1(S)]$, as before. Clearly, this expected utility is equal to $x_1 f^S(x_1)$, which expression is maximized at the Nash bargaining solution outcome. Thus, player 1 maximizes his expected utility by demanding $\nu_1(S)$. If player 2 has similar beliefs with respect to player 1, then player 2 will propose $\nu_2(S)$. Consequently, this "one-shot bargaining game" leads to the Nash outcome.

It is obvious that the results of this bargaining model are very sensitive to the beliefs of the players. Furthermore, the players may have beliefs not only concerning what the other player will demand, but also concerning the beliefs of the other player (possibly *ad infinitum*). Variations in this style are studied by Nakayama (1986) and Lahiri (1990).

9.6 Consistency and subgame perfectness for the RKS solution

A noncooperative game leading to the Raiffa-Kalai-Smorodinsky (RKS) outcome was developed in Moulin (1984). In this section we propose a related game that has the attractive feature of corresponding to an axiomatic characterization of the RKS solution in much the same way as the Krishna-Serrano game corresponds to Lensberg's axiomatization of the Nash bargaining solution (see section 9.4). The material in this section is based on Peters *et al.* (1991).

As in chapter 7, $I \subset I\!N$ denotes the (possibly infinite) set of all potential players, and $\mathcal{N}$ the class of all finite subsets of I. For $N \in \mathcal{N}$, $\mathcal{C}_*^N$ is the subclass of $\mathcal{C}_0^N$ consisting of all games S with $S = \text{com}(S \cap I\!R_+^N)$, and $\mathcal{C}^*$ is the union of all $\mathcal{C}_*^N$. The RKS solution on $\mathcal{C}^*$ is denoted by ρ. The solution ρ satisfies population anonymity (PAN, see section 7.2), weak Pareto optimality (WPO), scale transformation covariance (STC), and strong individual rationality (SIR). It is easy to see that ρ does not satisfy Lensberg's multilateral stability axiom. We will introduce another "reduced game property" that is satisfied by the RKS solution.

Let L, M be nonempty elements of $\mathcal{N}$, and let $S \in \mathcal{C}_*^M$. Then $S_L = \{y \in I\!R^L: \text{there is an } x \in S \text{ with } y = x_L\} \in \mathcal{C}_*^L$. Let $x \in S$, $x \geq 0$ with $x_L \neq 0$. Let

$$\lambda(S_L, x_L) := \min\{\lambda \in I\!R_+ : x_L \in \lambda S_L\}.$$

The *reduced game of S with respect to L and x* is the following bargaining game for L:

$$S_L^x := \lambda(S_L, x_L) S_L.$$

Because $x_L \neq 0$, $\lambda(S_L, x_L) > 0$ and therefore $S_L^x \in \mathcal{C}_*^L$. Note that x_L is an element of the weakly Pareto optimal subset of S_L^x. The reduced game S_L^x is a multiple of the game the players in L would be able to play if the players in M outside L could be sent off with nothing. This multiple is chosen in such a way that the players outside L may still obtain their payoffs according to the original outcome x, while leaving a weakly Pareto optimal outcome x_L for the players in the reduced game. The following axiom requires a solution φ on $\mathcal{C}_*$ to pick this point x_L in the reduced game if x is chosen in the original game. Thus:

Reduced Game Property (RGP): For all nonempty subsets $L, M \in \mathcal{N}$ and all $S \in \mathcal{C}_*^M$, if $L \subset M$, $\varphi(S) \geq 0$ and $\varphi(S)_L \neq 0$, then $\varphi(S_L^{\varphi(S)}) = \varphi(S)_L$.

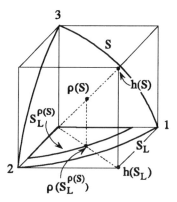

Figure 9.4: ρ has the reduced game property.

Although there are many definitions of reduced games and corresponding reduced game properties in the cooperative game theory literature (see Driessen, 1991, for a survey), RGP is the only axiom with that name in this book, so there is no confusion. For a game $S \in \mathcal{C}_*^M$, the projections S_L $(L \subset M)$ can be viewed as determining the interpersonal strength of the players in the coalition L, via the solution outcomes $\varphi(S_L)$. With scale transformation covariance as a natural condition in the background, RGP requires the solution outcome to be consistent with the coalitional outcomes $\varphi(S_L)$. If multilateral stability is interpreted as a "renegotiation proofness" condition: after an outcome has been reached no coalition has an incentive to renegotiate internally, then RGP can be seen as a "prenegotiation consistency condition": first each coalition prenegotiates, and then the outcome for the grand coalition should be proportional to the coalitional outcomes. The latter implies that interpersonal strengths as established in smaller coalitions are maintained through the grand coalition.

The RKS solution ρ has the reduced game property. This is a direct consequence of the fact that the utopia point of a game S_L is the projection of the utopia point of S. See figure 9.4 for an illustration with $M = \{1, 2, 3\}$, $L = \{1, 2\}$. Moreover, if the population contains at least three players, the solution can be characterized as follows.

Theorem 9.2 *Suppose $|I| \geq 3$. A solution φ on C^* satisfies WPO, PAN, STC, and RGP, if and only if φ is the RKS solution ρ.*

Proof We have already remarked that ρ satisfies the four axioms. Let now φ be a solution satisfying the four axioms. We first prove that if $|M| = 2$ and $S \in C_*^M$ then $\varphi(S) = \rho(S)$.

Let $M = \{i, j\}$ and $S \in C_*^M$ (cf. figure 9.5). By STC, we may assume $h_i(S) = h_j(S) = 1$. Let $k \in I\backslash M$ and

$$T := \text{comv}(O^{\{i,j,k\}}(S) \cup \{e^k\})$$

where $e^k \in \mathbb{R}^{\{i,j,k\}}$. By WPO and AN we have:

$$\varphi_i(T_{\{i,k\}}) = \varphi_k(T_{\{i,k\}}) = \varphi_j(T_{\{j,k\}}) = \varphi_k(T_{\{j,k\}}) = \tfrac{1}{2}.$$

By RGP and STC it follows that $\varphi_i(T) = \varphi_j(T)$, and applying RGP and STC again, we obtain $\varphi(S) = \rho(S)$.

If $|M| = 1$ and $S \in C_*^M$, then $\varphi(S) = \rho(S)$ by WPO of φ.

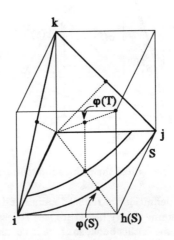

Figure 9.5: Proof of theorem 9.2

Suppose now $|M| > 2$ and $S \in C_*^M$ with (without loss of generality by STC) $h_i(S) = 1$ for every $i \in M$. Let $i, j \in M$ then $\varphi_i(S_{\{i,j\}}) = \varphi_j(S_{\{i,j\}})$ by the above and STC. Hence by RGP: $\varphi_i(S) = \varphi_j(S)$. Since this holds for all $i, j \in M$, we conclude by WPO: $\varphi(S) = \rho(S)$.   □

Theorem 9.2 does not hold if there are only two players in the player population I. In that case, any weakly Pareto optimal bargaining solution satisfies RGP, as well as MSTAB. RGP and STC together with strong individual rationality (SIR) imply weak Pareto optimality, as the following lemma shows.

Lemma 9.3 *Let φ be a solution on C_* satisfying RGP, SIR, and STC. Let $M \in \mathcal{N}$, $M \neq I$, and let $S \in C_*^M$. Then $\varphi(S) \in W(S)$.*

Proof Take $k \in I \backslash M$ and let $T \in C_*^{M \cup \{k\}}$ be the comprehensive convex hull of $O^{M \cup \{k\}}(S)$ and $e^k \in I\!\!R^{M \cup \{k\}}$. By SIR, $\varphi(T)_M \neq 0$. By RGP, $\varphi(\lambda(S, \varphi(T)_M)S) = \varphi(T)_M \in W(\lambda(S, \varphi(T)_M)S)$. So by STC, $\varphi(S) \in W(S)$. $\square$

An immediate consequence of lemma 9.3 and theorem 9.2 is the following corollary.

Corollary 9.4 *Let I be infinite. A solution on C_* satisfies PAN, STC, RGP, and SIR, if and only if it is the RKS solution.*

The infiniteness of I in corollary 9.4 is essential. Consider, for example the solution φ defined for $I = \{1, 2, 3\}$ by $\varphi(S) := \rho(S)$ if $S \in C_*^M$ and $|M| < 3$, and $\varphi(S) := \frac{1}{2}\rho(S)$ if $S \in C_*^{\{1,2,3\}}$. This solution satisfies all the axioms in the corollary.

It can easily be verified that for scale transformation covariant solutions RGP implies the population monotonicity axiom (PMON, see section 7.3). The converse is not true. We construct an example as follows. Let M be a nonempty finite subset of I, and let $n \in I$. Define a function $f : [0, 1] \to I\!\!R^M$ by $f_i(t) := t$ if $i \in M$, $i \neq n$ and $f_n(t) := t^2$, for all $t \in [0, 1]$. For $S \in C_*^M$ with $h_i(S) = 1$ for all $i \in M$, let $\varphi(S)$ be the unique point of $W(S)$ on the graph of f; φ is then defined on all of C_*^M be requiring it to be scale transformation covariant. We leave it for the reader to verify that this solution satisfies PMON but not RGP. Thus, under scale transformation covariance PMON is weaker than RGP. This is also suggested by the fact that in theorem 7.4, where the RKS solution is characterized with the aid of PMON, the infiniteness of I is essential.

A noncooperative model implementing the RKS solution

Next, corresponding to a bargaining game a noncooperative game in extensive form is introduced, the (unique) subgame perfect equilibrium outcome of which is the outcome predicted by the RKS solution. The subgames in this extensive form game correspond to the reduced games defined above, and the RGP axiom corresponds to the dynamic programming principle used to determine the subgame perfect equilibrium outcome.

Let M be a nonempty finite subset of the player population I, and let $S \in C_*^M$ be a bargaining game for M with $W(S) \cap I\!\!R_+^M = P(S)$ and with utopia point coordinates equal to 1 for all players. The latter assumption, which holds for the rest of this section, is inessential but makes the presentation easier. The former assumption is not harmless; see the final paragraph of this section. Without loss of generality let $M = \{1, 2, \ldots, m\}$. The following multistage game will lead to an outcome of S. A play of this game is described by sequences

$$M^0 := M, M^1, M^2, \ldots$$
$$S^0 := S, S^1, S^2, \ldots$$

as follows. Before stage k, M^k and S^k have been determined. Then stage k is played as follows:
(i) Each player $i \in M^k$ independently submits a *bid* p_i, $0 \leq p_i \leq 1$.
(ii) The player with the highest bid submits a *proposal* $x \in S^k$. In case there are two or

more players with the highest bid, the player with the lowest number submits the proposal.
(iii) Assume that player i has submitted the proposal $x \in S^k$ in (ii). Then each player
$j \in M^k\backslash\{i\}$ independently either accepts or rejects x. If all players accept, the game is
over.
(iv) Otherwise, let $M^{k+1} := M^k\backslash\{i\}$ and $S^{k+1} := \lambda(p_i)S^k_{M^{k+1}}$, where

$$\lambda(p_i) := \begin{cases} 1 & \text{if } (p_i\ldots,p_i) \notin S^k_{M^{k+1}} \\ \min\{\lambda : (p_i,\ldots,p_i) \in \lambda S^k_{M^{k+1}}\} & \text{otherwise.} \end{cases}$$

If $|M^{k+1}| > 1$ and $P(S^{k+1}) \neq \{0\}$, proceed to stage $k+1$. Otherwise, the game is over.
If the game stops with proposal $x \in S^\ell$ at stage ℓ being accepted, then the final outcome
is $\overline{x}$ where $\overline{x}_{M^\ell} := x$ and $\overline{x}_{M^k} \in W(S^k)$ for all $0 \le k < \ell$. So $\overline{x}$ is determined backwards by
each time adding the last player whose proposal was rejected. If the game stops because
$|M^\ell| = 1$, let $x := \max S^\ell$ and $\overline{x}$ as before. If the game stops because $P(S^\ell) = \{0\}$, let
$x := 0 \in S^\ell$ and $\overline{x}$ as before.

Thus, in this extensive form game, the players start by submitting bids, and the player
with the highest bid (say p_i) is entitled to submit a proposal. The game ends with this
proposal if it is unanimously accepted by the other players. If not, the remaining players
proceed by playing a multiple smaller than or equal to 1 of the projection of the original
game. If smaller than 1, this multiple is determined by the requirement that each of the
remaining players receiving p_i should be a Pareto optimal outcome. If this is not possible,
they just play the projection $S_{M\backslash\{i\}}$. In this last case, player i, who submitted the highest
bid, will end up with zero utility; otherwise, there will be something left for him. So, if a
player submits the highest bid, he has the advantage of being entitled to make a proposal,
but at the same time offers this bid to each of the remaining players as a Pareto optimal
outcome in their remaining game in case they refuse his proposal. Thus, alternatively, a
bid could be described as a vector — always a multiple of the utopia point — which is
offered by the highest bidder as a possible outcome for the remaining players if they refuse
his proposal. Consequently, this bid will put a constraint on the proposals acceptable for
the remaining players.

Observe that the rules of the game imply that a single player takes all he can get.
Allowing other possibilities, for instance the threat of complete disagreement if a single
player does not accept his own proposal, naturally would not upset the main result below,
which is concerned with subgame perfect equilibrium.

A *strategy* for a player is a complete description of the actions that player is going to
choose at any stage of the game given any history. We sat that a player $i \in L \subset M$ *plays*
Raiffa-Kalai-Smorodinsky (RKS) at a certain stage of the game, where the set of outcomes
is T, the player set is L, and $\rho(T) = (p,\ldots,p)$, if i bids p, proposes $\rho(T)$, and accepts a
proposal x if and only if $x_i \ge p$. Further, i *plays the RKS-strategy* if he plays RKS at any
stage of the game. The following observation is elementary but plays a central role in what
follows. Its proof is straightforward and left to the reader.

Lemma 9.5 *In a 2-player bargaining game S a player obtains a payoff of at least p, where*
$\rho(S) =: (p,p)$, *by playing the RKS-strategy.*

A *Nash equilibrium* (Nash (1951)) for the player set M in a bargaining game S is a combination of strategies such that each player's strategy maximizes that player's payoff, given the strategies of the other players. As is usual in games like this one, the Nash equilibrium concept is too weak to determine a unique outcome. Consider the following example.

Example 9.6 Let $M := \{1,2,3\}$ and $S := \text{com}\{x \in I\!R_+^M : x_1^2 + x_2^2 \le (1 - x_3)^2\}$. Then $S \in \mathcal{C}_*^M$ and $P(S) = (p,p,p)$ where $p := \sqrt{2} - 1$. Let $q := \frac{1}{3}$ and $z := (\frac{1}{3}, \frac{4}{9}, \frac{4}{9}) \in P(S)$. Note that $z_1 = q < p < z_2 = z_3$. Consider the following strategies. At stage 0, player 1 bids p, and players 2 and 3 bid q. Every player proposes z, and player $i \in M$ accepts a proposal x if and only if $x_i \ge z_i$. At stage 1 (where two players are left) player 1 always plays RKS. Player 2 plays RKS against 1, and also against 3 if player 3 deviated from his strategy at stage 0. If player 3 did not deviate from his strategy at stage 0, then, against player 3, player 2 bids 1, and proposes $(0, \alpha) \in W(S^1)$. Player 3, finally, plays RKS against player 1 and against a player 2 who deviated at stage 0. Otherwise, against player 2, player 3 bids 0 and accepts only $(0, \alpha) \in W(S^1)$.

We leave it for the reader to verify that the described strategies form a Nash equilibrium, but that this Nash equilibrium is not subgame perfect; that is, it does not induce a Nash equilibrium in every possible subgame. In the present model a subgame starts either if bids have to be made, or if some player has to make a proposal, or if the players have to accept or reject a proposal.

The equilibrium in example 9.6 is also not *stationary*: the actions of players 2 and 3 against each other at stage 1 depend on the way the subgame at stage 1 is reached. So the equilibrium would neither survive the stationarity nor the subgame perfectness criterion. In what follows, the latter is imposed because it seems to be more compelling.

Theorem 9.7 *Let S be a bargaining game for the player set M, and suppose S is played noncooperatively according to the procedure described above. Then there is a unique subgame perfect equilibrium outcome, namely the Raiffa-Kalai-Smorodinsky solution outcome $\rho(S)$.*

Proof The proof is based on induction with respect to the number of players. If $|M| = 1$, then the statement follows by definition of the bargaining procedure, and if $|M| = 2$, lemma 9.5 implies that the RKS solution outcome is (even) the unique Nash equilibrium outcome. Now suppose the statement in the theorem has been proved for all bargaining games with less than $m \ge 3$ players, and let $|M| = m$, $k \in M$, $\rho(S) = (p,p,\ldots,p)$. Let the strategy combination $(s_j)_{j \in M}$ be a subgame perfect Nash equilibrium. Suppose player k plays RKS instead at stage 0. If the game is over at stage 0, then player k obtains at least p, the RKS solution payoff. If not, there is a player $i \in M$ such that players in $M \backslash \{i\}$ play $\lambda S_{M \backslash \{i\}} \ni (p, \ldots, p)$. By induction, the strategy combination $(s_j)_{j \in M \backslash \{i\}}$ leads to the outcome $\rho(\lambda S_{M \backslash \{i\}}) \ge (p, \ldots, p)$, where we have equality if $i = k$. So again player k obtains at least p. Since k was arbitrary, the uniqueness part of the theorem follows. As to existence, each player playing the RKS-strategy is a subgame perfect Nash equilibrium. $\square$

As mentioned in this proof the obvious proposal to submit at stage 0 is the RKS solution outcome. However, this is not critical. If one or more players get offered less, the proposal will be rejected, but the remaining subgame leads to the same original RKS solution outcome. This is due to the principle of backward induction or, equivalently, dynamic programming used to calculate the subgame perfect equilibrium outcome. Note that this remaining subgame corresponds to the reduced game $S_{M\setminus\{i\}}^{\rho(S)}$ (if i is the player entitled to submit the proposal), and that the induction hypothesis based on backward induction corresponds to the RGP requirement in the axiomatic approach above.

The extensive form game described above has much in common with the procedure proposed by Moulin (1984). In the Moulin game, after a proposal has been made, each player at his turn has to accept or reject this proposal made by the highest bidder. As soon as a player rejects, the following lottery is performed: with probability p_i (the highest bid) the rejecting player receives his utopia payoff (implying zero for all the other players), and with probability $1 - p_i$ the game ends in disagreement, implying zero payoffs for all players. As Moulin shows, also in this game the subgame perfect equilibrium payoffs are given by the RKS solution. The relevant subgames correspond to two-person reduced games. In this respect, it is interesting to remark that the proof of theorem 9.2 also relies on two-person reduced games.

We conclude with the remark that for theorem 9.7 to hold the condition $W(S) \cap \mathbb{R}_+^M = P(S)$ cannot be dropped. The notion of Nash equilibrium entails individual optimization and therefore, in a model like the one under consideration, does not lead to the implementation of a bargaining solution which is only weakly Pareto optimal, like the RKS solution.

9.7   Noncooperative comparison of solutions

In the Harsanyi-Zeuthen procedure discussed in section 9.2, the players in a 2-person bargaining game make proposals, and if these are incompatible, the maximum risk criterion (see (9.1)) is used to determine which player has to make some minimal concession. This criterion implies that the proposals of a player should exhibit a certain coherence; in the Harsanyi-Zeuthen model, the Nash product should be increased by some minimal amount.

The Harsanyi-Zeuthen procedure is approached in a systematic way in van Damme (1986). In van Damme's model, the players in a 2-person bargaining game start by making simultaneous proposals. If these proposals are incompatible, they each make a new proposal, which should be a concession when compared to the old proposal, but in a weak sense: each player may repeat his previous proposal. This idea of weak concessions is interpreted as being equivalent to deleting those feasible outcomes that exceed the players' previous demands. A sequence of proposals made by a player thus implicitly defines a bargaining solution on a corresponding sequence of bargaining games with decreasing feasible sets; van Damme's key idea is that a player's proposals should be coherent in the sense that they should be attainable as outcomes prescribed by some *admissible* bargaining solution for 2-player games. The exact definition of admissibility may depend, for instance, on what the players regard as minimal properties a bargaining solution should have. Within the admissible class considered in van Damme (1986), it turns out that the Nash bargaining solution fares best.

In order to make this precise, consider the class $\mathcal{C}_*$ of 2-person bargaining games S in $\mathcal{C}_0$ with $S = \text{com}(S \cap \mathbb{R}_+^2)$. The restriction to $\mathcal{C}_*$ is merely for convenience. Let F denote the family of all bargaining solutions on $\mathcal{C}_*$ which are Pareto optimal (PO), anonymous (AN), and risk sensitive (RS). For the appropriate definition of risk sensitivity, see section

6.6, in particular lemma 6.20. Risk sensitivity can be interpreted as reflecting the intuition that a player should profit from a change in the feasible set which seems to be favorable for that player. This interpretation is justified, for instance, by theorem 6.26. F is the class of admissible solutions as announced above, but variations are possible and will be indicated later in this section.

By theorem 6.10 and remark 6.11, solutions in F are scale transformation covariant. Well-known members of F are the Nash, Raiffa-Kalai-Smorodinsky, and Perles-Maschler (cf. section 5.2) solutions.

Let $S \in C_*$, and let φ^1, φ^2 be bargaining solutions on C_*, not necessarily in F. Assume, however, that φ^1 and φ^2 are strongly individually rational — it is not hard to prove that all members of F have this property. For $t \in I\!N$, define $S^t(\varphi^1, \varphi^2)$ by

$$S^1(\varphi^1, \varphi^2) := S$$
$$S^{t+1}(\varphi^1, \varphi^2) := \{x \in S^t(\varphi^1, \varphi^2) : x_1 \leq \varphi_1^1(S^t(\varphi^1, \varphi^2)), \ x_2 \leq \varphi_2^2(S^t(\varphi^1, \varphi^2))\}.$$
$$(9.9)$$

Note that $S^t(\varphi^1, \varphi^2) \in C_*$ for all $t \in I\!N$. This bargaining procedure requires that if the proposals of the players at stage t are incompatible, viz. $(\varphi_1^1(S^t(\varphi^1, \varphi^2)), \varphi_2^2(S^t(\varphi^1, \varphi^2))) \notin S^t(\varphi^1, \varphi^2)$, then the players continue bargaining over the set of feasible outcomes not exceeding their previous demands. The idea is that a player i, by proposing x, gives up every feasible outcome y with $y_i > x_i$. Actually, procedure (9.9) not only reflects the idea that such an outcome should not be the final solution of the game, but, on top of that, that such an outcome should not *influence* the final solution outcome. The distinction between these two ideas is similar in nature to the distinction between the axioms of individual rationality (IR) and independency of non-individually rational outcomes (INIR); see subsection 2.5.2 and section 5.3.

We define

$$U(\varphi^1, \varphi^2; S) := \begin{cases} \lim\limits_{t \to \infty} \varphi^1(S^t(\varphi_1, \varphi_2)) \text{ if } \lim\limits_{t \to \infty} \varphi^1(S^t(\varphi_1, \varphi_2)) = \lim\limits_{t \to \infty} \varphi^2(S^t(\varphi^1, \varphi^2)) \\ 0 \text{ otherwise.} \end{cases}$$

By definition, $U(\varphi^1, \varphi^2; S)$ is the payoff vector from applying procedure (9.9). Based on procedure (9.9), we define for each bargaining game $S \in C_*$ a noncooperative game $\Gamma(S)$ where both players have F as strategy set, and where the payoffs are given by $U(., .; S)$. In this game, players 1 and 2 choose independently and simultaneously a bargaining solution from F, say φ^1 and φ^2, and then the payoffs are $U_1(\varphi^1, \varphi^2; S)$ and $U_2(\varphi^1, \varphi^2; S)$. A *Nash equilibrium* is a pair $(\overline{\varphi}^1, \overline{\varphi}^2) \in F \times F$ where, as usual,

$$U_1(\overline{\varphi}^1, \overline{\varphi}^2; S) \geq U_1(\varphi^1, \overline{\varphi}^2; S) \text{ for all } \varphi^1 \in F,$$
$$U_2(\overline{\varphi}^1, \overline{\varphi}^2; S) \geq U_2(\overline{\varphi}^1, \varphi^2; S) \text{ for all } \varphi^2 \in F.$$

It will be shown that (ν, ν) is a Nash equilibrium for every game $\Gamma(S)$ $(S \in C_*)$, where ν is the symmetric Nash solution. Furthermore, every equilibrium of $\Gamma(S)$ results in the outcome $\nu(S)$, and (ν, ν) is the only pair in $F \times F$ that is an equilibrium in every game $\Gamma(S)$. The key result needed to prove these statements is the following lemma.

Lemma 9.8 *Let* $S \in C_*$ *and* $\varphi^1, \varphi^2 \in F$ *with* $\varphi_1^1(S) > \varphi_1^2(S)$. *Let* $T \in C_*$ *be defined by* $T := \{x \in S : x_1 \leq \varphi_1^1(S), x_2 \leq \varphi_2^2(S)\}$. *Assume further that* $\nu_1(S) > \varphi_1^2(S)$. *Then* $\varphi_1^2(T) \geq \frac{1}{2} \min\{\nu_1(S), \varphi_1^1(S)\} + \frac{1}{2}\varphi_1^2(S)$.

An apparent criticism on procedure (9.9) could be that it seems to be tailor made for the Nash bargaining solution. Yet, it is quite surprising that in this procedure a player who demands more than what the Nash bargaining solution would assign to him, at the next stage has to yield by a relatively large positive amount; for this is what lemma 9.8 entails.

Proof of lemma 9.8 Write $\varphi^2(S) = (\alpha, \beta)$ and $\varphi^1(S) = (\gamma, \delta)$. Then $\gamma > \alpha$, $\beta > \delta$. By STC, we may assume $\beta = \gamma = 1$. We consider two cases.

Case (i) $\varphi^1_1(S) \leq \nu_1(S)$. From the definition of the Nash solution (or from applying IIE, cf. subsection 2.4.2) it follows that $\nu(T) = \varphi^1(S)$. Consequently, $\gamma\delta > \alpha\beta$, so $\alpha < \delta$, and there is a supporting line of T at $(1, \delta)$ with slope $-\delta$ (cf. lemma 2.2).

Let $R := \mathrm{comv}\{(1, \alpha), (\alpha, 1)\} \in \mathcal{C}_*$, then $R \subset T$. Consider the function $k^2 : [\alpha, 1] \to [\delta, 1]$ defined by $\xi \mapsto f^S(1 + \alpha - \xi)$. Thus function maps the second coordinates of points in $P(R)$ onto the second coordinates of points in $P(T)$, according to the arrows in figure 9.6. The function k^2 is the composition of an affine and a concave function and therefore concave. Also, k^2 is nondecreasing. Extend the function k^2 to $[0, 1]$ by $\xi \mapsto (\delta/\alpha)\xi$ for $\xi \in [0, \alpha]$.

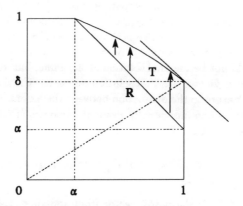

Figure 9.6: Proof of lemma 9.8

Then k^2 is nondecreasing on $[0, 1]$, and also concave on $[0, 1]$ because on $[0, \alpha]$ it is linear with slope δ/α, and at α there is a line supporting the graph of k^2 with slope δ, $\delta < \delta/\alpha$. Thus, $k^2 \in C^2(R)$ (see section 6.6 for notations), and by RS, AN, and PO

$$\varphi^2_1(T) = \varphi^2_1(k^2(R)) \geq \varphi^2_1(R) = \tfrac{1}{2}(\alpha + 1) = \tfrac{1}{2}(\varphi^2_1(S) + \varphi^1_1(S))$$

which completes the proof for case (i).

Case (ii) $\varphi^1_1(S) > \nu_1(S)$. Let $T^* := \{x \in S : x_1 \leq \nu_1(S), \ x_2 \leq \varphi^2_2(S)\}$. Then $T^* = k^1(T)$ where $k^1 \in C^1(T)$ is defined by $k^1(\xi) := \xi$ for $\xi \in [0, \nu_1(S)]$, $k^1(\xi) := \nu_1(S)$ for $\xi \geq \nu_1(S)$. By RS, $\varphi^2_2(T^*) = \varphi^2_2(k^1(T)) \geq \varphi^2_2(T)$, so by PO $\varphi^2_1(T^*) \leq \varphi^2_1(T)$. The proof is completed by combining this inequality with the inequality $\varphi^2_1(T^*) \geq \tfrac{1}{2}\nu_1(S) + \tfrac{1}{2}\varphi^2_1(S)$ following from the proof of case (i).   □

The following lemma is a consequence of lemma 9.8. It shows that the bargaining procedure underlying the game $\Gamma(S)$ will eventually lead the players to an agreement whatever solutions from F they choose.

Lemma 9.9 *For any $S \in C_*$ and $\varphi^1, \varphi^2 \in F$,*

$$\lim_{t \to \infty} \varphi^1(S^t(\varphi_1, \varphi_2)) = \lim_{t \to \infty} \varphi^2(S^t(\varphi_1, \varphi_2)).$$

Proof In view of PO it suffices to consider the case in which $\varphi_1^1(S^t(\varphi_1, \varphi_2)) > \varphi_1^2(S^t(\varphi_1, \varphi_2))$ for all $t \in I\!N$. If for all $t \in I\!N$

$$\varphi_1^1(S^t(\varphi^1, \varphi^2)) \geq \nu_1(S) \geq \varphi_1^2(S^t(\varphi^1, \varphi^2))$$

then by lemma 9.8 for all $t \in I\!N$ and $i \neq j \in \{1, 2\}$

$$\nu_i(S) \geq \varphi_i^j(S^{t+1}(\varphi^1, \varphi^2)) \geq (1 - (\tfrac{1}{2})^t)\nu_i(S),$$

so that both limits in the lemma are equal to $\nu(S)$. A similar argument can be used for the case in which a player sometimes asks for less than his Nash payoff.   □

Let $S \in C_*$. Since the Nash bargaining solution satisfies IIA, it follows immediately from lemma 9.9 that $U_1(\nu, \varphi^2; S) = \nu_1(S)$ and $U_2(\varphi^1, \nu; S) = \nu_2(S)$ for all $\varphi^1, \varphi^2 \in F$. From this observation the following theorem is immediate.

Theorem 9.10 *For every $S \in C_*$,*

(i) (ν, ν) is a Nash equilibrium of $\Gamma(S)$,

(ii) if $(\varphi^1, \varphi^2) \in F \times F$ is a Nash equilibrium of $\Gamma(S)$, then

$$U(\varphi^1, \varphi^2; S) = \nu(S).$$

Because of (ii) $\nu(S)$ can be called the *value* of the game $\Gamma(S)$, and ν is a *maximin strategy*, i.e., choosing ν guarantees the value of the game no matter which bargaining solution the other player proposes. Obviously, every maximin strategy of $\Gamma(S)$ is an equilibrium strategy; the converse, however, is an open question. Also the question of interchangeability of equilibrium strategies, as holds in zerosum games, is still open. Summarizing, we have the following corollary.

Corollary 9.11 *For every $S \in C_*$,*

(i) every maximin strategy of $\Gamma(S)$ is an equilibrium strategy,

(ii) ν is a maximin strategy in $\Gamma(S)$.

Although in some games there may exist other equilibria than (ν, ν), e.g., if the Nash bargaining solution outcome is an endpoint of the Pareto optimal set, (ν, ν) is the only one that is always available, as the following corollary shows.

Corollary 9.12 *Only (ν, ν) is a Nash equilibrium in $\Gamma(S)$ for every $S \in C_*$.*

Proof Assume that $(\varphi^1, \varphi^2) \in F \times F$ is a Nash equilibrium of $\Gamma(S)$ for every $S \in C_*$. Obviously $\varphi_1^1(S) \geq \varphi_1^2(S)$ for every $S \in C_*$, because otherwise player 1 could improve by proposing φ^2 in some game. On the other hand, if the inequality would be strict for some $T \in C_*$ then $\varphi_1^1(\pi T) < \varphi_1^2(\pi T)$ by AN, where $\pi(1) = 2$, $\pi(2) = 1$. Hence, $\varphi^1(S) = \varphi^2(S)$ for all S by PO, and therefore $\varphi^1 = \varphi^2 = \nu$ by theorem 9.10. $\square$

The key lemma, lemma 9.8, suggests that the Nash bargaining solution can be characterized by a weaker set of axioms; in particular, independence of irrelevant alternatives is not needed in its full strength. More precisely, IIA can be replaced by a recursivity principle which amounts to independence of alternatives that cannot be obtained as outcomes of solutions in F. Formally, for $S \in C_*$, let

$$S_F := \text{com}\{z \in S : z = \varphi(S) \text{ for some } \varphi \in F\}.$$

In lemma 9.14 below it is shown that $S_F \in C_*$. The recursivity principle for a solution φ on C_* announced above is defined as follows.

Recursivity (REC): $\varphi(S) = \varphi(S_F)$ for every $S \in C_*$.

The Nash solution ν is recursive because it satisfies IIA. On the other hand, if $\varphi \in F$ satisfies REC, then $\varphi(S^t) = \varphi(S)$ for all $t = 0, 1, 2, \ldots$ where $S^0 := S$ and $S^{t+1} := S_F^t$. From lemma 9.8 it follows that for $i = 1, 2$ and all $x \in P(S^t)$,

$$|x_i - \nu_i(S))| \leq (\tfrac{1}{2})^t \nu_i(S),$$

which shows that $\varphi = \nu$. We have proved the following theorem.

Theorem 9.13 *The Nash bargaining solution is the unique solution on C_* satisfying PO, AN, RS, and REC.*

It must still be proved that $S_F \in C_*$. This is an immediate consequence of the following lemma.

Lemma 9.14 *Let $S \in C_*$. Then the set $\{z \in S : z = \varphi(S) \text{ for some } \varphi \in F\}$ is closed and connected.*

Proof First, it is shown that the set is closed. Let $\{z^k\}_{k \in \mathbb{N}}$ be a sequence in this set with $z^k \to z$ as $k \to \infty$, and let $\varphi^k \in F$ with $\varphi^k(S) = z^k$ for all $k \in \mathbb{N}$. For $T \in C_*$ arbitrary, let $L(T)$ be the subset of $P(T)$ consisting of all limit points of $\{\varphi^k(T)\}_{k \in \mathbb{N}}$. For $i = 1, 2$ let $h_i(L(T)) := \max\{x_i \in L(T)\}$, so $h(L(T))$ is the utopia point of $L(T)$. Finally, let $\varphi(T)$ be the point of intersection of $P(T)$ and the straight line through 0 and $h(L(T))$, observing that this point exists. Then φ is a bargaining solution on C_*. Obviously, $L(S) = \{z\}$, so $\varphi(S) = z = \lim_{k \to \infty} \varphi^k(S)$. Therefore, to establish closedness, it suffices to show that $\varphi \in F$. Because PO and AN are easily seen to hold, we concentrate on RS.

Let $k^2 \in C^2(S)$ and write $T := k^2(S)$. Because every φ^k satisfies PO and RS, we have for all k

$$\varphi_1^k(S) \leq \varphi_1^k(T) \text{ and } k^2(\varphi_2^k(S)) \geq \varphi_2^k(T),$$

consequently

$$h_1(L(S)) \le h_1(L(T)) \text{ and } k^2(h_2(L(S))) \ge h_2(L(T)). \tag{9.10}$$

Write $s := \varphi_1(S)$, $t := \varphi_1(T)$. The inequalities in (9.10) imply

$$s \le \frac{h_1(L(T))}{h_2(L(T))} \frac{s}{h_1(L(S))} k^2(h_2(L(S))),$$

hence, by concavity of k^2 and $k^2(0) = 0$, $s \le h_1(L(S))$ implies

$$s \le \frac{h_1(L(T))}{h_2(L(T))} k^2 \left(\frac{h_2(L(S))}{h_1(L(S))} s \right) = \frac{h_1(L(T))}{h_2(L(T))} k^2(f^S(s)),$$

where the equality follows by definition of $\varphi(S)$. By definition of $\varphi(T)$, this implies

$$s \le \frac{k^2(k^S(s))}{k^2(f^S(t))} t$$

which is only possible if $s \le t$, i.e., $\varphi_1(S) \le \varphi_1(T)$. This shows that φ satisfies RS.

For the second property, connectedness, it is sufficient to prove (in view of closedness) that for $\varphi^1, \varphi^2 \in F$ with $\varphi^1(S) \ne \varphi^2(S)$, there is a $\varphi \in F$ with $\varphi(S)$ between $\varphi^1(S)$ and $\varphi^2(S)$. This can be shown by constructing a solution φ in the same way as above, now letting $L(S) := \{\varphi_1(S), \varphi^2(S)\}$. Then again $\varphi \in F$. □

Another consequence of lemma 9.14 is that the set F contains infinitely many elements.

We conclude this section with a few remarks concerning bargaining procedure (9.9) and the axioms. The proposed bargaining procedure implies a weak form of IIA, and a natural question is whether other procedures would lead to other bargaining solutions being optimal[2]. As to the axioms, van Damme (1986) shows that similar results can be obtained if risk sensitivity is replaced by the slice property (SL, see section 6.6) combined with scale transformation covariance. The other axioms (PO and AN) cannot be omitted without severely affecting the results. For some modifications, however, see van Damme (1986).

9.8 Arbitration games

Arbitration games were introduced by Nash (1953). See Tijs and Jansen (1982) for a general approach containing many earlier results as corollaries.

In this section we will give a brief informal account of arbitration games by way of the examples introduced in subsection 1.3.3. First consider the prisoner's dilemma, cf. figure 1.1, and the text that goes with it. Let the map f_S there be derived from the Nash bargaining solution ν. In this case, the *arbitration game* is the noncooperative game in which each player chooses a mixed strategy, say "T" with probability p for player 1 and "L" with probability q for player 2, and the corresponding payoffs are given by $\nu(S, d(p, q))$ where $d(p, q)$ is the pair of expected payoffs in the original bimatrix game; hence, $d(p, q) = (5q + 1 - p, 5p + 1 - q)$. Note that by choosing $p = 0$ player 1 can guarantee the outcome $\nu(S, d(p, q))$ to be in $P(S)$ with first coordinate at least the first coordinate of the point

---

[2]In an informal note, Chun has derived a similar result for the RKS solution.

$f_S(x)$ in figure 1.1. Similarly, by $q = 0$ player 2 secures himself of an amount of at least the second coordinate of the point $f_S(x)$. Therefore, these strategies are called the *optimal threat strategies*, and the point $f_S(x) = (5,5)$ is called the *value* of the arbitration game, in close analogy with zerosum games. In essence, by applying a bargaining solution, mapping threat outcomes to the Pareto optimal subset, the bimatrix game is effectively transformed into a zerosum-like, "strictly competitive" game. Applying the same line of reasoning to the battle of the sexes (cf. figure 1.2), we see that optimal threat strategies there are $p = 1$ and $q = 0$, and the value of the arbitration game is $(3/2, 3/2)$.

Obviously, the existence of optimal threat strategies and of a value depends on assumptions concerning the underlying noncooperative game and on the properties required of the bargaining solution that is being applied. With respect to the latter, it is interesting to note that the convexity axiom CONV (see subsection 2.5.2) plays a central role in the known existence results. See, in particular, Tijs and Jansen (1982).

Chapter 10

Solutions for coalitional bargaining games

10.1   Introduction

A natural extension of an n-person pure bargaining game is a *coalitional bargaining game*. In a coalitional bargaining game coalitions other than the grand coalition consisting of the whole player set N, or trivial coalitions consisting of single players, may form. Such a game is described by a characteristic function assigning to each coalition $M \subset N$ some subset of $\mathbb{R}^M$. We call these games coalitional bargaining games in order to keep in line with the main subject of this book; more often, however, they are called games without transferable utility or without sidepayments — the latter expression being more general, see Aumann (1967). There are many applications of these games to economic models, see Friedman (1986), Rosenmüller (1981), or the references in Aumann (1985b).

Three "solutions" for coalitional bargaining games will be considered in detail: the Shapley solution, known as the λ-transfer value or the NTU (nontransferable utility) value; the Harsanyi solution; and the Kalai-Samet proportional solution(s). These solutions extend the well-known Shapley value for transferable utility (TU) games to coalitional bargaining games. The Shapley and Harsanyi solutions coincide with the symmetric Nash bargaining solution for n-person pure bargaining games, whereas the Kalai-Samet proportional solutions reduce to the Kalai (1977b) proportional solutions — see section 4.5.

Almost any article on coalitional bargaining games gives a different definition of such games. Here, we will present the mentioned solution concepts in a framework that is unified as much as possible without imposing too much on generality — some of which is lost, however. Furthermore, our definition of a coalitional bargaining game admits the embedding of n-person pure bargaining games. For a comparison of the three mentioned solutions see also Hart (1985a), to which this chapter owes. Many additional details concerning these solutions and their axiomatizations can be found in the original articles. For the Shapley solution, see in particular Shapley (1969) and Aumann (1985a). The Harsanyi solution was proposed by Harsanyi (1959) and modified in Harsanyi (1963) after a comment by Isbell (1960); its axiomatization is by Hart (1985b). The Kalai-Samet proportional solutions were introduced and characterized by Kalai and Samet (1985).

This chapter is organized as follows. Section 10.2 contains definitions and some preliminary observations concerning the mentioned solutions. Sections 10.3 and 10.4 present axiomatic characterizations of the Shapley solution and of the Harsanyi solution, respectively;
these characterizations closely follow Aumann (1985a) and Hart (1985b). The Kalai-Samet
proportional solutions are treated in section 10.5; we give an axiomatization inspired by
Kalai and Samet (1985), but more closely related to the characterizations of the Shapley
and Harsanyi solutions. Section 10.6 concludes with a discussion of related literature.

10.2   Coalitional bargaining games and solutions

As usual, $N = \{1, 2, \ldots, n\}$ denotes the (fixed) set of players. A subset of N is called a
coalition, and 2^N denotes the set of all coalitions. Since all solution concepts to be discussed
extend the Shapley value for transferable utility games, we start with these.

Transferable utility games and the Shapley value

A *transferable utility* (TU) game is a pair (N, v) where $v : 2^N \to I\!R$ satisfies $v(\emptyset) = 0$. The
number $v(M)$ is called the *worth* of the coalition M.

The most prominent one-point solution concept for TU games is the *Shapley value*
(Shapley, 1953). This solution concept plays an important role in what follows. The Shapley
value assigns to each TU game v an allocation of the worth $v(N)$ of the grand coalition —
the implicit assumption therefore is that this coalition will form. In this allocation, each
player $i \in N$ receives

$$\text{Sh}_i(v) := \sum_{S : i \notin S} \frac{|S|!(n - |S| - 1)!}{n!} (v(S \cup \{i\}) - v(S))$$

which can be seen as player i's expected contribution if the grand coalition is formed by a
certain random process. The vector $\text{Sh}(v)$ is called the Shapley value of the TU game v,
and it can be checked that $\sum_{i \in N} \text{Sh}(v) = v(N)$. There exist many axiomatizations of the
Shapley value; here, we are particularly interested in a description with the aid of so-called
dividends (Harsanyi, 1963).

Let M be a coalition. The *unanimity game for* M is defined by

$$u_M(K) := \begin{cases} 1 & \text{if } M \subset K \\ 0 & \text{if } M \not\subset K \end{cases}$$

for every $K \in 2^N$. For TU games v and w, let $v + w$ and αv ($\alpha \in I\!R$) be defined by
$(v + w)(K) := v(K) + w(K)$ and $(\alpha v)(K) := \alpha(v(K))$ for every coalition K. With these
operations, the collection of all TU games is a $2^n - 1$ dimensional linear space with $\{u_M :
M \in 2^N \backslash \{\emptyset\}\}$ as a basis. To see this, check that this set is linearly independent, and that
the dimension of the linear space of TU games is $2^n - 1$ (for example, the collection of
all games assigning 1 to exactly one non-empty coalition and 0 to the other coalitions is a
basis).

Next, for a given TU game v define the real numbers ξ_M ($M \in 2^N$) recursively by

$$\xi_M := \begin{cases} 0 \text{ if } M = \emptyset \\ v(M) - \sum_{K \subset M, \, K \neq M} \xi_K \text{ otherwise.} \end{cases} \tag{10.1}$$

The number ξ_M is interpreted as the *dividend* added by the formation of the coalition M.[1] Obviously,

$$v(M) = \sum_{K \subset M} \xi_K \text{ for every } M \in 2^N. \tag{10.2}$$

Because $\{u_K : K \in 2^N \setminus \{\emptyset\}\}$ is a basis, we can uniquely write $v = \sum c_K u_K$ for $c_K \in \mathbb{R}$. With $c_\emptyset := 0$, this implies $v(M) = \sum_{K \subset M} c_K$ for every M. From (10.2) we deduce $c_K = \xi_K$ for every K, thus

$$v = \sum_{K \subset N} \xi_K u_K. \tag{10.3}$$

Now observe that the Shapley value is a linear functional on the space of all TU games. Therefore, (10.3) implies

$$\text{Sh}(v) = \sum_{K \subset N} \xi_K \text{Sh}(u_K). \tag{10.4}$$

From the definition of the Shapley value it is immediate that $\text{Sh}_i(u_K) = 0$ for all $K \neq \emptyset$ and $i \notin K$. Consequently, $\sum_{i \in K} \text{Sh}_i(u_K) = u_K(N) = 1$, and from considerations of symmetry, $\text{Sh}_i(u_K) = 1/|K|$ for every $i \in K$ and $K \neq \emptyset$. Combining this with (10.4), we have proved the following lemma.

Lemma 10.1 *For a TU game v, let the dividends ξ_M be defined as in (10.1). Then $\text{Sh}_i(v) = \sum_{K : i \in K} |K|^{-1} \xi_K$ for every $i \in N$.*

Thus, the Shapley value assigns to each player exactly the sum of the dividends of the coalitions to which that player belongs, divided by the cardinalities of these coalitions. Observe that this result only uses linearity of the Shapley value and the fact that $\text{Sh}(u_K) = e^K/|K|$ for every unanimity game u_K, where $e^K \in \mathbb{R}^N$ and $K \neq \emptyset$. Consequently, these two properties characterize the Shapley value. Next, we turn to the more general class of coalitional bargaining games.

Coalitional bargaining games

A *coalitional bargaining game* is a pair (N, V) where V is a map assigning to each coalition M a subset $V(M)$ of $\mathbb{R}^M$ (we define $\mathbb{R}^\emptyset := \emptyset$). With no confusion likely to arise, we write V instead of (N, V) and call V a *game*. We list the following possible conditions on V:

(G1) For every $M \in 2^N \setminus \{\emptyset\}$, $V(M)$ is nonempty, closed, comprehensive, convex, and $V(M)$ is bounded from above by a hyperplane with a positive normal.

(G2) $V(N)$ is *smooth*, i.e., at each boundary point there is a unique supporting hyperplane.

(G3) If $V(N)$ is bounded by a hyperplane with positive normal vector λ, then each $V(M)$ $(M \neq \emptyset)$ is bounded by a hyperplane with normal λ_M.

---

[1] Usually, the numbers ξ_M are divided by the cardinality of M, and the dividends interpreted as individual dividends. The definition given here is notationally more convenient.

The conditions in (G1) are more or less standard although, in particular, convexity is not needed to define the Kalai-Samet proportional solutions below; also, the axiomatization by Kalai and Samet does not need convexity of the feasible sets. Condition (G2) is important for the definition and axiomatization of both the Shapley and the Harsanyi solutions; it is discussed to some detail at the end of section 10.3. Condition (G3) could be viewed as a weak monotonicity requirement; it is only used in the axiomatization of the Shapley solution.[2] The class of all coalitional bargaining games for the player set N satisfying (G1) is denoted by $\tilde{\mathcal{G}}^N$. The subclass of $\tilde{\mathcal{G}}^N$ consisting of games satisfying also (G2) and (G3) is denoted by $\mathcal{G}^N$.

The obvious way to embed the class $\mathcal{C}^N$ of pure n-person bargaining games in $\tilde{\mathcal{G}}^N$ is to associate with each $(S, d) \in \mathcal{C}^N$ a game V^S by defining $V^S(N) := S$ and $V^S(M) := \text{com}\{d_M\}$ for every $M \in 2^N \backslash \{\emptyset\}$. If S happens to be smooth, then also $V^S \in \mathcal{G}^N$.

If $v = (N, v)$ is a TU game then the corresponding coalitional bargaining game V is given by

$$V(M) := \{x \in \mathbb{R}^M : \sum_{i \in M} x_i \leq v(M)\}$$

for every $M \in 2^N \backslash \{\emptyset\}$. In a coalitional bargaining game V, each coalition M can earn each point in $V(M)$ on its own. In a TU game v each coalition M can earn the worth $v(M)$ and split this amount among its members in any conceivable way; the corresponding coalitional bargaining game describes all such divisions. Let $\mathcal{G}^N_{TU}$ denote the subclass of all games corresponding to TU games.

A *payoff configuration* $x = (x^K) = (x^K)_{K \in 2^N \backslash \{\emptyset\}}$ is a collection of vectors x^K with $x^K \in \mathbb{R}^K$ for every $K \in 2^N \backslash \{\emptyset\}$. Let $\mathcal{G}' \subset \tilde{\mathcal{G}}^N$ be a class of coalitional bargaining games. A *payoff configuration solution* or *pc-solution* on $\mathcal{G}'$ is a map Φ on $\mathcal{G}'$ assigning to each $V \in \mathcal{G}'$ a (possibly empty) set of feasible payoff configurations; that is, if $x \in \Phi(V)$ then $x^K \in V(K)$ for every $K \subset N$. So a pc-solution describes a set of possible outcomes; each outcome consists not only of an allocation for the grand coalition N but also for all other coalitions. A *solution* on $\mathcal{G}'$ is a map Φ on $\mathcal{G}'$ assigning to each $V \in \mathcal{G}'$ a (possibly empty) set of feasible payoff vectors for the grand coalition, i.e., $\Phi(V) \subset V(N)$.

With $\lambda \in \mathbb{R}^N_{++}$ and V a game, we will associate two games in $\mathcal{G}^N_{TU}$ which play a central role in relation to the Shapley, Harsanyi, and Kalai-Samet solutions. First, suppose $v(K) := \max\{\lambda_K \cdot y : y \in V(K)\}$ exists for every $K \neq \emptyset$. Then v thus defined is a TU game; by V_λ we denote the corresponding game in $\mathcal{G}^N_{TU}$. Second, we recursively define the numbers ξ_K $(K \subset N)$ as follows: $\xi_\emptyset := 0$, and

$$\xi_K := |K| \max\{t \in \mathbb{R} : x^K(t) \in V(K)\}, \tag{10.5}$$

where $x^K_i(t)$ $(i \in K)$ is given by

$$x^K_i(t) = \lambda_i^{-1}(t + \sum_{L: i \in L \subset K, \ L \neq K} |L|^{-1}\xi_L), \tag{10.6}$$

and set

$$x^K := x^K(|K|^{-1}\xi_K).$$ (10.7)

Let V_λ^d ("d" from "dividend") denote the game corresponding to the TU game assigning $\lambda_K \cdot x^K$ to each non-empty coalition K.

As a final preliminary, for $V \in \mathcal{G}_{TU}^N$ let $\mathrm{Sh}(V)$ denote the Shapley value of the corresponding TU game.

The Harsanyi, Shapley, and Kalai-Samet solutions

The *Shapley solution* Λ is a solution defined on $\mathcal{G}^N$, as follows. For $V \in \mathcal{G}^N$, a vector $x \in V(N)$ is an element of $\Lambda(V)$ if and only if there is a $\lambda \in I\!\!R_{++}^N$ for which V_λ exists and $\lambda x = \mathrm{Sh}(V_\lambda)$.

The elements of $\Lambda(V)$ are also called (*Shapley*) *NTU values*, and were introduced by Shapley (1969). Aumann (1967) motivated NTU values as follows. If we assume that the players' utility functions are of the von Neumann-Morgenstern type (see section 11.2), then it should not really matter whether we apply some scale transformation $\lambda \in I\!\!R_{++}^N$. Suppose such a scale transformation has been applied. Next, for each coalition, maximize the sum of the players' utilities, and suppose that the Shapley value of the TU game thus obtained happens to be feasible. If the players believe in the Shapley value for TU games, why not believe in it now? Notice that his argument is particularly convincing if one believes in a version of independence of irrelevant alternatives; indeed, this is one of the characterization conditions in the next section.

We allow a solution to be empty-valued. In particular, $\Lambda(V) = \emptyset$ might occur for a game V. A general existence result can be obtained by imposing further restrictions on games, such as compactness of $V(N)$, and allowing weight vectors λ to have coordinates equal to 0. Such conditions enable the application of a fixed point theorem (e.g., Kakutani) to obtain nonemptiness of $\Lambda(V)$ for every V under consideration. See, for example, Shapley (1969) or Friedman (1986).

For each $\lambda \in I\!\!R_{++}^N$ the *Kalai-Samet proportional solution* E^λ is a pc-solution on $\tilde{\mathcal{G}}^N$ defined as follows: for each $V \in \tilde{\mathcal{G}}^N$, $E^\lambda(V)$ consists of the payoff configuration (x^K) defined by (10.5)–(10.7). Observe that $E^\lambda(V)$ always consists of a unique payoff configuration. Proportional solutions were introduced by Kalai and Samet (1985) as solutions, not as pc-solutions. We deviate from this because our characterization in section 10.5 involves axioms concerning the complete payoff configuration. If λ has all coordinates equal, then E^λ is called the *egalitarian solution* and denoted by E.

The final concept to be defined is the *Harsanyi solution* H, which is a pc-solution defined on $\mathcal{G}^N$. For $V \in \mathcal{G}^N$, a payoff configuration x is an element of $H(V)$ if and only if there is a $\lambda \in I\!\!R_{++}^N$ for which $x = E^\lambda(V)$ and $\lambda \cdot x^N = \max\{\lambda \cdot y : y \in V(N)\}$. The Harsanyi solution was proposed by Harsanyi (1959, 1963) in a different framework of noncooperative games. Also with respect to the Harsanyi solution, we do not bother about existence, viz., nonemptiness; similar remarks as for the Shapley solution are valid.

Let V be a game corresponding to a TU game. Then V_λ exists only for λ equal to a multiple of e^N, and then $V_\lambda = V$; consequently, $\Lambda(V) = \{\mathrm{Sh}(V)\}$. Similarly, by construction (10.5)–(10.7) and lemma 10.1, $H(V) = \{(\mathrm{Sh}(K, V_{e^N}^d)_{K \in 2^N \setminus \{\emptyset\}})\}$ where $(K, V_{e^N}^d)$ denotes the restriction of the game $(N, V_{e^N}^d)$ to subsets of K. Summarizing, we have the following lemma.

Lemma 10.2 *Let the game V correspond to a TU game. Then:*
(i) $H(V) = E(V) = \{(\mathrm{Sh}(K, V_{e^N}^d)_{K \in 2^N \setminus \{\emptyset\}})\}$
(ii) $\Lambda(V) = \{\mathrm{Sh}(V)\}$.

The payoff configurations in $E^\lambda(V)$ for arbitrary λ correspond to so-called weighted Shapley values, see Kalai and Samet (1985, 1987).

For coalitional bargaining games associated with pure bargaining games in C^N in the way described above, both the Harsanyi and the Shapley solutions coincide with the (symmetric, n-person) Nash bargaining solution; this can be seen by applying lemma 2.2. The proportional solutions coincide with the proportional solutions E^p, see section 4.5.[3]

10.3   The Shapley solution

This section is based on Aumann (1985a) and contains an axiomatization of the Shapley solution Λ on the class $\mathcal{G}^N$ (see section 10.2).

Let $\mathcal{G}'$ be some subclass of $\tilde{\mathcal{G}}^N$. For $V, W \in \mathcal{G}'$, define $V + W \in \tilde{\mathcal{G}}^N$ by $(V + W)(K) := V(K) + W(K)$ for every coalition K, and, for $\lambda \in \mathbb{R}_{++}^N$, define λV by $(\lambda V)(K) := \lambda_K V(K)$ for every K. Further, for every nonempty coalition K, let U_K denote the game corresponding to the (TU) unanimity game u_K. The axioms used in the announced characterization of the Shapley solution are as follows, stated for a solution Φ on $\mathcal{G}'$.

Strong Pareto Optimality (SPO): For every $V \in \mathcal{G}'$ and $x \in \Phi(V)$, $\{x\} = \{y \in W(V(N)) : y \leq x\}$.

Conditional Additivity (CA): For all $U, V, W \in \mathcal{G}'$ with $U = V + W$, for all $x \in \Phi(V)$ and $y \in \Phi(W)$, if $x + y \in P(U(N))$, then $x + y \in \Phi(U)$.

Unanimity (UN): For all $K \in 2^N \setminus \{\emptyset\}$, if $U_K \in \mathcal{G}'$, then $\{e^K / |K|\} = \Phi(U_K)$.

Scale Transformation Covariance (STC): For all $V \in \mathcal{G}'$, $\lambda \in \mathbb{R}_{++}^N$, if $x \in \Phi(V)$ and $\lambda V \in \mathcal{G}'$, then $\lambda x \in \Phi(\lambda V)$.

Weak Independence of Irrelevant Alternatives (WIIA): For all $V, W \in \mathcal{G}'$ and all $x \in \Phi(W)$, if $V(N) \subset W(N)$, $V(K) = W(K)$ for all $K \neq N$, and $x \in V(N)$, then $x \in \Phi(V)$.

Restricted Nonemptiness (RNE): If $V \in \mathcal{G}'$ and $V(N) = \{x \in \mathbb{R}^N : \sum_{i \in N} x_i \leq \alpha\}$ for some $\alpha \in \mathbb{R}$, then $\Phi(V) \neq \emptyset$.

Strong Pareto Optimality requires solution payoff vectors to be "interior" Pareto optimal points for the grand coalition. An alternative approach — as adopted in Aumann (1985a) — would be to require Pareto optimality and add a condition of "nonlevelness" (i.e., the non-occurrence of points that are weakly Pareto optimal but not Pareto optimal) to the definition of a game.

---

[3]More precisely, a Kalai-Samet proportional solution E^λ corresponds to a proportional bargaining solution E^p with $p_i = \lambda_i^{-1}$ for every $i \in N$.

Conditional Additivity is closely related to the restricted additivity axiom (RA) defined in section 5.5. Further comments are postponed until the end of this section.

Unanimity, Scale Transformation Covariance, and Restricted Nonemptiness, need no further comments. The adjective "weak" has been added in WIIA because, when applied to pure bargaining games, WIIA is strictly weaker than the IIA axiom for multisolutions defined in section 8.2 (see also section 8.4). The conclusion of WIIA can be formulated as "$\Phi(V) \supset \Phi(W) \cap V(N)$"; according to the IIA axiom for (pure bargaining) multisolutions, the inclusion sign would be an equality sign.

We first show that the Shapley solution on $\mathcal{G}^N$ satisfies these six axioms.

Proposition 10.3 *The Shapley solution Λ on $\mathcal{G}^N$ satisfies SPO, CA, UN, STC, WIIA, and RNE.*

Proof SPO follows, in particular, because by smoothness of $V(N)$ Pareto optimal points of $V(N)$ with supporting hyperplanes with positive normals must be "interior" Pareto optimal points. UN follows by lemma 10.2. STC and WIIA are straightforward, and CA can be proved in a way similar to the proof of restricted additivity of the Nash bargaining solution (see section 5.5, in particular lemma 5.12). RNE follows in view of condition (G3).   □

The proof of the converse of proposition 10.3 is based on a few lemmas.

Lemma 10.4 *Let Φ be a solution on $\mathcal{G}^N$ satisfying SPO, CA, RNE, STC, and UN. Let $V \in \mathcal{G}^N$ correspond to a TU game v. Then $\Phi(V) = \{Sh(V)\}$.*

Proof For any $\alpha \in \mathbb{R}$, let V^α correspond to the TU game αv. Let $x \in \Phi(V^0)$; such an x exists by RNE. Because $\Phi(V^0 + U_N) = \Phi(U_N)$, by SPO, CA, and UN, $x + e^N/n = e^N/n$. Therefore,

$$\Phi(V^0) = \{0e^N\}. \tag{10.8}$$

Next, let $y \in \Phi(V)$ and $z \in \Phi(V^{-1})$; such points exist by RNE. By SPO and CA, $y + z \in \Phi(V + V^{-1}) = \Phi(V^0)$. By (10.8) y and z are uniquely determined, say $y = \tilde{x}$ and $z = -\tilde{x}$. This, together with STC, implies for *all* $\alpha \in \mathbb{R}$:

$$\Phi(V^\alpha) = \{\alpha\tilde{x}\}. \tag{10.9}$$

In particular, (10.9) and UN imply $\Phi(U_K^\alpha) = \{\alpha e^K/|K|\}$ for all $K \in 2^N \setminus \{\emptyset\}$, thus (cf. section 10.2)

$$\Phi(U_K^\alpha) = \{ Sh(U_K^\alpha)\}. \tag{10.10}$$

Writing v as a linear combination $v = \sum \alpha_K u_K$ of unanimity games, we have $V = \sum U_K^{\alpha_K}$ for the corresponding coalitional bargaining games. Now SPO, CA, and (10.10) imply

$$\tilde{x} = \sum Sh(U_K^{\alpha_K}) = Sh(\sum U_K^{\alpha_K}) = Sh(V).$$

This completes the proof.   □

Lemma 10.5 *Let the solution Φ on $\mathcal{G}^N$ satisfy SPO, CA, UN, STC, and RNE. Then $\Phi(V) \subset \Lambda(V)$ for each $V \in \mathcal{G}^N$.*

Proof Let $V \in \mathcal{G}^N$ and $y \in \Phi(V)$. By SPO, $y \in P(V(N))$ and there is a unique supporting hyperplane of $V(N)$ at y with positive normal, say $\lambda \in I\!R_{++}^N$. By STC applied to both Φ and Λ it is without loss of generality to assume $\lambda = e^N$. Let V^0 correspond to the zero TU game as in the proof of lemma 10.4, then by condition (G3), $V + V^0 \in \mathcal{G}^N$. Moreover, $y \in P((V + V^0)(N))$ and $V + V^0 = V_{e^N}$. So by definition of Λ it is sufficient to show that $y = \text{Sh}(V_{e^N})$.

From lemma 10.4, $\Phi(V^0) = \{0e^N\}$. By CA, $y + 0e^N \in \Phi(V + V^0)$, hence $y \in \Phi(V_{e^N})$. The proof is complete by applying lemma 10.4. □

Lemma 10.5 states that the Shapley solution is the "maximal" solution satisfying the five axioms mentioned. By adding WIIA, the following result is obtained.

Lemma 10.6 *Let Φ be a solution on $\mathcal{G}^N$ satisfying SPO, CA, UN, STC, RNE, and WIIA. Then $\Lambda(V) \subset \Phi(V)$ for each $V \in \mathcal{G}^N$.*

Proof Let $V \in \mathcal{G}^N$ and $y \in \Lambda(V)$, and let $\lambda \in I\!R_{++}^N$ be a corresponding weight vector as in the definition of the Shapley solution; then $\lambda y = \text{Sh}(V_\lambda)$. Define the game W in $\mathcal{G}^N$ by

$$W(K) := \begin{cases} V_\lambda(N) & \text{if } K = N, \\ \lambda V(K) & \text{if } K \neq N. \end{cases}$$

Obviously, $\lambda y \in \Lambda(W)$.

Let V^0 correspond to the zero TU game, as before. Then $V_\lambda = W + V^0$. By RNE, $\Phi(W) \neq \emptyset$. For every $\tilde{x} \in \Phi(W)$, by SPO and CA $\tilde{x} + 0e^N \in \Phi(V_\lambda)$; so by lemma 10.4, $\tilde{x} = \text{Sh}(V_\lambda) = \lambda y$.

By definition, $W(N) = V_\lambda(N) \supset \lambda V(N)$, and $W(K) = (\lambda V)(K)$ for every $K \neq N$. Moreover, $\lambda y \in \lambda V(N)$. So by WIIA, $\tilde{x} \in \Phi(\lambda V)$ for every $\tilde{x} \in \Phi(W)$, hence, $\lambda y \in \Phi(\lambda V)$, and by STC, $y \in \Phi(V)$, which proves the lemma. □

The following corollary follows immediately from proposition 10.3, lemma 10.5 and lemma 10.6, and is the main result of this section.

Corollary 10.7 *The Shapley solution is the unique solution on $\mathcal{G}^N$ satisfying SPO, CA, UN, STC, RNE, and WIIA.*

In section 5.5, a class of bargaining solutions (viz., the solutions φ^H for $H \in \mathcal{H}^{\{1,2\}}$) was characterized by a set of axioms related to those occurring in corollary 10.7. See theorem 5.9, where adding an axiom of symmetry or anonymity would yield a characterization of the Nash bargaining solution — the theorem is formulated and proved for $n = 2$ but the symmetric case is easily extended for $n > 2$. Observe that no (W)IIA axiom is needed in theorem 5.9; but in fact, WIIA could be dropped above as well if the solutions were single-valued, as is straightforward from lemma 10.5. Further, there is no smoothness restriction on pure bargaining games in theorem 5.9; this restriction is built into the restricted additivity (RA) axiom. Because that axiom is therefore weaker, an axiom of continuity had to be added (Pareto continuity, PCONT). A similar approach might work in case of the Shapley solution, e.g., adding a continuity requirement, dropping condition (G2) on games, and building smoothness into the CA axiom. It is not clear, however, whether this would make the WIIA axiom redundant; it even is an open question whether this axiom can be dropped in corollary 10.7.

To conclude this section, we note that Kern (1981) presents a characterization also involving an axiom of independence of irrelevant alternatives; the main other axiom requires a solution to agree with the Shapley value on the class of games corresponding to TU games. Therefore, the obtained characterization is closer to the definition of the Shapley solution.

10.4   The Harsanyi solution

An axiomatization of the Harsanyi solution was first obtained in Hart (1985b), on which the present section is based. The axiomatization presented here is based on the following axioms formulated for a pc-solution Φ on $\mathcal{G}' \subset \tilde{\mathcal{G}}^N$. For $K \in 2^N \backslash \{\emptyset\}$ and $c \in \mathbb{R}$, let U_K^c be the game corresponding to the TU game that assigns c to coalitions containing K, and 0 to other coalitions.

Coalitional Strong Pareto Optimality (CSPO): For every $V \in \mathcal{G}'$ and $x \in \Phi(V)$, $\{x^N\} = \{y \in W(V(N)) : y \le x^N\}$, and $x^K \in W(V(K))$ for all $K \in 2^N \backslash \{\emptyset\}$.

Coalitional Conditional Additivity (CCA): For all $U, V, W \in \mathcal{G}'$ with $U = V + W$, for all $x \in \Phi(V)$ and $y \in \Phi(W)$, if $x^K + y^K \in W(U(K))$ for all $K \in 2^N \backslash \{\emptyset\}$, then $(x^K + y^K)_{K \in 2^N \backslash \{\emptyset\}} \in \Phi(U)$.

Coalitional Unanimity (CUN): For every $c \in \mathbb{R}$ and $K \in 2^N \backslash \{\emptyset\}$, if $U_K^c \in \mathcal{G}'$, then $\Phi(U_K^c) = \{(z^L)_{L \in 2^N \backslash \{\emptyset\}}\}$ where $z^L := ce^K / |K| \in \mathbb{R}^L$ if $K \subset L$, $z^L := 0 \in \mathbb{R}^L$ otherwise.

Scale Transformation Covariance (STC): For all $V \in \mathcal{G}'$, $\lambda \in \mathbb{R}_{++}^N$, if $x = (x^K) \in \Phi(V)$ and $\lambda V \in \mathcal{G}'$, then $(\lambda_K x^K) \in \Phi(\lambda V)$.

Coalitional Weak Independence of Irrelevant Alternatives (CWIIA): For all $V, W \in \mathcal{G}'$ and all $x \in \Phi(W)$, if $V(K) \subset W(K)$ and $x^K \in V(K)$ for all $K \subset N$, then $x \in \Phi(V)$.

Zero-Inessential Games (ZIG): If $V \in \mathcal{G}'$ with $0 \in W(V(K))$ for all $K \subset N$ and $\{0\} = \{y \in W(V(N)) : y \le 0\}$, then $0 \in \Phi(V)$.

Suppose the definition of the Shapley solution would be modified so that it becomes a pc-solution; an obvious way to do this is to allow those payoff configurations (x^K) with $x^N \in \Lambda(V)$ and, for every non-empty K, $\lambda_K \cdot x^K$ maximal on $V(K)$, where λ is the weight vector corresponding to x^N. This modified Shapley solution would satisfy all the axioms above except for CUN and ZIG. On the other hand, the Harsanyi solution (at least, its restriction to the payoffs for the grand coalition) satisfies all the axioms used in the characterization of the Shapley solution in the previous section except for Conditional Additivity (CA). Indeed, the premise of CCA is stronger than the premise of CA; in that sense, CCA is weaker than CA. The following example shows that H does not satisfy CA on $\mathcal{G}^N$ (cf. Hart, 1985b). Let $N = \{1, 2, 3\}$, and let V^0 be the game corresponding to the zero TU game. Let $V(K) := U_N(K)$ for every $K \ne \{1, 2\}$ and $V(\{1, 2\}) := \{x \in \mathbb{R}^{\{1,2\}} :$

$x_1 + 2x_2 \leq 0,\ 2x_1 + x_2 \leq 3\}$. Then $U_{\{1,2\}} = V + V^0$. Each of the three games $U_{\{1,2\}}$, V, and V^0 has a unique Harsanyi solution outcome with payoff vectors $z = (\frac{1}{2}, \frac{1}{2}, 0)$, $x = (\frac{1}{3}, \frac{1}{3}, \frac{1}{3})$, and $y = (0,0,0)$ for the grand coalition, respectively; but although $x + y \in P(U_{\{1,2\}}(N))$, $x + y \neq z$.

Proposition 10.8 *The Harsanyi solution H on $\mathcal{G}^N$ satisfies STC, CSPO, CCA, CUN, CWIIA, and ZIG.*

Proof CSPO follows in particular by smoothness of $V(N)$ for $V \in \mathcal{G}^N$. CUN follows by lemma 10.2. CCA can be proved by using an appropriate variant of lemma 5.12. The other properties are obvious.   □

We will show that the Harsanyi solution is uniquely determined by the six properties in proposition 10.8, starting with the following lemma.

Lemma 10.9 *Let Φ be a solution on $\mathcal{G}^N$ satisfying CSPO, CCA, and CUN. Let $V \in \mathcal{G}^N_{TU}$. Then $\Phi(V) = H(V) = \{(\mathrm{Sh}(K,V))_{K \in 2^N \setminus \{\emptyset\}}\}$.*

Proof The second identity to be proved follows from lemma 10.2.

Let V^0 be the game corresponding to the TU game that is identically zero. By CUN, $\Phi(V^0) = \{0\}$. For games U_K^c the lemma is obviously true in view of lemma 10.2 and CUN.

Next, recall (cf. section 10.2) that V can be written as a sum $V = \sum_{K \neq \emptyset} U_K^c$. By CSPO and CCA,

$$\Phi(V) = \Phi(\sum_{K \neq \emptyset} U_K^c) \supset \sum_{K \neq \emptyset} \Phi(U_K^c) = \{(\mathrm{Sh}(K,V))_{K \in 2^N \setminus \{\emptyset\}}\}, \qquad (10.11)$$

where the summation after the inclusion sign is interpreted coalitionwise, and the last equality follows from the second paragraph of this proof and the linearity of the Shapley value.

Finally, note that

$$\{0\} = \Phi(V^0) \supset \Phi(V) + \Phi(V^-)$$

where V^- is defined by $V^-(K) := -V(K)$ for every coalition K, and where the inclusion follows from CSPO, CCA, and the fact that $V^0 = V + V^-$. By (10.11), both $\Phi(V)$ and $\Phi(V^-)$ are nonempty, so each of these sets is actually a singleton. With (10.11), this concludes the proof.   □

Proposition 10.10 *Let Φ be a solution on $\mathcal{G}^N$ satisfying STC, CSPO, CCA, CUN, and CWIIA. Then $\Phi(V) \subset H(V)$ for every $V \in \mathcal{G}^N$.*

Proof Let $V \in \mathcal{G}^N$, let $x \in \Phi(V)$, and let $\lambda \in \mathbb{R}^N_{++}$ be a normal vector of the (unique) supporting hyperplane of $V(N)$ at x^N. In view of STC of Φ and H, we may assume $\lambda = e^N$. Define $V_1, V_2 \in \mathcal{G}^N$ by $V_1(K) := \{y \in \mathbb{R}^K : y \leq x^K\}$ for every $K \neq N$, $V_1(N) := V(N)$, $V_2(K) := \{y \in \mathbb{R}^K : e^K \cdot y \leq e^K \cdot x^K\}$ for all K. By CWIIA applied to V_1 and V, we obtain $x \in \Phi(V_1)$. Note that $V_2 = V_1 + U^0$, where as before U^0 corresponds to the zero TU game. By lemma 10.9, $\Phi(U^0) = \{0\}$, so CCA entails $x \in \Phi(V_2)$. Because V_2 corresponds to a TU game, by lemma 10.9 we have $x \in H(V_2)$. Then, by definition of H, $x \in H(V)$.   □

A complete characterization of the Harsanyi solution is obtained by adding the axiom for zero-inessential games.

Proposition 10.11 *Let Φ be a solution on $\mathcal{G}^N$ satisfying the axioms in proposition 10.10 and, additionally, ZIG. Then $H(V) \subset \Phi(V)$ for every $V \in \mathcal{G}^N$.*

Proof Let $V \in \mathcal{G}^N$, $x \in H(V)$ and $\lambda \in I\!\!R^N_{++}$ the corresponding weight vector. By STC, w.l.o.g. $\lambda = e^N$. Define the games V_1, V_2, and V_3 by $V_1(K) := \{y \in I\!\!R^K : e^K \cdot y \le e^K \cdot x^K\}$ for every K, $V_2(K) := \{y \in I\!\!R^K : y \le x^K\}$ for every $K \ne N$, $V_2(N) := V_1(N)$, $V_3(K) := V(K)$ for every $K \ne N$, $V_3(N) := V_1(N)$. Finally, define $U \in \mathcal{G}^N$ by $U(K) := \{y \in I\!\!R^K : y = z - x^K$ for some $z \in V(K)\}$ for all K. Because $x^K \in W(V(K))$ for every K, we have $0 \in W(U(K))$ for every K, so that $0 \in \Phi(U)$ by ZIG.

Because $x \in H(V)$, we have $x \in H(V_1)$ by definition of H. Since $V_1 \in \mathcal{G}^N_{TU}$, by lemma 10.9 we have $x \in \Phi(V_1)$; hence $x \in \Phi(V_2)$ by CWIIA. Because $V_3 = V_2 + U$, CCA implies $x = x + 0 \in \Phi(V_3)$. Applying CWIIA to V and V_3 yields $x \in \Phi(V)$, which completes the proof. □

We can now state the main result of this section as an immediate consequence of propositions 10.8, 10.10, and 10.11.

Corollary 10.12 *The solution Φ on $\mathcal{G}^N$ satisfies STC, CSPO, CCA, CUN, CWIIA, and ZIG, if and only if it is the Harsanyi solution H.*

10.5   The proportional solutions

The proportional solutions were proposed and axiomatized by Kalai and Samet (1985). Recall from section 10.2 that the proportional solutions are single-valued pc-solutions defined on $\tilde{\mathcal{G}}^N$ for exogenously given vectors $\lambda \in I\!\!R^N_{++}$.

Our characterization below is different from the characterization by Kalai and Samet, and more in line with the axiomatizations in the preceding sections. Furthermore, we restrict our attention to the egalitarian pc-solution E. A characterization of the nonsymmetric proportional solutions may be obtained by an appropriate modification of the CUN axiom used in corollary 10.16. We need the following additional axioms, defined for a pc-solution Φ on a subclass $\mathcal{G}'$ of $\tilde{\mathcal{G}}^N$ that is *single-valued*, i.e., $|\Phi(V)| = 1$ for every $V \in \mathcal{G}'$ (observe that non-emptiness of Φ is thus implicit). We write $x = \Phi(V)$ instead of $\{x\} = \Phi(V)$ for a single-valued pc-solution.

Weak Pareto Optimality (WPO): For every $V \in \mathcal{G}'$, if $\Phi(V) = (x^K)$, then $x^K \in W(V(K))$ for every non-empty coalition K.

Coalitional Monotonicity (CMON): For all $V, V' \in \mathcal{G}'$ and $M \in 2^N \backslash \{\emptyset\}$, if $V(K) = V'(K)$ for all $K \ne M$, $V'(M) \supset V(M)$, and $(x^K) = \Phi(V)$, $(y^K) = \Phi(V')$, then $x^K_i \le y^K_i$ for every $K \subset N$ and every $i \in M$; if, furthermore, $x^M = y^M$, then $(x^K) = (y^K)$.

For pure n-person bargaining games, CMON reduces to the combination of strong monotonicity (SMON) and disagreement point monotonicity, see subsection 4.5.3.

The final axiom we need is one of continuity. Let $V, V^1, V^2, \ldots$ be a sequence of games in $\mathcal{G}'$. We say that $\{V^k\}$ converges to V, denoted $V^k \to V$, if for every coalition M the sequence $V^k(M)$ converges to $V(M)$ (see section 8.8 for the definition of convergence in this context).

Coalitional Continuity (CCONT): For every sequence $V, V^1, V^2, \ldots$ in $\mathcal{G}'$, if $V^k \to V$ then $\Phi(V^k) \to \Phi(V)$.

Of the axioms used in the characterization of the Shapley solution, the egalitarian solution E satisfies UN, WIIA, and RNE, but not SPO, CA, and STC. Further, E satisfies CCA, CUN, CWIIA, and ZIG. For the axiomatization of E we use the axioms collected in the following proposition.

Proposition 10.13 *The egalitarian solution E on $\tilde{\mathcal{G}}^N$ satisfies CCA, CUN, WPO, CMON, and CCONT.*

We leave the proof of this proposition to the reader. (See also proposition 10.8 for CCA and CUN; CMON of E follows essentially by the fact that the egalitarian (pure) bargaining solution satisfies SDMON.)

The proof of the following lemma is identical to the proof of lemma 10.9 (where we can stop after formula (10.11)), and is therefore omitted.

Lemma 10.14 *Let Φ be a single-valued pc-solution on $\tilde{\mathcal{G}}^N$ satisfying WPO, CCA, and CUN. Let the game V correspond to a TU game. Then $\Phi(V) = E(V) = (\mathrm{Sh}(K, V))$.*

The next proposition establishes the converse of proposition 10.13.

Proposition 10.15 *Let Φ be a single-valued solution on $\tilde{\mathcal{G}}^N$ satisfying CCA, CUN, WPO, CMON, and CCONT. Then Φ is the egalitarian solution E.*

Proof Let $V \in \tilde{\mathcal{G}}^N$, and $(x^K) = E(V)$. We will show that $(x^K) = \Phi(V)$. By CCONT of E and Φ we may assume that $x^K \in P(V(K))$ for every non-empty coalition K.

Let the game U be defined by $U(K) = \mathrm{com}\{x^K\}$ for every non-empty coalition K. Let $\epsilon > 0$ and let, for every K, $U^\epsilon(K) := \mathrm{com}\{y \in \mathbb{R}^K : \|y - x^K\| < \epsilon,\ e^K \cdot y = e^K \cdot x^K\}$. Let V_0 be the game corresponding to the TU game assigning the number $e^K \cdot x^K$ to every coalition K. By lemma 10.14, $\Phi(V_0) = E(V_0) = (x^K)$. Let $M_1, M_2, \ldots, M_{2^n - 1}$ be an enumeration of all non-empty coalitions. Define, recursively, the game V_j by $V_j(S_j) = U^\epsilon(S_j)$ and $V_j(K) = V_{j-1}(K)$ for all $K \neq S_j$, for all $j = 1, 2, \ldots, 2^n - 1$. We will prove by induction that $\Phi(U^\epsilon) = \Phi(V_{2^n - 1}) = (x^K)$. As induction hypothesis, assume that $\Phi(V_i) = (x^K)$ for all $i < j$, where $1 \leq j \leq 2^n - 1$. (Observe that this is true for $j = 1$.) Let $(z^K) = \Phi(V_j)$. By CMON applied to V_j and V_{j-1} and the induction hypothesis, $x^{M_j} \geq z^{M_j}$; by WPO and the definition of $U^\epsilon(M_j)$, this is only possible for $x^{M_j} = z^{M_j}$, so by CMON: $(z^K) = (x^K)$. This completes the proof that $\Phi(U^\epsilon) = (x^K)$. By letting ϵ go to zero and CCONT, we conclude that $\Phi(U) = (x^K)$.

In a similar fashion, we can go from U to V by each time replacing a set $U(M)$ by a set $V(M)$; by CMON we prove, inductively, that $\Phi(V) = \Phi(U) = (x^K)$. $\square$

By combining propositions 10.13 and 10.15 we obtain the announced characterization of the egalitarian pc-solution.

Corollary 10.16 *A single-valued pc-solution on $\tilde{\mathcal{G}}^N$ satisfies WPO, CCA, CUN, CMON, and CCONT, if and only if it is the egalitarian solution.*

The characterization by Kalai and Samet also uses CCONT, and the weaker version CMON' of CMON obtained by omitting the second statement in its formulation.

We conclude this section with two arguments in favor of egalitarian solutions. The first argument consists of an example (Kalai and Samet, 1985, p. 309). Let $N = \{1, 2, 3\}$ and let the game V be given by $V(N) := \text{comv}\{(4, 4, 4), (7, 0, 0), (0, 12, 0)\}$, $v(M) := \text{com}\{0\}$ if $M \neq N$. For any $x^N \in \Lambda(V)$ or $x \in H(V)$, $x^N = (4, 4, 4)$, where Λ and H are the Shapley and Harsanyi solutions, as before. Let the game U be equal to the game V except for the coalition $\{1, 2\}$ which can now obtain $U(\{1, 2\}) = \text{comv}\{(7, 0), (0, 12)\}$. Then, for any $x^N \in \Lambda(U)$ or $x \in H(U)$, $x^N = (7/2, 6, 0)$. Consequently, although player 1 seems to have more power in the game U than in the game V, he suffers a loss of $1/2$. This lack of monotonicity is avoided by (say) the egalitarian solution, for which $E(V)^N = (4, 4, 4)$ and $E(U)^N = (4.421, 4.421, 0)$.

The second argument consists of presenting a noncooperative "prebargaining game" in order to justify the monotonicity axiom CMON'. Start with a given single-valued pc-solution Φ and a game V. A strategy for player i in the prebargaining game is a list $(\overline{V}^i(K))_{K:i\in K}$ where each $\overline{V}^i(K) \subset V(K)$ and where the conditions defining games in $\tilde{\mathcal{G}}^N$ should be obeyed. The interpretation is that player i could veto the alternatives in $V(K)\backslash\overline{V}^i(K)$ when he bargains with the coalition K. Given a combination of strategies of this type, one for each player in N, the game $\overline{V}$ given by

$$\overline{V}(K) := \bigcap_{i\in K} \overline{V}^i(K)$$

results. The outcome of the (noncooperative) prebargaining game is given by $\Phi(\overline{V})^N$. Then the following observations are immediate.

Proposition 10.17 *(i) If Φ satisfies CMON' then for every player $i \in N$ the strategy $(\overline{V}^i(K))_{K:i\in K} = (V(K))_{K:i\in K}$ is a dominant strategy in the above described prebargaining game.*

(ii) Suppose the strategies $(\overline{V}^i(K))_{K:i\in K} = (V(K))_{K:i\in K}$ are a Nash equilibrium of the prebargaining game for every game V. Then Φ satisfies CMON'.

Thus, monotonicity (CMON') of the solution prevents "manipulative" behavior in this prebargaining game, and, conversely, monotonicity is a necessary condition for Nash equilibrium behavior without manipulation in every (prebargaining) game.

10.6   Related literature

This book considers bargaining games from an abstract point of view. Obviously, if the theory is applied to specific economic situations, then more information is available that enables us to decide which assumptions are more appropriate; and solutions that seem to have some appeal in general, may lead to counterintuitive results in the presence of additional information or assumptions concerning the situation at hand. With respect to the Shapley solution ("NTU value"), there has been quite some discussion in the literature based on a few examples where the Shapley solution may be regarded to perform less well, depending on additional assumptions concerning the underlying model one might be willing to make. The interested reader is referred, chronologically, to Roth (1980), Shafer (1980), Harsanyi (1980), Scafuri and Yannelis (1984), Aumann (1985b), Hart (1985c), Roth (1986), Aumann (1986, 1987b). Especially the defensive papers by Aumann are quite stimulating.

Discussions as in the mentioned literature are natural in game theory. Even — or perhaps especially — in the clear framework of pure bargaining games they abound; for instance, just recall Kalai and Smorodinsky's criticism on IIA and the Nash bargaining solution (see section 4.2). The relatively complex definitions of the Shapley and Harsanyi solutions may have been the cause of the large number of critical papers written on these concepts. Also, there is not much general agreement on the appropriate definition of a coalitional bargaining game (or NTU game), and the existing axiomatizations are less clear-cut and less robust against small changes in the axioms or conditions defining the game, than most axiomatizations in (pure) bargaining theory or the theory of transferable utility games.

Other solutions for coalitional bargaining games were proposed by Owen (1972) and Lemaire (1973). Owen (1972) presents a so-called multilinear extension value (i.e., solution) for a class of coalitional bargaining games, which extends both the Nash solution for pure bargaining games and the Shapley value for TU games.

Lemaire (1973) proposes a solution that extends the Nash bargaining solution, but not the Shapley value for TU games. This solution is defined, recursively, by calculating for each coalition K in a game V the Nash bargaining solution outcome of $(V(K), d^K)$ where the "disagreement" point d^K is taken to be the average of the Nash bargaining solution outcomes of all strict subcoalitions; the "Nash outcomes" for singletons are their maximal attainable utilities. This solution is axiomatized by a (rather ad hoc) adaptation of Nash's characterization in Nash (1950).

Imai (1983a) provides a comparison between the Shapley and the Harsanyi solution. Winter (1991) extends the Harsanyi solution when coalition structures are given a priori. In this context we also mention Myerson (1980), who proposes a "fair" allocation rule for "conferences" (i.e., a kind of coalition structures). Hart and Mas-Colell (1989) provide an alternative characterization of the proportional solutions. Hart and Mas-Colell (1991) propose a new class of solutions for coalitional bargaining games; they start from a noncooperative model of coalitional bargaining. Lucchetti et al. (1986) study continuity properties of the Shapley and Harsanyi solutions.

Undoubtedly, this chapter does not provide the complete set of references concerned with solutions for coalitional bargaining games. In particular, the literature concerning the core is beyond its scope.

Chapter 11

Elements from utility theory

11.1 Introduction

This chapter reviews and sometimes modifies a number of concepts and results from utility theory needed elsewhere in this book. The reader already familiar with or not interested in these basics, which underly most of the other material in this book, may skip this chapter or the larger part of it. Only an understanding is required of the definition of a von Neumann-Morgenstern utility function, which is presented in section 11.2. Everything else in this chapter may be read upon references in other chapters.

Section 11.2 gives the definition of a von Neumann-Morgenstern utility function, and also presents Herstein and Milnor's axiomatic characterization. Section 11.3 is about risk aversion, and more specifically and of interest for game theory, about the notion "more risk averse than". A critical evaluation of the application of the risk aversion concept in general leads to the result in section 11.4, which provides an alternative interpretation of the technical equivalent of risk aversion — concavity of the utility function — and in particular of the technical implication of the notion "more risk averse than". The results of sections 11.3 and 11.4 are used in chapter 6, where risk properties of bargaining solutions are discussed.

The two final sections 11.5 and 11.6 are on additive and multiplicative utility, respectively. The section on additive utility provides a possible foundation for the use of axioms for bargaining solutions that deal with sums (for instance, but not exclusively, expectations) of feasible bargaining sets; see in particular chapter 5. A similar remark can be made for section 11.6 about multiplicative utility, see subsection 2.4.3. Reading these sections is not essential for understanding the applications.

11.2 Von Neumann-Morgenstern utility functions

Players in a game are confronted with the basic uncertainty about what their opponents will do, i.e., what strategies their opponents will play. They may, however, be able to assign probabilities to the strategy combinations that will be played, in which case they can calculate their expected payoffs and use these to guide their own behavior. This is, basically, what von Neumann and Morgenstern (1947) proposed to do. More generally, they provided a formal treatment of the existence of a so-called utility function linear with respect to probability distributions and measuring an individual's preferences, on the basis of a well-defined set of axioms.

This section is intended mainly to provide the formal definition of such a utility function in a framework appropriate for our purposes. For completeness' sake Herstein and Milnor's (1953) axiomatic treatment of the existence of a "von Neumann-Morgenstern" utility function will be briefly discussed in subsection 11.2.1. In subsection 11.2.2 their result is applied to the context of this book.

11.2.1 An axiomatic approach to measurable utility

This subsection is based on Herstein and Milnor (1953). A set $\mathcal{L}$ is a *mixture set* if there exists a map $\vartheta : \mathcal{L} \times [0,1] \times \mathcal{L} \to \mathcal{L}$ satisfying the following three properties:

$$\vartheta(\ell, 1, m) = \ell \tag{11.1}$$
$$\vartheta(\ell, \mu, m) = \vartheta(m, 1 - \mu, \ell) \tag{11.2}$$
$$\vartheta(\vartheta(\ell, \mu, m), \lambda, m) = \vartheta(\ell, \lambda\mu, m) \tag{11.3}$$

for all $\ell, m \in \mathcal{L}$ and $0 \le \lambda, \mu \le 1$. Such a map ϑ is called a *mixture operation*.

Examples of mixture sets are convex sets in real vector spaces (write $\mu\ell + (1-\mu)m$ instead of $\vartheta(\ell, \mu, m)$), and — of relevance in the present context — the set of finite probability distributions over a given nonempty set: see the next subsection.

A *weak ordering* $\succeq$ on $\mathcal{L}$ is a binary relation on $\mathcal{L}$ which is *complete*, i.e. $m \succeq \ell$ or $\ell \succeq m$ for all $\ell, m \in \mathcal{L}$, and *transitive*, i.e. $m \succeq k$ whenever $m \succeq \ell$ and $\ell \succeq k$, for all $k, \ell, m \in \mathcal{L}$. It is said that the function $w : \mathcal{L} \to I\!R$ *represents* the weak ordering $\succeq$ on $\mathcal{L}$ if $w(\ell) \ge w(m) \Leftrightarrow \ell \succeq m$ holds for all, $\ell, m \in \mathcal{L}$. Further, the function $w : \mathcal{L} \to I\!R$ is called *linear* if $w(\vartheta(\ell, \mu, m)) = \mu w(\ell) + (1 - \mu)w(m)$ for all $\ell, m \in \mathcal{L}$ and $0 \le \mu \le 1$.

Herstein and Milnor (1953) call a linear function representing the weak ordering $\succeq$ on the mixture set $\mathcal{L}$ a *measurable utility*. In order to ensure the existence of such a measurable utility, they impose the following axioms[1,2]:

Continuity: For all $k, \ell, m \in \mathcal{L}$, the sets $\{\mu : 0 \le \mu \le 1, \vartheta(k, \mu, \ell) \succeq m\}$ and $\{\mu : 0 \le \mu \le 1, m \succeq \vartheta(k, \mu, \ell)\}$ are closed.

The notation $k \sim \ell$ means that both $k \succeq \ell$ and $\ell \succeq k$ hold.

Independence: If $k, \ell \in \mathcal{L}$ with $k \sim \ell$, then for any $m \in \mathcal{L}$, $\vartheta(k, \frac{1}{2}, m) \sim \vartheta(\ell, \frac{1}{2}, m)$.

The intuition behind these axioms seems to be obvious. The latter axiom has also been called "strong independence axiom" and "sure-thing principle".

Herstein and Milnor derive the following result.

---

[1]These are axioms 2 and 3 in Herstein and Milnor (1953).

[2]In accordance with what has by now become common practice, the word "axiom" is used for a mathematical assumption (that is, no further proof is required) which is believed to have something to do with reality. For instance, an axiom may capture possible human behavior. This usage is a result from a long period of inflation. Necessity (as for instance claimed by Immanuel Kant with respect to the Euclidean world view) has since long ceased to be a necessary ingredient of an axiom.

Theorem 11.1 *Let $\mathcal{L}$ be a mixture set and $\succeq$ a weak ordering on $\mathcal{L}$ satisfying the axioms of Continuity and Independence. Then there exists a measurable utility.*

For a proof the reader is referred to the article of Herstein and Milnor. We also state the following result without proof. A proof is not too hard, and independent of Herstein and Milnor's existence result.

Theorem 11.2 *Let $\mathcal{L}$ be a mixture set, $\succeq$ a weak ordering on $\mathcal{L}$, and w and v measurable utilities. Then there exist real numbers $\alpha > 0$ and β such that $v(\ell) = \alpha w(\ell) + \beta$ for all $\ell \in \mathcal{L}$.*

Theorem 11.2 states that a measurable utility is unique up to a positive affine transformation. Actually, it is easy to verify that, in general, a monotonically increasing transformation of a measurable utility is not linear anymore and certainly does not represent the same weak ordering. Thus, measurable utilities are what are often called *cardinal* utility functions. See also Wakker (1989b, p. 42).

11.2.2 Von Neumann-Morgenstern utility functions

The situation prevailing in this book is that the mixture set $\mathcal{L} = \mathcal{L}(A)$ is the set of probability measures with finite support on a nonempty set A. A typical element of $\mathcal{L}(A)$ is denoted

$$\ell = (p_1; a^1, p_2; a^2, \ldots, p_n; a^n) = (p_i; a^i)_{i=1}^n$$

where $n \in I\!N$, $a^i \in A$ and $p_i \geq 0$ for every $i = 1, 2, \ldots, n$, $\sum_{i=1}^n p_i = 1$. Of course, ℓ is the *lottery* which results with probability $\sum_{j:a^j=a^i} p_j$ in a^i. By writing $(1; a)$ for $a \in A$, one has $A \subset \mathcal{L}(A)$.

It is now straightforward to show that $\mathcal{L} = \mathcal{L}(A)$ is indeed a mixture set, by defining the mixture operation ϑ as follows. For $0 \leq \mu \leq 1$, ℓ as above, and

$$k = (q_1; b^1, q_2; b^2, \ldots, q_m; b^m) \in \mathcal{L}(A)$$

define

$$\vartheta(\ell, \mu, k) := (\mu p_1; a^1, \ldots, \mu p_n; a^n, (1 - \mu)q_1; b^1, \ldots, (1 - \mu)q_m; b^m) \in \mathcal{L}(A).$$

$\mathcal{L}(A)$ is called the *lottery set* of A. Elements of A are called *riskless alternatives*, elements of $\mathcal{L}(A) \backslash A$ *risky alternatives*.

Let $\succeq$ be a weak ordering on $\mathcal{L}(A)$: $\succeq$ is called a *preference relation*. Assume further that $\succeq$ satisfies the Continuity and Independence axioms defined in subsection 11.2.1. Continuity is best interpreted as a mathematical requirement, while Independence is a kind of substitutability requirement. Then, by theorems 11.1 and 11.2 there exists a measurable utility, which is unique up to positive affine transformations. In other words, there exists a function $w : \mathcal{L}(A) \to I\!R$ with $w(\ell) \geq w(m) \Longleftrightarrow \ell \succeq m$ for all $\ell, m \in \mathcal{L}(A)$, and with

$$w((p_i; a^i)_{i=1}^n) = \sum_{i=1}^n p_i w(a^i)$$

for every lottery $(p_i; a^i)_{i=1}^n \in \mathcal{L}(A)$. The function w is called a *von Neumann-Morgenstern* (vNM) *utility function* (*for* $\succeq$, or: *representing* $\succeq$). In this book, utility functions are, often though not always, assumed to be of the vNM-type.

Note that a vNM-utility function on $\mathcal{L}(A)$ is completely determined by the values it takes on A. Therefore, it is convenient to introduce the notation $U(A)$ for the family of all functions $u : A \to \mathbb{R}$. For $\ell = (p_i; a^i)_{i=1}^n \in \mathcal{L}(A)$ and $u \in U(A)$, we then denote by

$$Eu(\ell) := \sum_{i=1}^n p_i u(a^i)$$

the *expected utility of ℓ* (*under u*).

This subsection is concluded by a simple example which links the present section to the following one. Let $A = [0,1] \subset \mathbb{R}$, and let $u \in U(A)$ be defined by $u : x \mapsto \sqrt{x}$. Then

$$u(\frac{1}{2}) = \frac{1}{2}\sqrt{2} > \frac{1}{2} = Eu((\frac{1}{2}; 0, \frac{1}{2}; 1)),$$

so an individual with this vNM-utility function u prefers obtaining $\frac{1}{2}$ (e.g., dollars) with certainty to a lottery in which he has a 50% chance of obtaining 0 and a 50% chance of obtaining 1. This kind of preference is exhibited by a *risk averse* individual. In the following section a related concept is discussed: the relation on $U(A)$ called *more risk averse than*.

11.3   Risk aversion

Suppose an individual may choose between receiving $5 for certain, and a lottery ticket which gives him $10 or nothing both with a 50% chance. An individual that is called risk averse (–neutral, –loving or –prone, respectively) in literature, will prefer the dollars (be indifferent, prefer the lottery ticket, respectively).

Here, interest is not so much in an absolute measure of risk aversion of a decision maker, but rather in a comparison of the aversion to risk of two decision makers. Such a comparison is entailed in the relation *more risk averse than*, which will be introduced and mathematically characterized.

Pioneering work in the area of risk aversion was done by Arrow (see Arrow (1971)) and Pratt (1964). Other important contributions are Yaari (1969) and Kihlstrom and Mirman (1974).

This section is based on Yaari's approach with a minor — but for the present purposes important — modification. Further, the characterization theorem (characterizing the relation more risk averse than) is more general than the characterizations usually found in the literature, since no continuity or differentiability properties of the utility functions are assumed, and (hence) no topological or algebraic structure on the set of alternatives.

In this section, A is a nonempty set of alternatives, with corresponding lottery set $\mathcal{L}(A)$.

Definition 11.3 (i) For $u \in U(A)$ and $a \in A$, the set

$$P_u(a) := \{\ell \in \mathcal{L}(A) : Eu(\ell) > u(a)\}$$

is called the *preference set of u with respect to a.*

(ii) Let $u, v \in U(A)$. (The decision maker with utility function) v is called *more risk averse than* (the decision maker with utility function) u (notation: $vMRu$) if $P_v(a) \subset P_u(a)$ for every $a \in A$.

As to (i) of definition 11.3, one sees that for $\alpha, \beta \in \mathbb{R}$ with $\alpha > 0$, we have $P_{\alpha u + \beta}(a) = P_u(a)$ for every $a \in A$, so preference sets are independent of the particular representation chosen (cf. theorem 11.2). Hence, also the relation MR is independent of the chosen representations u and v. Clearly, the definition of MR is based on the intuition that a more risk averse individual prefers less lotteries to each certain outcome than a less risk averse individual does.

Definition 11.3(ii) is a slight modification of the definition proposed by Yaari (1969), who uses so-called acceptance sets $A_u(a) := \{\ell \in L(A) : Eu(\ell) \geq u(a)\}$ instead of preference sets $P_u(a)$. The reason of this modification is, that (ii) of the following lemma would not hold with acceptance sets instead of preference sets in the definition of MR.

Lemma 11.4 *Let* $u, v \in U(A)$ *with* $vMRu$, *and* $a, b \in A$. *Then:*
(i) if $u(a) \leq u(b)$, *then* $v(a) \leq v(b)$,
(ii) if $u(a) = u(b)$, *then* $v(a) = v(b)$.

Proof (i) Suppose $v(a) > v(b)$. Then $b \in P_v(a) \subset P_u(a)$. So $u(b) > u(a)$.
(ii) In view of (i), if $v(a) \neq v(b)$, then $u(a) \neq u(b)$. $\square$

Before the announced characterization theorem can be formulated, it is convenient to extend the definition of concavity of a function. More precisely, concavity will be defined for functions defined on not necessarily convex domains. Next, it is shown how such functions can be extended to concave functions defined on at least the convex hull of the original domains. This result is used to prove the characterization theorem.

The subject will be treated with some generality, as in Peters and Wakker (1987). Let V be a linear space over the reals. Let T be an arbitrary subset of V, and f a function from T to $\mathbb{R} \cup \{-\infty, \infty\}$. The following definition adapts the definition of concavity given in the literature for convex sets T (see for instance Rockafellar (1970, section 4)) to general, possibly finite, sets T[3].

Definition 11.5 The function f is *concave* if for all convex combinations $\sum_{j=1}^n p_j x^j$ of elements x^j of T for which not both $-\infty$ and $+\infty$ are contained in $\{f(x^j)\}_{j=1}^n$, it holds that

$$\sum_{j=1}^n p_j f(x^j) \leq f\left(\sum_{j=1}^n p_j x^j\right), \tag{11.4}$$

whenever $\sum_{j=1}^n p_j x^j$ is in T.

As is usual, one defines: $\lambda\infty := \infty$ for $\lambda \in \mathbb{R}_{++}$, $\lambda\infty := 0$ for $\lambda = 0$, $\lambda\infty := -\infty$ for $-\lambda \in \mathbb{R}_{++}$, $\lambda + \infty := \infty$ for $\lambda \in \mathbb{R}$ or $\lambda = \infty$, and $\lambda + \infty$ is undefined for $\lambda = -\infty$;

---

[3]For compact sets, this definition was given in Peters and Tijs (1981), and for general sets in Wakker *et al.* (1985).

$\lambda(-\infty) := -\infty$ for $\lambda \in I\!\!R_{++}$, $\lambda(-\infty) := 0$ for $\lambda = 0$, $\lambda(-\infty) := \infty$ for $-\lambda \in I\!\!R_{++}$, $\lambda - \infty := -\infty$ for $\lambda \in I\!\!R$ or $\lambda = -\infty$, and $\lambda - \infty$ is undefined for $\lambda = \infty$.

A function f is *convex* if $-f$ is concave. All results derived below for concave functions f, can be reformulated for convex functions g, by setting $g := -f$.

Theorem 11.6 *Let V be a linear space over $I\!\!R$, and let $T \subset V$. Let $f : T \to I\!\!R \cup \{-\infty, \infty\}$ be concave. Then there exists a concave function $\tilde{f} : V \to I\!\!R \cup \{-\infty, \infty\}$ which extends f.*

Proof Define $\tilde{f}$ on V as follows:

$$\tilde{f} : x \mapsto \sup\{\mu : \mu = \sum_{j=1}^{n} p_j f(x^j), \ x \text{ is a convex combination}$$

$$\sum p_j x^j \text{ of elements } x^j \text{ of } T \text{ such that not } f(x^j) = \infty \text{ for some } j,$$

$$\text{and } f(x^j) = -\infty \text{ for some other } j\}. \tag{11.5}$$

Note that $\tilde{f}(x) \geq f(x)$ for all $x \in T$; by concavity of f, $\tilde{f}(x) \leq f(x)$ for all $x \in T$. So indeed $\tilde{f}$ extends f. It is left to prove that $\tilde{f}$ is concave. So let y be a convex combination $\sum_{i=1}^{m} q_i y^i$, with all $q_i > 0$. It must be proved that

$$\tilde{f}(y) \geq \sum_{i=1}^{m} q_i \tilde{f}(y^i) \tag{11.6}$$

whenever not $\tilde{f}(y^i) = \infty$ for some i, $\tilde{f}(y^i) = -\infty$ for some other i.

The case where $\tilde{f}(y^i) = -\infty$ for some i is immediate anyhow, so suppose $\tilde{f}(y^i) > -\infty$ for all i. This implies that every y^i is in $\text{conv}(T)$. Say y^i is the convex combination $\sum_k p_{ik} x^{ik}$ of elements x^{ik} of T. Then $y = \sum_{i=1}^{m} \sum_k q_i p_{ik} x^{ik}$. By definition of $\tilde{f}$,

$$\tilde{f}(y) \geq \sum_{i=1}^{m} q_i \sum_k p_{ik} f(x^{ik}). \tag{11.7}$$

Now first suppose $\tilde{f}(y^\ell) = \infty$ for some ℓ. Then, for every $M \in I\!\!N$, one can take the $x^{\ell k}$ above such that $\sum_k p_{\ell k} f(x^{\ell k}) > M$. Since $q_\ell > 0$, by (11.7) we obtain $\tilde{f}(y) = \infty$, and (11.6) follows.

Next suppose $\tilde{f}(y^i) < \infty$ for all i. Then, for any $\varepsilon > 0$ and every i, one can take the x^{ik} such that $\sum_k p_{ik} f(x^{ik}) \leq \tilde{f}(y_i) + \varepsilon$. This again implies (11.6). $\qquad\square$

Note that $\tilde{f}$ defined in (11.5) is the minimal concave extension. If $\tilde{f}$ in theorem 11.6 is real-valued, then even on $\text{conv}(T)$, it may be impossible to have $\tilde{f}$ real-valued, as the following example shows.

Example 11.7 Let $V = I\!\!R^2$, $T = \{(-1, -j)\}_{j \in I\!\!N} \cup \{(1, j)\}_{j \in I\!\!N}$, $f(x_1, x_2) = |x_2|$ for all $(x_1, x_2) \in T$. Then considering the pairs $(-1, -j)$ and $(1, j)$, one finds that $\tilde{f}(0, 0) \geq j$, for all $j \in I\!\!N$.

For bounded f, $\tilde{f}$ can be taken real-valued on $\text{conv}(T)$:

Corollary 11.8 *For $\tilde{f}$ defined in (11.5), $\sup \tilde{f}(\text{conv}(T)) = \sup(f(T))$, and $\inf \tilde{f}(\text{conv}(T)) = \inf(f(T))$.*

Proof Obvious from (11.5). □

If $V = \mathbb{R}$, then a real-valued f in theorem 11.6 can be extended to a real-valued $\tilde{f}$ on conv(T).

Corollary 11.9 *Let* $V = \mathbb{R}$, $T \subset V$, $f : T \to \mathbb{R}$ *concave. Then* f *has a concave extension* $\tilde{f} : \text{conv}(T) \to \mathbb{R}$.

Proof Obvious if T contains at most two elements, then $\tilde{f}$ can be taken affine (i.e., both convex and concave). So let $x_1 > x_2 > x_3$ in T. Let ℓ^1 be the affine function through $(x^1, f(x^1))$ and $(x^2, f(x^2))$, let ℓ^2 be the one through $(x^2, f(x^2))$ and $(x^3, f(x^3))$. Then, with $\tilde{f}$ as in (11.5), for all $x \in \mathbb{R}$ we have $\tilde{f}(x) \leq \max\{\ell^1(x), \ell^2(x)\} < \infty$.

Further, for all $x \in \text{conv}(T)$, $x \in [x^4, x^5]$ for some x^4, x^5 in T, hence $\tilde{f}(x) \geq \min\{f(x^4), f(x^5)\} > -\infty$ for such x. □

Even if $V = \mathbb{R}$ and the concave function f is real-valued and bounded on T, then still no concave real-valued extension $\tilde{f}$ of f to all of V may exist. For instance, let $T = [0, 1]$ and $f : x \mapsto \sqrt{x}$ on T. Then any concave extension $\tilde{f}$ of f on V must assign $-\infty$ to every $x < 0$.

Lemma 11.10 *Let* $V = \mathbb{R}$, *and* f *nondecreasing and concave. Then* $\tilde{f}$, *as defined by (11.5), is nondecreasing on* conv(T).

Proof By corollary 11.8, $\tilde{f}$ has the same supremum on conv(T), as f on T. Hence the supremum of $\tilde{f}$ can be found on the "right hand side" of conv(T): the concave $\tilde{f}$ must be nondecreasing. □

After this digression on the extension of concave functions, the theorem characterizing the relation "more risk averse than" can be formulated and proved.

Theorem 11.11 *Let* $u, v \in U(A)$. *The following two assertions are equivalent:*

(i) $vMRu$,

(ii) *There exists a nondecreasing concave function* $k : u(A) \to \mathbb{R}$ *with* $v(a) = k(u(a))$ *for every* $a \in A$.

Proof First suppose (i). Define the function $k : u(A) \to \mathbb{R}$ by $k(u(a)) := v(a)$ for every $a \in A$. This function is well-defined in view of lemma 11.4(ii), and nondecreasing in view of lemma 11.4(i). In order to prove that k is concave, let some element $u(a)$ of $u(A)$ be a convex combination $\sum p_j u(a^j)$ of other elements of $u(A)$. Then $Eu(\ell) = u(a)$, where ℓ denotes the lottery $(p_j; a^j)$, so $\ell \notin P_u(a) \supset P_v(a)$. One thus has $v(a) \geq v(\ell)$, hence $k(u(a)) \geq \sum p_j k(u(a^j))$. This proves concavity of k.

Next suppose (ii). Let $\ell = (p_j; a^j) \in \mathcal{L}(A)$ and $a \in A$ with $v(\ell) > v(a)$. Then $\sum p_j k(u(a^j)) > k(u(a))$, so $\sum p_j \tilde{k}(u(a^j)) > \tilde{k}(u(a))$, where $\tilde{k}$ corresponds to k in the way $\tilde{f}$ corresponds to f in theorem 11.6 and (11.5). Then the concavity of $\tilde{k}$ implies $\tilde{k}(\sum p_j u(a^j)) \geq \sum p_j \tilde{k}(u(a^j)) > \tilde{k}(u(a))$. Since $\tilde{k}$ is nondecreasing on conv$(u(A))$ by lemma 11.10, $\sum p_j u(a^j) > u(a)$, so $\ell \in P_u(a)$. It has been shown that $P_v(a) \subset P_u(a)$, hence $vMRu$. □

In Peters and Tijs (1981) this characterization theorem was proved under the additional assumptions of continuity of elements of $u(A)$, with A being a compact subset of some $I\!\!R^\ell$: for this case the extension theorem (theorem 11.6) is straightforward. A slightly more complicated proof of the characterization theorem was given in Wakker *et al.* (1985), without the use of the extension theorem, but with first-order-difference results concerning concave functions. Independently, a closely related result was derived by Nielsen (1988).

11.4   A criterion for comparing strength of preference

Cardinal utility functions uniquely describe a decision maker's preference up to positive affine transformations: see also subsection 11.2.1. A distinction is often made in the literature on cardinal utility between utility functions describing a decision maker's behavior in risky situations and those pertaining to situations where no risk is involved. Utility functions of the first kind are the vNM utility functions (see subsection 11.2.2 and section 11.3) and describe a decision maker's attitude towards risk by incorporating lotteries into the model. In case there is no risk involved, cardinal utility functions may measure something like strength of preference and are often called *value functions*[4].

Formally, there is no problem in distinguishing between the two utility concepts. Also, in a model without lotteries it is incorrect to explain theoretical results by referring to the risk attitude(s) of the decision maker(s). Still, such a phenomenon is common practice in many economic applications[5]. An example is given in section 6.5.

In the present section, attention is restricted to decision making under certainty. For utility functions measuring strength of preference, to be called value functions from now on, we propose a criterion to compare the rates of the changes in marginal value: a value function v will be called "improving faster than" a value function u if for the former marginal values are relatively higher for lower preferred alternatives and lower for higher preferred alternatives, than for the latter. We show that this is true if and only if v is a nondecreasing concave transformation of u. As such, the criterion and its characterization parallel the relation "more risk averse than" and its characterization for decision making under risk in the previous section.

As before, let A be a nonempty set, the *set of alternatives*, and let $\succeq^*$ be a weak ordering (cf. subsection 6.2.2) on $A \times A$. For a, b, c, and d in A, we interpret $(a, b) \succeq^* (c, d)$ as: the decision maker prefers the change from b to a to the change from d to c. We call $\succeq^*$ the *strength of preference relation*. The following assumption holds throughout this section.

Assumption   For every $\succeq^*$, there exists a function $u : A \to I\!\!R$ such that, for all $a, b, c, d \in A$:

---

[4]An even more frequently discussed issue has always been the controversial point of ordinality versus cardinality in economics. Ordinal utility functions are unique up to all monotonically increasing transformations. In many fields of economics, e.g. in equilibrium theory — see Hildenbrand and Kirman (1976) for an introductory text — ordinality of the utility functions is assumed. As regards the main theme of this book — the axiomatic approach to bargaining — ordinality of the utility functions would lead to a rather restrictive assumption on solution concepts: see section 8.7.

[5]Hanoch (1977) and Drèze (1982), criticize, for instance, the case where ordinal (e.g., consumer demand functions) and cardinal (e.g., risk aversion) concepts are mixed up.

$(a, b) \succeq^*(c, d) \Leftrightarrow u(a) - u(b) \geq u(c) - u(d)$.

Positive affine transformations of the function u, i.e., transformations of the form $\alpha u(\cdot) + \beta$ where $\alpha, \beta \in \mathbb{R}$ and $\alpha > 0$, preserve the equivalence in this assumption. Conditions for the existence of u are given in Wakker (1988, Theorem 5.3) or Shapley (1975).

From $\succeq^*$, we can derive the weak ordering $\succeq$ on A, the *preference relation*, by $a \succeq b : \Leftrightarrow$ $(a, b) \succeq^*(b, b)$ for all $a, b \in A$. Then u represents $\succeq$ since $u(a) \geq u(b) \Leftrightarrow a \succeq b$. u is called a *value function* representing $\succeq$ of $\succeq^*$.

Let v and u be value functions representing the strength of preference relations $\succeq_v^*$ and $\succeq_u^*$, respectively.

Definition 11.12 We call v *improving faster than* u (notation $v IF u$) if for all $a, b, c, d \in A$ with $a \succeq_u b \succeq_u c \succeq_u d$:

$$(c, d) \succeq_u^*(a, b) \Rightarrow (c, d) \succeq_v^*(a, b).$$

The expression "improving faster than" is perhaps best understood by considering the case where $(c, d) \sim_u^*(a, b)$ and $(c, d) \succ_v^*(a, b)$: here $\sim_u^*$ and $\succ_v^*$ denote the respective symmetric and asymmetric parts[6].

Theorem 11.13 *Let u and v be value functions with $u(A)$ an interval. The following two statements are equivalent:*

(i) $v IF u$

(ii) *There exists a nondecreasing concave function $k : u(A) \to \mathbb{R}$ with $v(a) = k(u(a))$ for every $a \in A$.*

Proof A more tractable formulation of $v IF u$ is:

$$u(c) - u(d) \geq u(a) - u(b) \Rightarrow v(c) - v(d) \geq v(a) - v(b) \qquad (11.8)$$

for all $a, b, c, d \in A$ with $u(a) \geq u(b) \geq u(c) \geq u(d)$.

First assume (ii) and the antecedent of (11.8). If $u(a) = u(b)$ or $u(c) = u(d)$, then the consequent of (11.8) is straightforward from the nondecreasingness of k. Otherwise, the concavity of k implies

$$\frac{k(u(c)) - k(u(d))}{u(c) - u(d)} \geq \frac{k(u(a)) - k(u(b))}{u(a) - u(b)}$$

— see for instance Wakker *et al.* (1985) for a formal proof of this fact — from which the consequent of (11.8) immediately follows.

Next assume (11.8). One has to prove the existence of a function k as in (ii). First note that, if $u(a) = u(b)$ for $a, b \in A$, then applying (11.8) to the sequence $u(a) \geq u(b) \geq u(b) \geq u(b)$ gives $0 \geq v(a) - v(b)$. Similarly, one shows $0 \geq v(b) - v(a)$, so that $v(a) = v(b)$. Hence the function $k : u(A) \to \mathbb{R}$ with $k(u(a)) := v(a)$ for all $a \in A$ is well-defined; furthermore, since $u(a) \geq u(b)$ implies $v(a) \geq v(b)$ by (11.8) applied to the sequence

---

[6]That is, $(c, d) \sim_u^*(a, b) \Leftrightarrow [(c, d) \succeq_u^*(a, b)$ and $(a, b) \succeq_u^*(c, d)]$, and $(c, d) \succ_v^*(a, b) \Leftrightarrow [(c, d) \succeq_v^*(a, b)$ and not $(a, b) \succeq_v^*(c, d)]$.

$u(a) \geq u(a) \geq u(a) \geq u(b)$, k must be nondecreasing. It remains to be shown that k is concave.

Let $\alpha, \beta, \gamma \in u(A)$ with $\beta = \frac{1}{2}(\alpha + \gamma)$, say $\alpha = u(a)$, $\beta = u(b)$, $\gamma = u(c)$, and $\alpha \geq \gamma$. Then $u(a) \geq u(b) \geq u(b) \geq u(c)$ and from $u(b) - u(c) = u(a) - u(b)$ we obtain by (11.8): $v(b) - v(c) \geq v(a) - v(b)$, hence $k(\frac{1}{2}(\alpha + \gamma)) \geq \frac{1}{2}k(\alpha) + \frac{1}{2}k(\gamma)$. Repeated application of this gives

$$k(t\alpha + (1 - t)\gamma) \geq tk(\alpha) + (1 - t)k(\gamma) \tag{11.9}$$

for every number t of the form $n2^{-m}$ where n and m are natural numbers with $n \leq 2^m$. In view of the nondecreasingness of k, it follows that (11.9) holds for every $0 \leq t \leq 1$. In other words, k is concave.   □

Unfortunately, the requirement in theorem 11.13 that $u(A)$ be an interval cannot be discussed (e.g., take $u(A) = \{0, 4, 5\}$, $k(0) = 0$, $k(4) = 4$, $k(5) = 6$). In particular, the characterization does not hold for finite A. Dyer and Sarin (1982, especially Theorem 1) present a similar result in a more restrictive setting; in particular, they impose differentiability assumptions on the value functions. This section is based on Peters (1992a).

11.5 Additive utility

Keeney and Raiffa (1976, p. 231), following Fishburn (1965), give a necessary and sufficient condition under which a von Neumann-Morgenstern utility function on the Cartesian product of two sets of alternatives, can be written as a scaled sum of coordinate utility functions. In this section, this result will be modified for the case where these coordinate utility functions represent *given* preference relations. The motivation for including this result is, that it provides a utility-theoretic foundation for additivity properties of solution concepts, see chapter 5. The result was published in Peters (1985).

In order to specify the problem let A and B non-empty sets of alternatives, and let $C := A \times B$ be the Cartesian product of these sets. $\mathcal{L}(A)$, $\mathcal{L}(B)$, and $\mathcal{L}(C)$ denote the corresponding lottery sets. Let $\succeq_C$ be a preference relation on $\mathcal{L}(C)$ representable by a vNM utility function w. Keeney and Raiffa (1976, p. 231) show that under the assumption of *additive independence* for $\succeq_C$ (see below) one can write $w = k_A w_A + k_B w_B$ where k_A and k_B are positive constants and w_A and w_B *induced* vNM utility functions on $\mathcal{L}(A)$ and $\mathcal{L}(B)$: i.e., they *induce* preferences on $\mathcal{L}(A)$ and $\mathcal{L}(B)$. This result will be modified for the case where w_A and w_B represent *given* preferences on $\mathcal{L}(A)$ and $\mathcal{L}(B)$.

Let now A, B, and C be as above, and let $\succeq_A$, $\succeq_B$, and $\succeq_C$ be preference relations on $\mathcal{L}(A)$, $\mathcal{L}(B)$, and $\mathcal{L}(C)$, respectively. It is assumed that

> Any preference relation occurring in this section is representable by a
> vNM utility function.   (11.10)

Below a weaker version of the *additive independence* property is introduced (cf. Keeney and Raiffa, 1976, p. 230). This version is weaker since only lotteries with probabilities $\frac{1}{2}$ are considered.

For all (a, b) and (a', b') in C : $(\frac{1}{2}; (a, b), \frac{1}{2}; (a', b')) \sim_C (\frac{1}{2}; (a, b'), \frac{1}{2}; (a', b))$

(*Additive independence*) (11.11)

Here $\sim_C$ denotes the symmetric part[7] of $\succeq_C$. We show that a decision maker with an additively independent $\succeq_C$ is indifferent between a lottery over C in which he receives $a^i \in A$ with probability p_i $(i = 1, 2, \ldots, m)$ and, independently, $b^j \in B$ with probability p_j $(j = 1, 2, \ldots, m)$; and the simultaneous distribution in which he receives (a^i, b^i) with probability p_i: i.e., $(p_i p_j; (a^i, b^j))_{i,j=1}^m \sim_C (p_i; (a^i, b^i))_{i=1}^m$.

$$
\begin{aligned}
&(p_i; (a^i, b^i))_{i=1}^m \\
&= (p_1^2; (a^1, b^1), \ldots, p_m^2; (a^m, b^m), p_1 \sum_{j \neq 1} p_j; (a^1, b^1), \ldots, p_m \sum_{j \neq m} p_j; (a^m, b^m)) \\
&= (p_1^2; (a^1, b^1), \ldots, p_m^2; (a^m, b^m), 2p_1 p_2; (\tfrac{1}{2}; (a^1, b^1), \tfrac{1}{2}; (a^2, b^2)), \\
&\quad 2p_1 p_3; (\tfrac{1}{2}; (a^1, b^1), \tfrac{1}{2}; (a^3, b^3)), \ldots, 2p_1 p_m; (\tfrac{1}{2}; (a^1, b^1), \tfrac{1}{2}; (a^m, b^m)), \\
&\quad 2p_2 p_3; (\tfrac{1}{2}; (a^2, b^2), \tfrac{1}{2}; (a^3, b^3)), \ldots, 2p_{m-1} p_m; (\tfrac{1}{2}; (a^{m-1}, b^{m-1}), \tfrac{1}{2}; (a^m, b^m))) \\
&\sim_C (p_1^2; (a^1, b^1), \ldots, p_m^2; (a^m, b^m), 2p_1 p_2; (\tfrac{1}{2}; (a^1, b^2), \tfrac{1}{2}; (a^2, b^1)), \ldots, \\
&\quad 2p_{m-1} p_m; (\tfrac{1}{2}; (a^{m-1}, b^m), \tfrac{1}{2}; (a^m, b^{m-1}))) \\
&= (p_i p_j; (a^i, b^j))_{i,j=1}^m. \quad (11.12)
\end{aligned}
$$

In (11.12), the $\sim_C$-step follows from additive independence of $\succeq_C$ and (11.10), and the other steps follows from elementary properties of lotteries.

The second condition used, relates $\succeq_C$ to $\succeq_A$ and $\succeq_B$[8].

There exists $(a^\circ, b^\circ) \in C$ such that for all $(p_i; a^i)_{i=1}^m$ and $(q_i; \tilde{a}^i)_{i=1}^n$ in $\mathcal{L}(A)$, and all $(p_i; b^i)_{i=1}^m$ and $(q_i; \tilde{b}^i)_{i=1}^n$ in $\mathcal{L}(B)$:

$(p_i; a^i)_{i=1}^m \succ_A (q_i; \tilde{a}^i)_{i=1}^n \Rightarrow (p_i; (a^i, b^\circ))_{i=1}^m \succ_C (q_i; (\tilde{a}^i, b^\circ))_{i=1}^n$

and

$(p_i; b^i)_{i=1}^m \succ_B (q_i; \tilde{b}^i)_{i=1}^n \Rightarrow (p_i; (a^\circ, b^i))_{i=1}^m \succ_C (q_i; (a^\circ, \tilde{b}^i))_{i=1}^n.$

(*Weak monotonicity*) (11.13)

The main result of this section is the following variation on Theorem 5.1 in Keeney and Raiffa (1976).

Theorem 11.14 *Let A, B and $C = A \times B$, be sets of alternatives and $\succeq_A$, $\succeq_B$, and $\succeq_C$, preference relations on the corresponding lottery sets, representable by vNM utility functions. Let A and B each contain at least two non-equivalent elements. Then the following two statements are equivalent.*

(i) *$\succeq_C$ satisfies additive independence, and $\succeq_A$, $\succeq_B$, and $\succeq_C$, satisfy weak monotonicity.*

(ii) *There are vNM utility functions u, v, and w, for $\succeq_A$, $\succeq_B$, and $\succeq_C$, respectively, and positive constants k_u and k_v, such that $w(a, b) = k_u u(a) + k_v v(b)$ for all $(a, b) \in C$.*

---

[7]So $\ell \sim_C m$ means $[\ell \succeq_C m$ and $m \succeq_C \ell]$.

[8]In (11.13), $\succ_A$ denotes the asymmetric part of $\succeq_A$: $\ell \succ_A m \Leftrightarrow [\ell \succeq_A m$ and not $m \succeq_A \ell]$.

Proof The implication (ii) $\Rightarrow$ (i) is straightforward. For (i) $\Rightarrow$ (ii), let $a°$ and $b°$ be as in (11.13), and take $\hat{a} \in A$ and $\hat{b} \in B$ such that $\hat{a} \not\sim_A a°$ and $\hat{b} \not\sim_B b°$. Choose vNM utility functions u, v, and w, for $\succeq_A$, $\succeq_B$, and $\succeq_C$, respectively, such that $u(a°) = v(b°) = w(a°, b°) = 0$ (cf. theorem 11.2). By weak monotonicity, $w(\hat{a}, b°)$ and $u(\hat{a})$ must have the same sign, so $k_u := w(\hat{a}, b°)u(\hat{a})^{-1} > 0$. Also, $k_v := w(a°, \hat{b})v(\hat{b})^{-1} > 0$. By additive independence of $\succeq_C$, for every $(a, b) \in C$, it holds that $\frac{1}{2}w(a, b) + \frac{1}{2}w(a°, b°) = \frac{1}{2}w(a, b°) + \frac{1}{2}w(a°, b)$, hence $w(a, b) = w(a, b°) + w(a°, b)$.

The proof is complete if we show that: $w(a, b°) = k_u u(a)$ and $w(a°, b) = k_v v(b)$ for every $a \in A$, $b \in B$. We only prove the first equality. Let $a \in A$, and distinguish three cases: $(a°, b°) \succeq_C (a, b°)$ and $(\hat{a}, b°) \succeq_C (a, b°)$; $(a, b°) \succeq_C (\hat{a}, b°)$ and $(a, b°) \succeq_C (a°, b°)$; $(a, b°) \sim_C (\mu; (\hat{a}, b°), (1 - \mu); (a°, b°))$ for a (unique) $0 < \mu < 1$ (where such a μ exists since $\succeq_C$ is representable by w). Only the third case is considered, the other ones are similar. In that third case, $(a, b°) \sim_C (\mu; (\hat{a}, b°), (1 - \mu); (a°, b°))$ implies $a \sim_A (\mu; \hat{a}, (1 - \mu); a°)$ by weak monotonicity, hence $u(a) = \mu u(\hat{a})$. So $w(a, b°) = \mu w(\hat{a}, b°) = u(a)u(\hat{a})^{-1}w(\hat{a}, b°) = k_u u(a)$, which is what had to be proved. $\qquad\square$

Remark 11.15 Of course, in view of theorem 11.2, u and v in theorem 11.14 can always be rescaled such that $k_u = k_v = 1$. If, in particular, $u(\hat{a}) = v(\hat{b})$ and $(\hat{a}, b°) \sim_C (a°, \hat{b})$ in the proof of theorem 11.14, then $k_u = k_v$, and one may set $k_u = k_v = 1$.

Theorem 11.14 and remark 11.15 are used in section 5.3.

11.6 Multiplicative utility

As in section 11.5, let A, B, and $C := A \times B$, be sets of alternatives, with corresponding lottery sets $\mathcal{L}(A)$, $\mathcal{L}(B)$ and $\mathcal{L}(C)$, respectively, and preference relations $\succeq_A$, $\succeq_B$, and $\succeq_C$, on these lottery sets. In this section, necessary and sufficient conditions are given under which a vNM utility function for $\succeq_C$ can be written as a (multiplicative) product of vNM utility functions for $\succeq_A$ and $\succeq_B$. Again, this result is a variation on a result obtained by Keeney and Raiffa (1976), namely their Theorem 5.2 (see also their subsection 5.4.3); it was also presented, in a slightly different form, by Binmore (1987a), and it is applied in subsection 2.4.3.

Let $A, B, C, \ldots$ be as in the first paragraph. Assume that $\succeq_A$, $\succeq_B$, and $\succeq_C$, are representable by vNM utility functions. Two conditions for $\succeq_A$, $\succeq_B$, and $\succeq_C$ are formulated.

If $(p_i; a^i)_{i=1}^n \sim_A (q_i; \tilde{a}^i)_{i=1}^m$ in $\mathcal{L}(A)$, and
$(r_i; b^i)_{i=1}^k \sim_B (s_i; \tilde{b}^i)_{i=1}^\ell$ in $\mathcal{L}(B)$, then
$(p_i r_j; (a^i, b^j))_{i=1, \, j=1}^{n, \, k} \sim_C (q_i s_j; (\tilde{a}^i, \tilde{b}^j))_{i=1, \, j=1}^{m, \, \ell}$ in $\mathcal{L}(C)$.
(*Weak utility independence*)   (11.14)

Condition (11.14) is a weaker version of the "Utility Independence" property in Keeney and Raiffa (1976, p. 224).

There exist $\bar{a} \in A$ and $\bar{b} \in B$ such that, for all $a, a' \in A$ and $b, b' \in B$:
$a \succeq_A \bar{a}$, $b \succeq_B \bar{b}$, $(\bar{a}, b) \sim_C (\bar{a}, b')$, and $(a, \bar{b}) \sim_C (a', \bar{b})$. Furthermore there exist $a^* \in A$ and $b^* \in B$ such that $a^* \succ_A \bar{a}$, $b^* \succ_B \bar{b}$, and
$(a^*, b^*) \succ_C (\bar{a}, \bar{b})$.   (11.15)

The first part of (11.15) requires that A and B both have "worst" alternatives, which make all combinations in C in which they occur, equivalent. The "furthermore" part of (11.15) serves to avoid triviality.

With these conditions, the following theorem can be stated and proved.

Theorem 11.16 *With notations as in the first paragraph of this section, and under the assumption of the second paragraph, the following two statements are equivalent.*

(i) (11.14) and (11.15) hold.

(ii) There exist vNM utility functions w, u, and v, for $\succeq_C$, $\succeq_A$, and $\succeq_B$, respectively, and $\overline{a}, a^* \in A$, $\overline{b}, b^* \in B$, such that for all $a \in A$ and $b \in B$: $w(a,b) = u(a)v(b) \geq 0$, $u(\overline{a}) = v(\overline{b}) = 0$, $u(a^*) > 0$, $v(b^*) > 0$.

Proof The implication (ii) $\Rightarrow$ (i) is straightforward. For (i) $\Rightarrow$ (ii), let $\overline{a}, \overline{b}, a^*, b^*$ be as in (11.15). Let w, u, v be vNM utility functions for $\succeq_C$, $\succeq_A$, $\succeq_B$, such that: $u(\overline{a}) = v(\overline{b}) = w(\overline{a}, \overline{b}) = 0$, and $w(a^*, b^*) = u(a^*)v(b^*) > 0$. Let $a \in A$, $b \in B$. The proof is finished if we show that $w(a,b) = u(a)v(b)$.

First consider $w(a, b^*)$. There are two cases: $a \sim_A (\mu; \overline{a}, (1-\mu); a^*)$ for some $0 \leq \mu \leq 1$; and $a^* \sim_A (\mu; \overline{a}, (1-\mu); a)$ for some $0 < \mu < 1$. Only consider the first case, the second one is similar. In that case, by (11.14): $w(a, b^*) = \mu w(\overline{a}, b^*) + (1-\mu)w(a^*, b^*)$, so, in view of (11.15), $w(a, b^*) = (1-\mu)w(a^*, b^*) = (1-\mu)u(a^*)v(b^*) = u(a)v(b^*)$.

Finally, consider $w(a,b)$. Again: either $b \sim_B (\mu; \overline{b}, (1-\mu); b^*)$ for some $0 \leq \mu \leq 1$; or $b^* \sim_B (\mu; \overline{b}, (1-\mu); b)$ for some $0 < \mu < 1$. And again, only consider the first case. Then, by (11.14), $w(a,b) = \mu w(a, \overline{b}) + (1-\mu)w(a, b^*)$, so, in view of (11.15), $w(a,b) = (1-\mu)w(a, b^*) = (1-\mu)u(a)v(b^*) = u(a)v(b)$. $\square$

References

Aliprantis, C.D., and O. Burkinshaw (1981): *Principles of real analysis*. Edward Arnold, London.

Anbar, D., and E. Kalai (1978): "A one-shot bargaining problem", *International Journal of Game Theory*, 7, 13–18.

Arrow, K.J. (1951): *Social choice and individual values*. Wiley, New York.

Arrow, K.J. (1959): "Rational choice functions and orderings", *Economica*, 26, 121–127.

Arrow, K.J. (1971): *Essays in the theory of risk bearing*. Markham, Chicago, Illinois.

Arrow, K.J., and A.C. Enthoven (1961): "Quasi-concave programming", *Econometrica*, 29.

Aumann, R.J. (1967): "A survey of cooperative games without sidepayments", in: M. Shubik (ed.), *Essays in mathematical economics, in honor of Oskar Morgenstern*. Princeton University Press, Princeton, 3–27.

Aumann, R.J. (1985a): "An axiomatization of the non-transferable utility value", *Econometrica*, 53, 599–612.

Aumann, R.J. (1985b): "On the non-transferable utility value: a comment on the Roth-Shafer examples", *Econometrica*, 53, 667–677.

Aumann, R.J. (1986): "Rejoinder", *Econometrica*, 54, 985–989.

Aumann, R.J. (1987a): "Correlated equilibrium as an expression of Bayesian rationality", *Econometrica*, 55, 1–18.

Aumann, R.J. (1987b): "Value, symmetry, and equal treatment: a comment on Scafuri and Yannelis", *Econometrica*, 55, 1461–1464.

Aumann, R.J., and M. Kurz (1977): "Power and taxes", *Econometrica*, 45, 1137–1160.

Aumann, R.J., and M. Maschler (1985): "Game theoretic analysis of a bankruptcy problem from the Talmud", *Journal of Economic Theory*, 36, 195–213.

Battinelli, A., P. Tani, and A. Villanacci (1986): "Harsanyi's axiomatic derivation of Zeuthen's principle: a critical examination", Universita degli studi di Firenze.

Billera, L.J., and R.E. Bixby (1973): "A characterization of Pareto surfaces", *Proceedings of the American Mathematical Society*, 41, 261–267.

Binmore, K.G. (1987a): "Nash bargaining theory", in: Binmore, K.G., and P. Dasgupta (eds.), *The economics of bargaining*. Basil Blackwell, Oxford, 27–46.

Binmore, K.G. (1987b): "Perfect equilibria in bargaining models", in: Binmore, K.G., and P. Dasgupta (eds.), *The economics of bargaining*. Basil Blackwell, Oxford, 77–105.

Binmore, K., and P. Dasgupta, eds. (1987): *The economics of bargaining*. Basil Blackwell, Oxford.

Binmore, K., A. Rubinstein, and A. Wolinsky (1986): "The Nash bargaining solution in economic modelling", *Rand Journal of Economics*, 17, 176–188.

Bossert, W. (1991): "Disagreement point monotonicity, transfer responsiveness, and the egalitarian bargaining solution", Department of Economics, University of Waterloo, Ontario.

Bossert, W. (1992): "Rationalizable two-person bargaining solutions", Department of Economics, University of Waterloo, Waterloo, Ontario.

Bradley, G., and M. Shubik (1974): "A note on the shape of the Pareto optimal surface", *Journal of Economic Theory*, 18, 580–538.

Buch, I., and Y. Tauman (1989): "Bargaining with a ruler", Ohio State University and Tel-Aviv University.

Butrim, B.I. (1976): "Modified solution of the bargaining problem", *Zh. vychisl. Mat. mat. Fiz.*, 16, 340–350.

Butrim, B.I. (1978): "*n*-Person games with an essential set of criteria", *Zh. vychisl. Mat. mat. Fiz.*, 18, 62–72.

Cayseele, P. van (1987): "Regulation and international innovative activities in the pharmaceutical industry", Nieuwe Reeks, Katholieke Universiteit Leuven, 63.

Christensen, F. (1989): "Two-person super-additive bargaining with interpersonal comparisons", Institute of Economics, University of Copenhagen.

Chun, Y. (1988a): "The equal-loss principle for bargaining problems", *Economics Letters*, 26, 103–106.

Chun, Y. (1988b): "Nash solution and timing of bargaining", *Economics Letters*, 28, 27–31.

Chun, Y. (1989): "Lexicographic egalitarian solution and uncertainty in the disagreement point", *ZOR-Methods and Models of Operations Research*, 33, 259–266.

Chun, Y., and H. Peters (1988): "The lexicographic egalitarian solution", *Cahiers du CERO*, 30, 149–156.

Chun, Y., and H. Peters (1989): "Lexicographic monotone path solutions", *Operations Research Spektrum*, 11, 43–47.

Chun, Y., and H. Peters (1991): "The lexicographic equal-loss solution", *Mathematical Social Sciences*, 22, 151–161.

Chun, Y., and W. Thomson (1988): "Monotonicity properties of bargaining solutions when applied to economics", *Mathematical Social Sciences*, 15, 11–27.

Chun, Y., and W. Thomson (1990a): "Nash solution and uncertain disagreement points", *Games and Economic Behavior*, 2, 213–223.

Chun, Y., and W. Thomson (1990b): "Bargaining with uncertain disagreement points", *Econometrica*, 58, 951–959.

Chun, Y., and W. Thomson (1990c): "Egalitarian solutions and uncertain disagreement points", *Economics Letters*, 33, 29–33.

Crawford, V.P., and H.R. Varian (1979): "Distortion of preferences and the Nash theory of bargaining", *Economics Letters*, 3, 203–206.

Crott, H.W. (1971): "Experimentelle Untersuchung zum Verhandlungsverhalten in kooperativen Spielen", *Zeitschrift für Sozialpsychologie*, 2, 61–74.

Damme, E. van (1986): "The Nash bargaining solution is optimal", *Journal of Economic Theory*, 38, 78–100.

Damme, E. van (1987): *Stability and perfection of Nash equilibria*. Springer Verlag, Berlin Heidelberg.

Debreu, G. (1959): *Theory of value*. Wiley, New York.

Derks, J. (1991): *On polyhedral cones of cooperative games*. Department of Mathematics, Maastricht, The Netherlands.

Drèze, J.H. (1982): "The marginal utility of income does not increase", CORE Discussion Series.

Driessen, T.S.H. (1991): "A survey of consistency properties in cooperative game theory", *SIAM Review*, 33, 43–59.

Dyer, J.S., and R.K. Sarin (1982): "Relative risk aversion", *Management Science*, 28, 875–886.

Eichhorn, W. (1978): *Functional equations in economics*. Addison-Wesley, Reading, MA.

Fishburn, P.C. (1965): "Independence in utility theory with whole product sets", *Operations Research*, 13, 28–45.

Freimer, M., and P.L. Yu (1976): "Some new results on compromise solutions for group decision problems", *Management Science*, 22, 688–693.

Friedman, J.W. (1986): *Game theory with applications to economics*. Oxford University Press, Oxford.

Furth, D. (1990): "Solving bargaining games by differential equations", *Mathematics of Operations Research*, 15, 724–735.

Gale, D. (1960): "A note on revealed preference", *Economica*, 27, 348–354.

Grout, P.A. (1984): "Investment and wages in the absence of binding contracts: a Nash bargaining approach", *Econometrica*, 52, 449–460.

Hanoch, G. (1977): "Risk aversion and consumer preferences", *Econometrica*, 45, 413–426.

Harsanyi, J.C. (1956): "Approaches to the bargaining problem before and after the theory of games: a critical discussion of Zeuthen's, Hick's, and Nash's theories", *Econometrica*, 24, 144–157.

Harsanyi, J.C. (1959): "A bargaining model for the cooperative *n*-person game", *Annals of Mathematics Studies*, Princeton University Press, Princeton, 40, 325–355.

Harsanyi, J.C. (1963): "A simplified bargaining model for the *n*-person cooperative game", *International Economic Review*, 4, 194–220.

Harsanyi, J.C. (1980): "Comments on Roth's paper, "Values for games without sidepayments" ", *Econometrica*, 48, 477.

Harsanyi, J.C., and R. Selten (1972): "A generalized Nash solution for two-person bargaining games with incomplete information", *Management Science*, 18, 80–106.

Hart, S. (1985a): "Axiomatic approaches to coalitional bargaining", in: A.E. Roth (ed.), *Game-theoretic Models of Bargaining*. Cambridge University Press, Cambridge, 305–319.

Hart, S. (1985b): "An axiomatization of Harsanyi's nontransferable utility solution", *Econometrica*, 53, 1295–1313.

Hart, S. (1985c): "Nontransferable utility games and markets: some examples and the Harsanyi solution", *Econometrica*, 53, 1445–1450.

Hart, S., and A. Mas-Colell (1989): "Potential, value, and consistency", *Econometrica*, 57, 589–614.

Hart, S., and A. Mas-Colell (1991): "*N*-person non-cooperative bargaining", Harvard University.

Hausman, J.A. (1985): "The econometrics of nonlinear budget sets", *Econometrica*, 53, 1255–1282.

Herrero, M.J. (1989): "The Nash program: non-convex bargaining problems", *Journal of Economic Theory*, 49, 266–277.

Herstein, I.N., and J. Milnor (1953): "An axiomatic approach to measurable utility", *Econometrica*, 21, 291–297.

Hildenbrand, W., and A.P. Kirman (1976): *Introduction to equilibrium analysis*. North-Holland, Amsterdam.

Hirsch, M.W., and S. Smale (1974): *Differential equations, dynamical systems, and linear algebra*. Academic Press, San Diego.

Houthakker, H.S. (1950): "Revealed preference and the utility function", *Economica*, 17, 159–174.

Hurwicz, L., and M.K. Richter (1971): "Revealed preference without demand continuity assumptions", in: Chipman, J.S., L. Hurwicz, M.K. Richter, and H.F. Sonnenschein (eds.), *Preferences, utilities, and demand*. Harcourt Brace Yovanovich, New York.

Imai, H. (1983a): "On Harsanyi's solution", *International Journal of Game Theory*, 12, 161–179.

Imai, H. (1983): "Individual monotonicity and lexicographic maxmin solution", *Econometrica*, 51, 389–401, 1603.

Isbell, J.R. (1960): "A modification of Harsanyi's bargaining model", *Bulletin of the American Mathematical Society*, 66, 70–73.

Jaffray, J.-Y. (1975): "Semicontinuous extension of a partial order", *Journal of Mathematical Economics*, 2, 395–406.

Jansen, M.J.M., and S.H. Tijs (1983): "Continuity of bargaining solutions", *International Journal of Game Theory*, 12, 91–105.

Kalai, E. (1977a): "Nonsymmetric Nash solutions and replications of 2-person bargaining", *International Journal of Game Theory*, 6, 129–133.

Kalai, E. (1977b): "Proportional solutions to bargaining situations: interpersonal utility comparisons", *Econometrica*, 45, 1623–1630.

Kalai, E., and D. Samet (1985): "Monotonic solutions to general cooperative games", *Econometrica*, 53, 307–327.

Kalai, E., and D. Samet (1987): "On weighted Shapley values", *International Journal of Game Theory*, 16, 205–222.

Kalai, E., and M. Smorodinsky (1975): "Other solutions to Nash's bargaining problem", *Econometrica*, 43, 513–518.

Kaneko, M. (1980): "An extension of the Nash bargaining problem and the Nash social welfare function", *Theory and Decision*, 12, 135–148.

Kannai, Y. (1977): "Concavifiability and constructions of concave utility functions", *Journal of Mathematical Economics*, 4, 1–56.

Keeney, R.L., and H. Raiffa (1976): *Decisions with multiple objectives: preferences and value tradeoffs*. Wiley, New York.

Kern, R. (1981): "Bargaining solutions and their independence from irrelevant alternatives", *Methods of Operations Research*, 41, 89–92.

Kihlstrom, R., A. Mas-Colell, and H. Sonnenschein (1976): "The demand theory of the weak axiom of revealed preference", *Econometrica*, 44, 971–978.

Kihlstrom, R.E., and L.J. Mirman (1974): "Risk aversion with many commodities", *Journal of Economic Theory*, 8, 361–388.

Kihlstrom, R.E., A.E. Roth, and D. Schmeidler (1981): "Risk aversion and solutions to Nash's bargaining problem", in: O. Moeschlin and D. Pallaschke (eds.), *Game Theory and Mathematical Economics*. North Holland, Amsterdam.

Kim, T. (1987): "Intransitive indifference and revealed preference", *Econometrica*, 55, 95–115.

Klemisch-Ahlert, M. (1988): "A note on the bargaining solution of Gauthier", Fachbereich Wirtschaftswissenschaften, Universität Osnabrück.

Klemisch-Ahlert, M. (1991): *Verhandlungslösungen als soziale Entscheidungsmechanismen*. Anton Hain, Frankfurt.

Koster, R. de, H. Peters, S. Tijs, and P. Wakker (1983): "Risk sensitivity, independence of irrelevant alternatives and continuity of bargaining solutions", *Mathematical Social Sciences*, 4, 295–300.

Krishna, V., and R. Serrano (1990): "Multilateral bargaining", Harvard Business School.

Lahiri, S. (1990): "Threat bargaining problems with incomplete information", Indian Institute of Management, Ahmedabad.

Lemaire, J. (1973): "A new value for games without transferable utilities", *International Journal of Game Theory*, 2, 205–213.

Lensberg, T. (1987): "Stability and collective rationality", *Econometrica*, 55, 935–961.

Lensberg, T. (1988): "Stability and the Nash solution", *Journal of Economic Theory*, 45, 330–341.

Lensberg, T., and W. Thomson (1988): "Characterizing the Nash bargaining solution without Pareto optimality", *Social Choice and Welfare*, 5, 247–259.

Livne, Z. (1987): "Bargaining over the division of a shrinking pie: an axiomatic approach", *International Journal of Game Theory*, 16, 223–242.

Livne, Z. (1988): "The bargaining problem with an uncertain conflict outcome", *Mathematical Social Sciences*, 15, 287–302.

Livne, Z. (1989a): "Axiomatic characterizations of the Raiffa and the Kalai-Smorodinsky solutions to the bargaining problem", *Operations Research*, 37, 972–980.

Livne, Z. (1989b): "On the status quo sets induced by the Raiffa solution to the two-person bargaining problem", *Mathematics of Operations Research*, 14, 688–692.

Lucchetti, R., F. Patrone, S.H. Tijs, and A. Torre (1986): "Continuity properties of Shapley NTU-value and Harsanyi value and an existence theorem", Department of Mathematics, Nijmegen.

Luce, R.D. (1979): *Individual choice behavior*. Greenwood Press, Westport, Connecticut.

Luce, R.D., and H. Raiffa (1957): *Games and decisions: introduction and critical survey*. Wiley, New York.

Maschler, M., G. Owen and B. Peleg (1988): "Paths leading to the Nash set", in: A.E. Roth (ed.), *The Shapley Value: Essays in Honor of Lloyd S. Shapley*. Cambridge University Press, 321–330.

Maschler, M., and M.A. Perles (1981): "The present status of the super-additive solution", in: *Essays in Game Theory and Mathematical Economics*. Bibliographisches Institut, Mannheim, 103–110.

Mayberry, J.P., J.F. Nash, and M. Shubik (1953): "Comparison of treatments in a duopoly situation", *Econometrica*, 21, 141–154.

McDonald, I.M., and R.M. Solow (1981): "Wage bargaining and employment", *American Economic Review*, 71, 896–908.

Moulin, H. (1984): "Implementing the Kalai-Smorodinsky bargaining solution", *Journal of Economic Theory*, 33, 32–45.

Moulin, H. (1990): "Cores and large cores when population varies", *International Journal of Game Theory*, 19, 219–232.

Myerson, R. (1977): "Two-person bargaining problems and comparable utility", *Econometrica*, 45, 1631–1637.

Myerson, R. (1979): "Incentive compatibility and the bargaining problem", *Econometrica*, 47, 61–73.

Myerson, R. (1980): "Conference structures and fair allocation rules", *International Journal of Game Theory*, 9, 169–182.

Myerson, R. (1981): "Utilitarianism, egalitarianism, and the timing effect in social choice problems", *Econometrica*, 49, 883–897.

Myerson, R. (1984): "Two-person bargaining problems with incomplete information", *Econometrica*, 52, 461–487.

Nakayama, M. (1986): "Justifiable beliefs in the Nash bargaining problem", Faculty of Economics, Toyama University.

Nash, J.F. (1950): "The bargaining problem", *Econometrica*, 18, 155–162.

Nash, J.F. (1951): "Non-cooperative games", *Annals of Mathematics*, 54, 286–295.

Nash, J.F. (1953): "Two-person cooperative games", *Econometrica*, 21, 128–140.

Neumann, J. von, and O. Morgenstern (1944): *Theory of games and economic behavior*. Princeton University Press, Princeton.

Neumann, J. von, and O. Morgenstern (1947): *Theory of games and economic behavior*. Princeton University Press, Princeton (2nd ed.).

Nielsen, L.T. (1983): "Ordinal interpersonal comparisons in bargaining", *Econometrica*, 51, 219–221.

Nielsen, L.T. (1984): "Risk sensitivity in bargaining with many participants", *Journal of Economic Theory*, 32, 371–376.

Nielsen, L.T. (1988): "Comparative risk aversion", *Economics Letters*, 27, 321–325.

Nydegger, R., and G. Owen (1975): "Two-person bargaining: an experimental test of the Nash axioms", *International Journal of Game Theory*, 3, 239–249.

O'Neill, B. (1982): "A problem of rights arbitration from the Talmud", *Mathematical social sciences*, 2, 345–371.

Osborne, D.K. (1976): "Irrelevant alternatives and social welfare", *Econometrica*, 44, 1001–1015.

Osborne, M.J., and A. Rubinstein (1990): *Bargaining and markets*. Academic Press, San Diego.

Owen, G. (1972): "Values of games without sidepayments", *International Journal of Game Theory*, 1, 95–109.

Perles, M.A. (1982): "Non-existence of super-additive solutions for 3-person games", *International Journal of Game Theory*, 11, 151–161.

Perles, M.A., and M. Maschler (1981): "The super-additive solution for the Nash bargaining game", *International Journal of Game Theory*, 10, 163–193.

Peters, H. (1985): "A note on additive utility and bargaining", *Economics Letters*, 17, 219–222.

Peters, H. (1986a): *Bargaining game theory*. University of Nijmegen.

Peters, H. (1986b): "Characterizations of bargaining solutions by properties of their status quo sets", University of Limburg, Maastricht, The Netherlands.

Peters, H. (1986c): "Simultaneity of issues and additivity in bargaining", *Econometrica*, 54, 153–169.

Peters, H. (1987): "Some axiomatic aspects of bargaining", in: Paelinck, Vossen (eds.), *Axiomatics and Pragmatics of Conflict Analysis*. Gower Publishing Company, Aldershot, 112–141.

Peters, H. (1992a): "A criterion for comparing strength of preference with an application to bargaining", *Operations Research* (forthcoming).

Peters, H. (1992): "Self-optimality and efficiency", *Games and Economic Behavior* (forthcoming).

Peters, H., and E. van Damme (1991): "Characterizing the Nash and Raiffa bargaining solutions by disagreement point axioms", *Mathematics of Operations Research*, 16, 447–461.

Peters, H., and S. Tijs (1981): "Risk sensitivity of bargaining solutions", *Methods of Operations Research*, 44, 409–420.

Peters, H., and S. Tijs (1983): "Probabilistic bargaining solutions", in: *Operations Research Proceedings DGOR*. Springer Verlag, Berlin, 548–556.

Peters, H., and S. Tijs (1984): "Individually monotonic bargaining solutions for n-person bargaining games", *Methods of Operations Research*, 51, 377–384.

Peters, H., and S. Tijs (1985a): "Characterization of all individually monotonic bargaining solutions", *International Journal of Game Theory*, 14, 219–228.

Peters, H., and S. Tijs (1985b): "Risk aversion in n-person bargaining", *Theory and Decision*, 18, 47–72.

Peters, H., S. Tijs, and R. de Koster (1983): "Solutions and multisolutions for bargaining games", *Methods of Operations Research*, 46, 465–476.

Peters, H., S.H. Tijs, and J. Zarzuelo (1991): "Consistency and implementation of the Kalai-Smorodinsky bargaining solution", University of Limburg, Maastricht, The Netherlands.

Peters, H., and P. Wakker (1987): "Convex functions on nonconvex domains", *Economics Letters*, 22, 251–255.

Peters, H., and P. Wakker (1991a): "Independence of irrelevant alternatives and revealed group preferences", *Econometrica*, 59, 1787–1801.

Peters, H., and P. Wakker (1991b): "WARP does not imply SARP for more than two commodities", University of Limburg, Maastricht, The Netherlands.

Pollak, R.A. (1990): "Distinguished fellow: Houthakker's contributions to economics", *Journal of Economic Perspectives*, 4, 141–156.

Pratt, J.W. (1964): "Risk aversion in the small and in the large", *Econometrica*, 32, 122–136.

Raiffa, H. (1953): "Arbitration schemes for generalized two-person games", *Annals of Mathematics Studies*, 28, 361–387.

Rawls, J. (1971): *A theory of justice*. Harvard University Press, Cambridge, MA.

Richter, M.K. (1971): "Rational choice", in: Chipman, J.S., L. Hurwicz, M.K. Richter, and H.F. Sonnenschein (eds.), *Preferences, utilities, and demand*. Harcourt Brace Yovanovich, New York.

Rockafellar, R.T. (1970): *Convex analysis*. Princeton University Press, Princeton, NJ.

Roemer, J. (1988): "Axiomatic bargaining theory on economic environments", *Journal of Economic Theory*, 45, 1–31.

Rose, H. (1958): "Consistency of preference: the two-commodity case", *Review of Economic Studies*, 25, 124–125.

Rosenmuller, J. (1981): "Values of non-sidepayment games and their application in the theory of public goods", in: *Essays in Game Theory and Mathematical Economics in Honor of Oskar Morgenstern*. Bibliographisches Institut, Mannheim, 111–129.

Roth, A.E. (1977a): "Individual rationality and Nash's solution to the bargaining problem", *Mathematics of Operations Research*, 2, 64–65.

Roth, A.E. (1977b): "Bargaining ability, the utility of playing a game, and models of coalition formation", *Journal of Mathematical Psychology*, 16, 153–160.

Roth, A.E. (1977c): "Independence of irrelevant alternatives, and solutions to Nash's bargaining problem", *Journal of Economic Theory*, 16, 247–251.

Roth, A.E. (1978): "The Nash solution and the utility of bargaining", *Econometrica*, 46, 587–594.

Roth, A.E. (1979a): *Axiomatic models of bargaining*. Springer Verlag, Berlin Heidelberg New York.

Roth, A.E. (1979b): "Proportional solutions to the bargaining problem", *Econometrica*, 47, 775–778.

Roth, A.E. (1980): "Values for games without sidepayments: some difficulties with current concepts", *Econometrica*, 48, 457–465.

Roth, A.E. (1986): "On the non-transferable utility value: a reply to Aumann", *Econometrica*, 54, 981–984.

Roth, A.E., and M.W.K. Malouf (1979): "Game-theoretic models and the role of information in bargaining", *Psychological Review*, 86, 574–594.

Roth, A.E., and U.G. Rothblum (1982): "Risk aversion and Nash's solution for bargaining games with risky outcomes", *Econometrica*, 50, 639–647.

Rubinstein, A. (1982): "Perfect equilibrium in a bargaining model", *Econometrica*, 50, 97–109.

Rubinstein, A., Z. Safra, and W. Thomson (1990): "On the interpretation of the Nash bargaining solution and its extension to non-expected utility preference", Tel Aviv University.

Safra, Z., L. Zhou, and I. Zilcha (1990): "Risk aversion in the Nash bargaining problem with risky outcomes and risky disagreement points", *Econometrica*, 58, 961–965.

Salonen, H. (1985): "A solution for two-person bargaining problems", *Social Choice and Welfare*, 2, 139–146.

Samuelson, P. (1938): "A note on the pure theory of consumers behavior", *Economica*, 5, 61–67, 353–354.

Samuelson, P. (1948): "Consumption theory in terms of revealed preference", *Economica*, 15, 243–253.

Scafuri, A.J., and N.C. Yannelis (1984): "Non-symmetric cardinal value allocations", *Econometrica*, 52, 1365–1368.

Schmeidler, D. (1969): "The nucleolus of a characteristic function game", *SIAM Journal of Applied Mathematics*, 17, 1163–1170.

Selten, R. (1965): "Spieltheoretische Behandlung eines Oligopolmodells mit Nachfragetragheit", *Zeitschrift fur die gesammte Staatswissenschaft*, 121, 301–324.

Sen, A.K. (1970): *Collective choice and social welfare*. Holden-Day, San Francisco.

Sen, A.K. (1971): "Choice functions and revealed preference", *Review of Economic Studies*, 38, 307–317.

Shafer, W. (1977): "Revealed preference cycles and the Slutsky matrix", *Journal of Economic Theory*, 16, 293–309.

Shafer, W. (1980): "On the existence and interpretation of value allocation", *Econometrica*, 48, 467–476.

Shaked, A., and J. Sutton (1984): "Unvoluntary unemployment as a perfect equilibrium in a bargaining model", *Econometrica*, 52, 1351–1364.

Shapley, L.S. (1953): "A value for *n*-person games", in: H. Kuhn, A.W. Tucker (eds.), *Contributions to the Theory of Games*, Princeton University Press, Princeton, 307–317.

Shapley, L.S. (1969): "Utility comparison and the theory of games", in: G.Th. Guilbaud (ed.), *La Décision*. Editions du CNRS, Paris.

Shapley, L.S. (1975): "Cardinal utility from intensity comparison", RAND Publication R-1683-PR.

Shubik, M. (1982): *Game theory in the social sciences: concepts and solutions*. MIT Press, Cambridge, MA.

Sobel, J. (1981): "Distortion of utilities and the bargaining problem", *Econometrica*, 49, 597–619.

Sprumont, Y. (1990): "Population monotonic allocation schemes for cooperative games with transferable utility", *Games and Economic Behavior*, 2, 378–394.

Sutton, J. (1985): "Non-cooperative bargaining theory: an introduction", *Review of Economic Studies*, 53, 709–724.

Svejnar, J. (1986): "Bargaining power, fear of disagreement, and wage settlements: theory and evidence from U.S. industry", *Econometrica*, 54, 1055–1078.

Thomson, W. (1980): "Two characterizations of the Raiffa solution", *Economics Letters*, 6, 225–231.

Thomson, W. (1981a): "Independence of irrelevant expansions", *International Journal of Game Theory*, 10, 107–114.

Thomson, W. (1981b): "A class of solutions to bargaining problems", *Journal of Economic Theory*, 25, 431–441.

Thomson, W. (1981c): "Nash's bargaining solution and utilitarian choice rules", *Econometrica*, 49, 535–538.

Thomson, W. (1983a): "The fair division of a fixed supply among a growing population", *Mathematics of Operations Research*, 8, 319–326.

Thomson, W. (1983b): "Problems of fair division and the egalitarian solution", *Journal of Economic Theory*, 31, 211–226.

Thomson, W. (1986): "Replication invariance of bargaining solutions", *International Journal of Game Theory*, 15, 59–63.

Thomson, W. (1987): "Monotonicity of bargaining solutions with respect to the disagreement point", *Journal of Economic Theory*, 42, 50–58.

Thomson, W. (1990): "The consistency principle", in: Ichiishi, T., A. Neyman, and Y. Tauman (eds.), *Game Theory and Applications*. Academic Press, San Diego, 187–215.

Thomson. W. (1992): *Bargaining theory: the axiomatic approach*. Academic Press (forthcoming).

Thomson, W., and T. Lensberg (1989): *Axiomatic theory of bargaining with a variable number of agents*. Cambridge University Press, Cambridge.

Thomson, W., and R.B. Myerson (1980): "Monotonicity and independence axioms", *International Journal of Game Theory*, 9, 37–49.

Tijs, S.H., and M.J.M. Jansen (1982): "On the existence of values for arbitration games", *International Journal of Game Theory*, 11, 87–104.

Tijs, S., and H. Peters (1985): "Risk sensitivity and related properties for bargaining solutions", in: A.E. Roth (ed.), *Game Theoretic Models of Bargaining*. Cambridge University Press, 215–231.

Varian, H.R. (1982): "The nonparametric approach to demand analysis", *Econometrica*, 50, 945–973.

Varian, H.R. (1984): *Microeconomic analysis*. Norton, New York.

Ville, J. (1946): "Sur les conditions d'existence d'une ophélimité totale et d'un indice du niveau des prix", *Annales de l'Université de Lyon*, 32–39.

Wakker, P. (1988): "The algebraic versus the topological approach to additive representations", Dept. of Math. Psychology, Nijmegen University.

Wakker, P. (1989a): "A graph-theoretic approach to revealed preference", *Methodology and Science*, 22, 53–66.

Wakker, P. (1989b): *Additive representations of preferences: a new foundation of decision analysis*. Kluwer Academic Publishers, Dordrecht.

Wakker, P., H. Peters, and T. van Riel (1985): "Comparisons of risk aversion, with an application to bargaining", *Methods of Operations Research*, 54, 307–320.

Weddepohl, H.N. (1970): *Axiomatic choice models*. Wolters-Noordhoff, Groningen.

Winter, E. (1991): "On non-transferable utility games with coalition structure", *International Journal of Game Theory*, 20, 53–63.

Yaari, M.E. (1969): "Some remarks on measures of risk aversion and on their uses", *Journal of Economic Theory*, 1, 315–329.

Young, H.P. (1988): "Consistent solutions to the bargaining problem", The Brookings Institution, Washington DC.

Yu, P.L. (1973): "A class of solutions for group decision problems", *Management Science*, 19, 936–946.

Zeuthen, F. (1930): *Problems of monopoly and economic warfare*. G. Routledge, London.

Author index

Subject index

Notation and symbols

A. General

Notation	(Sub)section		Notation	(Sub)section
$\leq, <, \geq, >$	1.2		int	2.4.2
$\mathbb{R}^N, \mathbb{R}^N_+, \mathbb{R}^N_{++}$	1.2		relint	4.5.2
$\mathbb{Q}^N_{++}$	3.5		cl	4.2

B. Games and classes of games

Notation	(Sub)section		Notation	(Sub)section
$\tilde{\mathcal{B}}^N, \overline{\mathcal{B}}^N, \mathcal{B}^N$	1.2		$\mathcal{G}^N, \tilde{\mathcal{G}}^N, \mathcal{G}^N_{TU}$	10.2
$\tilde{\mathcal{B}}^N_0, \overline{\mathcal{B}}^N_0, \mathcal{B}^N_0$	2.4.1			
			$\mathcal{I}^N$	4.2
$\tilde{\mathcal{C}}^N, \overline{\mathcal{C}}^N, \mathcal{C}^N$	1.2			
$\tilde{\mathcal{C}}^N_0, \overline{\mathcal{C}}^N_0, \mathcal{C}^N_0$	2.4.1			
$\tilde{\mathcal{B}}, \ldots, \mathcal{C}_0$	1.2		$(N,V), (N,v)$	10.2
$\overline{\mathcal{C}}^N_*$ etc.	2.4.5		$\mathcal{P}\mathcal{S}^N_0$	6.2
$\mathcal{C}^*$	7.2			
$\mathcal{C}\mathcal{S}^N, \mathcal{C}\mathcal{S}^N_0$	6.2		Σ^N	3.2
$\mathcal{C}_+\mathcal{S}_0$	6.4			
			$\mathcal{U}^N$	4.2
$\mathcal{D}^N$	1.2		$\mathcal{U}$	8.2
$\Delta^M, \overline{\Delta}^M$	2.3		$\mathcal{U}_K$	10.3
			u_M	10.2
			$\mathcal{V}\mathcal{S}^N_0$	6.5

C. **Axioms**

Notation	(Sub)section	Notation	(Sub)section
AN	4.3, 8.4.1	PAN	7.2
		PCONT	2.5.3
BSTAB	7.4	PMON	7.3
		PO	2.3, 8.2, 8.3
CA	10.3	PSA	5.4
CCA	10.4		
CCONT	10.5	RA	5.5
CIIA	8.3.2	RCONV	2.5.3
CMON	10.5	REC	9.7
CMON'	10.5	RGP	9.6
CONRAD	8.5.2	RM	4.2, 8.2
CONS	2.3	RMON	8.5.1
CONV	2.5.2	RNE	10.3
CSPO	10.4	RPO	6.2
CUN	10.4	RS	6.2
CWIIA	10.4		
		SA	5.2
DCAV	4.5.2	SARP	3.3
DCONT	2.5.2	SCONT	3.4, 8.4.1
DEC	4.5.1	SDMON	4.5.3
DLIN	2.5.2	SIR	2.2, 8.4.1
DPC	2.5.2	SL	6.6
		SMON	4.1
GIM	4.4	SMON*	4.6
		SPO	10.3
HOM	4.5.1	SSN	4.5.1
		STC	2.2, 8.8, 8.3, 10.3
IIA	2.2, 8.2, 8.3	STR	4.5.3
IIA*	4.8	SYM	2.2
IIE	2.4.2		
IM	4.2	TC	4.6
IMON	4.7	TS	6.6
IMON'	4.7		
INIR	2.5.2	UN	10.3
IR	2.2, 8.2, 8.3		
IS	6.5	WA	6.2
LOC	2.5.2	WARP	3.3
		WIIA	10.3
MCONV	2.5.3	WMON	4.8
MSTAB	7.4	WPO	2.2, 8.2, 8.3, 10.5
MUL	2.4.3	WSTAB	7.5
		ZIG	10.4

D. Solutions and related symbols

Notation	(Sub)section		Notation	(Sub)section
D^1, D^2	5.5		N^0, N^1	8.3.1
δ	8.3.1		N^t	5.5
$\underline{\delta}^t, \overline{\delta}^t$	8.3.2		ν	2.2
			ν^K	8.4.1
E	4.5.1, 10.2		ν^H	8.4.2
E^p	4.5.1			
E^*	4.6		$\overline{p}, \underline{p}$	8.2
E^λ	10.2			
			ψ^ϑ	4.4
φ^H	2.3			
φ^{PM}	5.2		ρ, ρ^λ	4.2
			ρ^p	4.3
H	10.2		ρ^L	4.7
$\varkappa^N$	2.3			
$h_S^{t,s}$	8.3.2		Sh	10.2
L	4.7		Θ	4.4
L^*	4.8			
Λ	10.2		υ, Υ	8.3.1
Λ^N	4.2			
			$\overline{w}, \underline{w}$	8.2
$\overline{M}, \underline{M}$	8.2		$\overline{W}, \underline{W}$	8.2
			$\overline{w}^t, \underline{w}^t$	8.3.2

E. Other notations

Notation	(Sub)section	Notation	(Sub)section
cc	3.3	MR	11.3
com	1.2	$M(S)$	8.3
comv	2.3		
conv	1.3, 2.3	N	1.2
		$\mathcal{N}$	7.2
e^L	2.3		
E^M	2.3	O^M	2.3
Eu	1.3, 11.2		
		pr^i	1.3
f^S	5.2	$P(T)$	2.3
$F(S)$	8.3	$\pi x, \pi V$	2.4.5
g^S	5.2	Q^k	8.3
$h(S,d)$	4.2	$\sigma(S)$	8.3
I	7.2	$U(A)$	11.2
IF	6.5	$u(S)$	1.2
$\mathcal{L}(A)$	1.3, 11.2	$W(T)$	2.2
$\ell(a,b)$	3.3		
$\ell_x(y)$	3.4		
$>^\ell, >^{\ell m}$	4.7		

THEORY AND DECISION LIBRARY

SERIES C: GAME THEORY, MATHEMATICAL PROGRAMMING AND OPERATIONS RESEARCH

Editor: S.H. Tijs, *University of Nijmegen, The Netherlands*

KLUWER ACADEMIC PUBLISHERS – DORDRECHT / BOSTON / LONDON